A Manager's Primer on e-Networking

A Manager's Primer
on e-Networking

An Introduction to Enterprise Networking
in e-Business ACID Environment

by

DRAGAN NIKOLIK

Maastricht School of Management,
Maastricht, The Netherlands

SPRINGER SCIENCE+BUSINESS MEDIA, LLC

A C.I.P. Catalogue record for this book is available from the Library of Congress.

ISBN 978-1-4020-1099-6   ISBN 978-94-007-0862-4 (eBook)
DOI 10.1007/978-94-007-0862-4

Printed on acid-free paper

CONTENTS

Contents   iii

List of Figures   viii

List of Tables   x

List of Cases   xi

Foreword   xii

Preface   xiii

Acknowledgements   xvi

Trademark notice   xviii

Introduction   1

Part I   5

Enterprise Infrastructure   5

Chapter 1   11

Enterprise Platforms   *11*
   Network Platforms   13
   Client/Server Transactions: Traditional vs. Transactional Contracts   15
   Client's Hardware   16
   Server's Hardware   19

Client's Software   22
Server's Software   26

Chapter 2   **29**

Network Infrastructure   *29*
Networking Paradigms   30
Network Ownership: Private vs. Public   33
Network Communications: Connection vs. Connectionless   34
Internet Hierarchy   36
Network Hardware   37
Network Software   38

Chapter 3   **41**

Network Architecture   *41*
Client/Server Concept: ACID Transactions Communication   42
Clients Participating in ACID Transactions   43
Servers Participating in ACID Transactions   44
Two-Tier Architecture   45
Three-Tier Network Architecture   46
Peer-to-Peer Network Architecture   46
Network Hierarchy   47
Persistent Transactions: Thin vs. Fat Systems   48
Applications Participating in ACID transaction: Sessions   50

Chapter 4   **55**

Network Connectivity   *55*
Distributed Computing Environment   56
MiddleWare Mechanisms   58
Transport Stacks   60
Network Agents   61

Part II   **65**

Enterprise Paradigm   *65*

Chapter 5   **69**

Enterprise Business Model   *69*
Order-entry Paradigm   75
Workgroup Paradigm   77
Personal Paradigm   79
Enterprise Paradigm   82
Collaborative Paradigm   86
Distributed Paradigm   88

Chapter 6   **95**

Virtual Enterprise   *95*
   Enterprise Communication: EDI, E-mail, Java, Teleconferencing   96
   Extended Enterprise: VE NIIIP standard   97
   Collaborative Computing: Workflow Integration   100
   Global Enterprise: e-Businesses vs. e-Portals   103

Chapter 7   **109**

Enterprise Management   *109*
   Network Efficiency vs. Total Cost of Ownership   111
   Network Costs   112
   Total Cost of Ownership (TCO)   113
   Network Change and Managing Complexity   115
   Network Growth   115

Chapter 8   **119**

Enterprise Development   *119*
   Business Process Re-Engineering   122
   Development Methodology   127
   Application Development Environment   132

Part III   **141**

Enterprise Networking   *141*

Chapter 9   **145**

Communications Networks   *145*
   Communication Techniques   147
   HDLC Networking Protocol   151
   Integrated Digital Network Services -ISDN   154
   Open System Interconnection - OSI   157

Chapter 10   **163**

Wide Area Networks   *163*
   Switched Wide Area Network Communications   165
   Packet Switching Network   166
   Circuit Switching Network   168
   High Speed Networking: Frame vs. Cell Switching   172
   Optic-optic Network: Next Generation Internet (NGI)   176
   Last Mile Alternatives: xDSL, Wireless, Mobile, Bluetooth, FSO   177

Chapter 11   **181**

Local Area Networks   *181*

LAN Topology: Bus vs. Ring   183
LAN Media: Twisted Pair, Coax, Fibre   183
LAN Layout: Linear vs. Star   184
Medium Access Control: CSMA/CD vs. Token Sensing   185
Fibre Distributed Data Interface: FDDI   186
IEEE 802 Suit of LAN Standards   186
Private Branch Exchange (PBX) LAN Alternative   187
Broadband Wireless   187
Digital PBX vs. LAN: Convergence Issues   188

Chapter 12   **191**

Distributed Network Management   *191*
Manager of Managers vs. Manager of Managing Agents   193
X/OPEN Network Management Applications   194
Network Object Management Framework   196

Part IV   **199**

Enterprise Computing   *199*

Chapter 13   **205**

Working with Databases   *205*
Database: A Conceptual View on Data   209
Why Database?   210
Database Models   212
Database Implementation   217
Database Manipulation - SQL   219
Alternative Database Models   220
OO Databases   220

Chapter 14   **223**

Database Functionality   *223*
Concurrent Transactions Processing   225
Database Recovery   227
Database Protection   228

Chapter 15   **233**

Distributed Application Interoperability   *233*
Distributed Application Paradigm Shift   235
Why Distributed Computing?   236
Evolution of Distributed Application Computing   236
Distributed Database Computing   239
ComponentWare - Java Applets   241
Distributed Transaction Processing   242

Chapter 16   **246**

Business Intelligence   *246*
  Data Warehouse Technology   248
  Multimedia Technology   251
  Document Standards: SGML, HTML, VRML, XML   251
  OLAP: Data Drilling, Mining, and Slicing   254
  Data Warehouse Development   255
  Data Warehouse Application Deployment   255
  Information and Intellectual Property Rights   256

Appendix   **262**

Networking Standards Overview   *262*

Communications Protocols Review   *265*

Glossary   **267**

Index   **274**

Website Bookmark   **279**

About the Author   **283**

List of Figures

Figure 1. Clients Accessing Internet Servers   15
Figure 2. Contemporary PC Client Architecture   18
Figure 3. Twenty-year's IT waves   19
Figure 4. Contemporary SMP Server Architecture   21
Figure 5. Large System Alternatives: SMP, MPP vs. NUMA   22
Figure 6. Generic Networks   36
Figure 7. Networking Software   39
Figure 8. Relationship Types   43
Figure 9. Two-Tier vs. Three-Tier Architecture   45
Figure 10. Thin Client Architecture   49
Figure 11. Fat Client Architecture   49
Figure 12. J2EE Architecture   52
Figure 13. DCE Network Layers   58
Figure 14. Message vs. RPC mechanism   59
Figure 15. Enterprise-wide Distributed Transactions Managers   60
Figure 16. Java Platform   84
Figure 17. A SMP Server Array Architecture   90
Figure 18. X/Open 1993 Transaction Processing Reference Model   90
Figure 19. NIIIP VE and CORBA Services   100
Figure 20. Workflow R3 patterns: Shipping Documents Workflow   102
Figure 21. e-Business Cube   105
Figure 22. Desktop TCO Breakdown   113
Figure 23. Development Processes and System Models   127
Figure 24. Boehm's Spiral Development Model   131
Figure 25. The DCE Architecture at IBM Transarc's Encina   135
Figure 26. Desktop Market Share (IDC Report, 2000)   136
Figure 27. Server Market Share (IDC Report, 2000)   136
Figure 28. Digitising Analogue Signals   149
Figure 29. Digital Signal Encoding   150
Figure 30. A Local/Remote Loop-Back with RS-449   151
Figure 31. Communication Network   151
Figure 32. Computer/Terminal Line Configurations   152
Figure 33. HDLC Frame Structure   153
Figure 34. Integration of Transmission and Switching   155
Figure 35. Network Communications Architecture   157
Figure 36. PDU - Protocol Data Unit   157
Figure 37. OSI Model   158

Figure 38. TCP/IP Architecture   159
Figure 39. Internetworking Devices   161
Figure 40. Generic Switching Node   166
Figure 41. Data Communications Alternatives   168
Figure 42. Bus-based Digital Switch   169
Figure 43. TDM Switching   170
Figure 44. CTI for Order-entry Processing   172
Figure 45. Frame Relays vs. X.25 Packet Switching   173
Figure 46. Frame Relays vs. ATM Cell Switching   175
Figure 47. Networking Hierarchy   176
Figure 48. All optical integrated network routing   177
Figure 49. X/Open DSM Management Platform   194
Figure 50. DME Object Management Framework   196
Figure 51. Relationship Types   210
Figure 52. EE/R Diagram for the Bridal Case Database   218
Figure 53. BEA Tuxedo   233
Figure 54. Host-based Distributed Computing   237
Figure 55. Desktop-based Distributed Computing   238
Figure 56. Traditional Client/Server Distributed Computing   238
Figure 57. Distributed Computing Environment Services   239
Figure 58. Distributed Java Applets using CORBA   242
Figure 59. Peer-to-Peer Transaction Processing   243
Figure 60. Data Warehouse   250
Figure 61. Spatial Data Hierarchy   253
Figure 62. Functional vs. Enterprise Database   254

List of Tables

Table 1. Device Networking   44
Table 2. ACID Properties of some Common Servers   45
Table 3. ACID Properties of some Common Networked Clients   45
Table 4. Taxonomy of Enterprise Architecture (3D tiers vs. 3P scope)   46
Table 5. Enterprise Business Paradigms   73
Table 6. Multi-tier Enterprise Paradigms   81
Table 7. Network Efficiency   112
Table 8. Enterprise Trends   113
Table 9. Breakdown of TCO – Operations (56%)   114
Table 10. Breakdown of TCO - Support (15%)   114
Table 11. Breakdown of TCO - Administration (14%)   115
Table 12. Signal encoding   148
Table 13. HDLC Related Data Link Control Protocols   154
Table 14. OSI Network Architecture   158
Table 15. Advantages and Disadvantages of CSN vs. PSN   167
Table 16. Comparison of WAN Communications Techniques   171
Table 17 Frame Relays vs. ATM   174
Table 18. Review of the '*Last Mile*' Communications   178
Table 19. LAN Topology vs. Transmission Media   184
Table 20. Review of LAN Standards   187
Table 21. Digital PBX vs. LAN Convergence   188
Table 22. An Instance Table of the Relation REFERENCE   215
Table 23. Compatibility Matrix for Data Locking   226
Table 24. Distributed Computing Systems   236
Table 25 SNA System Network Architecture   263

List of Cases

Case 1: **Linux Success Stories: Linux Making Inroads in Important Places** **6**

Case 2: **Novell's Simple Proposals of Generic C/S Architectures** **11**

Case 3: **Networked Computing with Beowulf Iridis Cluster** **29**

Case 4: **Xdrive Technologies, Inc. Acquires Businesses of Freedrive, Inc.** **41**

Case 5: **Novell NetWare at Beveridge & Diamond** **55**

Case 6: **Defining Peer-2-Peer** **63**

Case 7: **Peer-to-Peer Technology Exists Beyond Napster** **66**

Case 8: **Insignia Jeode Technology for Compaq iPAQ Home Internet Appliance** **69**

Case 9: **NIIIP Virtual Enterprise Project** **95**

Case 10: **Insignia Solutions apply NTrigue with Citrix WinFrame** **109**

Case 11: **CA AllFusion Harvest Manager Tool with IBM's WebSphere Studio** **119**

Case 12: **Nortel Networks Solutions to Power Taiwan's new eASPNet** **137**

Case 13: **Corvis All-Optical Network** **142**

Case 14: **CallWare's Callegra Advanced Messaging System** **145**

Case 15: **ACTnet Frame Relays Media Integration and Global Access** **163**

Case 16: **NetSpeed Copper-based High-speed WAN Link via ADSL** **179**

Case 17: **Tarantella Web-Enabling Software** **181**

Case 18: **What is Enterprise Networks?** **191**

Case 19: **Transition Associates wins Lotus Beacon Award at Hughes Christensen** **200**

Case 20: **Transition Associate and Lotus Notes at Foulks Lynch Virtual College** **205**

Case 21: **Dayton's Department Store Database** **217**

Case 22: **GemStone OO dBase in CONDIS Project** **223**

Case 23: **PGP Security Extends PGP Wireless Platform Support to Windows CE** **229**

Case 24: **CoreLAN - TP Services with BEA Tuxedo ™** **233**

Case 25: **Cognicase: Sold! Maximizer Enterprise for Notes Wins Bid for Management Solution** **246**

Case 26: **Privacy Guide: Steganography** **256**

Foreword

The implementation of Enterprise Networks or e-Networking is of paramount importance for organisations. Enterprise-wide networking would warrant that the components of information architecture are organised to harness more out of the organisation's computing power on the desktop. This would also involve establishment of networks that link the various but important subsystems of the enterprise.

Our firm belief is that in order to gain a competitive edge the organisations need knowledge and sound strategy. This conviction is particularly true today, considering the pressures from international competition, environmental concerns and complicated ethical issues. This book, entitled A Manager's Primer on e-Networking, negotiates the hyper dimensions of the Internet through stories from myriad of Web sites with its fluent presentation and simple but chronological organisation of topics highlighting numerous opportunities and providing a solid starting point not only for inexperienced entrepreneurs and managers but anyone interested in applying information technology in the business. I sincerely hope the book will help as well many small and medium size companies and organisations to launch corporate networking successfully in order to attain their strategic objectives.

Rajiv Jayashankar, Ph.D.

MIS Professor at MSM

Preface

"Enterprises should be planning for the future, because when
the recovery does occur, there will be renewed pressure on
the network to be able to rapidly handle new applications"
David Neil, Editor in Chief
Gartner Predicts 2002: Enterprise Networking

The challenges to write on *Enterprise Networks* have undoubtedly arisen from
obvious dynamic changes in the field entailing the most recent advances in
Information Technology. Moreover, faced with the growing interest in this
subject, it presents not only an opportunity to spread the knowledge but also to
instruct, consult, design and eventually implement enterprise wide networking
solutions. It is definitely a challenge and an opportunity one could hardly resist.
The book entails four integral parts. In the hypertext enabled mode the reader
could start reviewing the abstracts from any of the following topics presented.

The first part Enterprise Infrastructure is about to introduce the following topics:

Enterprise Platforms
A short review on contemporary computer hardware, system software architectures and IT trends. The
evolution of enterprise computing has been presented giving some insights into continuous development
of applied Information Technology (IT).

Network Infrastructure
A review of contemporary IT platforms of computer systems, user interfaces, access to servers,
communications, and networking, important components usually regarded transparent since do not
perform any business function but are essential in the implementation of variety of enterprise-wide
network architectures.

Network Architecture
Introduction to network architecture based upon a protocol that follows a rule according to which there
can be only one exchange of messages between two processes. The first process, called a client, sends a
message requesting a service to another process, called a server. The server can only respond once,
presumably with the results of performing the service, or launching an "agent" task.

Network Connectivity
A review of networking features provided by the set of software layers set between the Network
Operating System and enterprise applications. A number of transport stacks are transparently mapping
applications to resources hence enabling a wide range of networking services such as inter-process
messaging, remote processing, or transactions handling.

The second part Enterprise Paradigm is presenting the following topics:

Enterprise Business Model
Mapping business model into the corresponding enterprise network paradigms is the goal that leverages
current state-of-the-art in IT. It is possible to apply two-tier network architecture and build network

infrastructure in a variety of ways to support different business models. Most often, in order to meet growing business needs enterprise architecture demands a three-layer view of organisation. A proper decision on the enterprise networking, suitable hardware and software for the business environment more than often may first require conducting Business Process Re-engineering (BPR). A review on some basic business models and discussion on future convergence issue of these models and technology is of interest.

Virtual Enterprise
Introduction to collaborative model of enterprise computing that provides for group awareness of joint actions, tasks, transparent processes associated with creation, data update, and enterprise-wide distribution of free-structural information (grouper).

Enterprise Management
Review on network efficiency issues for a suitable cost containment. Together with network implementation they provide for efficient, flexible but reliable and secure, enterprise-wide operations.

Enterprise Development
A review of application tools used in software development processes and collection of software components used in OO-programming. Discussion on the functionality, simplified codes management, implementation of OO modules, object libraries, and code reuse exploited in enterprise applications.

The third part Enterprise Networking introduces some relevant networking topics closely following [Stallings & Slyke, 1996].

Communications Networks
Introduction to computer networking and communications, reviewing for instance on OSI, B-ISDN, TCP/IP, etc. the important standards and protocols regarded necessary to understand contemporary IT and its relationship to enterprise-wide networking.

Wide Area Networks
Introduction to telecommunications state-of -the-art IT covering large geographical distances, merging and extending extensively all around the world within WWW or Internet infrastructures.

Local Area Networks
Introduction to Local Area Networks state-of -the-art IT originally confined within a building or campus of buildings of an enterprise but increasingly extending beyond these boundaries.

Distributed Network Management
Review on open system DSM platforms applied to enterprise networks that efficiently manage DCE for multi-vendor enterprise networking, integrate systems and enterprise network management.

The last part, entitled Enterprise Computing, reveals some interesting topics on computing applications and data processing, namely:

Working with Databases
Introduction to data mapping models used for persistent data collections, including Relational DBMS and OO databases.

Database Functionality
Discussion on the functionality of relational database model in relation to the applications implementing particular business models. This is especially the case as database systems became an essential part of

mission critical applications throughout enterprises, influenced by concurrent processes, system recovery, and security issues.

Distributed Application Interoperability

Distributed application computing represents a new phenomenon in distributed network environments enabling enterprises to explore new brand of mission-critical applications. The distributed environment runs across different platforms, closely connecting networks and integrating enterprise wide business processes. It also introduces the component ware paradigm based upon expected widespread use of Java aware application, tools, and collections of OO-programming components. A new object paradigm of application development is introduced revolutionising the implementation of distributed applications in enterprise wide networks. X/Open, a distributed contemporary model of nested (complex) -transactions is also presented.

Business Intelligence

Introduction to the data warehousing as a modern Business Intelligence concept that has optimised the use of data complexes allowing for efficient data analysis, migration, smart decision support and reporting throughout the enterprise.

Acknowledgements

"Should you plan for a year - plant rice; should you plan for ten years
-do grow fruit orchards; but if you plan for life, do educate people".
Confucius, Chinese philosopher

The acknowledgements are most often prepared at the end of writing the text. It's more or less the same in this case. The only difference makes the message, the idea, which is to be conveyed to the reader. It has been planed action that was anticipated and also introduced for quite some time to my dear fellow students during the teaching classes, discussions and lectures, long before I even set to write this text. The Confucius' motto of *educating people* is therefore a philosophy, an idea that applies best to this endeavour.

It certainly gives the author the opportunity to reflect on its own work too. As usual, a series of questions comes to one's mind and that of the very reason have you achieved in writing the text. Are you going to change something in the reader's mind? Is it the way they perceive it, apply, or will they make use of today's information technology in the future? I wish I achieved it even to some extend. However, I'm certain that the new kids, the future generation of young executives, entrepreneurs, and managers will take Internet technology for granted, something very close to their ever known experience playing arcade games, browsing the Web, searching and fighting aliens, cyber monsters and Web tycoons. And only then comes the revelation that I had a wonderful chance of spending precious time, sharing my own experiences with them, my dear MBA and PhD candidates, students and participants of Maastricht School of Management all over the world, teaching and discussing information technology issues, Internet, connectivity problems, and enterprise networks.

Many people around me, my fellow colleagues and friends, and let me here mention my own family, all of them have made it possible and I'm enormously grateful to all them and proud to say that this endeavour could not be possible without them. However, if you say all of them and do not single out at least some that you find closest it's almost as if mentioning no one. My special thanks therefore, goes to my dear colleague and friend Prof. Rajiv Jayashankar, MIS Professor at MSM, who put confidence in me, the challenge I couldn't possibly miss. I'm very much indebted to my fellow colleagues at the MSM with whom I've spent numerous coffee breaks sharing ideas and networking experience. Special thanks goes to my dear friend Mrs. Karen Phillips, who spent time and patience to proof-read it through, and also to Prof. A. Beulens from LUW who's comments brought up valuable questions and issues regarding the contemporary trend of client/server technology and its applications. The list is much longer, but however limited the space might be, it allows me at least to thank my former fellow colleagues from the University of Skopje, R. Macedonia, I have been affiliated with, to share and enjoy the fruits of education being invested in me.

Following common Dutch expression, *last but definitely not least*, my sincere gratitude goes to my loving family, my dear and always caring mother, Gorjan, Bojan, and my loving and always supporting wife Pauline without whose understanding, endless love and support this endeavour could not possibly see the light and reach the hyper dimensions of the Web.

Maastricht, Christmas 2001

Dragan Nikolik

Trademark notice

ActiveX, FrontPage, Internet Explorer, J Script, NT Server, Office 2000, VBScript, VisualBasic, Visual InterDev, FoxPro, Windows 95, Windows NT, Windows CE, Windows NT SNA, Windows NT Workstation, Word are trademarks of Microsoft Corporation

Adabas, Bolero, EntireX, Natural, Tamino are trademarks of Software AG

AIX, APL, CICS TS, CICS/390, DB2, MQSeries, MVS, OS/2, OS/39, WebSphere are trademarks of International Business Machines Corporation

Alto, SmallTalk, Star are trademarks of Xerox Corporation

Arc/Info is a trademark of Environmental Systems Research Institute, Inc.

BeBox, BeOS are trademarks of Be, Inc.

Citrix, MetaFrame, WinFrame, are trademarks of Citrix Systems, Inc.

Delphi is a trademark of Borland International Inc.

Dreamweaver is a trademark of Macromedia

Eiffel is a trademark of Interactive Software Engineering Inc.

Elemental Software is a trademark of ESI Software, Inc. (dba Elemental Software).

EtherExpress is a trademark of Intel

Informix is a trademark of Informix Software, Inc.

Ingres of Ingres Corporation, and PowerBuilder are trademarks of Computer Associates Inc.

Fusion is a trademark of NetObjects

GemStone is a trademark of GemStone Systems, Inc.

HP-UX is a trademark of Hewlett-Packard Inc.

HyperCard, Macintosh, MacOS, Objective-C are trademarks of Apple Computer Inc.

Hotjava, Java, J2EE, JavaOS, Sun Solaris are trademarks of Sun Microsystems, Inc.

JavaScript, Netscape, Netscape Navigator are trademarks of Netscape Communications Corporation

Jolt, Tuxedo, WebLogic, are trademarks of BEA Systems, Ltd.

Jserv is a trademark of Apache

Modula-3 is a trademark of Digital Equipment Corporation

Mosaic is a trademark of National Centre for Supercomputing Applications

NetWare is a trademark of Novell Inc.

NTrigue is a trademark of Insignia Solutions Inc.

PalmPilot is a trademark of 3Com Corporation

PowerPlay is a trademark of Cognos Incorporated

Psion is a trademark of Psion Plc

SAP R/3 is a trademark of SAP

SyBase is a trademark of Sybase, Inc.

UNIX/SCO, Tarantella are trademarks of the Santa Cruz Operation, Inc., UNIX is a trademark of AT&T

Visa is a trademark of Visa International

X-Windows is a trademark of Massachusetts Institute of Technology

Introduction

What is this book about? It is about **organising enterprises** today and in the future; it's about current information demands and adjusting our response with respect to ever growing dynamic market changes. The book tries to satisfy hopes and often high expectations for collaboration efforts within enterprise-wide environments and performing among possible ways the Information Technology is expected to exercise its support.

WorldNet 1.5 Vocabulary Helper at http://www.notredame.ac.jp/cgi-bin/wn.cgi defines **organise** as *to begin, or enable someone else to begin, a venture by providing the means, logistics.*

Whether simple or complex an organisational task might be, it determines the way we work, the way we set up our efforts, access information, apply knowledge and available resources, use appropriate technology, software and the know-how to accomplish it.

Webster Dictionary at http://www.notredame.ac.jp/cgi-bin/wn.cgi defines **organise** as follows: *to arrange or constitute in parts, each having a special function, act, office, or relation; to systematise; to get into working order.*

Whether at our home working place or places we visit occasionally, more often our office, workgroup or department, company or worldwide enterprise, all are inevitably dependent on the way we organise or we wish to perform our business tasks.

WorldNet 1.5 Vocabulary Helper at http://www.notredame.ac.jp/cgi-bin/wn.cgi defines an *enterprise* as *the people belonging to an organisation created for difficult ventures.*

The IEEE Communications Society, the Technical Committee on Enterprise Networking introduces "the **Enterprise Networking** is the interconnection of corporate, departmental, local, and remote computing and communications resources to create an enterprise-wide information utility (an "enterprise" is an organization, such as a business, government, administration, institution, etc., having business or other operating needs) " [1].

The IT enables us to extend that reach beyond usual task boundaries: in time, right now, on-line, or as postponed action whenever convenient; in spatial dimensions too, through direct access or remotely, from anywhere. Moreover, the way we organise tasks influences not only us but also people we are working with or we are communicating to.

This book aims at presenting the readers, common end-users, business graduates perspective entrepreneurs, and business people, possible ways how to achieve efficient IT support in organising tasks. It goes beyond simple enterprise and introduces global, collaborative, distributed environment usually referred to -

---

[1]

http://www.sigda.org/Archives/CollectedInformation/NewsgroupHighlights/aug94/IEEE_Communications_Society_TC_on_Enterprise_Networking.txt *virtual enterprise.* It is therefore, about the ways we should be using Information Technology, the way we present the knowledge that could helps us organise and optimise the efforts to perform better and stay successful in this turbulent world.

The book is organized in four major parts. The first part introduces some basic concepts on *enterprise network infrastructures* related to enterprise computing. The second part elaborates on the organisational aspects associated with formal enterprise business models. It introduces *business paradigms* of organising common tasks and practices and the ways common enterprise environment is achieving the IT support. The third part aims on presenting the state-of-the-art in Communications and Networking Technology. It elaborates on some pragmatic issues end-users should be aware of, for instance, *CIT phenomenon* as a product of convergence of computer, communications and of telephony. The final, fourth part, introduces some information processing aspects of enterprise computing processes. It elaborates questions such as why are *databases* abundantly used in business tasks associated with large data complexes. It introduces some modern information concepts such as entities, objects, relations, and general multimedia documents as building blocks often used to manage complex information.

In our presentation we will follow simple subject overview and whenever possible provide support by *case-based* presentations. Whenever appropriate, we will introduce opening cases, most often simplifying real problem issues so that a specific subject related problem could be easily recognised, formulated and elaborated. Main topics will be introduced without elaborating on the complex technical issues but guiding through simple and practical knowledge that common user could benefit from. The emphasis will be on the state-of-the-art and the current information technology issues, both software and hardware solutions provided by the well-known market leaders for common business needs and satisfying enterprise end-users demands.

To find out more what is ahead, you could also check out the on-line <u>Contents</u> from the <u>MSM supporting Web site</u> that will provide brief HTML guide and update on some hot-issues elaborated in this book. The off-line readers may also benefit from the <u>Index</u> provided for downloading in Adobe Acrobat (PDF) format. Should you need a viewer, the *Acrobat viewer* free copy is available at http://www.adobe.com/acrobat/readstep.html.

Who is this book for? This will give you ideas on who might be interested in reading this book. Students, business graduates, MBA post graduates, everyone interested in IT issues: usual explorers of Internet, end-users of enterprise information systems, Intranets, business people, managers might find it interesting too. It addresses questions, which you would like to apply and make efficient use of IT or feel familiar with, as well as *virtual enterprise* readers connected from home or elsewhere on the Web. Feeling more confident, making sure all available information is at reach we learn as well not to loose information since, *there is no greater loss than late or missing information.*

Hypertext support. In order to provide answers to many relevant questions using the information technology as much as possible one could begin with the hypertext enabled <u>Preface</u> of the text. It enables readers exercise custom-made search through the hypertext content looking for a particular theme of interest, or for instance, by clicking the topic thus starting browsing through the <u>Contents</u>. Using Internet browsers the readers could access many interesting Internet sites too, either mentioned or in some way related to the themes discussed in the book. The <u>Bookmark</u> of these Web sites is provided too.

How to use the Hypertext Pointers? During the writing of the book I've been overwhelmed with the dynamic changes of the content. The information changes or becomes obsolete by the time you are reading it. Fortunately, the Internet provided a solution that seems might overcome or at least prolong the obsolescence by providing windows to the Internet sites related to the topics and protagonists mentioned in the book. The hypertext pointers have been introduced in the book in order to make full use of Internet windows. They are pointing to Internet sites of interest hence, extending the use of the book beyond present time of writing, through the windows of the future. All it needs is just to press a key at a specific Internet pointer indicated throughout the HTML version of the book. Conventional readers can still benefit from the Internet sites through the <u>Index</u> of pointer addresses generated from the List of Keywords and presented as the electronic <u>Website Bookmark</u> at the end of the book.

Do you need HTML support? The HTML or *hypertext* support associated with the book has been prepared for the non-experienced readers, not necessarily beginners, who are not that familiar with Internet and particular topic but may get direct and easy access to it at hand. It provides a glimpse of the most important themes elaborated in this book through multimedia access, at the same time guiding readers through the book and extends to the Internet as well. It captures the most important themes in somewhat different custom-made manner, by so-called optional or directed guide. Having the Internet access provides for an important starting point and opening Internet sites the book is just referring to or pointing to the hypertext documents where others have said and presented something more, commented, or added yet somewhat different arguments. However, for the readers who regularly access Internet, the common end-users, entrepreneurs, business people and enterprise managers this represents a shortcut to the hidden niches on the Internet where more relevant information could be found. And guess what? It also keeps the information in the book always updated, just like an open window to the world of Internet. Occasionally however, there might be some disappointments as well. Sometimes, the information we are looking for is just not at the right address, has been moved, updated, or just disappeared. In most instances all you need to do is to click the address provided and it will take you to the proper destination, reaching across dimensions of the Web.

So, why is the book than for? We have to start from somewhere, don't we? If you consider your would like to give a try and explore the hidden enterprise networks on the Web through the electronic <u>Bookmark</u>, please just click in the e-mail address provided via <u>Mail to form</u> and send me a note.

PART I

ENTERPRISE INFRASTRUCTURE

Case 1: Linux Success Stories: Linux Making Inroads in Important Places

LINUX SUCCESS STORIES: LINUX MAKING INROADS IN IMPORTANT PLACES
downloaded March 11, 2002, http://luna.flagstaff.az.us/success.html
(Reproduced by permission of LUNA, the Linux Users Of Northern Arizona)

Linux. You've heard of it on the news. You may know someone who uses it. Have you thought about using it, but were afraid to try it because the boss has been sold on another operating system? Are you the boss wondering if Linux can help your bottom line? Linux is too new, unstable, untested, can't be trusted with mission critical applications. Linux is open source and as such, is dangerous because it allows hackers to modify the software or to find bugs and holes to exploit by creating worms, viruses and trojans- and if someone quits after modifying the code then you are really in trouble, there's no way to go back. Linux is more expensive to administer because it is based on Unix and administrators demand more pay. You can't sell Linux based software because most of it falls under a viral, cancerous General Public License. Linux doesn't have the applications that are needed to get work done. There is no office suite; it can't be used to access the Internet.

All of these arguments have been used against using Linux in the workplace. One by one, we will dispel these myths or, as they are better known in the industry, FUD. FUD stands for fear, uncertainty, and doubt. This is a known marketing strategy when truth doesn't work. Details of use of FUD are available in the Halloween Documents.

Linux is not new. Linux has just celebrated its tenth birthday/anniversary. Linux was designed to be a free clone of the proprietary operating system Unix. Unix was developed by Bell Labs in 1969*. In the early 1970s Richard Stallman worked at MIT and by the mid 1980s had created the GNU Project, which aspired to create a free operating system. In 1991, Linus Torvalds released his version of a free Unix-like kernel-the very base of the operating system to the world. This kernel became known as the Linux kernel. The combination of the free tools, released by Richard Stallman, and the free kernel, released by Linus Torvalds, created the combination GNU/Linux and the free operating system known most commonly as Linux was born. Because the GNU project and the Linux kernel are both based upon Unix they were designed with multiple users, administration rights, and security in mind. Thus the maturity of the operating system is in part from the mid 1980s and partly from the early 1990s. The development method used for all parts of the operating system is described by Eric Raymond in his writings The Cathedral and the Bazaar where lots of people contribute to making software better-not because they have to, but because they want to. This helps to ensure that bugs are found, and, if there is a needed feature, it can be coded in.

Linux is stable. It is being used by Ameritrade Amex and NYSE. American Express and the NYSE are testing Sendmail, the most widely used Mail Transfer Agent in use to replace their current systems The Apache web server is the most widely used server on the internet with versions running on Linux as well as other operating systems.

Linux can save you money on the bottom line. Linux is being used to replace Win2k and to save over $10,000.00. That can be added to the bottom line- is the boss listening? And the City of Largo, Florida has chosen to use KDE as their solution of choice. With impending software audits by MS on customers large and small companies and governmental agencies are choosing to pay up rather than fight with MS over licensing. In our own county there are unconfirmed reports that the only machines that software can't be proven on are the ones installed by techs from MS itself. These will be the machines that MS will charge a new license fee for. Ironic (evil?) that the *only* machines that the county can't show proof of purchase for came directly from MS. Add to that reports- not in the paper of course- that our new emergency dispatch system doesn't work as advertised, techs blame the incompatibilities of the operating system to the software. Add MSs new licensing scheme and now you have users paying subscriptions for software that they could have just purchased once and upgraded when the time is right for that user.

Linux is not expensive to administer. While Unix and Linux administrators may demand more money, they also are able to admin more machines due to the scalability of the operating system and the availability of tools for Linux. Linux admins also don't have to spend as much time running around installing patches for IIS worms, Outlook viruses, or Explorer bugs. Linux does not suffer from the same problems as MS products. Some would have you believe it's because Linux is not as popular, and the most prominent operating system will be targeted. You did click the Apache survey link above didn't you? Apache runs on 60% of all web servers... why is it that Apache is **not** the most abused, *least* secure, web server in the world? It is because it was developed using the open source method of development subjecting it to peer review and quick bug fixes.

Need office suite functionality? Try StarOffice from Sun MicroSystems, koffice from koffice.org, openoffice to name a few. All of these options give you; a word processor, compatible with nearly all document formats, spreadsheet functionality, again with the multiple vendor format support, presentation/computer slide show, with multi-vendor support, import/export functions to save in additional formats. Web browsing with Netscape, mozilla, and konqueror part of the KDE.org project. The internet and web pages are based up standards that are agreed upon to be used by everyone so any browser should work, if it doesn't it's normally because the web site owner has chosen to ignore the previously agreed upon standards.

If you need to find out whether other applications are available for your needs browse applications at linux.org or search for a specific tool on freshmeat

We hope you have found this page to be informative. If you need help, we have a mailing list luna@infomagic.net with many knowledgeable individuals who are willing to help with installing and using GNU and Linux.

> *History of Unix development
> *Linux is TM Linus Torvalds. GNU is TM Richard Stallman.*
> *Other copyrights and trademarks may apply to their respective owners*

The main topic discussed in this part is the state-of-the-art of Information Technology (IT) and its role in contemporary business enterprises. Following the introductory *Case 1:* Linux Success Stories: Linux Making Inroads in Important Places, there is a short review of what constitutes an enterprise infrastructure. It has been especially important to small and medium size business enterprises (SMSE) and has scaled up nicely across large worldwide enterprises. We will elaborate on the need for integration, consolidation, sharing, and most of all, the efficient use of information. In the industry, there exists a wide opinion that these issues are fundamental for the existence of any organized business activities. Most often they are seen as organizational requirements, constraints which any information infrastructure is to meet in response to information processing demands. Due to constant changes, IT architecture plays an important part in configuring individual offices, but its role is even greater in configuring SMSE enterprise networks.

The introduction takes a short overview into some common client and server hardware, and proceeds with the necessary software requirements. The emphasis is mainly on hardware-related software issues in regard to common networking infrastructures. A specific networking software suite, networking middleware, further emphasizes its present trend, the role and importance of software in appropriate configuration of networking paradigms implemented for and by distributed business enterprises. Our goal is to achieve better understanding of the relationships that exist among different technologies that play key roles in enterprise networking subject to the phenomenal pace of IT change.

The opening chapter Enterprise Platforms provides a short review over contemporary computer hardware and related system software architectures in the light of to-date IT trends. The evolution of enterprise computing on the other hand gives some insights into the continuous development and fast changes of Information Technology (IT) recently.

The following chapter Network Infrastructure entails contemporary IT platforms of computer systems, user interfaces, access to servers, communications, and networking, important components usually regarded as transparent that do not perform any business function but are essential in the implementation of a variety of enterprise-wide network architectures.

Likewise, the subsequent chapter Network Architecture introduces the Client/Server concept. This concept is based upon a protocol used in the past to manage traditional software applications and accordingly there can be only one exchange of messages between two related processes. The first process, called a *client*, sends a message requesting a service from a host process, called a *server*. According to this protocol, the server can only respond once, presumably with the results of performing the service, or launching an "*agent*" task on its behalf, which actually performs the requested service.

Lastly, the chapter on <u>Network Connectivity</u> elaborates on networking features provided by a set of software layers set between Network Operating Systems and enterprise applications. A number of transport stacks are transparently mapping applications to resources, hence enabling a wide range of networking services such as inter-process messaging, remote processing, and transactions handling.

CHAPTER 1

ENTERPRISE PLATFORMS

MS Windows vs non-Windows OS

Case 2: Novell's Simple Proposals of Generic C/S Architectures

---

PEOPLES FIRST COMMUNITY BANK
Novell Customer Case Study

Peoples First Community Bank is a large commercial bank, founded and federally chartered in 1983. Since then, Peoples First has grown to 16 branches throughout Florida with assets of more than $640 million. Headquartered in Panama City, the bank loaned $388 million for construction, residential, commercial and consumer loans during fiscal year 1996.

In addition to loans, Peoples First offers its customers a variety of financial products, including checking, savings and money market accounts, credit cards and speciality accounts tailored to businesses, senior citizens and 18-24 year- olds. The bank's diverse customers expect complete and immediate customer service and rely on the bank's tellers, loan officers and customer representatives to furnish this service upon request. Peoples First enabled its employees to deliver outstanding customer service by depositing its trust in Novell.

Network Overview

Peoples First Community Bank powers its enterprise with NetWare 4.1. Sixteen NetWare servers connect 250 users across 18 sites through a frame relay. Most client machines are IBM-compatible PC's although the bank's advertising and marketing groups work on Macintosh computers supported by NetWare for Macintosh. Motorola MPR routers channel communications via a 64kbps line--56k for data, 8k for voice--and connect network users to the company's UNISYS A-4 mainframe in Orlando.

Like most banks, Peoples First used separate systems to process the different services they offered: teller transactions, loan origination and approval, and the sharing of information. Loan applications completed at any of the company's branch offices were physically sent--by fax or mail--to Peoples First headquarters for processing and approval. And because customer information is stored on the company's mainframe, employees would have to dial-in across leased lines, which rendered documents on their desktop inaccessible during the remote connection.

Systems engineers were resolving network issues, managing user accounts and providing for disaster recovery--at each of the bank's 18 sites throughout hurricane-prone Florida.

Needs Analysis: An Integrated Solution

Peoples First realized that to offer its customers one-stop banking and to remain competitive in the banking industry:

− Employees would need complete and transparent access to all information and resources on the enterprise.

− Network administrators must be able to manage the entire network from a single central location and to resolve issues before they arise.

Working with its Novell Authorized Reseller, Peoples First Community Bank selected NetWare 4.1 as its network computing platform and ManageWise 2.0 to help manage and optimize its enterprise.

The Novell Solution: Pervasive Computing

Since implementing NetWare 4.1 in April 1996 as its enterprise computing platform, Peoples First has found that its business operations have become significantly more efficient. "Formerly we'd have employees in front of dumb terminals who were able only to open an account, for example," explains Eddie Creamer, senior vice president of Finance and Administration and Chief Financial Officer for Peoples First. "NetWare has made possible a single intelligent terminal that will do everything the company has to offer."

Hardware Platforms. Whenever a new information technology has been introduced, common users usually feel disoriented since they are unfamiliar with the current terminology. Often, there are new acronyms to be acquainted with, strange words are concatenated together, or grouped into unrecognizable acronyms that mean very little to very few enthusiasts and are confusing rather than helping explain. Actually, it usually gives quite the opposite impression. Instead of attracting, it deters end-users, making them very much reluctant to accept newer technology, albeit it may offer favorable features, benefits and advantages.

To enable users to feel more comfortable in applying and using contemporary *Information Technology* (IT), we shall start by bringing up the necessary terminology. Let us first, introduce IT terminology, related to the state-of-the-art in contemporary computer hardware and thereafter, proceed with software systems presently in use.

Software Platforms. There are significant changes on this front. The dominant trends are the consolidation of enterprise-wide networking and *Intranet* platform integration. Consequently, present trends in networking software are *consolidation* and *integration with migration*. The consolidation involves both, various enduser types at the client side, as well as multi layering with structuring at the server side of an enterprise network. By the end of the millennium, the client software entered a migration phase heading towards Microsoft *Windows '9x/00* OS and its application suite. The only serious client OS-challenge at this moment represents Symbion/Psion *EPOC* 32-bit OS primarily targeting Personal Digital Assistant (PDA) devices and smart phones[2] for mobile clients (WAP). Servers' platforms however, have fewer alternatives. Consolidated UNIX OS (e.g. UNIX SCO, HP-UX, Sun's Solaris, IBM AIX, etc.), including *Linux* which grows enthusiastically on various platforms, are moving in, closing in on some former *Network OS* (NOS). However, the greatest challenge of all represents the new version of NOS *MS Windows 2000/NT*. It is well supported at the client side by MS Windows 2000 and XP and its suite of end-users' *MS Office* applications. *MS Windows 2000/NT,* surpassingly even for Microsoft, took over the place intended for *Windows Cairo Object OS.* After almost a decade of development, from *VMS, Digital VAX* roots, within less then five years, modern OS Windows NT advanced through several versions, 3.1, 3.51, 4.0, 5.0 and 2000 in both EE (Enterprise Edition), as well as the EE OEM editions. Determined to fight for greater market share, it is eventually gaining market dominance against many versions of UNIX systems and other proprietary OS. The volatile SMSE market, presently shared by Mac OS, UNIX, Novell NetWare, Banyan Vines, and other proprietary OS contenders on the enterprise-networking scene, is therefore under constant competitive pressure. According to the most recent market polls[3] the outcome is certain: *Window 2000/NT* is gaining firm grounds, closing on UNIX.

Network Platforms

It has been mentioned that enterprise-wide computing relies strongly on specific hardware platforms. The contemporary computer platform today is also known as *Client/Server* (C/S) network architecture. The underlining computing concept involves at least two distinct agents (known as systems, objects, or applications) determined to co-operate in establishing various communication paradigms.

The *client* side usually plays a role of common end-user system (i.e. objects and front-end applications in software domain). For instance, the client system may apply for services offered by *Internet Service Providers* (ISP) through specific *network interfaces*. We will elaborate on some network interfaces later on. Just in a sequel, let us say that we would like to access the network, *World Wide Web* (WWW) or *Internet* for instance. As a particular client, i.e. computer-equipped device, it calls upon some device-specific *Internet Protocol* (IP). As expected, the IP performs a programmed set of rules, hence ensuring correct interface actions between the client system and the networking device. For instance, a dial-up modem-equipped PC establishes network access with the *Internet Service Provider* (ISP) server system. During a trip for instance, a laptop connected by *PCMCI* communication card (*FirstFone)* to a mobile phone network enables easy access through *Communications Service Provider (CSP)* server to the network. At the bus stop, an enduser using palm-held client *Psion5* PDA, i-

---

[2] BYTE, Dec./1997, *Smart Phones Make the Grade.*
[3] Butler Group Report, *Enterprise NT*, August 1998

MODE 3G mobile phone, or *Nokia* 9000i Communicator smart-phone may get an easy access to the email or even browse the *Web*[4]. Back at home, an ordinary TV set may just as well become a common client. Using *Broadband Wide Area* (WBA) set-top box via its tele-text mode for instance, allows users to get connecting to the *TV Cable Services Provider* (CAT) server and the *Web*[5]. The client/server paradigm applies similarly in cases of applications interactions. For instance, MS Word text editor in process of creating a drawing object either linked or embedded in its document acts as a client. It calls upon *Object Linking and Embedding* (OLE) as the *Application Program Interface* (API) to establish object sharing among itself and other applications, Excel, or Power Point for instance.

The *server* is a synonym for a contemporary computer system but also common application. It plays the role of a universal service provider, enabling many types of services such as executing applications, system support and file management, backup, printing, database or network access, etc. Depending on its role, either played by the server, or assigned by the network to a particular node to which a particular server is attached to, the server is to provide specific functionality in accordance with the network design.

In order to enable clients getting connected to a server or a network, appropriate *communication interfaces* are required. They include specific hardware and software implementing a *networking protocol*. The NOS or Network Operating System provides basic network connectivity by default. In general, connectivity protocols are divided into three groups: media, transport and client-server protocol. For instance, *Ethernet* and *FDDI* are media type protocols. Internet connectivity on the other hand is based on *TCP/IP transport protocol*.

Among client-server protocols the prominent ones are *NetBIOS*, and *Advanced Program-to-Program Communication* (APPC) protocol. Moreover, the network management, security and connectivity still remain NOS' responsibility. Present communication protocols provide networks with diverse bandwidth range, from number of 64 Kbps channels up to some tens of Gbps in multiples of 52Mbps or 155Mbps high bandwidth channels (e.g. *ISDN, FR,* xDSL, SDH, or *ATM*) as shown in *Figure 1*. Traditional Circuit Switching Networks (CSN) use switching technology between clients with pre-established connections. Packet Switched Networks (PSN) however, apply IP computer routing technology for connection-less information packets. Presently, network communication trends are in favor of IP computer routing technology both for data and voice as well.

---

[4] E-mail utility of *Symbion* – a joint venture of Psion, Ericsson, Motorola, and Nokia.

[5] Swisscom's microwave 32-channel video broadcasting system for Val d'Herens.

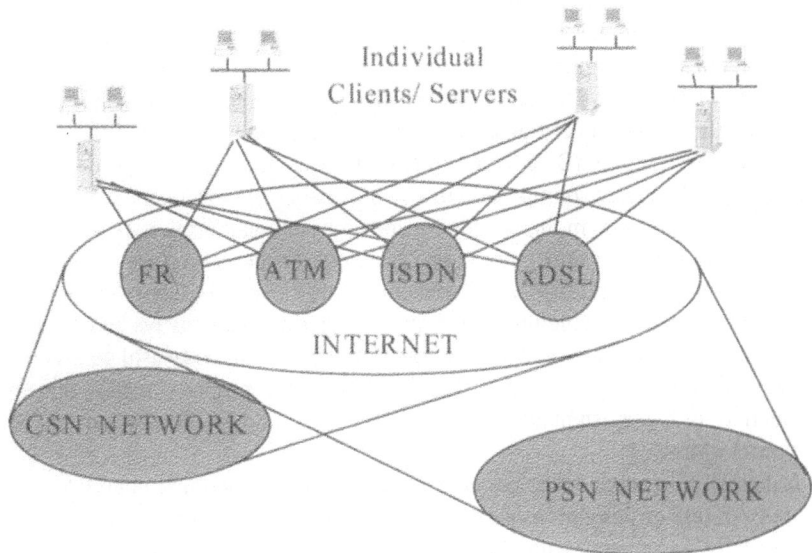

Figure 1. Clients Accessing Internet Servers

Depending whether network connectivity functions are implemented at server side, at client side, or as separate *middleware* functionality enabling transparent mapping to both sides, there are *two-tier* and *three-tier platforms*, often extended to *n-tier* enterprise networking platforms; see *Figure 9*.

In *two-tier* enterprise model the clients are connected directly to servers. Usually it applies for smaller size networks, less than 50 clients. In larger networks however, the *three-tier* enterprise model is more suitable. The additional *middle layer* of the third-tier model corresponds to an intermediary server that takes care of *networking* processes (also called *"agents"* by the NOS related processes it initiates) and provides for transparent distribution of enterprise computing among large numbers of clients and various types of distributed servers.

Client/Server Transactions: Traditional vs. Transactional

Contracts

Client/Server transaction has been powerful and remains dominant networking concept. Early in the 1970s, it was introduced into computer networks through transactional databases (please check Database Functionality) during the *on-line wave* of computer networks evolution. Traditionally, a *simple transaction* has been defined as any independent, coherent unit of work in Client/Server environment. A computerized business transaction represents a dialog between a human and one or more applications, which produces a change of the state of the business system. Unlike simple ones, a *conversational transaction* consists of multiple exchanges of information between an operator and one or more applications. From client/server point of view transactions are actions requesting a service by Clients and only in some instances can Servers initiate them as well. Nowadays, transactions have evolved into more complex entities thus allowing service-requests to originate from any side, Client or Server alike. However, for simplicity of operations today's network management recognizes mainly Client-to-Server and Peer-to-Peer transactions. There are several key properties, known under the acronym ACID, which explains the way transactions are dealt with, which makes this term so important in any networking environment.

The ACID is an acronym that stands for four transactional properties: Atomicity, Consistency, Isolation and Durability. *Atomicity* property implies that "*all-or-nothing*" principle applies to any transactional unit of work. *Consistency* means that a correct state is stable under frequent changes and can always be preserved. *Isolation* means that any concurrent transactions are mutually isolated, coexist and do not influence each other. Finally, *Durability* property means that any transaction is a persistent unit of works that can and is able to survive any system's failures.

In principle, Clients and Servers adhere to general transactional contracts either in *one-to-many* or in *many-to-many* communication relationships with the *'many'* part usually associated with the Server side. The one-to-many C/S has been implemented mainly in 2-tier and 3-tier networks, whereas many-to-many and peer-to-peer relationships are found primarily in 3-tier+ and n-tier networks. Both sides, the client and the server side, attain the so-called 3P properties: *Presentation, Processing,* and *Persistence.* Presentation has gradually improved from simple ASCII text, through text strings, X-Open and X-Windows to nowadays, complex GUI, sophisticated OOUI, and GNOME features. Processing has evolved from single up to multiple treaded processes. The implementation has been carried out by mono processor, SMP clusters, and parallel processing architectures. Finally, document persistency has advanced too, from shared-all to shared-nothing primarily in distributed and federated networking environments. Presently, enterprise networks trends are geared to many-to-many C/S and Peer-to-Peer relationships maintaining rich OOUI presentation features and distributed shared-nothing persistency in SMP or parallel processing network environments.

Client's Hardware

From ACID point of view there are mainly three types of clients: terminals, PC (laptop or desktop*)* and mobile communicators. Conventional dumb terminals apart from data presentation are unable to process information supplied through network communication. For information processing, the terminal relies heavily on server's support, which means that any processing, data access, or any application execution actually runs at the server's side. The server is actually sending only the presentations' parts of application to the terminal. The server takes care of all the responses or feedback either from the terminal's keyboard or its pointing device (e.g. mouse). It's evident that terminals are rather weak regarding the ACID compliance. Due to its dependency on Server side, most of

ACID features are either delegated to or performed by the Server, and therefore highly dependent on the availability and reliability of its network connection.

Take for instance an Internet user using Nokia *Wireless Application Protocol* (WAP) mobile phone acting as a terminal to Internet Portal or email host. The all-or-nothing transactions' feature solely depends on the news-portal or email-host server. Consistent transaction means mainly preservation of the state of current transactions by the server. For mobile users equipped with larger active memory it's possible to have transactions with local state preservation but still it has to be backed up frequently at the server side, which eventually requires much higher availability and more reliable network connectivity. The isolation feature though, e.g. the independence of concurrent transactions, has been delegated to the transactional service provider. Finally, the transactions' durability in most cases will depend on the availability and reliability of service providers.

In many respects PC architecture is similar to that of a server. Equipped with substantial main memory, processor boards often supported by several types of external memories, etc. Moreover, a modern PC can share most of the processing burden hence, performing tasks or even processing large applications within its own memory address domain, for more please see <u>IBM, Monterey Project</u>[6]. Whenever access to shared resource is required, a PC client asks for server's support. It makes requests for server's tasks distribution, calls for file or print-management services, demands for resource allocations or network connectivity, all subject to some server's availability, reliability, and security requirements. Sophisticated clients are even able to perform actions usually initiated by some triggering event, the so-called *event-driven* response. For instance, it only takes a mouse click, or a keyboard key-press to initiate client-server session. Old type clients, so-called legacy ASCII terminals were mostly *character-driven*. This means that servers had to frequently poll them (by hardware or software-based polls) and ask them if services were necessary. Today, event-driven clients make use of *multi-tasking, multi-tread OS* with *Graphical User Interfaces (GUI)* enabling them to perform several tasks at a time. GUI are often initiated through separate screens or through active *Windows* sessions. Same GUI Windows interfaces have been implemented for dumb terminals via UNIX *X-Windows* clients. Similarly, PC terminals can make effective use of *Citrix WinFrame* support for MS Windows net-centric clients or GNOME UNIX/Linux clients, see *Case 1:* Linux Success Stories: Linux Making Inroads in Important Places.

Contemporary PC architecture is built around high-speed communication bus interconnection structures, e.g. *Peripheral Component Interconnect* (PCI). PCI bus allows fast Gbps interconnection communications exchange among building blocks. Effectively, the PCI bus today can generate Gbps rate of bus traffic. If allowed the burst of traffic generated may actually spill over causing a bottleneck to any but multimedia-range high-bandwidth networks. The PC building block today often includes few processor boards, internal as well as external memory modules, multifunction controllers for various I/O interfaces

---

[6] IBM ships Project Monterey 64-bit alpha code
http://www.infoworld.com/articles/pi/xml/00/02/29/000229pimonterey.xml

such as: keyboards, mouse, monitor, CD-ROM, printer, scanner, Network Interface Card (NIC) for networking, modems, etc. A PC represent highly compact, easy to upgrade programmable device with simple modular architecture. *Figure 2* presents common computer architecture of PC client, i.e. laptop or desktop PC.

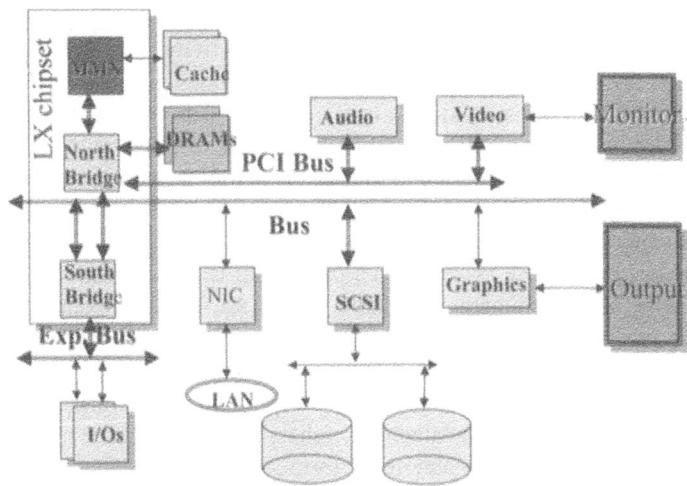

Figure 2. Contemporary PC Client Architecture

A slim or thin PC client is the most recent trend in client architectures to date[7]. A *thin PC* is considered a client associated with the least *Total Costs of Ownership* (TCO) in regard to its pre-loaded applications, OS, and its necessary software maintenance. Since being a hybrid between conventional terminals and PC-based clients it takes a new role with a lower price tag. Nevertheless, it is still equipped with high performance processor board, substantial main memory and all the necessary networking interfaces. Unless required for virtual memory support, there might be no need for local hard-disk memory or local OS support. Most files, data, and applications are maintained and shared across the network. The applications may as well be initiated by Java-aware NOS or network browsers, or even may run using the distributed-memory address-space concept; see *Case 3:* Networked Computing with Beowulf Iridis Cluster. In terms of ACID compliance, thin PC clients have traded some of its functionality, mainly the persistence, in order to achieve lower TCO. However, provided high availability of network connections is guaranteed and assuring large disk-arrays distributed throughout the network may provide simple and inexpensive but highly reliable solutions for persistent data with information sharing. See *Case 3:* Networked

---

[7] *Worldwide Enterprise Thin Client Unit Shipments to Reach 1.4 Million in 2002*, IDC says, 8/14/00

Computing with Beowulf Iridis Cluster . For more on new PC architectures please refer to *BeBox architecture.*

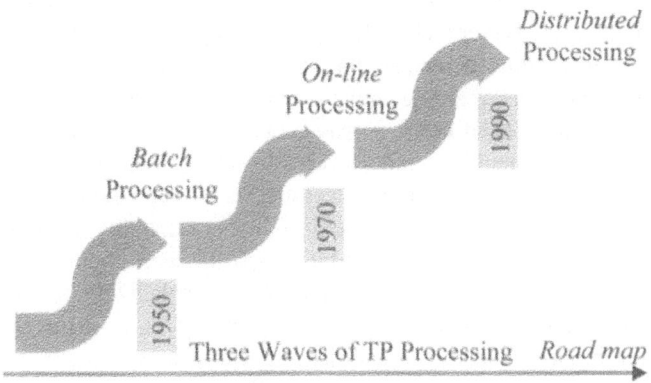

Figure 3. Twenty-year's IT waves [8]

Server's Hardware

A contemporary server architecture traces back to the roots of classic computer architecture, that of mainframe computer systems. There were several important stages in the historical development of server systems. *D. Vaskievitch* from Microsoft refers to this phenomenon as *"twenty-year's IT waves"*; see *Figure 3.*
During the first twenty-year wave known as *batch processing,* the old mainframe systems of the 50's (the so-called *legacy systems)* run mainly centralized operations using dumb and/or character-based terminal processing. The second twenty-year wave brought in *on-line processing.* It started around 1970's introducing decentralized, mini-size modular computer architecture, soon to be followed by the first *Personal Computer* or PC. The last twenty-year wave that we are surfing on began during the last decade of the last century. It brought in the *distributed network* paradigm and with it the *Symmetrical Multi Processing* (SMP) server. Along with it actually came the *Network Computer* (NC). In both cases, the new computer architectures have applied *Reduced Instruction Set Computer* (RISC), which have enabled servers to balance the workload by distributing CPU processing among clusters of processors. Moreover, IBM server R/6000, DEC Alpha server, MIPS 4000, and Sun SPARC servers have been upgraded to 64-bit CPU technology. Intel is expected to join the club soon with its Merced 64-bit processor. The expectations of running up to 8 64-bit Processors in a cluster is to surpass the remarkable overall performance that has been reported on similar SMP servers with clusters of up to 4 Intel's PentiumPro 32-bit processors (e.g. *Compaq ProLiant servers*). At the highest end of the

---

[8] Adapted from UVC Video on Client/Server Architecture, *D. Vaskievitch,* Microsoft, 1994

spectrum are the real *super-servers*. They implement loosely coupled, parallel, or mesh-computer architecture, in an attempt to eliminate SMP bottlenecks. It allows *Massive Parallel Processors* (MPP) supper-servers run some hundreds, even thousands of processors simultaneously, such as Fujitsu AP 1000+, T3D or *Connection Machine CM-5* for instance.

This contemporary server architecture provides solutions to two key issues:

- Increased *availability*. It reduces the system's downtime from several days to only few minutes per year, e.g. approx. 5min/year for 99.999 reliability. Highly dependent on associated costs, it may range from conventional to high, either fault resilient, or fault tolerant levels. In fact, it enables enterprise users uninterrupted access to network services and server-supported resources.

- System *reliability*. It is possible to achieve higher reliability implementing usual data-correction mechanisms such as bus bit-parity checking or relying on *Error Correction Code* (ECC) memories. Moreover, reliable SMPs are equipped with external disk memory using *Redundant Arrays of Inexpensive Disks* (RAID) drives for higher data-store reliability especially in server-array and cluster-based *Multilevel Organisation Memory* (MOM) architecture.

Contemporary server architecture is built with very high bandwidth in mind and multi-bus interconnection structures. Some recent cutting age microprocessors are equipped with crossbar CPU connections on the chip[9]. CPU arrays use multi-tier bus architecture thus integrating several SMP processor boards together with some internal, as well as, secondary cache memory modules. It is highly scaleable system that enables fast access to distributed *RAID* disk drives. A number of network segments may be connected via *Network Interface Cards* (NIC), routers, switches, shared printers, scanners, etc. in distributed, scaleable, easy to upgrade, and highly modular computer architecture. *Figure 4* depicts common computer layout of SMP server architecture. For instance, SMP array and PC cluster implementation are found in *Compaq ProLiant SMP* servers to date. These servers make use of at least two levels of interconnection buses. The high-speed *system bus* integrates multiple processor boards together with Gbyte-range internal memory. More complex hierarchies organized around high-speed *PCI buses* usually include higher tiers of host-to-client bridges integrating wider segments of enterprise network. Similar PCI bus is found in client PC architectures. The difference is primarily in their dedication to network segment integration hence, assisting the management of shareable resources throughout the enterprise network. They may also be coupled with Intel's *Fast Ethernet* NIC thus providing high-bandwidth networking capability.

---

[9] AviON Microprocessors, Butler Group Report, Enterprise NT, Aug. 1998

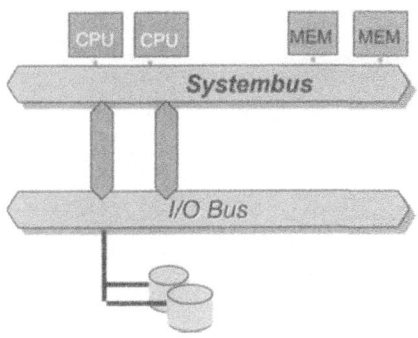

Figure 4. Contemporary SMP Server Architecture [10]

More demanding network configurations may include larger system alternatives:
- SMP in low scaleable clusters with limited number of 4-8 standard CPUs, sharing the main memory; see *Figure 4.*
- *Massive Parallel Processors* (MPP) is highly scaleable, almost unlimited number of processors, sharing no resources, however it runs on non-standard, expensive, parallel application programming code.
- *Non Uniform Memory Access* (NUMA) architecture as a compromise to SMP software availability and MPP scalability implements the state-of-the-art distributed main memory concept by sharing private 'nearer' main cluster's memories among all 'distant' clusters of processors via high speed *Scaleable Coherent Interface* (SCI) backbone ring. *Figure 5* shows simple comparison of characteristic features among different multi processors' alternatives.

---

[10] Adapted from Compaq ProLiant SMP, http://www.compaq.com/newsroom/

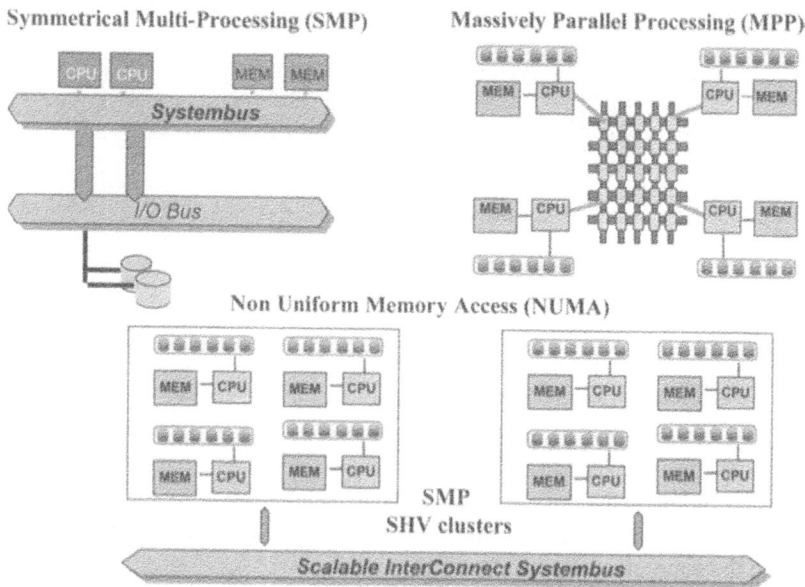

Figure 5. Large System Alternatives: SMP, MPP vs. NUMA[11]

Client's Software

Client software platforms have evolved a long way from dump and ASCII terminals, which were fully dependent on its mainframe. The OS used ranged from first standalone versions of DOS, 16-bit MS Windows 3.x, to 32-bit IBM OS/2, MS Windows '9x/NT, and occasionally MacOS, BeOS or Linux. Today, in the new millennium, MS Windows 2000/NT remains the market leader heading its way to small and medium size servers. However, most recent market reports[12] suggest that Linux is getting even more convincingly.

Interestingly in the mobile client market, Symbion/Psion 32-bit EPOC OS is in close race against MS Windows CE. Are we going to see yet another OS war? The current contest has MS Windows 2000/NT and Linux as main contenders. Hence, a natural question arises. What makes an *Operating System* so important? It is the OS 'intelligence', the virtual resources' model that the OS builds around particular hardware that helps users manage system resources, data, or run applications? Besides being a resource manager, the OS monitors, integrates, and co-ordinates all the processes associated with any computer applications run by the client system.

In order to keep this presentation simple we will discuss only the OS currently in use by majority of clients. Eventually, any OS becomes obsolete giving way to more versatile, more sophisticated and more advanced OS. Advances in IT give

---

[11] Source: Siemens-Nixdorf, [1996]

[12] Corporate Presentation on IBM Linux Platform, CeBit 2000, Hanover

rise to new OS, attracting end-users either through strong market position, or offering attractive features such as responsiveness, efficiency, availability of resources, concurrency, independence of platforms, and application's portability. To date, the main software-selling feature turns to be the affordable *Total Cost of Ownership* (TCO). TCO is a price tag that protects user's investments against ever changing and most demanding application software, so-called *"killer-apps"*. The latter has been overwhelmingly used in the advertising logos therefore, acknowledging the fact that the IT investments have moved away from hardware and more towards user's application domain. The recent software trends include not only application building blocks, components, but also user's knowledge and know-how stored in data *warehouses* and software development *repositories*.

Remembering first OS for desktops, PS DOS and later MS DOS provided clients rather limited resources' support. DOS ran simple unprotected file management system; quite restrictive memory management allowing applications all but less than MByte memory footprint. Being a single-user OS, no provisions were made for concurrent processing. DOS provided neither multiprogramming nor multitasking support. Moreover, both features were necessary to allow multiple users attain concurrent access and efficiently share limited network resources.

Compared to the superior multi-user UNIX OS old timer, MS DOS was rather primitive. However it was easy to manage by end-users. It was low complexity system, providing stand-alone PC processing, unprotected to many threats, but offered at bargain prices. Moreover, due to its independent local mode of processing it provided end-users a wide range of easy to use and inexpensive application software (widely illegally copied too). Combined with the ease of building and supporting various types of I/O devices DOS represented a viable alternative for mainly non-UNIX, home, and variety of common, *small and medium enterprise* (SME) end-users.

Building on DOS, Microsoft introduced the Windows 3.x OS and its *'windows'* look primarily following the Macintosh OS primer. However, the so-called *threads* and threaded applications concept, firstly implemented in MS Windows, was very much dependent on its unreliable DOS predecessor. Sometimes it was actually built on some DOS undocumented features. During runtime, single-user Windows sessions relied heavily on DOS running in the background. It claimed some pre-emptive multitasking features, but no real provisions for concurrency were provided. Additional client networking layers were necessary in order to provide for concurrent processing. Although rather limited segmented memory concept survived several updates.

It was not until full 32-bit architecture memory addressing was adopted, and Windows 3.x was finally replaced by the 32-bit multithreading Windows '9x. Today, it is hard to find real DOS clients anymore, leaving the only two real 32-bit OS alternatives for a client:

- MS Windows 2000/XP, a 32-bit full multi-user multitasking OS has replaced MS Windows '9x and MS Windows 2000/NT 5.0/client workstation OS. MS Windows 2000/XP in many ways stays the OS of the future basically due to its supreme features: reliability, availability, efficiency of its *new technology file system* (NTFS) management, application richness, Internet support, robustness, and mostly due to the refined security, all in one for bargain price tag.

- IBM Metrowerks OS/2, BeOS, and Macintosh OS were possible choices but due to their marginal market share had no chances competing with Windows 2000.
- UNIX is multi-user, multitasking OS used traditionally by mainframes. *Linux OS* is its 32-bit PC variant, a rather interesting option for all kinds of desktops. Linux is full-featured POSIX-based UNIX-like OS designed for inexpensive PCs (Intel 386, 486, Pentiums or PowerPC alike) back in 1991 by Linus Torvald, a student from Finland. Being fully open-code OS, Linux has been developed and improved not just by Linus Torvald, but also by a myriad of unknown Linux followers around the world. Interestingly, as freely down-loadable OS Linux has got an overwhelming support not only by the academia but recently, throughout the industry. Linux has matured over the years provoking the interest of system integrators like Caldera, Red Hat, SuSa, and software giants like IBM, SUN, or BEA. Numerous software vendors are following suite. For more, please refer to *Case 1:* Linux Success Stories: Linux Making Inroads in Important Places
  What is the main functionality that any client needs from an OS?
- *Multitasking* feature turns out to be the most important. At the beginning, a client will start an application. Then, it will eventually switch to another one, leaving the first application dormant. Possibly, it may start some background tasks such as file printing or downloading, or initiate some communications related tasks like e-mail, or some file management tasks such as file searching, copying, or file delete, etc. All these tasks basically rely on transparent, highly responsive request/reply mechanisms by the server system. Consequently, both *pre-emptive multitasking* and *task prioritization* rely on reliable inter-process communication as necessary mechanism for *concurrency* control.
- *OS file management* and shared main *memory protection* is equally important feature. Basically, most OS file management schemes are based either on *File Allocation Table* (FAT) or some other sophisticated schemes, for instance, NTFS for Windows 2000/NT, or NPFS in case of IBM OS/2. The actual differences come from the underlying file indexing structures applied in the file management schemes: linear in case of FAT, or more advanced binary B-tree like schemes in case of NTFS and NPFS. Without going into technical details, FAT turns to be much simpler, and common scheme that any OS could access by default. However, it is rather inefficient with limited addressing, unsafe, and frequently prone to data losses. NTFS on the other hand is sophisticated, highly reliable, secure, and most efficient to date. The MS Windows 2000/NT OS makes use of it by default. The memory allocation mechanisms, enabled by reliable and secure multitasking OS are able to provide efficient concurrent access to shareable system resources.
- *Object Oriented* framework is contemporary trend in the software development best practices allowing for greater reuse of software building components. It introduces specific interface standards that any client's OS system is to provide in order to allow clients share the benefits of *reuse* in everyday computing. The OO computing paradigm will be elaborated later on in **OO Databases**. Building

applications with reusable component, based on platform independent processing are basic features of *Java* programming that according to many programming experts is currently the leading application development environment. Java and Java *applets* derived from *Enterprise Java Beans* (EJB) libraries are now widely accepted trend in component-based OO programming. EJB provides so much desired *computing platform independence* and at the same time *program reliability,* due to highly reliable reused building components. Backed up by the strong *Sun Microsystems* alliance EJB brings in the Internet and full enterprise-wide support by giant vendors such as SUN, IBM, DEC, HP, Netscape, BEA and Oracle. For more see *Java* topics in Enterprise Communication: *EDI, E-mail, Java, Teleconferencing.*

The hottest issue for any client platform to date is by no means the *thin client* model that caters for Java-aware OS and Internet-based distributed component applications. Simply stated, any clients equipped with Internet Java browser can easily obtain network access to various applications developed and deployed by distributed Java components - *applets.* Microsoft being aware of the marketing implications of thin client model acquired Citrix *WinFrame* software and came up with its own terminal net-server that provides an alternative for thin-client networking. SCO UNIX's Tarantella provides similar, but rather effective slim-lined solution for thin client platforms. A thin client establishes its connectivity either through the existing enterprise LAN networking or through the wide range of services provided by *Internet Service Providers* (ISP) for standalone users, home or mobile clients alike. Thus, the new computing paradigm extends the functionality of the existing enterprise networks to so-called *Intranet* environment. Often, this approach seams to be much simpler then achieving connectivity through local area service providers. IBM Lotus *Domino/Notes,* and Novell *IntranetWare* are two networking operating systems (NOS) for extended connectivity in enterprise Intranet networks relying on Internet connectivity. Novell incorporated the Intranet in its NetWare essentially extending the existing *file-print, directory, security,* and *management* services. In addition the IntranetWare package introduced *messaging, Web publishing,* and *wide-area connectivity.* It offers convenient, affordable, networking solution suitable for SMSE, and independent, highly distributed pool of clients whose connectivity requirements are to assist enterprise-wide business functions under minimal total ownership software price tag; see *Case 2:* Novell's Simple Proposals of Generic C/S Architectures. In contrast, the net-centric connectivity by Citrix *WinFrame* downloads on demand the necessary portion of Windows OS and the requested applications from the Terminal Server to the end-user's thin-clients. For more; see *Case 10:* Insignia Solutions apply NTrigue with Citrix WinFrame.

From the TCO point of view, the net-centric paradigm is especially suitable and adequate for e-Business start-up SMSE and large distributed enterprise networks. Paradoxically, the end-users have not shown the expected enthusiasm of the new thin-client NC/terminal hardware released by *Sun Microsystems NC* [13]. It may look as if NC technology is ahead of time, a bit premature primarily due to lack

---

[13] The NC market fate so far has been rather slim; *IC* Sept. 1998: *And so farewell then*

of adequate applications support and rather low demand for introducing and integrating new business activities through the Intranet. However, new palm-held and NC devices are gaining overwhelming Internet market support from mobile communicators such as Nokia, or *Palm-held Digital Assistants* (PDA) like *Velo* by Philips, *Palm V* by HP, Casio, Sony, and Intel hence softening the reluctance of end-users towards thin and NC clients. The established Intranet infrastructure provides thin clients the aforementioned network capability based on extended local connectivity or at the expense of the existing Internet bandwidth. The later issue and how to gain most from it within the *"last mile"* range is elaborated in Last Mile Alternatives: x*DSL, Wireless, Mobile, Bluetooth, FSO*.

Server's Software

In fact, it is the server system that has experienced major changes during the last twenty-year technology wave. Starting with large mainframe, expensive, rather perplexed system in comparison to its simple clients, terminals and early PC-like clients, it become robust, reliable, but still much similar in size and comparable price to a desktop. A server to date encompasses complete, reliable computer system, highly available, not cheap but relatively inexpensive, and scaleable on-demand both in terms of memory and its processing power due to the excellent features of multi-processor architecture. In fact, it's the new breed of servers that the Web-based Application Service Providers (ASP) rely upon to date.

Historically, early mini-computers by DEC might be considered primeval servers to the *file servers* to date engaged primarily in file management related activities. Somewhat similar client-server relationship existed among enduser terminals and departmental mini-computers. Central mainframes however, were on different, higher hierarchical level. Having established full control of information flow in enterprises, they integrated many departmental minis and thousands of terminals together in centralised lacework.

Most mainframes today are running highly proprietary OS. IBM, Cyber, ICL and Unisys are well known mainframe vendors dominating top enterprise networks. The OS provided real multi-user environment, since everything that ran on the mainframe somehow were to be shared by everyone else. In 70's, DEC and its followers introduced PDP later known as VAX, the first mini-computer. It also had to share resources, but smaller in size and cheaper it remained strongly departmental. It was the time when UNIX OS was introduced throughout the computing community. Proliferation of UNIX clones was exceptional. Thirty years later, some 40 different UNIX clones still co-exist.

The second generation of servers that provided unlimited access to corporate databases was usually referred to as *SQL database server*. The vendors are still organised into powerful alliances such as *Open Software Foundation* (OSF) or UI, which are gathered around some important players, *SCO UNIX,* HP, IBM, or *Sun Microsystems.* It is worth mentioning the important role the Object Oriented paradigm (OOP) played with its distributed objects and services. OOP has been early recognised and brought in via *Common Object Request Broker Architecture* (CORBA) standard.

One of the last generation of servers, known as *TP Monitors,* are used mainly to monitor and control complex, nested transactions due to their supreme control over ubiquitous distributed objects. For more please refer to the **Case** *24:* CoreLAN - TP Services with BEA Tuxedo ™. The e-business trend to date, both business-to-customer and business-to-business support, is driving force behind the proliferation of these powerful TP servers.

As *multi-user,* kernel-based OS, UNIX requires substantial technical support. UNIX runs equally well on servers, supercomputers, and on individual PCs. Enterprise servers often run UNIX OS. As mentioned earlier, *Sun Microsystems Linux* alliance has successfully introduced Linux OS to the PC-user world too. The latter is very much in line with the First law of *Dvorak* for Client/Servers: '*If you could run the same OS on both clients and servers - do it!*' Both Linux and Windows 2000/NT proved no exception to this rule.

The remaining alternatives for server OS are shared among *MS Window 2000/NT* now *Windows NT/XP suit, IBM OS/2,* and many proprietary OS like *Sun Solaris, BeOS* and similar. They all have many features in common such as pre-emptive multitasking with multithreading, multiprocessing and SMP support, networking, flexibility, EJB and Java compliance, transparency, reliability, and security.

Bibliography

High-availability Internet servers: Linux clustering on a CompactPCI platform; *Harald Mueller*; Edn, Boston; Dec 7, 2000; Vol. 45, Iss. 25; pg. 143, 4 pgs

Server Appliances -- A Platform of A Different Colour -- Cobalt's Qube 3 isn't merely an appliance any more; *Alan Zeichick*; **InternetWeek**, Manhasset; Nov 27, 2000; pg. PG.44

Decomposing legacy programs: A first step towards migrating to client-server platforms; *Gerardo Canfora*; **The Journal of Systems and Software**, New York; Oct 15, 2000; Vol. 54, Iss. 2; pg. 99

New servers expand, integrate Web apps platform; *Russell Kay*; **Computerworld**, Framingham; Jun 12, 2000; Vol. 34, Iss. 24; pg. 69, 1 pgs

IBM servers: Mainframe features on Intel platform; *Paul McDougall*; **InformationWeek**, Manhasset; Mar 20, 2000, Iss. 778; pg. 93, 1 pgs

HP scales back thin-client program, eyes server model; *Joseph F Kovar*; **Computer Reseller News**, Manhasset; Nov 22, 1999, Iss. 870; pg. 91, 2 pgs

Too many servers? Try a consolidation program; *Marc Songini*; **Network World**, Framingham; Oct 25, 1999; Vol. 16, Iss. 43; pg. 21, 2 pgs

Platform debuts Web server manager; *Brian Riggs*; **InformationWeek**, Manhasset; Jun 23, 1999, Iss. 740; pg. 18, 1 pgs

Intel's Real Server program helps end server confusion; *Marcia Savage*; **Computer Reseller News**, Manhasset; Jun 21, 1999, Iss. 847; pg. 99, 2 pgs

IBM morphs OS/2 warp server into e-business platform; *John Fontana*; **Network World**, Framingham; Jun 7, 1999; Vol. 16, Iss. 23; pg. 19, 1 pgs

Active server pages freed from platform; *David Orenstein*; **Computerworld**, Framingham; May 24, 1999; Vol. 33, Iss. 21; pg. 64, 1 pgs

Server platform to power mobile transactions; *Bob Curley*; **Bank Systems & Technology**, New York; May 1999; Vol. 36, Iss. 5; pg. 24, 1 pgs

Linux: Application server platform of choice?; *Dana Gardner*; **InfoWorld**, Framingham; Jan 25, 1999; Vol. 21, Iss. 4; pg. 26, 1 pgs

The future of tape in enterprise storage--server or mainframe media platforms?; *Sig Tullmann*; **Computer Technology Review**, Los Angeles; Jan 1999; Vol. 19, Iss. 1; pg. 46, 2 pgs

Power In Numbers -- Trio bets on portals as the enterprise platform for hardware, software, content, services; **InternetWeek** *Richard Karpinski*; Nov 30, 1998

The extranet habit: The Web becomes the new business platform; **Fortune** *Anonymous*; Summer 1998

Sybase plans five business platforms, buys Intellidex Systems; **Computer Dealer News** *Jacqueline Emigh*; Mar 2, 1998

Your intranet: Dancing icons or enterprise platform?; **Telecommunications** *Chris Dallas-Feeney*; Mar 1998

Stuart McClure: Enterprise platforms manager; **InfoWorld** *Stuart McClure*; Jan 19, 1998

CHAPTER 2

NETWORK INFRASTRUCTURE

Connection vs Connectionless Paradigm

Case 3: Networked Computing with Beowulf Iridis Cluster

SOUTHAMPTON UNIVERSITY'S PREMIER COMPUTE FACILITY
http://www.sucs.soton.ac.uk/research/iridis/
(Copyright © 2002, Southampton University Computing Services.
Reproduced by permission of Southampton University Computing Services)

Beowulf is a well-known research project to produce software for off-the-shelf clustered workstations based on commodity PC-class hardware, a high-bandwidth internal network, and often based on Linux operating system.

Iridis is one of the largest computational facilities in the UK. Funded by HEFCE and purchased from Compusys Plc, Iridis is what is commonly known as a Beowulf cluster. The price/performance ratio of these platforms is exceptional and has attracted attention and investment worldwide. Iridis is the latest and largest of a growing number of Beowulf clusters at Southampton. Access to Iridis provides high performance computing facilities in a professionally managed service environment to a wide spectrum of the University's researchers.

Iridis contains
- 404 processors; consisting of 292 1000Mhz Intel Pentium III's; 80 1800Mhz Intel Pentium IV's and 32 1500Mhz Intel Pentium IV's
- 192Gb of memory
- 8.5Tb of local disk storage
- 2.8Tb on RAID5 disk array

Iridis is capable of 484 billion floating-point calculations per second

Beowulf installations
The increase in performance achieved by desktop PCs over the last few years has been accompanied by a growth in the use of such computers in numerically intensive scientific applications. The Beowulf Project has used the convergence of

mid-range proprietary workstations and desktop PC's to produce commodity super-computers.

The basic idea is to connect together a number of headless PCs via some network whether it be simple Fast Ethernet or a more specialised interconnect and using the flexibility of the operating system create an environment wherein the individual workstations, appear to the user, to behave as one multi-CPU computer. Since all of the components in such a machine are off-the-shelf and mass-produced the cost benefits of such an approach are clearly apparent.

The number of Beowulf installations around the world has grown significantly in the past few years. Most of these installations use Intel IA-32 CPUs and the free operating system Linux. Although, Compaq's Alpha and AMD's Athlon CPUS and the Microsoft Windows clusters are also taking a share in this arena.

Here at Southampton a number of departments have chosen this method to fulfil there own high performance computing needs, and the collection of clusters extends across the range of platforms and operating systems mentioned above.

Linux Platforms
- Southampton University Computing Services run Iridis a 172 node Intel cluster which provides high performance computing facilities to researchers throughout the University.
- Southampton University Computing Services administer Metropolis a 19 node Intel cluster for ECS and Social Statistics.
- The Chemistry Department has the Magic Roundabout, which contains a mixture of 39 AMD Athlons and 4 dual Intel nodes.
- Electronics and Computer Science has an 8 node AMD Athlon cluster.
- The Computational Engineering and Design Centre and have two clusters a 21 dual node and a 10 dual node Intel cluster.
- Aerodynamics and Flight Mechanics have an 11 dual node Intel cluster.

Windows Platforms
- Aeroacoustics have a 9 dual node Windows-2000 cluster.
- The High Performance Computing Centre (HPCC) has constructed a Windows NT based cluster with 16 533Mhz Alpha nodes.
- In addition the High Performance Computing Group also runs the Windows Cluster web site with support from Microsoft.

Networking Paradigms
Networks are everywhere around us. Internet for instance, has been gaining users with 95% growth rate per year[14]. Despite warnings for saturated growth at the beginning of the century, from 8.6 million Web servers by the middle of 2000[15]

[14] Information Strategy with Novell and INSEAD, *The Global Internet 100 Survey 1998 Special Report*
[15] CW International, Aug.10, 1998, *Future Internet Services, The End of the Web?*

has reached 36 million in Aug. 2002 following the Netcraft Survey Report[16]. The growth of enterprise networks therefore is no exception but a fact.

Small offices are embarking on networking in order to share files and data, printers, scanners, etc. Collaborative computing, remote processing, global reach, virtual offices in large enterprises, distributed outlets, *POSIX* based terminals, information inquiry offices etc., all rely on efficient and low-cost networking.

The prospect is to reach the customer as soon as possible through fast network deployment, efficiently networking our offices remotely, distributed workgroups, and ultimately virtual global enterprises. One thing is certain, *desktops* are becoming ubiquitous networking clients shaping up a new enterprise networking. Depending on how much networking support one could possibly achieve, there are two types of clients: *thin clients* and *fat clients,* or software run on-demand and software loaded respectively. The choice between thin and fat clients is all but academic and turns to be rather important, since it affects not only the TCO enterprise networking price-tag but also the usual client's response in relation to client's ACID properties.

Terminals and some PC-emulated versions were considered software lean since very little was required for very simple networking (mainly centralised though). Today however, according to any criteria a PC in our office when compared to a terminal is fully loaded, therefore exceptionally fat client. Take for instance PC's main memory. In many cases it approaches some server's standards with at least 128 MB of RAM, often to 256MB, guiding the present trend to 512MB or more. What kind of *Central Processing Unit* (CPU) or processor board does it acquire? Usually single, high-speed, Intel's PentiumPro, AMD or Motorola's PowerPC processor at 2000 MHz or more, becomes a PC standard. Commonly, there is built-in SMP support, often with Intel Pentium, AMD or Motorola PowerPC dual processors onboard. For more, please refer to *BeBox*. Regarding the client system configuration, by default, it comes fully loaded with multimedia, networking, communications, huge external memory support etc. Despite current doubling of client's performance per year for the same price, the threat of obsolescence and software investment loss is present more than ever. Therefore, it is necessary for PC hardware and especially application software to follow the IT pace and be fully updated in less than 12 months! Changes in networking and the associated costs with software maintenance become even more pronounced. No wonder the most recent trend promotes new enterprise networking paradigms with *low TCO*.

Following marketing policies of major PC suppliers, for instance Microsoft present networking relies still on fat, heavily loaded PC clients. It represents a compromise solution for high availability of local, often home or mobile clients, independent, stand-alone PC processing, and necessity for reliable but simple, low-costs enterprise-wide networking. Eventually, the price tag for this constant migration and pursuing the technology pace is rather high. Apparently, the

---

[16] Netcraft Survey Results, http://www.serverwatch.com/news/article.php/1451411, Aug. 23, 2002

advances and constant IT improvements once implemented in PCs are managed functionality rather than leveraged opportunity. However, changes for the better are expected according to overwhelming reactions to *MS Windows 2000/NT/XP.* SMSE have adopted the new networking paradigms built following the concept of low total cost of ownership in mind, actually adopting the thin-client model. In order to provide necessary flexibility and free choice for different business models, the expectations are that SMSE will adopt either *three-tier, peer-to-peer* networks, or follow much simpler conventional *two-tier* net-centric solution. Regardless, any choice will be in favour of *connectionless* IP packet switching. For more see *Case 10:* Insignia Solutions apply NTrigue with Citrix WinFrame.

Apparently, net-centric model becomes a viable trend. Is the net-centric model comeback of the old mainframe-terminal paradigm, a *'deja vue'*, or *'back to the future'* concept? The increased functionality introduced by the ubiquitous Internet presence calls for new *Network Computer* architecture. It seems we are back to the future, are we not? For instance, a *thin-client* system configuration comprised of fast, dual processors with at least 128 MB of RAM main memory comes fully equipped for networking capability. The OS, applications, data, and network management overhead data is downloaded on-demand from appropriate networking or application servers through usual network interfaces. For more, please refer to *Sun Microsystems NC* and most recent thin-client market reports [7]. However, the common PC-centric model is not giving up. It has demonstrated its success in wide-distributed computing too. Accordingly, Beowulf Project has experimentally shown the viability of distributed networked PC paradigm with a *pool of PopC*; see Case 3: Networked Computing with Beowulf Iridis Cluster.

Moreover, Linux *how to* Beowulf document defines the Beowulf PC architecture as following: 'Beowulf is a multi computer architecture, which can be used for parallel computations. It is a system, which usually consists of one server node, and one or more client nodes connected together via Ethernet or some other network. It is a system built using commodity hardware components, like any PC capable of running Linux, standard Ethernet adapters, and switches. It does not contain any custom hardware components and is trivially reproducible. Beowulf also uses commodity software like the Linux operating system, Parallel Virtual Machine (PVM) and Message Passing Interface (MPI). The server node controls the whole cluster and serves files to the client nodes. It is also the cluster's console and gateway to the outside world. Large Beowulf machines might have more than one server node, and possibly other nodes dedicated to particular tasks, for example consoles or monitoring stations. In most cases client nodes in a Beowulf system are dumb, the dumber the better. The nodes are configured and controlled by the server node, and do only what they are told to do. In a diskless client configuration, client nodes don't even know their IP address or name until the server tells them what it is. One of the main differences between Beowulf and a Cluster of Workstations (COW) model is the fact that Beowulf behaves more like a single machine rather than a workstation-cluster. Often client nodes do not need keyboards or monitors, and are accessed only via remote login or possibly a serial terminal. Beowulf nodes can be thought of as a CPU + memory package which can be plugged in to the cluster, just like a CPU or memory module can be plugged into a motherboard.

Beowulf is not a special software package, new network topology or the latest kernel hack. Beowulf is a technology of clustering Linux computers to form a parallel, virtual supercomputer.'

The early experimental networks comprise of a cluster of 16 PCs, off-the-shelf Pentium commodity microprocessor systems and a custom-built network OS. Each node consists of a 1.2 GB hard drive, 32 Mbytes DRAM of main memory, and a couple of 100 Mbps *Fast Ethernet* channels. The project has successfully shown the networking ability and advantages of actual distributed network-processing of single-user client environment at lower costs than that achieved through conventional network of high-end workstations and servers competing even with supercomuters[27].

In order to understand current developments of networking paradigms, two important networking issues are to be elaborated on: the *ownership* of providing networking services, and the way *connectivity* is implemented, whether by *connectionless*, or through *connection-oriented* communications techniques.

Network Ownership: Private vs. Public

Depending on network complexity, clients in one tier of the network and servers in the other may implement simple, centralised, *two-tier architecture*. However, *three-tier architecture* is also viable alternative, especially in case of large numbers of non-homogeneous clients. Servers as usual provide for various types of services including networking, whereby, intermediate tiers of servers provide for transparent connectivity of tiers of mainly non-homogeneous users. Hence, it is the *ownership of service-functions,* not the ownership of networking assets that actually makes the difference between private and public networks:

– *Private network*, as the name suggests, is usually owned by a single enterprise. It entails networking infrastructure as well as associated services. Usually, it is the option chosen by SMSE units, few offices, often within a single location, a cluster of buildings, or a network node. It consists of a certain networking infrastructure, *a network and file server*, a number of clients, and networking services offered to all users within the enterprise domain. It is self-sufficient network in terms of networking support, since it provides users access to shareable resources and often some access to networking services beyond its own environment.

– *Public networks* offer services to consumers through public communication interfaces: fax/modem equipped dial-up phone lines, *Packet Switching Networks* PSN X.25 connections and *TCP/IP* leased lines, *Broadband Wireless Access* (BWA) [17] for fixed to mobile convergence, or via *Cable TV* (CATV) microwave, terrestrial or satellite. With overwhelming presence of the Internet, a user can access the Web, irrespective of place, time, or type of client system. Besides some basic networking it is also possible to get services such as wide

---

[17] IC, Sept. 1998, Broadband Wireless Access, *Radio Reassessed*

connectivity, or network inquiry services. It may resemble in many aspects to a private network service. However, there is some difference. With overwhelming presence of public networks on the market, a client makes use of the existing networking infrastructure.

Networking access is all it needs: TCP/IP, ISDN, or xDSL with multifold increase in bandwidth on copper POT lines, or CATV on coax or fibre distribution lines offered by many *Internet Service Providers* (ISP). Communication implemented by many public networks is in *broadcasting* mode, as in case of Web access via CATV and BWA or most often as *Peer-to-Peer IP routing* communications used in commercial PSN inter-node connections.

Peer-to-Peer networks provide clients with *Serial Line Internet Protocol* (SLIP) or *Point-to-Point Protocol* (PPP) connections. PPP is superior and regularly used since SLIP is often unreliable over error-prone dial-up lines and requires its IP addressing configuration set. Windows 9x for instance, doesn't support peer-to-peer networking over SLIP connections. It means that both parties have to use the same communication protocol interface, in order to initiate and conduct symmetrical network conversation. The underlying architecture can be either two-tier for individuals and relatively small numbers of users, or three-tier for medium and large numbers of corporate SMSE users. The enterprise networks have early recognised the advantages of this low-cost networking alternative.

Internet and many similar public networks are offering common information services, very much similar to common consumer services, just like electricity, water, phone and other communal services. The drop in ownership costs for networking services with the economy of scale expected with large numbers of users makes this type of networking paradigm appealing equally well to individual users, SMSE or even large enterprises. Eventually, the associated cost of network infrastructure for public networks falls dramatically. A paraphrase of a song title by Beatles '*all you need is a PC*' may look like Microsoft logo, but still, it may be considered rather expensive networking solution. If keen for networking services, an *Internet Computer* provides an affordable alternative for less than third of the equivalent Win PC price. It is to be expected that the new *Internet equipped TV set* offered by many Cable TV providers would provide inexpensive network access too. Besides being used mainly for browsing with abundance of Java applications coming into it, it promises more than mere TV Tele-text on the Web. Refer to *Asymmetrical Digital Subscribe Line* (ADSL) and **Case 16: NetSpeed** Copper-based High-speed WAN Link via ADSL for high bandwidth local loop networking alternative.

Network Communications: Connection vs. Connectionless

Eventually, networking technology to date becomes much more closely related to communications techniques. The convergence process involves the telephony too. The legacy of old communications systems is undergoing a change either as digital voice over IP, or via multimedia merger of voice, data, image and video in mobile telephony. Telephony has evolved from traditional connection-oriented communications technology such as *Plain Old Telephone Systems* (POTS) to the connectionless communications alternatives as voice mail, teleconferencing, or *Internet Phone*. Actually, network nodes and IP routing could easily perform channel switching and become a viable channel or a circuit-switching alternative. Digital technology, besides doing real *channel switching,* is also able to do *cell-switching*. It actually sends or broadcasts *frames and cells*, packets of digitised information, fast enough via virtual channels using common communications technology. What are main differences between two communications networks?

– *Connection-oriented* networks were mainly used in the past for *voice traffic*. Nowadays, the improved reliable digital technology enables sharing of available channel capacity via base/broadband *virtual-channels*. Not only voice, but also computer data and all media types are easily transmitted using digital encoding. The transport service guarantees that all data will be delivered to the other end as continuous stream following the same order as sent and without duplication. Usual communication session proceeds through three phases: connection set-up, data transfer and connection release, e.g. *Transmission Control Protocol* (TCP).

– *Connectionless* networks are widely used for data but also for digital voice, TV, radio and wireless communications. It is used for a variety of *communication bus* connections or *drop-line* communications in older mainframe-based centralised computer networks connecting *pool of terminals* via single line. Today, it is primarily used in PSN for IP routing. IP is an example of connectionless, packet switching protocol with optimal use of bandwidth that can tolerate an arbitrarily long delay. The data link layer is responsible for packet routing, fragmentation and re-assembly. The network layer for TCP/IP protocol suite is widely used on Ethernet and Internet networks.

The two types of networks use inherently different communications technology. Not only simpler, connectionless technology is also independent of number of clients and communications pool size. Network switching may require complex many-to-many communication. The pair-wise conversation links rely heavily on local environments. It is often limited to mainly one-to-many conversation (e.g. broadcasting based radio or TV communications).

Networking technology permitted technological shifts to both networking paradigms, implemented so far with a variable success. Enterprise networks have successfully used either connectionless communications such as *Ethernet LAN* networks and *TCP/IP* based Internet or connection-based communications such as virtual circuits in *ATM* cell-switching or *X.25* PSN networks. Any network infrastructure thus assumes distinct, different interfaces, protocols, standards, and specific requirements.   Check Networking Standards Overview in the Appendix.

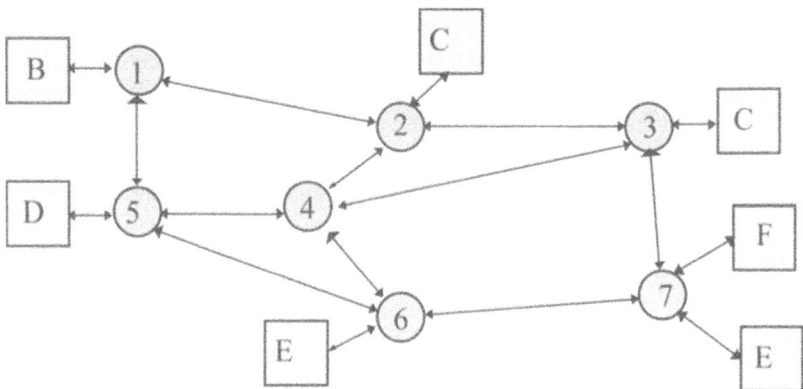

Figure 6. Generic Networks

The concept of computer networks is illustrated in *Figure 6*. The generic network consists of *nodes* connected by a set of *communication links*. The hardware systems associated with nodes and links correspond to concepts presented in Network Hardware. The software solutions, interface protocols, and standards are presented in the Appendix: Communications Protocols are related to a particular networking implementation and required for network integration referred to as Network Software.

Internet Hierarchy

As mentioned earlier, the Internet has become the fastest growing public network in the world. Internet is based on TCP/IP communication protocol. In relation to OSI the TCP/IP encompasses both networking and data link layers. Interestingly, IP provides simple and efficient connectionless packet switching whereas TCP on IP enables flow-control and reliable connection-oriented communication. In principle, the nodes, links, and host components, all three could be networks. The only difference is their IP addressing. The IP v. 4 addressing scheme entails four numbers each one in the range of [0-255], for instance IP:[137.120.96.89]. Accordingly, there are three classes of networks: class A uses one number only in the range of [0-126] as its host address so that the rest can be allocated to its clients; class B uses two numbers in the range [128.0 – 191.255], and class C uses three numbers in the range [192.0.1 – 223.255.255]. It is clear that class A may allocate the remaining three numbers to its clients thus become very large network with as much as 16 million clients; B can allocate two with less than 16 thousand clients; and C only one number with support to at most 253 clients. As far the number of networks is concerned, due to IP address there can be only 128 A network types, as much as 16 thousand B network types, and almost 2 million C network types. For readability purposes the IP address is always associated with corresponding Internet Domain Names (IDN), such as .com, .edu, .org, .gov, .biz etc. For instance, www.mit.edu has [18.181.0.31] for IP address of A class network, www.ibm.com has [129.42.18.99] IP address of B class network, and similarly www.odci.gov [198.81.129.100] is IP address of C class network. These networks entail a hierarchical Internet structure. The IP address translation to IDN is the responsibility of a *Domain Name Server* (DNS) in accordance with *Address Resolution Protocol* (ARP). Some networks constitute the Internet *backbone*, yet others represent *transient* networks that connect the end-users or *stub* networks to the backbone. The inter-networking devices at the nodes where networks meet are known as *routers, network bridges* or *gateways*. They connect hosts to at least two of its neighbouring networks therefore need at least three IP addresses, one to the host, and two to the links. Since distribution of IP addresses within networks is sparse and rather inefficient, contributed to the shortage of IP addresses. A solution to the unprecedented Internet growth, starting from 2000, the W3C has introduced an extended IP addressing scheme known as IP v.6 or IP *next generation* protocol. It extends the four [0-255] range address numbers to 16 numbers, at the same time preserving the present Internet hierarchical structure. The Internet and the Web are open standard protocols. Tim Berners-Lee, CERN, invented the Web and associated protocols in 1990. The URL assigns a unique address to any information entity on the Web. HTML is its universally accepted format, and HTTP is Web delivering protocol over the TCP/IP Internet platform.

Network Hardware

Networking hardware simply entails network channels, nodes, and interfaces.
- *Network channels,* whether real or virtual, represent communications *links* between network nodes or among associated clients. It is possible to have more simultaneous links between same pairs of nodes called network *paths*. Links and paths are considered shareable resources. Dedicated links assigned to a single user have restricted shareability. Virtual links or paths provide bandwidth on-demand, via shareable network links (e.g. virtual channels in ATMs).
- *Network nodes* are particular sites that host active processing devices called network *switches* and/or *servers*. Network nodes are usually linked by high bandwidth communication links, e.g. 64 Kbps channels, 2 Mbps Frame relays, A1 to 4/T1 to 4 lines, 100/10 Mbps Ethernet links, or as in case of **NGI** super networks even tens of Gbps links. The nodes in switching networks connect ATM and PBX switches through host switching devices or Point-to-Point links. Whenever connectionless communications is used hosts are computer *servers* or sometimes inter-networking devices such as *routers, gateways,* or *bridges.*
Depending on site allocation of enterprise offices throughout the network and the type of implemented networking, the network channels comprise of *switched* Point-to-Point links, and *broadcasting* network links such as LAN segments.
Networking hardware associated with these links use either copper or optic fibre conducts for *guided media* communications channels. *Unguided* and *wireless* communication channels such as radio, TV, satellite, and terrestrial microwave transmission, extend existing networks beyond stationary and local boundaries

into mobile[18] and global networks. For more refer to Mobile networking in *Case 14:* CallWare's Callegra Advanced Messaging System.

— *Networking interfaces* represent a generic name for a set of specific devices used to connect users to networks. End-user systems, terminals, PC and NC make use of *Network Interface Cards* (NIC), a computer hardware card that are placed into the extension-bus slots. NIC implements specific networking protocols, which together with the associated interface standards provide desired connections to the network. Some common NIC used to connect clients to networks are *10 Base-T2* for 10 Mbps coax Ethernet LAN clients (refer to *Cisco, 100 Base-TX* for FastEthernet over 100 Mbps Unshielded Twisted Pair (UTP) cable category 5 (refer to *Intel)*, also *28.8 Kbps Fax/Modem Card* for dial-up access, and *128 Kbps ISDN Card* (refer to *Motorola)* for dial-up phone/fax/network interface.

Network Software

Middleware is a generic name for a set of networking software used for mapping client applications to network resources; see *Figure 7*. Middleware implements necessary connection protocols among network OS, databases, and applications clients may want to use. It plays an important integrating role, especially if used with heterogeneous hardware, different software systems across networking environments. Middleware is especially valuable in three-tier and higher n-tier networks providing an appropriate environment for specific application servers. Middleware products are also aiming at solving the application-to-database connectivity. Some alternative solutions for connectivity include messaging, communications, mail services, etc. On the client side middleware takes care of various *Application Program Interfaces* (API) used to invoke specific actions in applications. It also manages transmission requests by clients' responses, which may also include appropriate servers' responses e.g. *Remote Procedure Call* (RPC), messaging, or queuing services. Some specific middleware products are NetBIOS, NetWare, LAN Manager, Vines, or OSF's DCE. Middleware consists of three layers: *transport stacks*, NOS, and service-specific *network agents*:

---

[18] IC, Sept., 1998, The growth of GSM, *Ain't no stopping us now.*

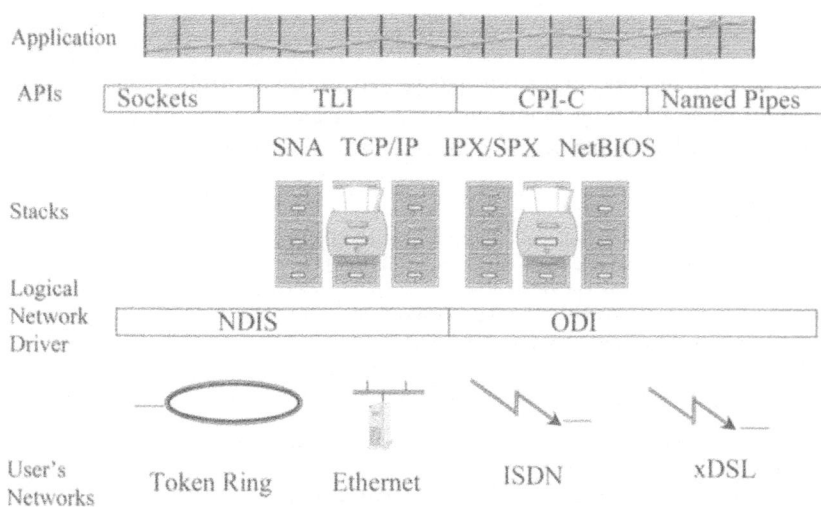

Figure 7. Networking Software

– *Network Operating System* (NOS) refers to a OS running on a network server and responsible for managing services provided by the server. It offers certain availability and reliability, performance, security, and internetworking within the enterprise network. It provides networking services such as routing, distribution, messaging, also sharing common resources like files or printers, and including some network management services. More on NOS, refer to *IntranetWare* from Novell in the *Case 5:* Novell NetWare at Beveridge & Diamond. Other NOS are IBM *OS/2 LAN Server*; Microsoft *Windows 2000/NT, LAN Manager*; Artisoft's LANtastic, Banyan's *VIrtual NEtwork System (VINES)*, Novel's *NetWare* etc.

– *Transport Stacks* role is to establish the necessary transport protocols such as NetBIOS, TCP/IP, IPX/SPX, DECnet, etc. for reliable network communications. For more see Network Connectivity and Networking Standards Overview.

– *Network agents* are relatively new autonomous software entities. Agents are usually launched by specific applications, Web servers, and Network Managers capable of executing commands remotely on behalf of dispatching applications in an open, multi-vendor, host environment. Residing or running on different network platforms, network agents are able to provide Network Management applications valuable information and current status reports. Some examples of network agents include: *firewall* that is *responsible* for implementing enterprise security rules*; mail agent* that monitors and reports on current status of network mail resources, mail boxes, address lists, mail queues; *time agent* in charge of synchronisation of the global time services in open distributed networks, etc. There are also some rather sophisticated '*intelligent agents*' acting autonomously on behalf of Web service providers, either ISP or ASP used for remote information gathering. For instance, they help fulfil the goals and objectives of some e-Business solutions such as the *Customer Service Management* (CSM) policies, *Supply Chain Management* (SCM) virtual Web catalogues, *Knowledge Management/Messaging* (KM/M) services, and *Business Intelligence* (BI) surveys. For more, please see *Portal-in-a-Box™,* automated online information Portal by Autonomy. Ltd., or *Neugents*, ANN software agent technology applied by Computer Associates *Jasmine ii* application.

Bibliography

Network Infrastructure -- A Complete Solution -- Enterasys Networks proves its mettle in enterprise-class switching; *Keith Schultz*; **InternetWeek**, Manhasset; Jan 22, 2001; p.33

Network Infrastructure -- The All-In-One VPN Router -- Cisco's 7140 VPN router offers advanced site-to-site routing for your enterprise; *Keith Schultz*; **InternetWeek**, Manhasset; Sep 18, 2000; pg. PG.40

Safeguard Your Network -- ClearTrust provides scalable infrastructure for e-business; *Diane E. Levine*; **InternetWeek**, Manhasset; Mar 27, 2000; pg. PG.35

Network infrastructure to support application technology; **Telecommunications** *Bill Yarborough*; Aug 1998

SET makes inroads at N. American banks, readies to blend into Web infrastructure; **Bank Systems + Technology** *Alison F Orenstein*; Mar 1998

Network infrastructure: The superconductor for retail innovation; **Chain Store Age** *Jeffery Siegal*; Jul 1997

CHAPTER 3

NETWORK ARCHITECTURE

Transactions and Sessions

Case 4: Xdrive Technologies, Inc. Acquires Businesses of Freedrive, Inc.

XDRIVE TECHNOLOGIES, INC. ACQUIRES BUSINESSES OF FREEDRIVE, INC.
http://www.xdrive.com/press/releases/pr_20020225.shtml

"We needed access to a virtual drive that would be shared with our vendors. Due to security concerns, we couldn't grant outside companies access to our network. Our IS&T group was also strapped for resources, so to minimize their involvement, we required a contract provider. We use Xdrive to exchange log data, reports, schedules... instead of e-mail, CDs, diskettes, hard copies and other methods of communication. I am confident that this method of communication will be adopted by other Texaco business units."
IT Manager Texaco Research, April 2001

MARINA DEL REY, Calif., February 25, 2002 -- Xdrive Technologies, Inc., a leading provider of Internet information management software and services, announced today the acquisition of the businesses of FreeDrive, Inc., a leading Enterprise Storage Application Provider. The acquisition brings together FreeDrive's consumer and commercial web-based storage applications with Xdrive's software and services that provide secure access, storage, backup, sharing, synchronization and transactional management of information distributed via the Internet.

"This acquisition establishes Xdrive as the clear market leader in a solid growth market with strong demand from large enterprises, carriers, small and medium businesses and consumers," said Karl Klessig, president and CEO, Xdrive Technologies. "Combining our businesses promises increased benefits for all of our customers, partners and investors." Among the benefits he mentioned were enhanced technical expertise, combined leadership and an expanded range of services.

These expanded resources will help Xdrive to meet the growing demand for online storage and the technology that eases sharing of information from different devices and locations. Already, Xdrive's convenient offering allows users to leverage the Internet as an environment for storing and sharing information, which is becoming increasingly rich with text, images, music and video.

Since last fall, Xdrive's services have been bundled with Microsoft's Windows XP, offering online storage as a Web service accessed via the Web Publishing Wizard. Currently, users in 30 countries are using Xdrive's services to upload, download and share their files from anywhere, at any time, using any wireline or wireless Internet-ready device, including personal computers, PDAs, WAP phones and public Internet terminals.

"The consolidation of Xdrive and FreeDrive forms a stronger base of talent, technology and partners, making the combined business a more robust software and services platform for customers," said Dean DeBiase, CEO of FreeDrive. "This alliance also allows Xdrive to further leverage FreeDrive's strategic partners, EDS and Motorola, in the enterprise marketplace." He also said that Xdrive, as a stronger market leader, will be good for the industry and will further stimulate the demand for secure online storage, access and collaboration services.

Combining the businesses expands Xdrive's reach into key vertical markets and augments its business categories, adding to the consumer, small business and corporate base and further extending into the enterprise business market. The acquisition also extends Xdrive's geographic reach, adding a Chicago link to its network of sales and support offices in Atlanta, Boston, New York, San Francisco and Salt Lake City. The corporate headquarters will remain in the Los Angeles area.

About Xdrive Technologies

Xdrive Technologies, Inc. is a privately held company headquartered in Marina del Rey, Calif. Known as the Internet Information Management Company, it provides software products and services for access, storage, sharing and transactional management of information distributed via the Internet. Strategic investors include SOFTBANK CORP., VERITAS Software, VeriSign, Inc., StorageNetworks, Inc., EMC Corporation, Network Appliance, Aether Systems, Mitsubishi Corporation, NEC Corporation, C-Networks, Inc. and AOL/Time Warner. Financial Investors include Goldman Sachs Group, Wit SoundView Ventures, Deutsche Banc Alex. Brown, Centre Partners, eCompanies-Evercore Venture Management (E2VM), Pacific Capital Group, David Bohnett's Baroda Ventures, Davis Companies, Amos Hostetter's Pilot House Associates and J. & W. Seligman & Co. Inc.

About FreeDrive

FreeDrive, an Enterprise Storage Application Provider, develops and markets online storage and information management solutions through its CompanyDrive (sm) and FreeDrive (sm) brands, which enable users to securely store, retrieve, share and distribute audio, video and data files from Internet and wireless devices from anywhere at any time.

Client/Server Concept: ACID Transactions Communication

The *client/server* is a networking model and a relationship concept established between two processes or systems running these processes. A *client process* once initiated by the client system makes a request for a service to be provided by another system, so-called *server process*. Usually, the server may respond once, presumably providing the results of performing the service or by launching subsequently an "*agent*" task, which in turn can perform specific actions in order to complete the client's request.

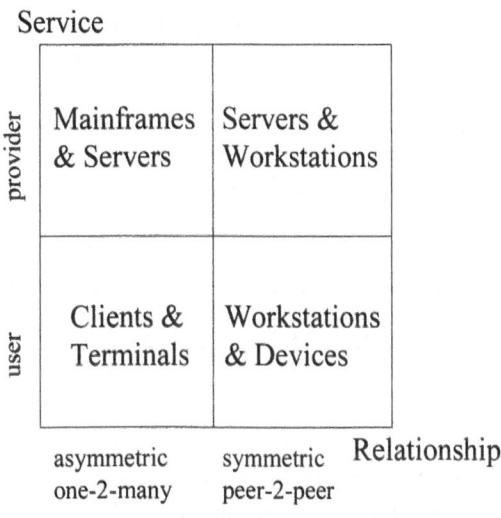

Figure 8. Relationship Types

Clients Participating in ACID Transactions

The *client* is a system or an application running on that system. For instance, a client can be a simple computer terminal equipped with a monitor that may also include some I/O devices such as, a keyboard, or a mouse, which could perform simple data presentation tasks. Also, a common PC able to perform some higher information computing processes may initiate client processes too. PC client processes may often request services from file/print, network, and Web servers, therefore establishing a specific client/server relationship; see *Figure 8*. There are many client devices to date that could be networked based upon C/S concept; see *Table 1*. Along with traditional cable interfaces to the network, the trend today is geared towards wireless and mobile-networked devices supported by *Wireless Access Protocol* (WAP). In order to keep devices as much as possible physically compact a compromise has taken place.

There is a trade-off between the rich functionality and occasional connectivity, hence negotiating some well-established ACID properties in order to get more functionality. For instance, thin NCs, wireless PDAs, or mobile WAP phones may require a kind of *permanent storage's support* in order to provide data *persistency*[26]. Other clients may lack *atomicity*, i.e. all-or-nothing transaction execution due to unreliable or occasional rather than *permanent connectivity*[23].

This might be as a result of deteriorated quality of wireless connection, which in turn may result in *inconsistent* transactions[24]. Often, it may not been able to process transactions *concurrently*, i.e. in *isolation* due to *lack of concurrent processing mechanisms* and/or lack of transactional monitor's support required for such *complex transactions*[25]. In all these cases where the ACID properties are violated it might result in *inconsistent* transaction processing; see *Table 3* that gives some insights in *Atomicity*[19], *Consistency*[20], *Isolation*[21], and *Durability*[22] properties for some frequently used clients. Eventually, the new-networked devices have changed the conventional networking paradigms introducing much richer forms of functionality and at the same time broadening the communications variety C/S networking are able to establish. This is mainly due to the *stateless feature* of HTTP Web protocol that requires an additional agent at application level responsible to provide sustainable ACID properties of clients.

Table 1. Device Networking

Networking Types	Device	Client	Workstation	Server
Device (WAP, PDA)	limited	limited	C/S	C/S
Client (NC, fat PC)	limited	Pear-2-Peer	C/S	C/S
Workstation (fat WS)	C/S	C/S	Pear-2-Peer	Pear-2-Peer
Server (thin WS)	C/S	C/S	Pear-2-Peer	Pear-2-Peer

Servers Participating in ACID Transactions

Similarly, a *server* is a computer system able to perform tasks, run processes, or do higher information processing in response to clients' requests. It also provides services, which are either requested, or initiated on behalf of client's processes. Single server could also execute processes in parallel, concurrently thus, provide services simultaneously. The whole concept may be viewed as an extension and an alternative implementation of distributed programming concept, according to which, individual sub-programs in complex environment may execute in distinct, even remote, memory address-spaces. Servers are engaged predominantly in ACID transactions. There are just few exceptions such as for on-line dynamic transactions where serves may need other servers' support such as TP Monitors in order to provide for ACID functionality. *Table 2* gives some insights in the *Atomicity*[23], *Consistency*[24], *Isolation*[25], and *Durability*[26] properties for some common servers.

---

[19] Provided a *real-time Two-Phase-Commit* (2PC) dbase is applicable, remotely or on-line.

[20] Provided transactions are within a *single dbase 2PC domain* or unless under a *TP Monitor's support.*

[21] Provided the *OS supports concurrent processing* running on single or multiple CPUs

[22] Provided the *real-time permanent storage* is accessible, remotely or on-line.

[23] Provided a *real-time Two-Phase-Commit* (2PC) dbase is applicable, remotely or on-line.

[24] Provided transactions are within a *single dbase 2PC domain* or unless under a *TP Monitor's support.*

[25] Provided the *OS supports concurrent processing* running on single or multiple CPUs

[26] Provided the *real-time permanent storage* is accessible, remotely or on-line.

Table 2. ACID Properties of some Common Servers

Device/Property	A	C	I	D
Mainframe	Yes	Some	Yes	Yes
TP Monitor	Yes	Yes	Yes	Yes
Server	Yes	Yes	Some	Some
Web-Server	Yes	Some	Some	Some
Database Server	Yes	Some	Some	Yes
File/Print Server	Some	Yes	Some	Some
Thin Server	Yes	Some	Some	Some
Router (thin server)	Yes	Yes	Some	Yes
Workstation (WS)	Some	Some	Some	Some

A: Atomicity, C: Consistency, I: Isolation, D: Durability

Two-Tier Architecture

Two-tier architecture is an enterprise-networking concept where clients are *directly* connected to network servers in order to receive application support or other services. This simpler, single layer type of networking is mainly implemented within smaller pool of clients where application support and network connectivity functions are closely integrated together. Any substantial increase in number of servers or clients would lead to exponential rise in network complexity. A *three-tier* network provides an alternative solution. In this case, servers specialised for certain application services and servers providing network integration or wide connectivity are naturally separated into two independent but closely related tiers, thus leaving the clients in the third tier. Usually, two-tier networks operate under single NOS. A generic representation of two-tier versus three-tier networks is presented on *Figure 9*.

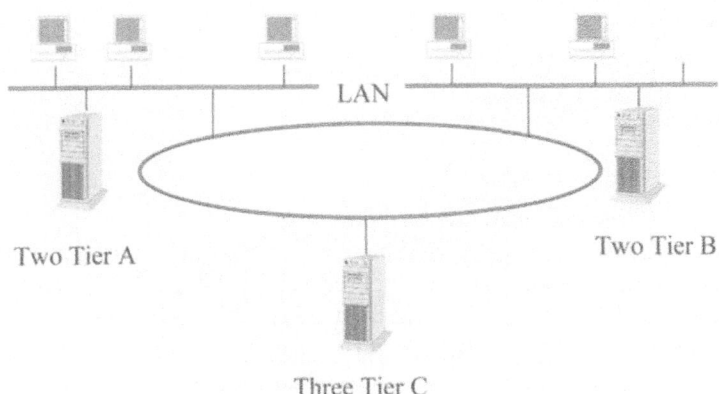

Figure 9. Two-Tier vs. Three-Tier Architecture

Table 3. ACID Properties of some Common Networked Clients

Devices/Properties (ACID)	A	C	I	D
Smart Appliances (JINI)	Some	Ltd.	N/A	N/A
Mobile phone (WAP)	Some	Ltd.	N/A	Ltd.
PDA/PalmHeld Computer	Some	Ltd.	Ltd.	Ltd.
Net-Computer (thin PC)	Yes	Ltd.	Ltd.	Some
Personal Computer (fat PC)	Yes	Yes	Ltd.	Some
Workstation (fat PC)	Yes	Yes	Yes	Some

A: Atomicity, C: Consistency, I: Isolation, D: Durability

Three-Tier Network Architecture

The *three-tier* model introduces additional layer between clients and its servers. Three-tier networks therefore, provide configurations rich in functionality and often are segmented in number of distinct NOS workgroup domains. The new server layer is responsible for networking functions and communications among pool of application-specific servers. The application servers usually take care of clients, providing them with services offered through specific applications. The three-tier remains a natural model for most enterprise networks. It could easily manage network complexity especially in case of larger numbers of servers or numerous clients at several sites, which expect a number of applications or type of services to be provided throughout the network. This is the case for specific middleware software. It may also provide for appropriate CRM, SCM, or ERP solutions as in the case of e-business applications. The three-tier architecture is also used in cases with great number of clients accessing distributed databases such as, *on-line Transaction Processing* (OLTP) type of enterprise computing. It represents a viable solution applied in system-migration cases too, a conversion of legacy mainframe applications to enterprise computing paradigms, known as *downsizing,* or *rightsizing*, an euphemism meant to avoid negative associations.

Table 4. Taxonomy of Enterprise Architecture (3D tiers vs. 3P scope)

Tier/Scope	Presentation	Processing	Persistency
Individual	Terminal (ICA)	Desktop PC/NC	WS
Workgroup	X-Windows/GUI	File/Network Server	Db Server
Enterprise	ActiveX/ Java	Web/Application Server	OLTP Monitor

Peer-to-Peer Network Architecture

Peer-to-Peer is contemporary networking concept such that every participating entity has symmetrical and equivalent networking capabilities that pertains equal responsibilities. This is rather different from the prevailing client/server concept, which in fact models an asymmetrical relationship. For instance, some systems are dedicated to providing services, whereas others are playing subordinate client roles. Additionally, peer-to-peer networks are generally simpler and less expensive, but they usually do not offer the same performance under heavy loads. The success of peer-to-peer and its client-to-client direct connection rather than client-to-server networking has a promising future in the Napster-style MP3 and similar media distributed computing environments[27]. Peer-to-peer networks come in two basic versions: *Napster-style* models, which use servers to re-direct traffic, and Intel's server-free implementations, which directly connect desktops over IP networks. According to the reports[27] 'Amerada Hess, in New York, has been experimenting with *peer-to-peer networking and resource sharing* for a year. Its Beowulf Project strings together with 200 desktop PCs Ethernet and Linux to handle complex seismic data interpretation, and replaced a pair of IBM supercomputers'. For more; see Case 3: Networked Computing with Beowulf Iridis Cluster as well as *Case 6:* Defining Peer-2-Peer and *Case 7:* Peer-to-Peer Technology Exists Beyond Napster.

Network Hierarchy

The richness of networking hierarchy to date can clearly be seen in *Table 4*. A simple dumb *terminal* is able to do individual presentation. However, some processing logic is still necessary to support communications, data processing, or data persistency. It looks after processes executed either locally or at remote sites. For collaborative tasks the choices are among following client solutions:

- GUI or UNIX based *X-Windows* terminals which could handle limited presentation features and partially some networking logic
- *ActiveX* or *Java NC* does presentation, local processing, and rich networking logic
- *PC* or *WS* integrates these functions together with local data-persistent storage. However, simple *File Servers* (DOS/Windows or UNIX based) are able to organise some data-persistent tasks. More advanced applications may need a *DBMS Server* to provide for multi-user back-end logic, two-phase-commit (2PC) and data-persistent storage. In case of substantial transaction processing that eventually may involve on-line transactions over several databases and serving large number of database clients throughout the enterprise, it may require support from an *on-line Transaction Process Monitor* (OLTP) server. For multi-user and GroupWare application support it requires *Application Servers* for processing stage. To date, due to e-business hype and overwhelming access to individual and corporate Web pages there is high demand for *Web Servers* that provide Web presence and support. We should also not forget *Networking Servers* that actually allow for integration of networking capabilities and networking services throughout the enterprise. It is important to note that the right-hand diagonal of the 3D/3P hierarchy-table (**in bold**) represents a separating line between different types of clients and servers. We will come back on this issue later in Enterprise Business Model.

---

[27] The Power of Peer-to-Peer by Paul McDougall,
http://www.techweb.com/wire/story/TWB20000828S0014

Persistent Transactions: Thin vs. Fat Systems

Concerning clients and servers alike, we are to come up with a decision how wide the actual scope should be with regard to presentation, application and networking, and should the persistency logic be included in the system?

With respect to the client paradigms this decision is usually referred to as a choice between *thin vs. fat* client model, also known as a decision between *Net-centric* vs. *Desktop-based* approach.

The choice of *thin-client* ranges from almost obsolete character-based terminal, ICA or X-Windows, PC emulated terminal, to the most recent ones - Java NC Networking Computer; see *Figure 10*. The NC model assumes that eventual client is only able to do presentation, or initialise further tasks and processes through events generated at client side (character, ICA, GUI, or ActiveX or Java-applet actions). Subsequent processing takes place either *locally* at client side, in case of PC and NC, or remotely at server's side, in case of ICA, X-Window terminal, PDA, WAP-based communicators, Java NC, and *across* pool-of-PopC. To date, due to network bandwidth constraints and more than 1000 times slower hard-disk latencies, NCs are targeting a specific niche in enterprise networks that requires smaller memory footprint and depends substantially on built-in cache memory and Java components downloaded on-demand to overcome the existing latency problem. For more refer to Oracle NC[28] and the latest interview from Thin Planet[29] over IBM support to Thin Clients. According to the interview, 'thin clients are attractive in the marketplace for: ease of use, very fast application deployment; and the ability to run in the client, the browser, Java Virtual Machine (JVM) and emulators'. Eventually, they see two broad classes of clients: one that *uses and updates information*, and another that *creates information*. Essentially, this leads to four different classes of end-users: *transactional workers* such as, reservation and booking clerks, call-centre and help-desk employees etc.; *general office workers*, which include marketing and sales, office, middle and senior management administrators; *knowledge workers*, such authors, analysts and consultants; and finally, *power users* from various fields, including R&D, engineering, graphic designers, etc.[29]

---

[28] Ellison signs off on latest version of network appliance,
http://news.cnet.com/news/0-1006-200-2214799.html
[29] ThinPlanet: Executive Interview with Howie Hunger [IBM's Director for Thin Clients],
http://alllinuxdevices.com/news_story.php3?ltsn=2000-09-13-001-03-IN-LF-TC

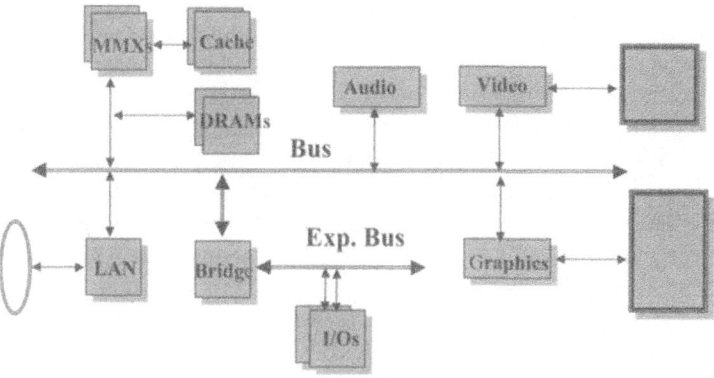

Figure 10. Thin Client Architecture

A PC as representative of fat-client model is presented on *Figure 11*. In addition to the necessary presentation software and common networking logic usually, there are overwhelming number of user's applications. Regularly, PCs are equipped with spacious persistent storage primarily in support of its elaborate file directory system and databases that makes the PC a rather *fat* client. The hard disk drive, potentially with Gbps transfer rate and sub-10-millisecond range of disk-latency, provides support to many applications with increased availability and high bandwidth demands.

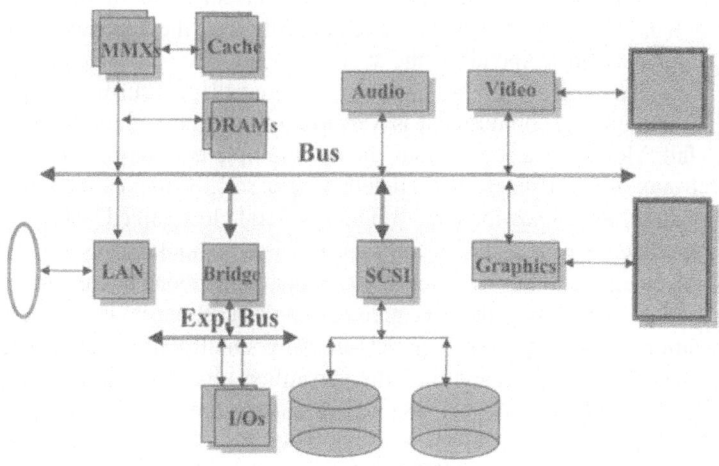

Figure 11. Fat Client Architecture

The *thin* architecture model applies to servers too. Servers can as well be specialised for networking or some specific applications, for instance, file/print servers, database servers, Web servers, or communications servers. Traditionally, old mainframe systems were overwhelmingly rich in all types of software. There are also servers, usually in two-tier network architectures that are rather rich in presentation, supporting many applications, networking types, persistent and store logic. Whenever possible, this kind of network architecture should be avoided since inherently introduces many-to-many type of complexity; see *Figure 55*. In order to simplify the overloaded two-tier architecture, simple network reorganisation leads to a natural three-tier architecture; see *Figure 59*. The 3-tier architecture makes clear separation between applications' processing at one level and networking with persistency logic at another. The introduction of *Java-NC* clients and *Network Computer* has actually emphasised this functional separation. Whatever presentation and application processing is required it is usually done *locally*. All the necessary networking, transactions, file, and persistency functions are performed *remotely* mainly in the *server's domain,* therefore, at higher level of networking hierarchy.

Applications Participating in ACID transaction: Sessions

An *application* is a computer program, a spreadsheet, a macro-instruction, or a script of predefined actions required in order to perform a task, run a process, or perform information processing. We know that Web applications can run either on server, or on client side. Nevertheless, running a Web application is a kind of transaction - an active session, open and close, start and end, but not exactly. Actually, it incorporates a transaction but in qualitatively novel way due to very problems of determining its start and especially the end. Since, it might not have one at all, or it may be lost in the Web space. For instance, the dial-up modem might be down, the connection might be temporarily lost, the application might fail, the server may not respond, or the Web user may have just abandoned the Web site without saying a word, no goodbye, no farewell. Just surfing the waves of the Web without any commitment is a recipe for our transaction's two-phase commit to fail. Moreover, a session may include multiple transactions as in many Web storefronts and cart-based virtual-shopping cases. Complex transactions may also include several sessions, like running several close linked tasks, as in a workflow application, or a flight-itinerary-car-hotel-room booking system.

There are advantages and disadvantages of running applications in contemporary Web transaction world on whichever side of the transaction environment. The first applications, based on Java-1 applets used by small platform independent programs, have claimed for some time the versatility, ubiquity, and most of all, the security. It was based on very innovative and secure Java Virtual Engine developed and supported by Sun Microsystems; see *Figure 16*. However, due to the *statelessness* property of the HTTP and the *all-or-nothing* secure computing model, the Java-1 failed to ascertain full Web transaction support. Albeit the attempts to maintain the state in Web sessions based on dynamic URL, various authentication mechanisms, hidden fields in HTML pages, and browsers-based cookies, it is of little help to thin clients, NC, smart JINI appliances, and WAP phone users of Web applications unless there is a support by the server-side application or by a Java applet Repository. But most of all, the reason Java-1 has failed on its promises is mainly due to the lack of full PC market support and has been influenced by the competition between Sun Microsystems Java alliance and Microsoft DCOM initiative for VBScript-based *ActiveX* program components.

The later and the growing interest in Web-based applications made application developers turn their eyes to server-based rather than client-based applications. However, running applications on the server-side has its own problems too such as, decline in performance, platform dependence, communications dependence, or OS dependence, just to mention a few. Also, in order to run applications on the server-side, several new Web technologies have been introduced.

Common Gateway Interface (CGI) that facilitates both the client-side as well as the server-side logic is based on scripting code often written in *Perl* 4GL. For faster response and more efficient use of server's resources CGI scripts are often implemented by Netscape Server API (NSAPI) or Microsoft Internet Server API (ISAPI) technology. It enables applications to maintain its state information and database connection in conversational Web transactions and between interactions with the browser. Netscape's NSAPI and similarly Microsoft's ISAPI are Server-based APIs used by Sun Java Sever Pages (JSP) and by Microsoft Active Server Pages (ASP) respectively. To date, most successful across open platforms are Java *servlets* - i.e. Java components, a sever-side equivalent of Java applets. Most recently, Sun has successfully introduced the new Java Enterprise Application Model based on the Java-2 Enterprise Edition (J2EE) applying the *four-tier architecture* and allowing either side, clients and serves alike, to run applications in reliable Web sessions. An interesting example is Driveway.com; see *Case 4:* Xdrive Technologies, Inc. Acquires Businesses of Freedrive, Inc., a reliable Internet file-storage for individuals, and a private-label service for ASPs running BEA WebLogic Server[30] applications and providing file-sharing solution used by more than six million people worldwide.

Within individual sessions a number of transactions may call on each other, hence performing required applications and tasks; see *Figure 12*. The *iBus* JSP solution is a server-based messaging server by Software AG.

---

[30] http://www.beasys.com/press/releases/2000/0823_Driveway.html

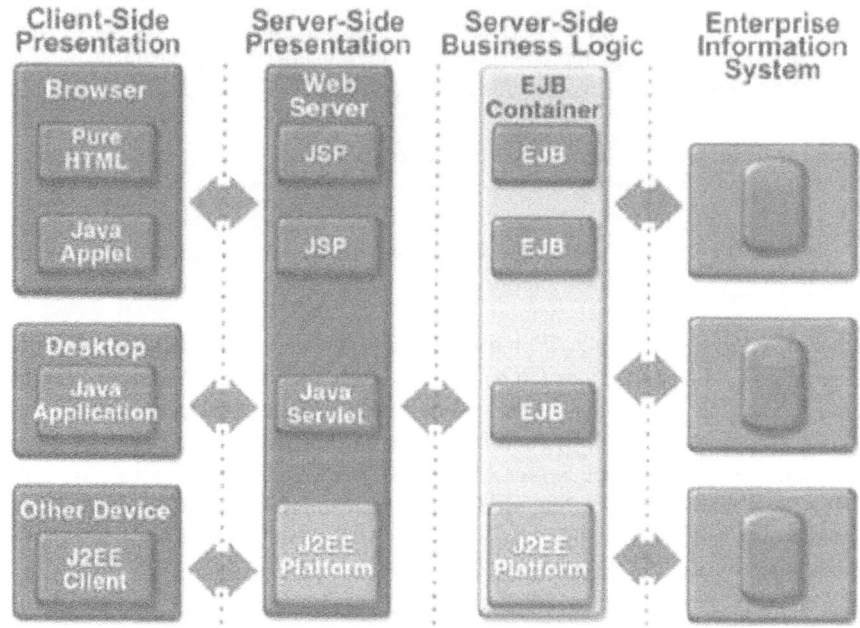

Figure 12. J2EE Architecture [31]

Bibliography

App servers strategic tool in Web architecture; *Mario Morejon*; **Computer Reseller News**, Manhasset; Nov 6, 2000, Iss. 919; pg. 131, 1 pgs

Fat network architectures will have a chance to shine--but this isn't their year; *Bob Lewis*; **InfoWorld**, Framingham; Mar 20, 2000; Vol. 22, Iss. 12; pg. 80, 1 pgs

Microsoft Protocol Shows Promise; Leverages Existing Web Architecture; *Jamie Lewis*; **InternetWeek**, Manhasset; Mar 6, 2000; pg. PG.27

In a flood of mail, readers both attack and defend fat-network architectures; *Bob Lewis*; **InfoWorld**, Framingham; Aug 30, 1999; Vol. 21, Iss. 35; pg. 68, 1 pgs

On design of a survivable network architecture for dynamic routing: Optimal solution strategy and an efficient heuristic; *Ouveysi, Iradj*; **European Journal of Operational Research**, Amsterdam; Aug 16, 1999; Vol. 117, Iss. 1; pg. 30, 15 pgs

Wideband Network architecture explained; *Roger E Billings*; **Computer Technology Review**, Los Angeles; Apr 1999; Vol. 19, Iss. 4; pg. 22, 1 pgs

New Network Architecture; **Aviation Week & Space Technology**, New York; March 29, 1999; Vol. 150, Iss. 13; pg. 92

Web architectures rule future development; *Michael Vizard*; **InfoWorld**, Framingham; Mar 22, 1999; Vol. 21, Iss. 12; pg. 5, 1 pgs Setting Objectives For Web Architectures; **InternetWeek** *Nick Evans*; Oct 5, 1998

Switched Services Access Network Architecture; **Telecommunications** *Paul Berkowitz*; May 1998

Network architectures and performance; **Information Systems Management** *Sharp, Duane E*; Spring 1998

Data Network Handbook: An Interactive Guide to Network Architecture and Operations; **Technovation** *Bailey, Brian*; Apr 1998

A second option on network architecture; **Public Utilities Fortnightly** *Chris S King*; Feb 1, 1998

---

[31] Source: Sun Microsystems, http://java.sun.com/j2ee/blueprints

Cabletron versus Cisco: Evaluating network architectures; **Telecommunications** *Axner, David*; Feb 1997
Paul E. Renaud, Introduction to Client/Server Systems, John Wiley, 1996
Evans et all, Client/Server: A Handbook of Modern Computer Design, Prentice Hall, 1995
Gary Gagliardi, C/S Computing,, Prentice Hall, 1994
Butler Report, Client/Server Computing, McGraw-Hill, 1994
Orfali, Harkey, Edwards, Essential Client/Server, John Wiley, 1994
Dawna Travis Dewire , Client/Server Computing, McGraw-Hill, 1993
Pine, B. J., Mass Customisation. Harvard Business School Press, Boston, 1993

CHAPTER 4

NETWORK CONNECTIVITY

Middleware

Case 5: Novell NetWare at Beveridge & Diamond

BEVERIDGE & DIAMOND
Novell Customer Case Study
http://netware.novell.com/nwnews/beveridg.htm
(Copyright © 2002, Novell, Inc. All rights reserved.
Novell's Beveridge & Diamond cases used with permission from Novell, Inc.)
When Fortune 500 companies need legal advice on complex regulatory matters regarding the environment, they turn to Beveridge & Diamond, P.C., a law firm that delivers legal services with an environmental emphasis. And when the attorneys of Beveridge & Diamond needed to work and communicate with greater flexibility and security, they turned to the NetWare environment.

Network Overview
Beveridge & Diamond's 175 employees are located in Washington, D.C., New York and San Francisco. Six NetWare 4.1 servers power the firm's enterprise, connecting 200 IBM-compatible PCs across three time zones via a fractional T-1 line, used for both voice and data transmission. The group sends email and schedules meetings using GroupWise 4.1 and, using technology from Novell, connects to its intranet and Internet through WorldNet Intranet Connect Service from AT&T.

Needs Analysis: Fast, Flexible and Secure Communications
Beveridge & Diamond works on complex cases with such government offices as the Environmental Protection Agency, the Departments of Energy and Transportation and the Food & Drug Administration. The information the firm handles is highly sensitive and subject to the confidentiality of attorney-client privilege. Employees therefore must be able to:
–   Access and share secured information at all three of the firm's offices, at anytime of the day or night.

- Communicate quickly and confidentially with clients, co-counsellors and business partners from anywhere in the world.
- Connect to the Internet from any local or remote point on the network.

Network supervisors needed to ensure the security of their enterprise and to increase the firm's disaster recovery capabilities--while minimising the time they spend administering the network across the three Beveridge & Diamond sites.

The Novell Solution

In 1994, Beveridge & Diamond migrated from NetWare 3.11 to NetWare 4.1 as part of a network upgrade. The following year, the firm decided to implement a wide area network (WAN) between its offices, using frame relay to improve communications capabilities and reduce the time spent on network administration. Working with Novell and AT&T; Beveridge & Diamond determined that the features of AT&T. WorldNet Intranet Connect Service were best aligned with the firm's business plan for remote connectivity.

GroupWise 4.1 was selected as the workgroup productivity platform because it combines local, WAN and Internet email access, personal calendaring and group scheduling in a single application, and was implemented using the SMTP gateway NetWare Loadable Module (NLM).

Distributed Computing Environment

It is essential that users see the network as *transparent* as possible, yet ensuring high level of confidentiality and security. As in many similar cases, all the network resources can be considered virtual objects, hence ensuring the required transparency. In practice, there are two ways to implement transparency: either by server's OS, for instance, using the built-in support by MS *Windows 2000*, or following the DCE concepts rely on an enterprise NOS such as Novell NetWare. The *Open Software Foundation* (OSF) *Distributed Computing Environment* (DCE) proposal represents a comprehensive integrated set of tools and services, which support creation, use, and maintenance of distributed applications in a heterogeneous computing environment. Yet, the full acceptance of OSF DCE is still uncertain. Sun has introduced its own *Open Network Computing* (ONC) as an alternative to the OSF DCE. Neither Novell nor IBM has fully endorsed DCE. Microsoft has supported only part of DCE. Still, it is important to review the OSI X.500, OSF DCE, and C2 network standards in order to understand the DCE:

- *X.500* is the industry standard for global network directory, based on replicated distributed database, designed to run under the OSI communication protocol. X.500 network directory follows Object Orientation. Each object in the directory belongs to a member class. Any client or server derives its attributes using appropriate API from the class hierarchy. The communication among clients and servers makes use of directory agents, DUA and DSA, the user and server agents respectively. They require appropriate protocols, DAP and DSP, respectively. In addition to X.500, TCP/IP and IPX/SPX can coexist as important proprietary standard alternatives, still in wide use by enterprise networks. Periodically, time agents synchronise clocks within the systems to maintain and handle the unique time across the network. Similarly, DCE makes use of *time clerks*.

- *C2* is a government security standard for NOS. It is based on user's *authentication* prior to allocating network resources to anyone, clients, or servers. DCE comes very close to meeting the requirements set by this standard. There are many other security standards presently in use by network community. *Kerberos* for instance, follows the "*trust no one*" principle. Together with DCE it fulfils strictly the C2 requirements. Kerberos is often used by trusted third-party security systems. It provides passwords used by *authentication procedure* that allows users access to resources. It maintains a list of shared session-specific private passwords based on *Data Encryption Standard* (DES) approach. Despite recent 56-bit encryption failure [32], DES is still needed, regardless whether used by Kerberos or by the *RSA public key encryption* standard. For short messages the *RSA electronic signatures* are superior since there is no need of third party authentication. Having completed thus far, servers still need to make sure their clients have passed proper *authorisation* for using network resources. Novell's NetWare *Intranet* for instance, checks client's inherited domain attributes in order to simplify the *authorisation procedure*. However, most recent reports on computer-based *stegonography* have proven that the data encryption technology and cryptography are still far away from a foolproof secure system. For more please refer to the *Case 26:* Privacy Guide: Steganography.

- The OSF DCE standard, shown in *Figure 13*, provides the OS-independent network layers support on distributed directory services, RPC, threads, distributed time, and network security services. Lined up with OSI *Application and Presentation* the DCE layer includes Messages, RPC, Named Pipes or Peer-to-Peer DCE. The *Session* layer entails Sockets, NetBIOS, TLI, and SNA CPI-C. The *Transport and Network* layer contains NetBEUI, TCP/IP, SPX/IPX and APPN. The *Logical Link Control* layer incorporates IEEE 802.2; NDIS and ODI supporting *Medium Access Control* protocols: Ethernet, Token Ring, SDLC, and ISDN. For more, please refer to DCE in the Appendix.

---

[32] CW, DES failure, Aug. 10, 1998, *IETF set to turn its back on DES encryption standard*

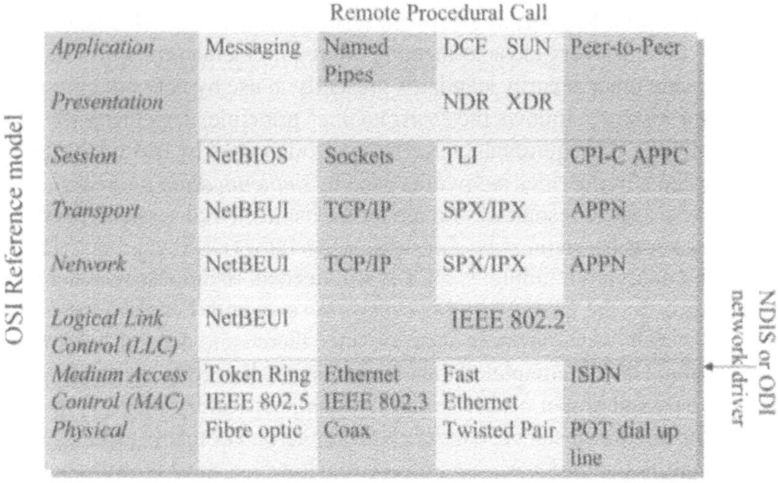

Remote Procedural Call

OSI Reference model				
Application	Messaging	Named Pipes	DCE SUN	Peer-to-Peer
Presentation			NDR XDR	
Session	NetBIOS	Sockets	TLI	CPI-C APPC
Transport	NetBEUI	TCP/IP	SPX/IPX	APPN
Network	NetBEUI	TCP/IP	SPX/IPX	APPN
Logical Link Control (LLC)	NetBEUI	IEEE 802.2		
Medium Access Control (MAC)	Token Ring IEEE 802.5	Ethernet IEEE 802.3	Fast Ethernet	ISDN
Physical	Fibre optic	Coax	Twisted Pair	POT dial up line

NDIS or ODI network driver

Figure 13. DCE Network Layers

MiddleWare Mechanisms

Messaging, Remote Procedure Call, and *Peer-to-Peer communications* are common networking solutions used to create co-operative, enterprise-wide applications:

— *Peer-to-peer* conversation interface protocol enables variety of two-way symmetric communication among clients and servers. It's also referred to as *client-to-client,* or *program-to-program* communication, *Figure 59. Transport stacks* represent more refined choice.

— *Remote Procedural Call* (RPC) makes use of a well-known programming approach that allows connection or link of two entities - processes using *parameter-passing* techniques. It binds clients to servers automatically and dynamically in real-time. A fast *call-return* is guaranteed by balancing the load and service requests by either *synchronised* execution of processes or *concurrent* threads. Whether connection-oriented or connectionless communication version is used, the RPC provides flexible, secure data conversion across the network (e.g. Sun's XDR for neutral vs. DCE NDR for multiple data representation). Connection-oriented RPC is well suited for robust environments. However, a complex Web transaction processing combined with persistent data is not a favourable networking environment for RPC communication paradigm and might be better to use *TP Monitors*[33]. Instead of RPC, using ORB-based objects and components is preferred communication method to date; see *Figure 58.*

---

[33] BYTE, Jan./1998, Tech'98 Outlook: *Transacting On the Web.*

- *Messaging* or *Message Oriented Middleware* (MOM) provides for real *Distributed Application Development* (DAD). It is an essential tool for large, distributed enterprise networks. Its implementation is based upon asynchronous re-distribution of requests and loads, a common communication technique for asynchronous, queued transactions[34]. It enables creation of *concurrent* type (*many-to-one* or *one-to-many*) relationships (e.g. *persistent, local, filtered, or protected*) among clients and servers. It is regarded as an effective network messaging in the event-driven and *frame-based connectionless* communications providing minimum transactional safety.

Connectionless MOM is a complementary communication paradigm to the RPC, the later being used predominantly in *connection-oriented* paradigms. MOM vs. RPC relationship is akin to plain telephone vs. ordinary mail communications. This analogy helps distinguish the advantages and limitations of MOM or RPC used in various connection-oriented or connectionless network communications. See *Figure 14*.

Remote Procedural Call vs. *Messaging*

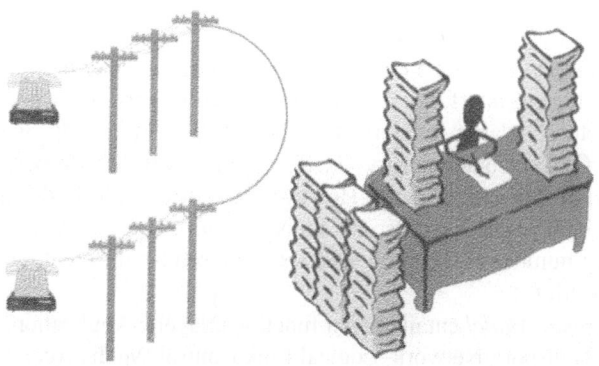

Figure 14. Message vs. RPC mechanism

To date, *Transaction Processing Monitor* (TPM) and *OLTP* are predominantly used in enterprise-wide mission-critical applications, *Figure 15*. The *DLL funnelling act model* is considered best suited for transaction processes and transactions management. It guarantees transactional *ACID properties* for fast and reliable response to OLTP, load balancing, backup, and recovery services under tight security constraints. The *International Standard Organisation* (ISO) *OSI* standard and *X/Open Distributed Transaction Processing* (DTP) are the most important standards for TP Monitor implementation. For more, please refer to *Tuxedo* in the *Case 24:* CoreLAN - TP Services with BEA Tuxedo ™. It is successfully used in mission critical applications providing OLTP support,

---

[34] Publish-&-Subscribe business events are the new MOM alternative using CORBA 3.0. ORBs.

enterprise scalability, firewall security and protection, high availability, simple MOM integration, and low total ownership costs.

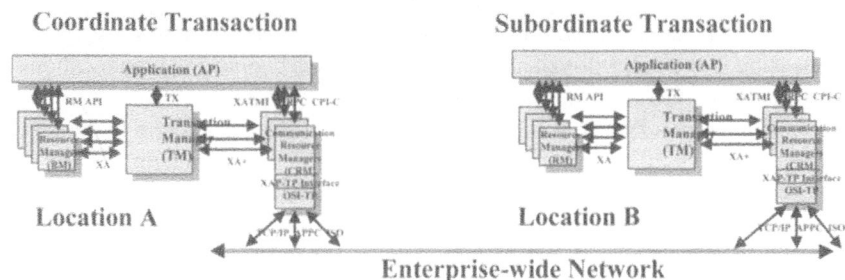

Figure 15. Enterprise-wide Distributed Transactions Managers

Transport Stacks

Transport stacks provide a necessary communication layer between multi-vendor NOS and logical interfaces for network device drivers. They are also supported by de facto standards for network adapters (e.g. Microsoft, 3Com's NDIS, or Novell's ODI). Contemporary NOS provides full peer-to-peer API support, mostly within its native stacks. However, it is difficult to find a solution equally good for both connectionless and connection-oriented communications. Instead, we rely on number of transport stacks specialised for different modes of network communications:

- *OSI Reference Model* entails seven functional layers: Application, Presentation, Session, Transport, Network, Logical Link Control, Media Access Control, and Physical layer, from top down respectively. The model simply shows where the transport stacks fit in. Top of the stacks comes right below the NOS interaction. It is responsible for application interface through messaging, RPC, or Peer-to-Peer communications. At the OSI MAC level, the transport stacks interfaces the network hardware through IEEE protocols. SNA, the IBM proprietary network architecture, also entails seven functional layers. However, its alignment is quite differently than that of OSI. It too allows applications to run transparently across IBM proprietary networks, Token Ring for instance.
- *Named Pipes* interface as part of basic inter-process communication services runs on top of TCP/IP, IPX/SPX, and NetBIOS stacks. Named Pipes are very suitable for *many-to-one pipelines* taking care of synchronisation and scheduling tasks therefore providing reliable two-way communications between clients and servers.
- *TCP/IP,* as mentioned previously, is the communication protocol of the Internet. Initially, it was introduced in the ARPA network set for US government

agencies and universities. Later, it evolved into public or commercial domain as Internet. The TCP/IP supports X.500 and is a constituent part of any UNIX OS. Through "*sockets*" it runs on virtually any OS, providing clients peer-to-peer API support required for session and presentation services. The socket types, e.g. streams, or datagrams are often specified at creation time.

– *Transport Layer Interface* (TLI) introduced by AT&T and presently owned by Novell represents a more sophisticated version for a socket interface.

– *Winsock* is Windows' socket API that provides Windows OS clients the TCP/IP interfaces to the Internet. Unlike older Windows, new Windows 2000/NT/XP ensures non-blocking handling of operations through pre-emptive multitasking. The *Internet socket address* for TCP/IP consists of two address parts separated by a dot. The first part sets a 32-bit *Internet address* uniquely assigned to any host interface to the Internet. The second part is a 16-bit *Port address* assigned to an application entry point. Commercial applications may assign specific port addresses, e.g. Oracle dB.

– *IPX/SPX* supported by the Novell's NetWare enterprise networks is frequently used transport stack. Novell NetWare provides reliable *datagram* type services using TLI, Named Pipes, and NetBIOS peer-to-peer networking protocols on top of its IPX/SPX stacks.

– *NetBIOS* and NetBEUI, i.e. NetBIOS Extended User Interface in IBM/Microsoft LAN use broadcasting *one-to-all* or multicast *one-to-some* mechanism in order to provide *connection-oriented* and powerful *datagram* services. NetBIOS is de facto portable standard for LAN-based protocol stacks and program-to-program communications.

– *Common Programming Interface for Communications (CPI-C)* for IBM SNA networks enables *advanced peer-to-peer networks* (APPN) transparent and flexible access to resources, cross-network directory-service support, including integrated network management. Hence, it creates a distributed SNA network in place of a traditional centralised mainframe-based network. Running between applications and on top of stacks, the CPI-C API becomes "de facto" standard for *robust API* peer-to-peer communications. Having licensed CPI-C from IBM, the X/Open consortium has endorsed the CPI-C standard throughout the industry to enable application portability and interoperability across network platforms.

Network Agents

The networking agents are small autonomous programs playing rather interesting roles in process of monitoring and performing normal network integration tasks. To illustrate, there are several common cases that involve characteristic features of particular networking services supported by network agents:

– *Mail* services in networks such as *e-mail*; see Virtual Enterprise: Collaborative Computing is of ultimate importance for internal and external enterprise services. For more; see *Case 19:* Transition Associates wins Lotus Beacon Award at Hughes Christensen as well as *Case 20:* Transition Associate and

Lotus Notes at Foulks Lynch Virtual College . To date, there is wide proliferation of standards in this domain, among them, the *X.400 international standard*, Novell *Message Handling Service* (MHS), and Internet *Simple Message Transport Protocol* (SMTP). Still the most successful is X.400 standard that endorses the separation of mail functions: *front-end* at the client side and the *back-end* mail engines at the server side. It supports, but should not be confused with, the X.500 standard, i.e. distributed directories over multiple nodes. X.400 supports the exchange *of Binary Large Object Block* (BLOB) that is especially important for images, fax, digital sound and multimedia, and any ordinary binary attachments to electronic messages. It also provides support for *Electronic Data Interchange* (EDI) option that is traditionally used in commercial document exchanges. For more please refer to *Case 9:* NIIIP Virtual Enterprise Project

− *Firewall solution* for network security remains an important topic for discussion in any enterprise network community. The concern over network security is not only appropriate, but also necessary, considering the explosive growth of the I-net, e.g. *Internet* and *Intranet*, and more recently, the new e-Business solutions. So, what is a firewall anyway? A firewall is a networking device, e.g. a firewall router usually placed between two separate computer networks responsible for implementation of organisation's security policy. For instance, an enterprise may wish to connected its network to an external network, that of its business partner, or more likely to the Internet. The enterprise is to decide who may have access to and what kind of access is to be allowed from the inside out, from the outside in, or not at all. A firewall router is programmed to implement the access "rules" the enterprise has established. Firewall routers have been widely used as protecting mechanisms implemented between the distributed network applications and the corresponding resource managers. For instance, TP Monitors provide support for *two-phase commit* ACID transaction firewalls and for simple MOM transaction *queuing* firewalls. See *Case 24:* CoreLAN - TP Services with BEA Tuxedo ™

− *Backup systems* perform valuable management tasks by removing any network points prone to data disaster and enabling efficient disaster recovering strategies. The network *recovery* systems entail *backup* systems, archiving, scheduling, planning, and recovering tools. The backup policies include remote interface for scheduling any of the operations in unattended mode, usually during off business hours, weekends, holidays, or special sessions. The backup systems make use of almost all data media types. With regard to archive price/performance features, *streamer DAT tapes* are considered superior. However, due to falling prices of high performance, highly reliable *Redundant Array of Inexpensive Disks* (RAID) hard-disks drives has made them very common to date, affordable, and suitable data media not only for on-line data storage but data archiving too.

− *Conferencing (PC and teleconferencing)* is a *GroupWare technology* that enables groups of users to share electronic messaging services, simultaneously, or at any time. See *Case 14:* CallWare's Callegra Advanced Messaging System

Case 6: Defining Peer-2-Peer

DEFINING P2P

Posted by shelley at May 23, 2002 06:01 PM

http://p2psmoke.org/archives/000272.html#

(Copyright (C) 1996 - 2002 Shelley Powers. All Rights Reserved.
Reprinted by permission herein.)

May 23, 2002

In P2P, a peer both provides and consumes services. A group of peers then can provide and consume services to and from each other without dependence on any one server. With this understanding there's an assumption that this consumption and distribution occurs when the peer is connected.

Within some P2P enabled applications, the communication may be cached or queued when the peer is not connected. I know this the way Groove works.

Within Freenet, any one of the nodes within the network can consume or supply files. But if a peer is not connected, it's not part of the network, it isn't a participant and files are consumed and supplied through other participants. Either you're a peer, or you're not. Again, the assumption of 24 hour access is not a factor.

Some systems support a hybrid cloud whereby service requests are cached at a remote location (usually hidden from the peer), waiting for the other peer to connect. When the other peer connects, the communication is concluded. The results of the service call can then be communicated back to the originating peer, or cached itself if the originating peer is offline.

In a true P2P system, any one of the peers within the network could act as a cloud (intermediary) for other peers. Within a hybrid system, such as Groove, the system itself might provide these types of intermediary services.

As for firewall issues, most P2P tools can work from within firewalls, or be made to work within firewalls.

Bibliography

Xircom bets on network connectivity for Windows CE; *Joe Wilcox*; **Computer Reseller News**, Manhasset; May 3, 1999, Iss. 840; pg. 47, 1 pgs

Bluetooth reborn as network connectivity tool; *Denise Romberg*; **Computing Canada**, Willowdale; Jun 4, 1999; Vol. 25, Iss. 22; pg. 17, 1 pgs

StarNine technologies WebStar: Mac-based Web connectivity; *Lori MacVittie*; **Network Computing**, Manhasset; Jul 12, 1999; Vol. 10, Iss. 14; pg. 32, 2 pgs

CNC/PC network connectivity; *Anonymous*; **Manufacturing Engineering**, Dearborn; May 2000; Vol. 124, Iss. 5; pg. 36, 1 pgs

YesTrader to offer ASP model, Web connectivity; *Cristina McEachern*; **Wall Street & Technology**, New York; Jul 2000; Vol. 18, Iss. 7; pg. 60, 2 pgs

New appliances will focus on network connectivity; **Network World** *John Cox*; Aug 10, 1998

Dell's PowerEdge 6300: Sharp edge over network connectivity; **Network Computing** *Jonathan Feldman*; Aug 1, 1998

PART II

ENTERPRISE PARADIGM

Case 7: Peer-to-Peer Technology Exists Beyond Napster

PEER-TO-PEER TECHNOLOGY EXISTS BEYOND NAPSTER
http://www.pcworld.com/news/article/0,aid,44670,00.asp
*(Reproduced by permission of the IDG News Service and
International Data Group, Inc.)*

You may already be using P2P; if not, you will be soon, says Intel expert.
Douglas F. Gray, IDG News Service
Thursday, March 15, 2001

SAN FRANCISCO--If you're not running a peer-to-peer (P2P) application already, the chances are you will be soon, according to Bob Knighten, Intel's peer-to-peer evangelist.

When P2P comes up in conversation these days, it's usually referring to Napster. But P2P is about more than free music; it includes such applications as instant messaging and the SETI@home project, which uses idle computing resources in home PCs to search for intelligent extraterrestrial life.

"Peer-to-peer is something that's moving the focus of computing," Knighten said, speaking on the first day of a peer-to-peer conference put on here by the Digital Consulting Institute. "The variety of computers that become peer-to-peer clients is expanding."

Clients already taking part in P2P systems include PCs and PDAs (personal digital assistants), and the network is already moving toward the support of cell phones and fixed-line phones, according to Knighten.

P2P can be grouped broadly into three models, he says. They are "client-server computing," where the servers provide services and the clients request them; "pure peer-to-peer," which operates independently of central servers; and a hybrid model, where servers assist clients to find information stored on other clients. Most well-known peer-to-peer programs, including Napster and SETI@home, are hybrid types.

Distributed computing systems, which connect a large network of computers to create a single supercomputer, are used for everything from aerospace design to automobile crash test analysis, Knighten says. They are also used for analyzing sound patterns from outer space and working on the human genome project.

In fact, distributed computing is used for so many things that Intel decided it had to try something with it, too.

The company wanted to give employees access to training materials on demand, but there were logistical problems of doing so worldwide. Shipping out the material on CDs would prove too costly, and letting people download it on demand was too taxing on both Intel's WAN (wide area network) and on the nerves of users using dial-up modem connections.

So Intel did its best at merging the two models. When one user requests training materials--in the form of a video stream, for example--the materials are stored on his or her hard drive. When another user wants to view the same video stream, the network points that user to the first user's machine rather than back to the original source.

Already more than 200 companies offer peer-to-peer technologies of some form, and the technology has been around for a lot longer than Napster, Knighten says.

"Peer-to-peer computing was not invented a year ago," he says. "Some of the aspects have been around for 20 years or so. Others have been in development for three or four years."

Commonly, enterprise networks provide support in several networking aspects:
- *User interface* that enables local or remote, and fixed or mobile network access,
- *Service request* with notification of acceptance for on-line or batch transactions,
- *Information presentation* logic that allows for simple or complex media types,
- *Processing and application* logic that supports individual or collective sessions,
- *Physical data management* for access, retrieval, update, delete, or modification,
- *Information/data integrity*; persistency, availability, completeness, and security.

The opening *Case 7:* Peer-to-Peer Technology Exists Beyond Napster introduces new peer-to-peer networking alternative, a rather interesting networking model. In contrast to usual clients or servers, peers may assume both client and server roles, therefore implementing by default decentralized networking. Unlike traditional C/S applications, the peer applications are either monolithic or often distributed processing applications. Presenting few contemporary networking models we will try to introduce a virtual enterprise model. It will provide a better understanding of the enterprise-computing framework. It is essential to recognise the relationships among various networking paradigms and understand the way they match and correlate to the corresponding enterprise business models. The business process may exhibit specific features regarding enterprise organisation, its business functions, data volume, particular application choices, whether data persistency is required or not, or whether the distribution of program components across the network is essential or not. These issues may become even more complex due to requests for a particular implementation or network architecture. Usually, there is a choice of having functions performed either at client or at server side. For instance, it is possible to execute a transaction that is presented either at client side using a desktop, NC, or an X-terminal; from a remote using a dumb terminal, *Personal Digital Assistant* (PDA) communicator, or a *Palm-Held* computer. The former is often a scenario seen in *order-entry* and *Point-Of-Sale* (POS) applications. Clearly, it is the data presentation that requires support by the presentation logic at the server side. For more; see SCO UNIX *TermVision*.

Chapter Enterprise Business Model will introduce a number of interesting *enterprise business models* and related *business environments*. The attention will be focused mostly on business *process distribution*. In order to compare the alternatives of distributed processing, some characteristic features of *distributed processing* will be elaborated as well.

In response to growing Business-to-Business e-Commerce trends and the follow up on new enterprise business models, the chapter <u>Virtual Enterprise</u> introduces *virtual* enterprise model renown by its *collaborative* features and *GroupWare processing applications.* It incorporates features of previous distributed models.

Chapter <u>Enterprise Management</u> touches upon some important relationships that exist between networking TCO, i.e. the networking technology *Total Cost of Ownership* and the enterprise networking efficiency.

Chapter <u>Enterprise Development</u> re-examines the development of *distributed enterprises* with respect to the new wave of *server-side development* using the XML database Web-server technology and other forms of publish-&-subscribe *Component-based software Development* (CBD). The UML approach and related catalyst methodologies are presented since they apply well to managing change and application legacy problems and the understanding of *Business Process Re-engineering* (BPR). We recognize that distributed data and online transactions may significantly influence the choice of appropriate enterprise paradigms. Specific cases of data distribution are presented in order to illustrate the variety and possible alternatives of developing distributed information systems.

CHAPTER 5

ENTERPRISE BUSINESS MODEL

Thin vs Fat Clients and Servers

Case 8: Insignia Jeode Technology for Compaq iPAQ Home Internet Appliance

JEODE TECHNOLOGY ENHANCES THE ART OF WEB BROWSING ON THE COMPAQ
IPAQ HOME INTERNET APPLIANCE
http://www.insignia.com/products/ch.asp - compaq
(Copyright © 2002, Insignia Solutions, Inc. Reproduced by Permission)

Once limited to PCs and workstations, the art of browsing the Web has extended to a new class of devices – some of which were built strictly for accessing e-mail and surfing the World Wide Web. As users browse from one website to the next, they expect the experience to be the same as using their desktop computers. They expect web pages to open and functionality that is meant to enhance the Internet experience to do just that.

This is especially true for Internet terminals, sometimes known as "dedicated Web browsers." These devices are intended to provide a simple and easy to use mechanism to get people on the Internet and provide e-mail, instant messaging and chat capabilities. The target audience for this type of product tends to be:

- Inexperienced computer users that are worried about setting up and maintaining a complex PC
- People or families that already own a PC but want additional affordable devices to access the Internet from elsewhere in their home, such as the kitchen or kids' bedrooms

While users expect all the Internet functionality of their personal computers, meeting this expectation is a challenge. Internet terminals are fundamentally different than PCs. They don't have the resources of a desktop computer. They don't have a hard drive. The amount of available RAM is limited. The processors these devices employ may not be as powerful so that they can be built more economically.

The barriers to overcome in delivering a rich and complete Internet experience to consumers are especially apparent in ensuring that they can leverage the many popular Java-enabled websites that have become increasingly prevalent on the World Wide Web.

The Art of Web Browsing Mandates Java Functionality

Since being introduced in 1995, Java has quickly built a reputation as "the language of the Internet." The Java programming language is one of the most robust, fully featured, user-friendly languages used by software developers today, and its popularity is growing. International Data Corporation estimates that there are currently 2.5 million Java developers and expects that this number will grow to 4 million by 2003. According to the Gartner Group, 79 percent of the universities offer Java courses with 50 percent requiring Java coursework in their computer science curriculums.

According to Hotbot, more than 5.6 million web pages are Java-enabled – and that number is growing quickly every day. As a point of comparison, use of Java technology on the Web is nearly twice that of the much longer established .pdf technology, which is the standard in document display and printing.

According to both the Web 100 poll and MediaMetrix usage ratings, 70 percent of the ten most popular websites on the Internet are Java-enabled. The top Java-enabled Web 100 sites include Disney, senior.com, National Geographic Online, USA Today, CNN, ZDNet, PBS Online and the Wall Street Journal. The top Java-enabled MediaMetrix sites include Microsoft, Yahoo, AOL, Lycos, Excite, About - The Human Internet, c/net and Real.com network.

The increasing interest in deploying Java technology in information appliances, such as an Internet terminal, is due to its many benefits to both consumers and developers. The most visible benefit of Java technology for consumers is the rich, complete Internet experience it provides by providing the ability to run the many Java applications and applets available over the Web, including games, chat, personalized news tracking, real-time stock quotes and sports headlines, financial calculators and other dynamic content.

Developers appreciate the attributes of Java as a programming language, as well as its portability and cross platform support (write once, run anywhere) the Java platform provides. They also like its high degree of security, dynamic extensibility, and Internet savvy.

To provide these types of consumer and developer benefits, Internet terminals and other types of information appliances need to be Java-enabled, which requires a Java Virtual Machine (JVM). But JVMs that were built for desktop computers do not effectively operate in the constrained-memory environments that are typical of these devices. Only a JVM that is tailored for the unique requirements of limited-memory is suitable for these types of devices.

Enter the Compaq iPAQ Home Internet Appliance

While the personal computer has found its way into a large percentage of U.S. households, a significant number of people still don't own one. There are also some households that have a PC, but need additional ways to access the Internet as more family members go online for information and communication.

Recognizing the need for a simple, affordable device that offers rich browsing functionality, instant messaging, and e-mail capabilities, Compaq Computer teamed up with Microsoft to create the Compaq iPAQ Home Internet Appliances IA-1 and IA-2, powered by Windows CE with MSN® Web Companion software.

When Compaq introduced the iPAQ Home Internet Appliance IA-1 in August 2000, it became the first company to offer an Internet terminal with Microsoft's MSN Web Companion service and to provide a built-in Java Virtual Machine to enhance the Internet experience for its users.

An Accelerated, Responsive Java Runtime Environment

Compaq chose Insignia Solutions to provide the Java virtual machine technologies for both the IA-1 and IA-2 with the Jeode™ platform, PersonalJava™ edition, which is tailored for information appliances.

The Jeode platform has earned industry-wide acclaim for its accelerated, responsive Java application performance and robust, efficient memory management. The Jeode Embedded Virtual Machine™ (EVM™) provides the Java runtime environment that enables IA-1 and IA-2 users to run popular Java-enabled financial content such as:

- Dynamic charting from Yahoo Finance, Metastock Online
- Real-time charts from Quote.Com
- Nasdaq's custom logo ticker
- Smart Money's Map of the Market
- Datek Online Streamer real-time quote
- Social Security retirement benefit calculator

Sports fans can view popular programs that were created as Java applets, such as Major League Baseball "GameChannel" and "NFL Gameday Live" –mini-programs that graphically depict game action and provide accompanying statistical information.

The Jeode platform allows users to leverage the popular chat and survey facilities that were developed using the Java programming language, including those provided by:

- Yahoo!
- Excite
- Lycos
- EarthWeb
- Quote.Com
- Stock Talk Live
- CBS Sportsline Poll Tool, Java Chat and Live Score Center

Gamers also benefit from the incorporation of Jeode technology in the Compaq devices. Java technology is becoming extremely popular for developing online games. According to Chris Melissinos, business development manager for electronics entertainment at Sun, Java technology gives "users in the game community the ability to personalize the game to their liking. What we are beginning to see now is player-based add-ons to the game that completely redefine the story, the script, the graphics, the movement – everything about the game is completely customizable if you can program in the Java language." [*]

---

[*] Source: java.sun.com, "Gadgets, Games, Gizmos and Gas Pumps" by Martin Hardee, Jan. 8, 2001

Jeode technology enables IA-1 and IA-2 users to play such popular Java-based games such as Jellyvision's "Who Wants to be a Millionaire" and "You Don't Know Jack"; Activision's "Vampire: The Masquerade"; real-time games such as Monopoly, Sorry!, Battleship, Clue and more at Hasbro's games.com; and Road Rash, Jungle Strike and other multiplayer games at Electronic Arts online gaming center, ea.com.

To make the experience seamless for users of Windows CE-powered devices, Insignia makes Jeode technology available as a plug-in that is integrated with Internet Explorer (IE) 4.0. This allows Java applets to execute inside of the IE browser.

"In selecting a JVM supplier, we were interested in both the technology and the business relationship," said Randy Cooper, Engineering Program Manager, Platform Development with Compaq's Consumer Inter-Connected Products Group. "Insignia's Jeode platform met our product needs by providing the compatibility, small memory footprint and performance we required. But just as important, Insignia has proven its effectiveness as a business partner by responding very quickly to our early inquiries, cooperating with us to meet special requirements and working very hard to meet our schedule and cost goals."

"With the Jeode platform, users of our iPAQ Home Internet Appliance products enjoy a responsive and rich experience as they access Java technology-based applications and applets," said Jim Ganthier, director and general manager, Inter-Connected Products Group, Compaq Computer Corporation. "We're pleased to provide customers with this important functionality as a result of Insignia's excellent technology."

Jeode Technology-Enabled iPAQ Home Internet Appliance Wins Acclaim
Compaq's innovation in delivering the first MSN Companion and Java-enabled device is being recognized by the industry. The iPAQ IA-1 has won several awards, including the PC Magazine 5 Star Rating, the Silver IDEA 2000 Design Award, Top Rated and Family PC Recommended, Consumer's Digest Best Buy Award and Best of What's New in the Computer and Software category in Popular Science magazine's thirteenth annual Best of What's New issue.
For more information on the iPAQ Home Internet Appliance, visit http://athome.compaq.com/showroom/static/ipaq/intappliance.asp.
For a Microsoft-sponsored case history on the iPAQ Home Internet Appliance, visit http://www.microsoft.com/Windows/embedded/ce/guide/casestudies/compaq.asp.

Enterprise business models have developed a long way from simple data *order-entry* systems running centralised *mainframe* networks to the present complex mixtures and varieties of *peer-to-peer* networks, *Intranets,* and *Extranets* alike. The driving force behind the proliferation of these models came from a variety of business enterprise paradigms. In order to meet the needs and requirements of many types of businesses, new models have emerged from ever-changing business environments. It is of no surprise that the *three-tiered* and subsequently, *n-tier* enterprise architecture, turned out to be the most versatile organisational mapping that satisfies all three views of the enterprise:

1. The *functional model* that reflects the use of system functionality and its organisational responsibilities. Often, it is closely associated with the end-user network *interface*.
2. The enterprise *process model* that entails the core business functions. It can be mapped well by its object-oriented interactions among suitably defined *business processes*.
3. The *information model,* based on existing data and information flows through the enterprise, allows the system to function properly. It is often presented as an *information infrastructure*; see Working with Databases.

The centralised, hierarchical organisations, proved to be the most appropriate for old legacy *mainframe* architectures. The patterns of business organisation to date have evolved from *centralized* through *workgroup* model and *matrix* enterprise organisation, in thoughtful, self-sufficient, task-oriented *individual* organisation that is primarily seen today in offices and individual production systems. They were also the building blocks of early information systems. Woven into complex forms of network organisation and often guided by resource sharing goals rather than information-sharing objectives they finally matured into a worldwide open, *enterprise network* to date.

In order to understand these new features, appreciate the advantages, prevent eventual drawbacks, and raise the awareness of differences that exist between enterprise business models we need to review the basic paradigms. Following the client/server taxonomy shown in *Table 4*, it is easy to derive the features of enterprise paradigms: *Presentation, Processing,* and *Persistence* (3P) shown in *Table 5*. As possible *clients* we may consider the shaded table entries in *Table 4*, above the right-hand diagonal. However, the table entries on the diagonal and below belong to the corresponding server models.

Table 5. Enterprise Business Paradigms

Paradigm	Order-entry	Workgroup	Personal	Enterprise	Collaborate	Distributed
CLIENT	Terminal	X-Window	Desktop	Java NC	Desktop	WS
Presenting	shared	at client	at client	at client	at client	shared
Processing	at server	at server	at client	at client	shared	shared
Persistence	at server	at server	shared	at server	shared	shared
SERVER TYPE	dBase Mainframe	File/Apps Server	Web/Print Server	EJB/Java Server	GroupWare Server	OLTP Monitor

Historically, the *order-entry* paradigm was the earliest. Often used in large enterprises it was based on *mainframe* computer systems. As its client name suggests, the *Intelligent Console Architecture* (ICA) terminal's primary role was to support databases and handling large data complexes such as data-order and data-entry in highly centralised mainframe-based information systems. Nowadays, this paradigm is still in demand especially in large enterprises, providing information systems support in corporate and financial centres, large warehouses, store chains, or mail-order retail businesses. Due to the introduction of *PDA hand-held computers* equipped with bar-code readers and modern *CTI communications*[35] features, providing praiseworthy on-line customer support, makes character-based terminals and X-Windows terminals possibly obsolete hence, paving the way to contemporary distributed order-entry applications.

The *workgroup paradigm* on the other hand stems from former minicomputers. To date, these legacy systems are still in use. Closely related to departmental applications, it actually relied on mini-frame computer support often backed up by a mainframe system at corporate level. However, the mini systems introduced an additional level of networking, hence, have enriched the existing enterprise hierarchy. To date, the mini systems correspond very well with conventional matrix of workgroup organisational structure in medium and large enterprises that rely on n-tier networks with X-Windows or thin PCs as clients.

Notorious as it is, we believe it is necessary to elaborate on the ubiquitous, individual or *personal paradigm*. Constantly evolving, not only within enterprise networks but also at home, it still represents a general worldwide phenomenon. It may be interesting to remind on number of alternatives offered by this paradigm, especially when related to enterprise computing and various forms of *virtual office*[36] implementations.

The most recent client is the NC. It has been introduced by the Oracle and Sun Microsystems alliance. At first rejected by consumer's market, it has received undisputed conceptual support even by its fierce competitors, Microsoft for instance. Its *Java-based NC* networking is relatively new net-centric enterprise concept. Closely dependent on *Internet* technology it is instrumental in providing support to *Intranet* and *Extranet*[37] implementation. Some find it similar to the *workgroup* model that made use of first ICA and X-Windows "dumb" terminals. Except, there are few major advantages. Namely, its multitasking support, high performance, lowest TCO, platform independence, and unique response to task distribution issues. Eventually, the NC represents quite an interesting, low-cost, efficient alternative for enterprise-wide networking.

We have previously defined the necessary conditions for entities to play a client role. Interestingly, the *collaborative* paradigm too has extended the client role to some new types of servers, EJBs and GroupWare servers for instance The collaborative computing today represents a prevalent paradigm in SMSE enterprises always keen for application of new trends in virtual and rich organisational structures. It will be elaborated in Collaborative Paradigm.

Finally, the *distributed* paradigm introduces a sophisticated model designed to meet the most demanding requirements of contemporary enterprise computing. Communications have been challenged internally by the enterprise Intranet, but also externally, through the enterprise value chain Extranet[38], enabling global access, and mobilizing network assets in response to high information demands.

---

[35] Butler Group Report, 3/98, *CTI-Computer Telephony Integration & Convergence*

[36] Badr El Din, D. Nikolic, *The Object Model for a True Virtual Enterprise*, SCI'98, Orlando, Florida, '98

[37] BYTE, Dec./ 1997, *Extending the Enterprise: The Extranet Revolution.*

[38] Hikkanen et all, 1997, *Distributed DSS for Real-time Supply Chain using Agent Technologies.*

There are many other enterprise-networking paradigms, combined, or taken as close alternatives to the aforementioned ones. This only proves that the way enterprises organise their businesses and operations changes very much due to the specific conditions and the environment that influences their very existence. For more on these topics please refer to the Chapter Virtual Enterprise presented and also the *Case 9:* NIIIP Virtual Enterprise Project

We will proceed with a review on the most prominent features of basic enterprise paradigms. Whenever possible, we will provide an update on related technology and present a case or an environment where a particular enterprise model is best implemented. Some alternative models will be reviewed as well, presenting as complete as possible real cases where particular enterprise paradigms pertain to be the most advantageous.

Order-entry Paradigm

The data order-entry enterprise paradigm has been successfully applied to a large number of SMSE business environments especially those closely associated with large data entry or point-of-sale (POS) terminals. Typical cases of data order-entry systems are used often in store warehouses, retail, banks, supermarkets, department stores, distributions & logistics etc. There are several features, which make this specific paradigm easily recognisable and attractive to the end-users. Common to our reviews, the features presented consider three specific point of views: *data presentation* requirements, application and *processing issues*, and the need for *data persistency*. It also unveils how these features influence either the client, or the server support side. In general, more sophisticated enterprise business models demand more perplexing networking paradigms. However, in order to reduce the inherent organisational complexity, a multi-level network organisation may prove to provide a desired solution. The opposite is also true. Downsizing to simpler two-tier network paradigms can be achieved by negotiating the enterprise complexity. However, once the separation of functions has been somehow assured, the eventual distribution of information presentation, processing, or persistency of clients among multiple tiers of servers turned out to be a praiseworthy task to be accomplished.

Data Presentation

Data presentation requirements in the order-entry enterprise paradigm are very simple, with low-level volume of data exchange, mostly through standardised data formats governed by universally accepted data exchange standards (e.g. EDI, POSIX, etc.). It provides for use of very simple data-entry terminals as enterprise clients, for instance, character based terminals, PDA communicators, palm-held bar-code readers, POSIX terminals, UNIX based X-Windows, often by PC and desktop emulated terminals, and alike. Usually, the communications requirements depend on the level of randomness of data bursts and data volume. The order-entry data volume remains generally low when compared to image, video, or multimedia data traffic. This in turn enables *clustering* of data terminals for efficient use of the available communications bandwidth. It also provides for efficient, combined implementation of *multiplexing* and *data compression* that can further cut the demand on nevertheless scarce communications bandwidth.

Remote Applications Processing

Due to simple data communication requirements and in many cases a substantial large number of clients distributed throughout the enterprise, often scattered at many distinct sites, we naturally assume that the actual application processing is done remotely, i.e. at the server's side. Whether single or multiple applications are running simultaneously depends on the variety of tasks and the complexity of the enterprise. In general, the larger the number of terminals running in the enterprise network, the smaller is the poll of different applications demanded by the end-users. As a consequence, a proportional increase in efforts dealing with interactive application complexity is to be expected as well.

However, it is often desirable to process applications at the client side. For instance, in data inquiry information systems it is possible to perform a query or a list processing at the client side using a PC-emulated terminal; through the Internet using mobile WAP clients and Java-based NC; or running an enterprise *Intranet* platform. We will elaborate on this issue in our next enterprise paradigm of networking. However, in case there is more than a single application running on the enterprise network, it is advisable to introduce an additional networking level rather than overloading the existing two-tier enterprise infrastructure. It will provide an additional networking tier to accommodate for additional application servers. Thus, they could cope with more applications that are simultaneously distributed throughout the enterprise network. Again, it is advisable to keep the networking architecture as simple as possible and introduce the *distributed processing only if necessary*. In many cases, the existing servers can provide both networking as well as application support. In large networks however, it is advisable to separate the two functions and introduce several *parallel tiers* or groups. They maintain different functions from traditional hierarchical or vertical tiers. The actual server distribution is according to *specific criteria*: locality of site, applications and functional similarity, applications concurrency, security constraints, etc. The number of application servers actually deployed depends on the size of the enterprise network and usually is constrained by the accepted level of distributed processing response, e.g. real-time, batch, etc. Yet another network design rule suggests that the *distribution of databases* should be carried out with respect to their *closest point of data creation* and *maintenance*.

Which networking design issues actually will be drawn in an enterprise *Business Process Re-engineering* (BPR) represents the key decision point. However, *data distribution* and *distributed processing* alternatives remain the key determinant strategy issues. For more, please refer to **Business Process Re-Engineering**.

Persistent Data

An important concern in data processing applications is whether data persistency is required or not. In many cases involving order-entry enterprise networking this requirement is essentially anticipated or taken for granted, for instance, due to two-phase commit requirement in *Transaction Processing* environments. More on *data persistency* issue and *database functionality* will be elaborated later in the Chapter <u>Working with Databases</u>. However, it should be noted that data persistency represents an important requirement essential to the core enterprise processes, usually, closely related to the implementation of order-entry business applications. To date, any serious implementation of data persistency in an order-entry application often requires a real database management system support. Small, data order-entry applications in simple networks may share these services or gain support from the existing File & Print servers. If file sharing and network printing is small in volume it is possible to achieve this objective using only local OS or network OS support. However, in more demanding cases, often in mission-critical, TP applications, the support of *TP Monitor*[39] is essential. For, TP Monitors are able to successfully manage and control eventual increase of transaction complexity and still maintain distributed data persistency. In fact, it is the close co-operation of DBMS, NOS and TP Monitors that could successfully manage distributed resource allocation for data transactions in mission-critical database applications and maintain the network performance concurrently at the optimum level throughout the enterprise. For more; see *Case 24:* CoreLAN - TP Services with BEA Tuxedo ™ and Oracle8™ TP Monitor database application [40].

Workgroup Paradigm

Frequently, the enterprise business model attains a familiar matrix organisation in order to manage the complex relationships required in performing its core business processes. Examples of such enterprise models are abundantly found everywhere around us. Most prominent ones are found in public domains and government organisations. Offices in business and public domain institutions often involve *'heavy'* administration, such as insurance companies, banks and similar financial institutions, universities etc. However, the introduction of the enterprise IS to this environment has reduced the depth of functional and information hierarchy. Though the departmental structure still persists in enterprises worldwide, it is rather shallow, streamlined, and more efficient than ever before. Years after the successful debut in Japan enterprises, the *'task-force'* enterprise organisation model has gained a limited public acceptance anywhere but in virtual enterprise networks. An alternative to former departmental model, it basically introduces *loose* horizontal enterprise networking hence making the vertical channels almost outdated, often on a temporal basis, and usually for the duration of a task, or a project; see *Case 9:* NIIIP Virtual Enterprise Project.

---

[39] BEA Tuxedo, *Hongkong International Terminals*, http://tuxedo.novell.com/actions
[40] Distributed Transaction Processing using Oracle 8™,
   http://technet.oracle.com/products/oracle8/htdocs/xdtptwp7.htm

The *workgroup* enterprise model assumes somewhat weaker relationship among the constituent parts of an enterprise that is clearly reflected in its information system layout. The workgroup and departmental IS become rather involved. In fact, it makes a well-balanced network able to manage the overall enterprise IS integrity including the independent, workgroup-specific core-business processes. The corresponding workgroup paradigm maintains a variety of applications in order to support a number of business processes, a mix of operational data that arrive from all departments to enterprise headquarters, and in turn, managing the information disseminated via different levels of enterprise hierarchies. For instance, take the case of a University IS network. A common University campus IS comprises of a number of workgroups across departments and supporting institutions each running its own core business processes. The related IS cater for relatively smaller, but in many instances, parallel administration tasks within each workgroup and similar, but wider, more complex, higher administrative functions at the University HQ. The MIS is essential in maintaining a variety of curricula, tracks, course programs, exam dates, current events, lectures, resource schedules, student lists, premises, library items, etc. Still, there are at least few, among many information activities of individual University departments, which are to share the information burden with the rest of the University IS [41].

What is the most suitable enterprise network paradigm that meets the demands of a particular business model and still maintains the operational efficiency and low computing overhead? The following review is to shed some light on data presentation methods, applications process support, and data persistency issues.

GUI Presentation

In order to support a large number of different applications to many users, the enterprise networks usually run a multi-user, multi-tasking Network OS. In many cases UNIX/Linux may be the preferred OS. For instance, a UNIX X-Windows presentation support that runs entirely at the client side often requires smaller server overhead, provides lower costs, and more reliable, prompt response to a number of applications running simultaneously at the server side.

Application Processing

The introduction of contemporary NOS allows clients transparent, remote access to all network resources across the enterprise network from anywhere, anytime. Usually, applications provide a set of service levels and often an automatic task continuation by maintaining the environment parameters set during the last point of entry. Multi-user computing environment is therefore, able to support a range of core business process requirements at lowest cost per user. A full range of industry-specific applications, in finance and accounting, productivity and automation tools are available to end-users across the enterprise network. In fact, the clients are even not aware of any departmental boundaries. It is the NOS that manages the complexity of the enterprise network and remains transparent to all

---

[41] SAP, *IQ-CAMPUS Solution*, Press Releases, Dec./98, http://www.sap.com/press/

workgroup clients. The enterprise network we are looking for, should be highly scaleable, with reliability, availability, and security meeting our requirements and providing sufficient performance level to business processes, networking support, and advanced resource sharing (e.g. file and printing, backup, etc.).

Persistent Information

Persistent data stores are frequently required in workgroup networks in order to store local data created by departmental business processes. Later, they are often replicated and made remotely accessible throughout the enterprise. For instance, shared RAID date stores provide for reliable and efficient, but still global data access. Unless transactional, the speed and data access may not be too critical. Main data persistency model remains *remote access* to a *replicated database*. Since most of enterprise processing takes place within workgroups any uplink information channels may provide sufficient bandwidth for database replication across the enterprise. The applications that require persistent data with higher bandwidth are of multimedia, desktop publishing, or videoconferencing type. They usually require an installation of network fibre *backbone* in order to access massive enterprise data archives (e.g. RAID disks, tapes, or CD-ROM libraries).

We may consider more complex *distributed database* as a viable alternative provided *on-line transaction processing* is demanded. This particular application type will be briefly examined in the Distributed Paradigm.

Personal Paradigm

Personal computers are becoming ubiquitous throughout SMS enterprises, as are they among common individual home users worldwide. For more than twenty years PCs have been gaining in popularity due to the affordability and richness of applications hence improving the efficiency of individual office productivity tools. Personal home networking has followed suit. Presently, it is still booming due to the Web access and ease of connectivity provided by the local *Information Service Provider* (ISP). The Web provides an easy, remote, ubiquitous access, and information availability to individual PC/desktop users equipped just with a simple modem for Web access. The remote network access trend was noticed early in the development of enterprise networks giving rise to and emergence of various forms of *virtual offices* concepts. The PC/desktop or personal enterprise-networking paradigm therefore, represents most common solution to a variety of businesses, individual, as well as *Small and Medium Scale Enterprises* (SMSE).

Regardless the variety of implementations of enterprise networking paradigms, it is the *ownership of networking infrastructure* that makes the difference. For instance, a *private network ownership* is the fundamental issue of well known *Local Area Networks* and PC LANs. Still, *public network ownership* as common solution is gaining enormous recognition to date. This is the case with *Internet* technology imbedded into enterprise network infrastructures and the emergence of a number of *Intranet* and *Extranet* business solutions. These solutions rely on Internet networking technology provided by *Network Service Providers* (NSP) either through proprietary or public network infrastructures. Most recently, the *Application Service Providers* (APS) are trying to fill in the service gap and provide number of Web applications on demand, outsourced remotely. The trend is slower than expected since users are still reluctant on accepting service offers that attempt to *'lock'* them in to a specific service provider. Due to the disputable reputation of *'intelligent'* networks providing *'value-added'* services that serve suppliers best, as a result gave rise to so-called *'stupid'* IP networks i.e. global networks providing all but bare network access [42]. Presumably, these trends are going to open up the service networks for other players willing to provide end-to-end services both to individuals and corporate enterprises alike providing Internet networking infrastructure at lowest costs of ownership. The debate over these and similar issues are still open and without consensus so far.

Multimedia Presentation

The Window 95 *Plug-and-Play* technology has enabled desktops to easily use all sorts of available information media types. Sound and video have excited not only video-game addicts, but desktop enterprise users as well. To date, most desktops are capable of some *multimedia* (MM) support. Besides, the processors have often some MM chips built-in. For *MMX processors* please see **Enhanced Multimedia Processing - MMX**. This technology provides client side with full MM presentation support. Thus, the PC is able to run most demanding MM applications. It should be noted though that the anticipated introduction of *MM applications* is still lagging behind the outstanding MM hardware development. Moreover, the successful debut of most recent versions of Java aware browsers is facilitating the acceptance of desktops as common network clients. The development towards the full integration of different CD-ROM media and MM standards made its contribution as well. The end result is a client that can serve: mobile users, laptops, home desktops, NC and ICA terminals, PDA, hand-held computers (HHC) either coupled with GSP or WAP-based phones, and *'smart'* emulators. New voice-activation mobile clients will definitely contribute to the wealth of multimedia applications implemented in enterprise networks to date.

Application Multitasking

During the last decade PC has encountered enormous improvement in hardware and software platforms. However, by all measures, the major breakthrough has been achieved on the applications front. Plain character-based, data-processing applications, predominately used during the 60's evolved into pure document processing during the 70's. During the 90's and especially following the unprecedented growth of information base during the Internet revolution, the demand of individual users as well as the enterprise end-users had definitely turned in into a wide range of multimedia applications. This trend has been followed by two major software developments. The first is *Object Oriented* (OO) platform enabling innovative top-down application development. It resulted in

---

[42] Communication Week International, *"Stupid" Network*, Sep./98

emergence of *component based application development* (CBD) paradigm and subsequently, the *Java phenomenon.* The second one is a real *multitasking* OS support, enabling applications simultaneous execution of several tasks at a time. Microsoft Windows 2000/NT, Symbion/Psion EPOC, BeOS, and UNIX/ Linux are but few representatives of that trend. To date, event-driven applications are able to run on any desktop platform. The most prominent ones, Windows and UNIX platforms provide for *pre-emptive multitasking.* It enables desktop users to run several applications at a time, switching among applications, sharing resources, and allowing processes background execution under OS supervision. However, the aforementioned flexibility and ample applications availability took its toll, the abundance of installed PC resources on *fat desktop* client architecture.

Persistent Data and Islands of Information

Yet another phenomenon in the PC evolution trend was the introduction of small desktop-based databases. The mainframe systems of the 70's were the realm of databases. However, the PC introduced smaller, user convenient databases as successful in prevailing desktop-based applications, such as *DBase4, FoxPro, Paradox,* or *MS Access.* They provided desktop users a full persistent data store. As a result, the enterprise networks have early recognised the value of desktops as individual data stores for persistent data and thus, have widely accepted the personal *desktop enterprise paradigm.*

Thanks to personal networking paradigm, the desktop clients are able to share the burden of persistent information store thus, enabling end-users to merge their own individual data with the corporate data. Real-estate agencies, legal advice offices, employment agents, small solicitor organisations, rental and tourist offices, mail-order inquiries, etc. are just a few cases that have found this type of enterprise networking very attractive and supportive to their business processes. However, the database applications often could not provide end-users distributed data support. Even though desktop applications have accomplished shared access to the corporate database, they have left behind smaller, independent databases, scattered across the enterprise desktops. The individual database access and the unclear data responsibility has prevented efficient use of available information across enterprises, hence contributing to database proliferation and existence of many small, parallel, persistent data stores. The *lack of data integration* and data consistency resulted in the *"island of information"* phenomenon. The increased awareness of data availability and the widespread concern related to data security made data availability and data security the major drawbacks of the personal paradigm affecting and limiting the functionality of enterprise networks to date.

Table 6. Multi-tier Enterprise Paradigms

Tier/Paradigm	Enterprise	Collaborate	Distributed
CLIENT System	Java NC	Fat desktop	POS/Workstation
Presentation	at client	at client	shared
Processing	at client	shared	shared
Persistence	at server	shared	shared/at server
NETWORK Server	ISP/ASP	Network	DB/Application

Tier/Paradigm	Enterprise	Collaborate	Distributed
Processing	at server	shared	shared
Persistence	at server	shared	at server
APPLICATION	EJBs Java	GroupWare	OLTP Monitor

The aforementioned three paradigms of enterprise network, presented in *Table 6*, are often implemented in a *multi-tier network* environment. It is interesting to note that the client/server concept allows any system to play either role interchangeably, i.e. either client or server at a time. Network Computers (NC) and most recently Java-based NC introduced by Oracle[28] and Sun Microsystems are considered thin clients. However, an enterprise Java Beans (EJBs) server, a GroupWare server, or a TP Monitor plays the server role. Sometimes servers may play clients' roles, for instance DB server vs. TP Monitor. Depending on the enterprise size, there may exist a number of subsequent network tiers allowing clients and servers to communicate using C/S or peer-to-peer mode. For instance, in public networks cases, it is the ISP and ASP that provide the necessary networking services. For GroupWare collaborative enterprise applications it is the responsibility of GroupWare application servers to provide the required functionality. Transaction applications however, often run across several tiers, thus distributing data and services throughout the enterprise network. For these enterprise-wide applications the network-server processing and a reliable OLTP Monitor-support remains essential. An interesting transaction case arises in the distributed Point-of-Sale (POS) networks with clients running on a Database or Application server in the second tier under the OLTP Monitor's 2PC supervision.

Enterprise Paradigm

Regardless of its sluggish widespread acceptance, the *enterprise paradigm* in fact introduces an innovative idea, improving an earlier form of workgroup paradigm with somewhat redesigned role of former UNIX/X-Windows client. However, the enterprise paradigm is radically different from the prevalent personal paradigm that relies on the broad use of Windows PC/desktop clients. The enterprise paradigm essentially is a revival of the net-centric model we used during the mainframe days. Nevertheless, it has been received enthusiastically by the entire enterprise networking community. It anticipates that clients are already networked, and that application's suite is always accessible and available across enterprise network. The difference between dumb terminals or formerly used X-Windows clients and presently Java-based NC clients is that most of application processing and the overall middleware communication processing required to provide network accessibility takes place at the client side. Since applications are in fact running at the client side, the NC clients are equipped with the substantial main memory. Looking from the cost-benefit perspective, the NC clients benefit best from the current IT trend of continuous constant fall in chip price per bit and the exponential increase in density of DRAM memory chips; a phenomenon usually attributed to Gordon Moore[43] as *Moore's Law.* Having provided the NC with reliable networking support, it is able to furnish full networking access and obtain services offered via enterprise networks. Due to its open architecture and platform independence modern Java-aware browser technology allows full inter-operability and scalability. It also enables easy access to Java-based applications, portability across platforms, provides reliable, scalable, mobile solutions[44], and ubiquitous access by any client throughout the enterprise network; see *Figure 16.* Once within the reach of a browser, applications are easily downloaded, re-compiled, linked, and executed at the client side. The *Java applets,* i.e. Java components (likewise ActiveX components in MS Windows environment) are open, platform independent, and pre-compiled program objects that reside and are distributed throughout the Internet address space. Once downloaded at client side, the application runs as usual under the multitasking OS control. Eventual data input or output is performed under the application's control. There are no specific restrictions as to what type of applications can run at the client side since it supports MM presentations. In principle, there is no need for local data store since data is normally distributed and accessed through the network. In view of increasing trends leading to virtual computer organisations it is interesting to see *Case 9:* NIIIP Virtual Enterprise Project. Some enterprise paradigm variants may eventually ask for some sort of internal disk memory in order to provide for client's OS virtual memory support. The media types applicable for document exchanges comply with the *HyperText Markup Language* (HTML) *standard* for Web document presentation and data formatting. Following the HTML wide acceptance the overwhelming response comes for XML, the newest upgrade of the SGML document standard. The long awaited *Extensible Markup Language* (XML)[45] as data content-based standard provides the Web-documents content structuring and document-labelling support. The XML is the latest improvement of HTML document data formatting and structuring approach, a successful solution for simple virtual catalogue processing and Web-store content labelling.

---

[43] Gordon Moore, a semiconductor engineer, co-founded of Intel, held until the late 1970s
[44] Mobilising Enterprises, http://www.centurasoft.com
[45] BYTE, Jan./1998, Tech'98 Outlook: *Extensible Markup Language*

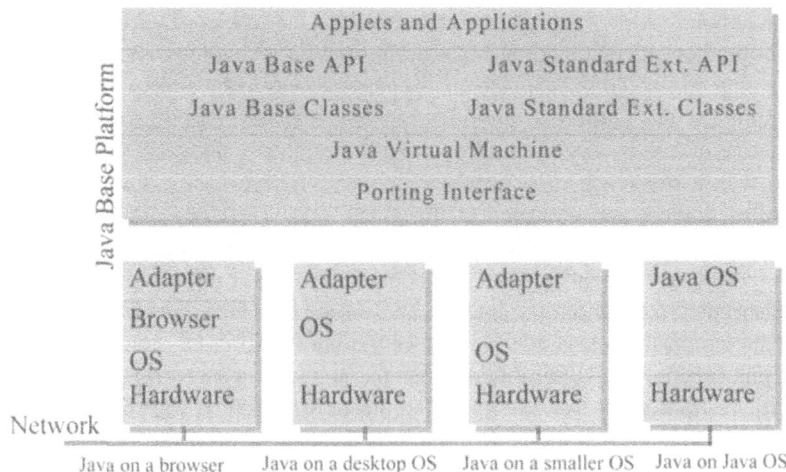

Figure 16. Java Platform [46]

Yet another breakthrough in the hypermedia data representations represents the *Virtual Reality Modelling Language* (VRML) standard. Enabled by Web Java-aware browser the VMRL applications are able to perform rich visualisation, 3D image representation, on-line 3D rendering and animation, and interact with user's models of reality in their own 3D cyberspace. No media type has been forgotten. Hypermedia drivers can access text, graphics, images, sound, or video. The high performance that is required for such hypermedia processing is fully supported by Matrix *Math eXtension* (MMX) processors, e.g. Intel's brand name processor, often a standard component in contemporary computer configurations. Due to the overwhelming user acceptance the networking paradigm of enterprise computing is expected to become de-facto standard for enterprise *Intranets*. It will replace and empower the obsolete dumb terminals and UNIX X-Windows clients by the intelligent, high performance NC stations. Moreover, it will also assure the lowest ownership costs of application processing across the enterprise.

HTML vs. SGML Presentation

HTML is document independent standard for hypertext, multimedia, and display of simple Web documents. It presents the content of a document based on *Document Type Definition* (DTD) standard as part of a more general *Standard Generalised Markup Language* (SGML*)* and the recent XML Web-document standard. Presently, there are many HTML editors in use creating documents in a *'What You See Is What You Get'* (WYSIWYG) form. The HTML documents written in plain ASCII text formats are not only editor-independent but also

---

[46] Source: Sun Microsystems, *The White Paper on Java*

presentation-independent and can be produced by common text editors. HTML browsers are also able to make necessary conversions allowing users to exchange almost any type of documents. This feature has been widely used by browsers on the Internet and *Wide World Web* (WWW), or just *the Web,* for document store in Web repositories, publish & distribute document exchange using downloading and uploading, and information presentations contained in most types of mixed MM documents.

Unlike the HTML document-content concerns, the common SGML as accredited *ISO standard* provides internationally accepted rules that enable defining not only the content but also the particular structures and formats of Web documents. This is especially important in document management and the exchange of large, complex documents, document archives, and information repositories.

Web servers and clients have to conform with relevant standards for document structuring, content preparation, fragmentation and item pointing, rendered in accordance with optional style-sheets and correctly interpreted by the hypertext semantics in order to be able to exchange SGML documents transparently. *W3C SGML* is the international group responsible for Web-document standardisation.

Applets - Java Application Components

Java applets are in fact program components written in an object-oriented Java language. Java applets are made available either by the browser's virtual Java platform, or downloaded through the network in the same manner as any HTML documents. The inherent program intelligence makes important difference. Once downloaded and executed at the client side they perform a specific programmed action. Like other program components, applets are able to dynamically respond to user actions, perform the desired input or output functions, run predefined program code, and perform program flow control in the usual way conventional programs do. This enables the intelligent information processing much easier than using elaborate pre-programmed animation of HTML documents. Java language belongs to the *object-oriented* group of programming languages and has inherited its best features from C++ and Smalltalk OO languages. In many respects, it has streamlined many OO features hence, enabling simple but powerful, interactive, portable, and easy to use programming language. Running the Java *virtual machine* interpreted the *byte code* on a native processor's code provides for even higher program performance. Sun Microsystems announced NC and intelligent consumer electronics running native *Java RISC processors*[47].

Besides robustness and platform independence of Java, special emphasis has been dedicated to ensure data and application security in *Java Virtual Machine* (JVM) especially if running in mixed *Internet* and *Intranet* environments. Unquestionably, Java applets are becoming most valuable program building blocks, basic components for *platform-independent* applications across the Web. Java NC networking paradigm furnishes users with required functionality on

---

[47] JavaTM Processors Supercharge the Next Generation of Java-Powered Networked Consumer Electronics, http://www.sun.com/970722/cover/javace.html

demand throughout the enterprise networks therefore, assuring the Intranet and Extranet users the lowest costs of application ownership.

Persistent Information

Should the need arise the Network Computers could easily handle local disks as persistent data store. However, it is often not the case since persistency is usually attained by servers running at the higher networking tiers, such as application or file/print network servers, or associated with on-line transaction applications and OLTP Monitors. Java NC has extended the thin client concept further so that in some cases the NC can assume some forms of local data persistency. Therefore, the data persistency is regarded mainly as responsibility of enterprise paradigm in maintaining data and applications globally, throughout the enterprise, providing regular application update, procurement of standards, enterprise-wide data integrity, and consistency. In addition to the lowest total costs of application ownership these features will certainly advocate toward greater acceptance of the enterprise paradigm.

Collaborative Paradigm

A collaborative networking paradigm supports business processes within an enterprise providing an important feature – a powerful *collaboration* among the users. The integration of business processes through collaboration is an essential feature claimed by most advocates of computerisation and virtual office elite. However, it is not only the office processes that can benefit from the introduction of networking paradigms. There is a suite of business activities where the sharing of intellectual know-how, information, and applications is of ultimate importance for the efficient, and productive business environment. Most information creative processes that need sharing and individual contribution such as design, process analyses, document authoring and text proofreading, consulting, education and learning, rich-information media presentation and system modelling, etc. are just few domains of collaborative computing applications which are supported by the collaborative enterprise networking paradigm. In fact, the collaborative paradigm takes responsibility of all aspects of enterprise network commuting. Mutual collaboration and sharing of creative endeavours across the enterprise introduces significant changes in the way users communicate with each other, which not only transforms the enterprise culture, but also more importantly sets its mind.

The collaborative processing requires mutual support by both, the client side as well as the server side. Moreover, some applications may require high network bandwidth in the anticipation of full networking support by the enterprise networking servers. Usually, the applications are equally shared and supported by both, clients and servers. The market leader[48] in integrated collaborative environment (ICE) remains IBM *Lotus' Notes/Domino* which according to IDC reports (July, 2002) has gained 49% ICE market share on more than 75,000

[48] Ed Brill, *Domino continues leadership in Integrated Collaborative Environments*, July 23, 2002, http://www.lotus.com/news/news.nsf/link/edbrill3, http://www.netcraft.com/Survey/Reports/0206/

enterprise servers world-wide. For more; see Virtual Enterprise: **Collaborative Computing** and *Case 20:* Transition Associate and Lotus Notes at Foulks Lynch Virtual College . IBM *Lotus' Notes* entails an OO enterprise database that supports GroupWare applications managing information of general document type across the enterprise. For instance, it manages executives' meeting minutes, assignment reports among various groups of users, collaborating, sharing tasks, and workloads across the enterprise. The individual document contributions are appropriately indexed, labelled, stored, and accessed in distributed manner, enabling the information to be shared, disseminated, and distributed to corresponding GroupWare partners across the enterprise. More than empowering individual users, it creates a responsive network layer that eliminates the need for any intermediary agents. It also enables enterprise business process integration and workflow consolidation. In fact, it is a powerful enterprise BPR tool that can be instrumental in flattening and streamlining any top-heavy enterprise structure. The business process integration is a decisive reason that makes the collaborative paradigm an overwhelming choice among all other networking paradigms.

Shared Processing

It is important to recognise that the collaborative paradigm is able to provide many-to-many, client-to-client communications, still based on very simple one-to-many client-server relations. The reason is that the collaborative paradigm implements an intensive shared processing at both, clients' and servers' side. Having a number of applications running simultaneously in a distributed environment across the enterprise it is essential that clients can easily access the portfolio of applications offered by the application servers. This kind of shared processing may require rather advanced clients and powerful application servers. Only few OS such as, Windows 2000/NT, OS/2, or UNIX/Linux suite could efficiently support the high demand for multi-user applications and at the same time safely meet the multitasking requirements. This advanced form of enterprise computing makes full use of enterprise-wide networking recourses and provides high level of computing and collaboration thus empowering the enterprise users.

Shared Applications

To date, there are suites of attractive GroupWare applications shared among clients and implemented by collaborative networking paradigm. Frequently, they cover several important application domains, for instance *multimedia* document processing, *workflow* and *scheduling* analysis, *e-mail* communications, and modern form of electronic on-line multimedia information exchange (e.g. *PC conferencing, teleconferencing*). For more; see *Case 19:* Transition Associates wins Lotus Beacon Award at Hughes Christensen.

Virtual *document archiving and imaging* is yet another shared application running behind the large document repositories and virtual Libraries. It has been successfully used to scan, compress, store and retrieve, and distribute any type of multimedia documents. Building document virtual libraries for many SMSE is an important task in their quest for the efficient organisation of documents, retrieval systems, and information archiving. The enterprises that have adopted electronic document archiving and paperless document processing have also found these systems cost efficient and beneficial for their environmental awareness policy.

Shared Database

Almost all the applications implemented by the collaborative paradigm depend on some sort of persistent data store. In order to provide high performance support to the individual collaborative contributions, a document is either stored locally, or in common libraries shared across the enterprise. The choice of document library features depends mostly on the GroupWare application used, the document-sharing type, and safety features implemented. However, it is important to recognise that the current workflow model implemented by the GroupWare document sharing tools is rather different from the one used by transactional database systems, from functional and data integrity point of view. Basically, the basic *document* type can be regarded either as unstructured or as highly hierarchical entity. For instance, a Lotus' Notes document entails highly elaborate structure with rather involved architecture. The data is tagged on many properties such as client, region, subject, or multiple data types respectively. It allows for simple extension for document attachments, therefore implementing embedded multimedia objects. Besides persistent store, the GroupWare offers a number of applications specific for multimedia documents. Undoubtedly, the collaborative computing technology in many aspects complements the database functionality and contributes to the wider use of common database technology.

Distributed Paradigm

The distributed computing represents one of the most attractive enterprise wide computing paradigms. Historically, it can be related to the former *transaction processing* used on the traditional mainframe systems and old-fashioned dumb terminals. Present distributed systems have evolved into more perplexing, sophisticated data transaction paradigms. An important feature is the *distributed processing*, i.e. distributing the processing load, by default, across processors in different address spaces. Moreover, it is possible to run *distributed applications* across several servers (e.g. database, file, or print server) so that two or more applications, for instance, few SQL related queries could contribute to a common transaction-processing task. With respect to data sharing, the implementation of *distributed databases* across the enterprise becomes a common approach for reducing the complexity of enterprise business processes. Controlling the data occurrences and its update frequency, a suitable data distribution policy can contribute best in order to select the enterprise domain with particular data-prone business process. This remarkable feature of the distributed paradigm tends to be rather important as the number of clients becomes large. Many network sub-layers are needed in order to reduce the complexity of such a large network. It may need three-tier or sometimes multi-tier network architecture. A number of application servers can provide the necessary application processing power for large pool of simple, but mostly thin clients. Frequently, few specialised network servers equipped with TP Monitors can furnish the required OLTP support or help execute the *On-Line Analytical Processing* (OLAP) task.

Distributed Processing

There are three distinct types of distributed data processing that the distributed paradigm of enterprise networking may benefit from:

1. *Symmetric*, i.e. distributing the processing to a small set of on-board processors with symmetric load share, sharing the same address space, also known as *symmetrical multiprocessing* (SMP). Its simple layout is presented in *Figure 4* and *Figure 17*. This is common enterprise architecture used by transaction servers in order to balance a variable enterprise-processing load.

2. *Parallel*, enabling the distribution of processing power across myriad of processors in a *Multiple-Instruction Multiple-Data* (MIMD) processing mode. The processors rarely share the same memory address space. Since they share the common processing logic through special distribution and communications processors with parallel code execution, this type of parallel data processing it is also referred to as *Massive Parallel Processing* (MPP), check *Figure 5*. Thanks to the immense processing power provided under the specific parallel programming constraints, this type of distributed processing supports distinct applications that are beyond the scope of our interest. For more; see *Massive Parallel Processors* (MPP) .

3. *Clustered* SMP *server arrays,* or *pool of servers,* distribute the processing across enterprise processors, each one being a server within its own distinct address space. Often equipped with few SMP boards, it represents yet another type of distributed processing, which nowadays becomes rather attractive for enterprise-wide OLTP applications; see *Figure 5*. The SMP clusters are used mainly to balance the processing power of already existing servers within the enterprise network, by sharing the processing load and integrating, possibly optimising the access to distributed enterprise RAID data stores. A successful experiment for networking a *pool of common desktops* running Linux OS is presented in Case 3: Networked Computing with Beowulf Iridis Cluster .

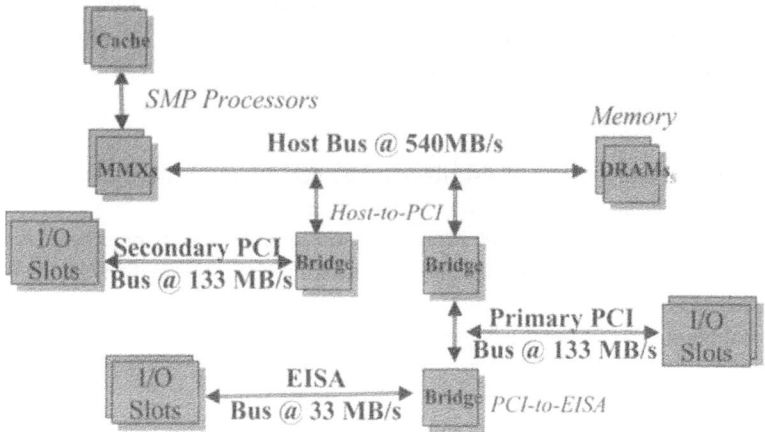

Figure 17. A SMP Server Array Architecture [10]

Distributed Applications

Distributed applications often run on many different platforms and provide access to several databases running under the supervision of particular resource managers. This is usually the case in transaction environments. Thus, the role of TP Monitors becomes indispensable since it integrates the transaction processing across different platforms. There are two standards that specify the TP Monitor's activity. The first is *FAP*, i.e. an ISO-OSI standard that calls on the message protocol allowing different TP Monitors to co-operate. The second is the familiar *X/Open Distributed Transaction Processing* (DTP) 1993 specification; see *Figure 18*. It allows multiple application programs to share resources under the control of particular resource managers, hence supervising the coordination of enterprise-wide transactions.

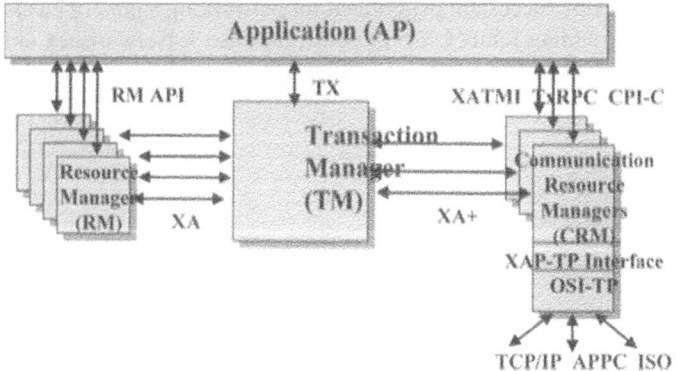

Figure 18. X/Open 1993 Transaction Processing Reference Model [49]

The 1993 update of the X/Open DTP Reference Model entails four components:

1. A *resource manager* (RM) manages shared resources. For instance, a database manager may allow external updates and co-ordination of concurrent activities by applying the *two-phase commit* database protocol.

2. A *transaction manager* (TM) co-ordinates and controls all the necessary resource managers communicating via the X/Open's XA interface (updated in 1993).

3. An *application program* (AP) makes use of general APIs. The resource managers provide support and co-ordinate the transactions calling on transactional manager via X/Open's TX interface. The TX interface drives the XA interface, therefore providing an application independent access within the distributed environment.

4. A *communication resource manager* (CRM), controls communications between different distributed applications. For instance, it may allow a transaction manager to control remotely a resource manager in a different domain, therefore supporting global transaction information flow across the entire enterprise. At the application level the CRM supports all three existing interface standards: for transactional version of DCE RPC, peer-to-peer CPI-C with APPC, and conversational interface based on *Application Transaction Management Interface* (ATMI). For more on related Tuxedo applications; see *Case 24:* CoreLAN - TP Services with BEA Tuxedo ™.

The X/Open committee has added another update to the X/Open 1993 standard[49], a *message queuing interface.* It confirms the well-known practice in the IT industry that frequent changes of existing standards actually make them obsolete.

Distributed Database

The distributed database concept comes as a promising solution to the current trend of integration of data processing across the enterprise. Therefore, data processing assumes *local* data creation, *remote* data update, and *global* data access. many advanced database applications to date claim transparent, flexible, and efficient global data processing, hence ensuring high network performance throughout the enterprise without compromising system's security or information safety constraints. We will elaborate on the distributed data issue in more details later in Distributed Applications. However, we should emphasize that the *data distribution* issue remains of utmost importance for any enterprise since it may directly influence its *data availability*, *network bandwidth*, actual *network performance*, and the overall *systems' security*. Aforementioned issues often determine the enterprise organisation structure and serve as key requirements for the introduction of the *Business Process Re-engineering* (BPR)

---

[49] The OSF TP work group continues with its DCE-based transaction RPC proposal that most probably will not be based on the OSI-TP.

initiative. It is illustrative to quote D. Vaskievitch, Microsoft[50], *"Distribute the business process and the data will follow"* that recognizes the perplexing relationship and the importance of BPR initiatives and distributed computing in enterprises to date.

Bibliography

Internet business models that work; *Alex Garden*; **New Zealand Management**, Auckland; Dec 2000; Vol. 47, Iss. 11; pg. 140, 1 pgs

The converging business models of Internet and bricks-and-mortar retailers; *Albrecht Enders*; **European Management Journal**, London; Oct 2000; Vol. 18, Iss. 5; pg. 542

Business models for Internet-based E-commerce: An anatomy; *B Mahadevan*; **California Management Review**, Berkeley; Summer 2000; Vol. 42, Iss. 4; pg. 55, 15 pgs

Internet-driven business models; *Ann Grackin*; **Manufacturing Systems**, Oak Brook; Jun 2000; Vol. 18, Iss. 6; pg. 56, 1 pgs

Adopting new business models key on Web; *Stephen Campbell*; **Bank Systems & Technology**, New York; Feb 2000; Vol. 37, Iss. 2; pg. O4, 3 pgs

Internet Anxiety; Part in envy, part in fear, Corporate America is embracing a radically new business model; *Nanette Byrnes in New York and Paul C. Judge in Boston, with bureau reports*; **Business Week**, New York; June 28, 1999, Iss. 3635; Industrial/technology edition; pg. 78

Winning Internet business models; *Marc E Brown*; **Electronic Business**, Highlands Ranch; Apr 1999; Vol. 25, Iss. 4; pg. 10, 1 pgs

At Milia, a search for new Web business models; *Herbert R Lottman*; **Publishers Weekly**, New York; Mar 1, 1999; Vol. 246, Iss. 9; pg. 18, 2 pgs

Internet zoo spawns new business models; *Alan Mitchell*; **Marketing Week**, London; Jan 21, 1999; Vol. 21, Iss. 45; pg. 24, 2 pgs

Don't reinvent wheel for IP business model; **Electronic Engineering Times** *Mark Templeton*; Dec 14, 1998

Viable e-business model is still a closed book; **Computing Canada** *Rosie Lombardi*; Dec 7, 1998

Vance mines new business model; **Advertising Age's Business Marketing** *Dana Blankenhorn*; Dec '98

A business model of one's own; **Inc** *Leigh Buchanan*; Nov 1998

Predicting business failure of retail firms: An analysis using mixed industry models; **Journal of Business Research** *McGurr, Paul T*; Nov 1998

The business excellence model: Will it deliver?; **Management Services** *John Seddon*; Oct 1998

Model business processes; **InformationWeek** *Nick Wreden*; Sep 28, 1998

The business model for teleconferencing; **America's Network** *Debbie L Sklar*; Sep 15, 1998

Automating the discovery of AS-IS business process models: Probabilistic and algorithmic approaches; **Information Systems Research** *Datta, Anindya*; Sep 1998

A model management approach to business process reengineering; **Journal of Management Information Systems** *Levent V Orman*; Summer 1998

Development of a business process re-engineering model applicable to the public sector; **Total Quality Management** *Rodney McAdam*; Jul 1998

It's Time To Examine Your Company's E-Business Model; **InternetWeek** *Bill Frezza*; Jun 22, 1998

A shift in business model; **Electronic Engineering Times** *Len Perham*; May 27, 1998

New business models proliferate; **Pensions & Investments** *Linda Sakelaris*; Apr 20, 1998

Business: Model business; **The Economist** *Anonymous*; Apr 18, 1998

MicroAge reworks business model; **Computer Reseller News** *Craig Zarley*; Apr 6, 1998

Searching for the right business model; **The Practical Accountant** *Anonymous*; Apr 1998

Extranets come in different styles. Do you know which is best for serving your business partners? The model extranet; **Network World** *Julie Bort*; Mar 30, 1998

Choosing a business model; **Best's Review** *Richard K Berry*; Mar 1998

---

[50] D. Vaskievitch, *Reengineering Business: The Shift to Client/Server*, Microsoft '94, http://murl.microsoft.com/videos/cmhc/leaders7/7-vaskTitle.htm

Enterprises' perceptions on business process re-engineering: A path analytic model; **Omega** *Hsi-Peng Lu*; Feb 1998

E-Commerce security: An alternative business model; **Journal of Retail Banking Services** *Roger Alexander*; Winter 1998

Formulating the new business model; **Telecommunications** *Bill Henry*; Jan 1998

The Nike Macro: It's the business model, stupid; **MC Technology Marketing Intelligence** *Michael Schrage*; Nov 1997

Reference Bibliography

CHAPTER 6

VIRTUAL ENTERPRISE

e-Business

Case 9: NIIIP Virtual Enterprise Project

VIRTUAL ENTERPRISES REQUIRE OMA/WWW INTEGRATION
Position Paper by Craig Thompson, NIIIP Project Office
http://www.w3.org/OOP/9606_Workshop/submissions/38-W3COMG.htm
(Reprinted by permission of the author and Object Services and Consulting, Inc.)

About the NIIIP Consortium.
The National Industrial Information Infrastructure Protocols Consortium (NIIIP) is developing technology to enable *industrial virtual enterprises* (VEs). An industrial VE is a temporary consortium of independent member companies which come together to quickly exploit fast-changing worldwide product manufacturing opportunities. Virtual Enterprises assemble themselves based on cost effectiveness and product uniqueness without regard for organization size, geographic location, computing environments, technologies deployed, or processes implemented. Virtual Enterprise companies share costs, skills, and core competencies which collectively enable them to access global markets with world class solutions that could not be provided individually.

In order to enable VEs, NIIIP is developing protocols and a reference implementation that ties together several emerging infrastructure technologies: Internet, web, OMG object technology, workflow, KBMS, rules, agents, and STEP product data. Rather than standardize protocols itself, NIIIP works through memberships in standards organizations, principally OMG (Internet SIG, Manufacturing TF), WfMC, and STEP. Much of the NIIIP work involves "harmonizing" the many sets of existing protocols, and then doing pilot projects to prove out the approach. NIIIP has ongoing work in many of the areas the W3C-OMG workshop is focused on. Three are described here.

NIIIP Desktop. The purpose of the NIIIP Desktop is to provide an interface for VE clients to create and manage VE tasks and sessions. Tasks, tools, and data are modelled as OMG IDL objects. The modelled entities are consistent with CAD Framework Initiative and Workflow Management Coalition protocols. One of our experiments involving web-object integration was to use a WWW browser as a VE client interface. In the initial demonstration, html-forms were used by a VE client to render and browse NIIIP Desktop objects. User selected method calls were sent to the web server and a CGI binary program used to interpret the message and make an IDL call. Drawbacks of this approach include that it required the user to request refreshes and that the CGI program was started for each selected method call. We are now working on a follow on variant in which a Java applet on the web client calls the server and Java on the server calls C++ ORB clients.

VE Repository Browser. The STEP community is standardizing product data descriptions. As part of its NIIIP effort, STEP Tools, Inc. developed a web-based data. The repository lets web clients browse an AP203 data set and download parts of that data set into their CAD and visualization systems. The data is translated from STEP Express to HTML using a set of STEP to HTML templates (STML). The ST-Visualizer was used to create VRML files for each of the parts and assemblies in the database. ST-ACIS was used to create ACIS files for AutoCAD for some of the parts. The STEP to CATIA translator in CATIA was used to create CATIA format files for some of the parts. An advanced version of the demo uses OMG CORBA (Orbeline) plus custom code at the VE client site.

Crossing Firewalls. VEs must share information but VE members are separated by corporate firewalls. Eventually OMG ORB/OS Task Force and/or the IETF Authenticated Firewall Traversal Working Group will propose a Secure Peer-to-Peer Internet Messaging standard. In the meantime, Enterprise Integration Technologies (EIT), a NIIIP member, is experimenting with a Post-and-PickUp (PPU) messaging scheme which can be extended to allow data encryption, digital signature, delivery certification, return receipt, message urgency. The PPU scheme relays a message through firewalls via third party called an Exchange Server located in the open outside of any firewall-protected VE client. Client A posts messages to the Exchange Server to the Individual Message Box of client B; Client B independently picks up messages from the Exchange Server. Both the Post and the PickUp protocols initiate from the client-side to the Exchange Server, making it more compatible with commonly accepted access control policies. Different PickUp schemes are being explored: polling, connect-and-hold (involves holding a TCP connection; may not scale) and out-of-band notification (e.g. via email). HTTP and Secure HTTP can readily be adapted to use PPU.

Enterprise Communication: EDI, E-mail, Java, Teleconferencing

One of the most important achievements of the enterprise-wide computing trend is certainly the leveraging role of the IT in the process of integration that goes beyond the core business processes, thus enabling transformations of wide range of business process across enterprise boundaries.

Enterprise networks are becoming so pervasive that the process of removing traditional barriers becomes quite natural, hence establishing the entire new paradigms of co-operation among business entities, both at the individual, as well as, at corporate level. New strategic alliances and partnerships are growing in number by redefining the scope of business processes in traditional enterprises and introducing a new paradigm – the *virtual enterprise*. This trend is supported by the *Virtual Enterprises* (VE) network standards introduced by the NIII[51]. The VE standard establishes necessary IT infrastructures hence enabling enterprises appropriate networking solutions providing almost unlimited *modus vivendi*, i.e. ways to operate. Among the technologies taking part in VE are certainly *Intranet* networking technology, *EDI standard* for electronic commerce support, *Java* browsers, and UML-based development methodology for business applications. All of them bring the scope of integration beyond that of a local area network or simple enterprise networking provisions. The VE IT solutions provide full-scale integration of existing enterprise networks geographically or across worldwide areas, temporarily for a limited time period, or for a specific task, thus sharing mutual project resources. VE enables new forms of joint ventures and extends the scope of their core business process activities. It is also necessary to establish a new strategy that will incorporate individual strategic plans, co-ordinate each partner's activities, and perform business processes transparently, in close co-operation with other business partners, hence creating a sort of loosely coupled *virtual enterprise* environment with clearly defined individual responsibilities.

Virtual enterprise concept has extended the enterprise stereotype beyond its physical boundaries into enterprise-wide networking. VE organisation integrates geographically dispersed entities into much broader form of enterprise, acting as a single entity with respect to its counterparts, but sharing joint business tasks and resources that are provided in response to a specific market opportunity. Once initiated the virtual enterprises may develop further into more permanent forms of business relationships, forging individual strengths to cater for increased market opportunities. Some forms rely on external enterprise networks, extending the traditional *EDI* technology initiatives to some sort of *outsourcing* and *franchising* organisation model. The new virtual enterprise entity adds value throughout its value chain, to the products and services of each and every VE member, but still bearing its own original trademark, brand name, and its distinct business processes' behaviour. In order to accomplish these goals the virtual enterprise depends on the application of few information-related technologies:

–   Communication technology support for individual *enterprise networks*
–   Information technology support for application-to-application *connectivity*
–   Workflow and knowledge management support for *collaborative* computing
–   OO development support for business processes *compatibility* across platforms
More on VE technology support will be elaborated in <u>Distributed Applications.</u>

Extended Enterprise: VE NIIIP standard
This virtual enterprise integration idea eventually has evolved into a standard. In September 1994, the *National Industrial Information Infrastructure Protocol[51]*

---

[51] <u>National Industrial Information Infrastructure Protocols (NIIIP) Consortium, http://www.niiip.org</u>

(NIIIP) was introduced by the NIIIP Consortium, a group of 18 organisations[52] led by IBM. The aim of the NIIIP is to integrate the work and knowledge management, objects, communications, and information technology and enable the proliferation of *Virtual Enterprises* (VE) concept[53]. The NIII defines Virtual Enterprise as follows: "*A temporary consortium of companies which come together quickly to explore some fast changing opportunity. Within the virtual enterprise, companies share costs, skills, and access global markets with each participant contributing its core competence. NIIIP technology will enable virtual enterprises without regard to size or organisational, geographic or technical boundaries to provide the most cost-effective, timely, and competitive products and services in the world*".

It extends the individual *Intranet* beyond the enterprise boundaries into its value chain and its *Extranet*. VE allows individual industrial partners to communicate together on a project-by-project or a task-force base. It also enables sharing of information among enterprises. For instance, it allows for updating the product-ordering status automatically, exchange of joint business rules, distribution and tracking of supplies, hence making effective use of its local *Intranets* and global *Extranet* networks. It also makes use of *Open Systems*[103] standards, premeditated industrial models of information and activities, and adheres to the ISO *STandard for Exchange of Product data* (STEP) and *WorkFlow Management Coalition (WFMC) standards*. Moreover, following the OMG's *object oriented* technology guidelines the disparate resources are named and modelled as global enterprise objects. Furthermore, the NIIIP protocols provide effective infrastructure for the inter-operation of *Commercial-Off-The-Shelf* (COTS) products in the industrial domain. For more, check Case *9:* NIIIP Virtual Enterprise .

The NIIIP VE standard entails a set of 13 interrelating objects. Various VE schemas are possible depending on actual selection of interrelating objects. VE is also compliant both with CORBA protocol and STEP product data (EXPRESS) descriptions; see *Figure 19*.

During the process of interaction, clients and servers usually follow a four-step protocol: *ask, agree, deliver*, and *accept*. The NIIIP infrastructure maintains the *routing* of eventual requests and furnishes the following services: project control, project management, knowledge and rule management, task and session management, and decision support. The VE infrastructure entails several NIIIP components organised hierarchically into several levels of functionality:

– Level 1 or *user level* provides end-user applications support such as: *project control* composed of *desktop* and *agent* components, *project management*, and *virtual enterprise services*. The *desktop* entails user interface to multiple VE, sessions and roles. The *session* performs user authentication, resource allocation, transaction logging, simulation, and long-transaction control. The *agent* component is responsible for VE organisational structures, resource ownership, etc. The *STEP services* provide support for STEP *Data Access Interface* and SDAI for VE *Industrial Models*. Among the levels, there is the *Transport*

---

[52] http://www.niiip.org/consortium-members.html
[53] Virtual Enterprises Require OMA/WWW Integration, http://www.objs.com/niiip/W3COMG.htm

component that provides non-CORBA mediated object access, replication, caching, DFS, SHTTP, and TCP/IP protocol support.

– Level 2 or *middleware level* renders co-ordination services to the level 1 such as *task and session management* and *knowledge and rule management* that help share and monitor the resources distributed across enterprises within its *firewall* domain. The task and session management includes a *Workflow* that provides cross-product workflow management. *Rule and Knowledge Management* makes use of the *VE Knowledge DBMS* that resolves semantic problems and provides active semantic network database for the VE.

– Level 3 or *mediation service* is responsible for the *resolve and decision support* for other two levels and helps the *negotiation* between disputing agents. The involvement of *negotiator* component enables impartial multiparty negotiation. The role of the *mediator* component is to provide a resolution of semantic ambiguity, summarising, abstracting, validating data, localised knowledge, local ontology maintenance, etc.

Adhering closely to the OO reuse, the NIIIP Consortium has adopted elements of the following methodologies:

– STEP development methodology;
– OMG development methodology,
– Object Analysis & Design (OA&D) methodologies,
– SEI Capability Maturity Model [78] (CMM) or Clean Room,
– Taligent Coding Guidelines, and
– Work Management tools.

Excluding legal and cultural issues, the NIIIP focus is on integrating IT needed to enable *Industrial Virtual Enterprises* (IVE) to form, schedule and complete projects, share information, collaborate on solving problems, communicate with those outside the IVE, negotiate, mediate, and resolve disputes, and then dissolve. The relationship between the NIIIP components and CORBA facilities and corresponding CORBA service-building blocks is illustrated on *Figure 19*.

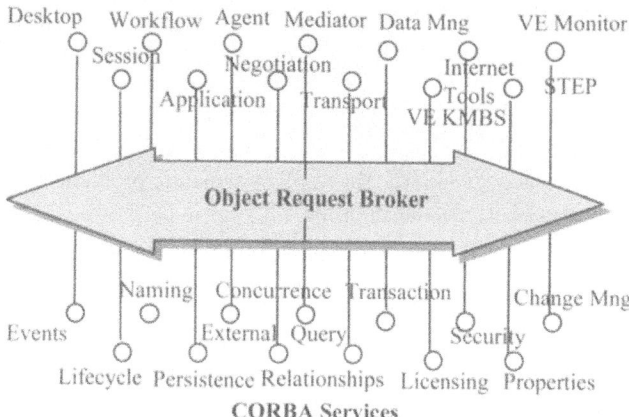

Figure 19. NIIIP VE and CORBA Services [54]

Collaborative Computing: Workflow Integration

The enterprise i-Net, i.e. *Intranet* and *Extranet,* incorporates the potential of present client/server technology that combined together provides significant advantages over traditional legacy systems usually, traditional mainframe-based systems. Unquestionably, the i-Net increases the efficiency of programmable, repetitive tasks, something legacy systems were very good at. Moreover, the i-Net also maintains efficient operational feedback inherited from C/S systems. However, it is the *integration* ability of the GroupWare technology that remains the distinct *Intranet* feature. It also enables workflow and teamwork support for most enterprise-wide collaborative tasks. Therefore, the collaborative computing involves a suite of software applications that help enterprise-wide organisation to manage asynchronous distribution of information, and maintain efficiently the number of task-related GroupWare activities across the enterprise. Components of collaborative computing include *workflow* and multimedia *document* support, enterprise *email/messaging facility*, individual and group *task scheduling*, and electronic *conferencing*; see *Case 5:* Novell NetWare at Beveridge & Diamond.

Besides the e-mail and messaging support mentioned in our GroupWare review and a number of frequently used applications related to either simple databases applications or complex information retrieval, there is a number of GroupWare support utilities, management tools, task organisers, event visualisation and other useful tools. The main feature of all these collaborative applications and tools is its inherent hierarchical information architecture based upon - *the document.* Unlike *tables* - the building blocks of conventional common relational database, the *document* is the basic building block of GroupWare document repositories. Whether storing transactional records, simple email, fax, or large binary images,

---

[54] Adapted from VE NIIIP http://www.rdrc.rpi.edu/virt-ent.html

the database *table* assumes *flat-file* data structure that allows no *data hierarchies*. In contrast to common flat-file architecture the GroupWare document entails a *hierarchical* organisation; see *Case 22:* GemStone OO dBase in CONDIS Project The market leaders for GroupWare software are IBM *Lotus Notes,* Novel's *GroupWise,* and Microsoft *Outlook,* providing a number of collaborative support features. An *OO document* component type represents a hierarchical information container that entails rich formatted text, highly structured binary data, and a set of multimedia types including image, digital sound, movie clips etc. The XML has extended the HTML and STML standards for Web document *format and presentation* with its XSL style and XQL database labelling support. The XML standard has enabled Web document *content* a full database support. For more on general *object document* type and its concepts see Oberon *Component Pascal* [55].
The collaborative systems like TP Monitors, designed to manage distributed, conversational transactions across enterprise networks, also provide substantial support for complex document-based transactions, sometimes even competing with the mainline GroupWare software. The GroupWare is also designed to provide enterprise *workflow* support in addition to the existing *collaborative* software functionality. Recent product developments for the i-Net, e-Business GroupWare, and TP Monitor applications show considerable convergence in that direction. A GroupWare document repository combined with a solid TP Monitor complex ACID transactions' support becomes a dominant feature of an i-Net collaborative system; see *Case 24:* CoreLAN - TP Services with BEA Tuxedo [TM]
The management of collaborative document roots back to copying and photo imaging that has replaced and revolutionised traditional paper-based information archives. First, it used the microfilm to scan, or otherwise digitise the images. Later, it was the paperless document retrieval system that revolutionised the document archive. To date, an IBM *Lotus Notes/Domino* document management server uses similar hierarchical tagging for all types of document properties such as *client, region,* and *subject.* It can handle any number of document *attachments* as embedded objects. Shared and collected works by collaborating authors are stored in original *hierarchical databases* that provide full text support, content-wise indexing across documents, and efficient document retrieval.
GroupWare supports both structured and unstructured work-task environments. A GroupWare *workflow* application introduces a new enterprise technology that can automatically route any individual or group workflow, and organise the enterprise-wide events into continuous, scheduled workflows. Presently, the collaborative workflow tools provide a low-cost GroupWare support integrating objects from different collaborative applications across enterprises. They also provide facilities for tracking any work in progress, loosely coupled forms of communication among applications, such as e-mail, or MOM events, and support tools that perform programmed tasks and complete the requested actions. The workflow tools clearly defines and traces who does "what, when, and to whom". It illustrates the very idea presented as the *three R's* by Ronni Marshak

---

[55] ETH Oberon, http://www.oberon.ethz.ch/

[Workgroup Computing Report Editor][56]. The *routes* define paths to objects in space and time. The *rules* define the information routed and to whom. The *roles* define the assignments to actors who perform the tasks. Applying the *three R's* a workflow tool is able to create, join, fork, and split the tasks into sequential and parallel actions, and organize the feedback, circular, and fully connected process-oriented workflows; see *Figure 20*.

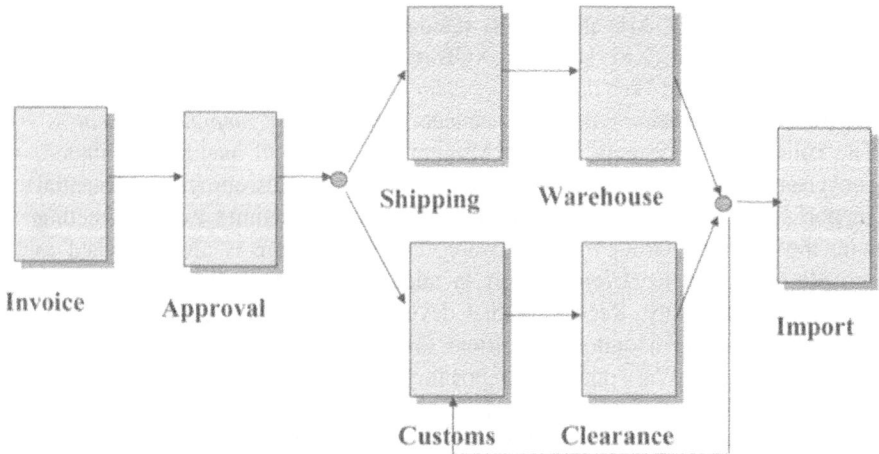

Figure 20. Workflow R3 patterns: Shipping Documents Workflow

The workflow tools comply with the *WorkFlow Management Coalition (WFMC) standards*. They are often used together with other collaborative applications like *messaging* and common *e-mail*. For more, please refer to <u>Network Connectivity</u>: *Network Agents*. In conjunction with the appointment and task *scheduling* with timetable and *calendar* support they play an important role in creating a dynamic workflow enterprise environment, e.g. Novell *GroupWise*; see *Case 5:* Novell NetWare at Beveridge & Diamond.

No doubt, the *Intranet* has become a valuable and for many business enterprises even a mission-critical asset. In addition to providing e-mail services as common popular collaborative computing application, the GroupWare can offer support and integration to the enterprise-wide mission-critical business applications. Still the power of collaborative computing starts with basic messaging. Presently, the e-mail tools entail application features that facilitate integration of scheduling, appointments, meetings and message exchange among enterprise employees. It can help maintain the individual calendars, collaboration in creation of shared document, processing, and workflow supervision. It is also possible to control the workflow complexity of a number of enterprise-wide business tasks. Novell *GroupWise* is certainly one of the top-rated collaborative computing groupware

---

[56] Marshak, Ronny T.: *InConcert Workflow*. Article in Patricia Seybold's Workgroup Computing Report, 1997, <u>http://www.inconcert.com/press/articles/iar_ seybold.html</u>, <u>http://www.inconcert.com/products</u>

applications. Novell GW provides a cross-platform support, remote access, Web access, gateways to both foreign-based and host-based systems, full integration of calendaring, scheduling and task management, real-time conferencing support, database access, development tools, consolidated system administration, and reliable enterprise network integration using efficient Novell *NetWare Directory System* (NDS). It also provides email, voicemail messaging, integrated document management, workflow, imaging, shared library folders, and other features.

To date, especially with the widespread use of powerful *MMX processors* for multimedia processing and substantial video compression, there is an enormous interest for yet another form of collaborative applications - *the electronic conferencing*. Creating asynchronous replicas out of individual contributions the GW makes them available and shareable to all group members across the enterprise. The individual contributions thus become part of a *group document library* in timely, but still real-time environment. Some forms of *conferencing* provide GW conferencing with e-mail, electronic bulletin board, and treaded discussions support. *Real-time conferencing* or *teleconferencing* however, allows for individual and multi-group simultaneous collaboration. It also provides document presentation, electronic whiteboards, and motion video support.

Global Enterprise: e-Businesses vs. e-Portals

In our review of the global nature of enterprise networks we mentioned an interesting relationship that exists between the on going changes in the enterprise organisation and the electronic market place that shares that information known as e-Portal. The former is primarily due to the high pace of changes in the IT infrastructure whereby the later is mainly influenced by the advantages of virtual enterprises. Undoubtedly, the e-Business remains a significant trend in the development of the contemporary enterprise networking solutions. Some may argue that e-Business is more of a hype. Something that comes and goes, leaving its inevitable marks due to organisational changes and the IT impact on the enterprise paradigms. It has been said that the history repeats itself. Enterprise networks are the very example. For instance, the mainframe networks maintained its dominant position in the value chain. Therefore, the locking in of the trading partners could easily apply, e.g. EDI networks, mainframe support systems etc. To date, this very idea is re-invented by many e-businesses, e.g. MS Network, Hotmail, and similar e-business solutions, *free* business offers that require only to get registered. Recently, the development of virtual marketplaces becomes a new networking trend. From a simple Web presence, via business-to-consumer solution, it develops into a full business-to-business inter-organisational network; e-Portals provide virtual marketplaces that port and connect enterprises together.

Most experts believe that the success (or failure) of the present e-Business trend will depend whether the new solutions will more efficient in reducing the costs of co-ordination of business processes in virtual enterprise or will it be due to lower entry barriers and lower costs of competitiveness of virtual marketplaces.

It is the efficient use of networking hierarchies that will eventually help reducing the co-ordination costs. For more on outsourcing and e-Business' ASP solutions; see *Case 12:* Nortel Networks Solutions to Power Taiwan's new eASPNet.

The e-Portal solution achieves the same goal of reducing the costs of co-ordination among business partners using much simpler and traditionally proven marketplace laws of supply and demand. However, a substantial enterprise network re-organisation is required in order to apply e-Portal or virtual enterprise solutions. For more on e-Portals and virtual catalogues see *Case 25:* Cognicase: Sold! Maximizer Enterprise for Notes Wins Bid for Management Solution

e-Businesses: Inter-organisational Networks for e-Commerce[57]

Enterprise networks, i.e. e-Networks, are usually used in electronic marketplaces in order to steer the execution of business transactions among business partners. Transactions are necessarily found in any value-added or supply-chain activity that requires procurement of components to be transformed into products or provided as services. It is done either in-house or by contractors (outsourcing)[58]. According to Porter[59] there are three ways the enterprise can strategically achieve competitive advantages; e-Networks play a decisive role in accomplishing them:

- Gain *cost/benefit advantage*, e.g. launch an ERP solution, or *lock in* to a browser
- Achieve *product differentiation*, e.g. *Otis-line* support, or Dell.com *Web-store*
- Render *market focus-niche*, e.g. Ariba.com e-Procurement, or Cisco.com *On-line*
  In fact, taking into account the role of market share one is to be added to the list.
- Attain *market leadership*, e.g. MS Windows, IBM Lotus' Notes, or Oracle dBase
  Consequently, inter-organisational and e-Networks infrastructures are commonly used to support new e-Business solutions. The range of e-Business initiatives can be wide, starting from simple business-to-customer or e-Commerce applications to most complex forms of business-to-business or e-Business solutions. Due to the inherent internal links among e-Business applications it might be useful to present them as comprehensively as possible. The architectural framework in *Figure 21* presents a simple outlook of internal communication and relationships among individuals, corporate parties, and corresponding e-Business applications.

---

[57] Steinfield C., Kraut R., and Plummer A., *The Impact of Interorganizational Networks on Buyer-Seller Relationship*, JCMC, vol. 1, #3.

[58] *Hierarchy* refers to in-house production, while *Market* refers to outsourcing subject to supply/demand laws.

[59] Porter, Michael, *Competitive Advantage: Creating and Sustaining Superior Performance*, London, Free Press, 1985

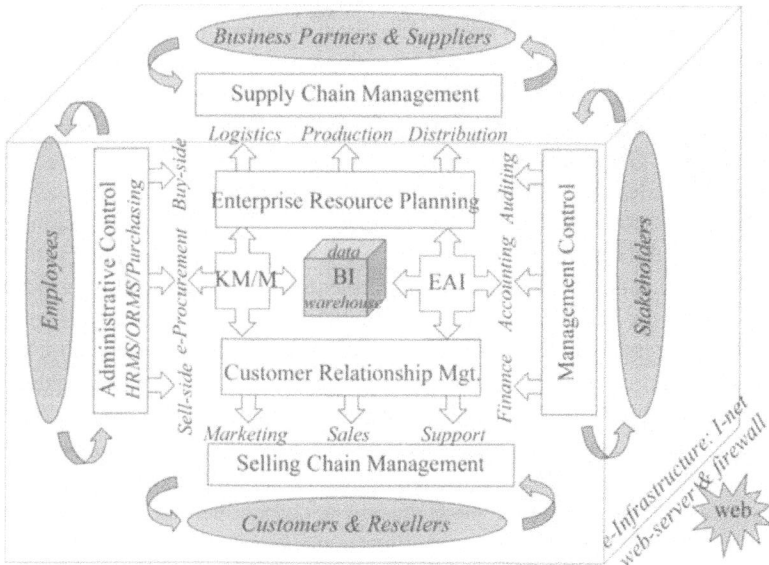

Figure 21. e-Business Cube [60]

Customer Relationship Management (CRM) is closely associated with marketing channels, customers, and/or resellers. Business partners and value-added chain suppliers are linked through the Supply Chain Management (SCM) application. The Management and the Administrative Control run its own application that brings Stakeholders and Employees together. An application that integrates them all and manages enterprise resources is the *Enterprise Resource Planning* (ERP). Some technologically advanced enterprises achieve higher integration benefits introducing Enterprise Application Integration (EAI) solutions. It allows EAI to be closely linked to Knowledge Management and Massaging (KM/M). Together with Business Intelligence (BI) applications they are at the hart of the e-Business cube. The BI relies on data warehouse technology; OLAP for instance for data mining is responsible for competitive advantages support, whereas, OLTP allows for higher competitive advantages and on-line transactions processing support.

The benefits due to improved co-ordination of transactions and the reduced costs of co-ordinating the production process throughout the value chain comes as the consequence of the improved electronic communication (e.g. EDI, EFT) among e-Networks and e-Business applications.

However, the open network standard is a prerequisite for market-like relationship among trading partners. Due to the low-costs trend and the adherence to open networks, the benefits gained from electronic brokerages and global integration are even provided to small-size enterprises and end-users. The *dot.com* hype and the growing interest in the e-Business are overwhelming evidences of this trend.

---

[60] Adapted from Kalakota, Robinson M.: *e-Business: Roadmap for Success, AWL, 2000*

e-Portals: Electronic Marketplaces[61]

Unlike e-Business solutions, the electronic marketplaces use much simpler supply/demand market mechanism. The flow of materials, products, services, finances, and information throughout the value-chain is self-regulated by market-based pricing system. Assuming perfect market information the systems remains stable. The introduction of e-Networks affects the costs of acquiring information or obtaining actual goods and services through information media distribution and electronic delivery. Virtual marketplaces and e-Portals already established provide the electronic brokerage of information, but also delivery of information-related goods and services (e.g. news casts, e-books, music, e-catalogues, motion pictures, e-manuals, etc.). The electronic dissemination of information in various business domains illustrates the role and the importance of virtual marketplaces. E*Trade.com remains an important financial broker. eBay.com leads the group of growing number of electronic auction providers. Ariba.com is an established e-Procurement broker and the market leader in creating virtual market places. Yahoo.com is certainly the pioneer as information portal. Amazon.com is well known as the e-Portal for trading all kinds of information-related products, books, CDs etc. Interestingly, some music exchanges such as Napster.com and Gnutella.com introduced a new client-to-client (C2C) P2P-based transactional trade model, eventually bypassing eventual intermediaries. The C2C e-business model relies on the extensive use of Web-browser technology and the e-Markets information media. The C2C debate has produced a lasting impact over the acceptance of the traditional intellectual copyright issues in the electronic market places. For more; see *Case 7:* Peer-to-Peer Technology Exists Beyond Napster.

The electronic market or e-Market[62] is the electronic marketplace where business partners assemble to do business over the Web. The e-Markets have specialised and spread across industries. They focus on specific class of products or services, from raw materials and spot markets in oil and gas industry, to pharmaceuticals and lab equipment for scientific research.

According to the previous review[62], the e-Network hierarchies and the e-Market portals have been established equally well in practice. The e-Network presence is pronounced in business-to-business environments. The prevalence of e-Network hierarchies is because extending the e-Network infrastructure to trading partners is only economically viable provided there is a substantial transaction volume. However, the e-Market portal remains an alternative in cases where large number of occasional trading partners is expected with frequent transactions, and growing, but uncertain consumer base dispersed across network environments. Depending on the scale of applications and the market size some e-Business solutions can implement either of the two alternatives. For instance, a virtual enterprise that makes use of the e-Networking hierarchical solution[63] may launch a SCM application using a virtual catalogue for products and services from an

---

[61] Hoffman L. D., Novak P. T., and Chatterjee P., *Commercial Scenarios for the Web: Opportunities and Challenges*, JCMC, vol. 1, #3.

[62] A comprehensive list of e-Markets can be found at http://www.line56.com/b2bprofiles.

[63] http://www.softwareag.com/corporat/products/default.htm

XML-shared database. Similarly, a million-dollar e-Procurement application like Ariba.com[64], a third party financial clearing application like NetBill.com[65], a spot market for crude oil products, an online storefront like Dell.com[66], or a Web stockbroker like E*Trade.com[67] may rather use the e-Market or e-Portal solution.

Bibliography

Electronic Commerce: Control Issues for Securing Virtual Enterprises; *Richard A Selg*; **Cost Engineering**, Morgantown; Nov 2000; Vol. 42, Iss. 11; pg. 13, 1 pgs
Learning e-commerce through 'virtual enterprise'; *Anonymous*; **IIE Solutions**, Norcross; Jun 2000; Vol. 32, Iss. 6; pg. 9, 1 pgs
NTT pays cash for virtual business; *Anonymous*; **International Financial Law Review**, London; Jun 2000; Vol. 19, Iss. 6; pg. 8
Virtual business; *Tony Jordan*; **Asian Business**, Hong Kong; Nov 1999; Vol. 35, Iss. 11; pg. 31, 1 pgs
As E-Business Evolves, Boundaries Will Give Way To Virtual Enterprise Networks; *Jamie Lewis*; **InternetWeek**, Manhasset; Sep 13, 1999; pg. PG.25
Finance and economics: The real virtual business; *Anonymous*; **The Economist**, London; May 8, 1999; Vol. 351, Iss. 8118; pg. 71, 2 pgs
Virtual business school opens; *Anonymous*; **Works Management**, Horton Kirby; May 1999; Vol. 52, Iss. 5; pg. 9, 1 pgs
Visual assessment of engineering processes in virtual enterprises; **Association for Computing Machinery. Communications of the ACM** *Thomas Rose*; Dec 1998
Virtual business realities; **InformationWeek** *Judith S Hurwitz*; Nov 23, 1998
Virtual business, real concerns; **Midrange Systems** *Larry Greenemeier*; Nov 9, 1998
Aurora Public Library Business Resource Centre Virtual Business Library; **Library Journal** *Susan C Awe*; Sep 1, 1998
The virtual enterprise gets real; **Telecommunications** *Annelise Berendt*; Apr 1998
Building the virtual enterprise; **InformationWeek** *Sean Gallagher*; Feb 23, 1998
Sending Files to Faraway Places--for Far Less; Infonet's Virtual Enterprise VPN service cuts the cost of connecting remote offices and telecommuters; **Data Communications** *Joanna Makris*; February, 1998
The industrial virtual enterprise; **Association for Computing Machinery. Communications of the ACM** *Martin Hardwick*; Sep 1997

---

[64] http://www.ariba.com/corp/home
[65] http://www.netbill.com/consumer/usage.html
[66] http://www.dell.com/us/en/gen/default.htm
[67] http://www.etrade.com/cgi-bin/gx.cgi/applogic+Home

CHAPTER 7

ENTERPRISE MANAGEMENT

Total Cost of Ownership (TCO)

Case 10: Insignia Solutions apply NTrigue with Citrix WinFrame

*Insignia Solutions Spotlights a Real-World Problem Solved by **NTrigue***

A major northwestern utility that supplies electricity to 70,000 metropolitan residents and businesses has a lot to keep track of. It has over 2,000 employees, 14 major substations and 3,654 miles of power distribution lines -- and it's not all transmission lines and fuse boxes. The utility had a computer compatibility problem. Excel Data Corporation, a regional software consulting and systems integration company, was brought in to help solve it.

At the utility, there are over 1,600 computers on the network; virtually all of them PCs. However, there are about 55 non-PCs on the network -- UNIX workstations and Macintosh computers. These non-PC users are mostly engineers using UNIX and graphic designers on Macs who need their platforms to get their jobs done. But when it came to getting access to Windows applications, these non-PC workers were in the dark.

The 1,600 workers on PCs are fully networked and have access to a common set of applications -- including some in-house custom applications that are mission critical. The utility employs WinFrame by Citrix to deliver this access to remote users and telecommuters. But system administrators had to find a solution that would bring the 40 UNIX workstations and the 15 Macintosh users into the fold.

For ease of administration, a directive was issued requiring users to standardize on the same electronic mail system, cc:Mail. Accommodating the Macintosh users would have been a cinch -- there is a version of cc:Mail for the Mac. But the UNIX users would still have been left out in the cold.

The utility needed a system-wide solution, not just a patch. It needed to give users on all platforms the same access that WinFrame gave the PC side of the house. Essentially, the company was looking for a solution similar to Citrix's WinFrame, which extended to UNIX and Macintosh platforms.

The answer: NTrigue

NTrigue, which includes Citrix Systems' WinFrame product, delivers Windows 95, Windows 3.x and Windows NT applications to all enterprise desktops, including UNIX workstations and Macintosh computers. NTrigue is the tool that the utility needed to bring cc:Mail to the UNIX and Macintosh platforms. But it goes well beyond just that. With NTrigue, the engineers on UNIX workstations and the creative service workers on Macs now have access to the entire world of Windows applications. These workers can now access the custom applications, designed in-house, that were previously accessible only from the PC domain, as well as any standard Windows applications the company implements. NTrigue welcomed the UNIX workstations and the Macintosh computers into world of Windows.

By deploying NTrigue Excel Data Corporation saved the utility over $150,000 -- the cost the utility would have incurred to put PCs on all of the 55 non-PC desktops. NTrigue also saved the utility's investment in its Macintosh computers and UNIX workstations by adding Windows functionality to the non-PC computers.

"The most glorious moment was when I got the product on my desk and had it up and running three hours later" said systems analyst Erick Watson of Excel Data Corporation. "With NTrigue I got it up and running in a matter of hours! It was a real watershed event."

Things have been going very smoothly ever since.

NTrigue made it possible.

"From the day we installed it, we haven't had a single problem," Watson said. "We turn it on. It runs. We never touch it. It works."

As mentioned earlier, the IT today supports fundamentally different computing enterprise environments enabling significant business transformations to take place. The IT not only helps reengineer its business processes, it ultimately helps the enterprise extend its business scope[73]. The appropriate application of IT can boost the enterprise performance and enable new organisational paradigms. The IT also helps enterprise sustain its initial success. Often, it represents a challenge to the competitors, always eager and waiting for a single opportunity or a chance to penetrate the market. Enterprise partnerships and enterprise *Mergers & Acquisitions* (M&A) of weaker and smaller enterprises become a dominant organisational change contributing to the enterprise growth and integration. Yet another symptom the *information-centric paradigm* [Renaud, 1996] is at its peak.

In fact, the global networking enables enterprises easy access to everything they need, from components provided by suppliers, to products and services offered to the market. A closer look at virtual enterprise life-cycles reveals that it entails product financing, product contracting, often outsourcing the supply and product delivery, manufacturing, assembling, setting up third-party distribution channels, maintaining retail network, and offering product distribution logistic support. Actually, at each and every step there exists an information-centric process that retains the coordination of business processes.

In fact, the *virtual enterprise* paradigm treasures the entrepreneurial creativity as an intellectual property solely responsible for transforming the entire business processes and potentially able to manage most enterprise concepts, ideas, products, and services.

Customer-focused enterprise approach however, is a response to market forces favouring responsiveness, product and service customisation in cost competitive output. Hence, the customisation of product/service and increased *economy of scope* along with process efficiency of *economy of scale* becomes the key to the business success. The *economy of scope* accordingly [Pine, 1993] is "*the application of a single process to produce a greater variety of products or services more cheaply and more quickly*". In contrast, the *economy of scale* means *mass production using large-scale resources* usually built around large enterprises. It follows that the economy of scope approach is smaller in scale, more customer-oriented, and is able to react quickly on market demands, rapidly changing production, customizing a variety of products and services, cheaper and faster. The *OTIS Elevators* case with its OTIS-line network application remains a well-known example. Despite its break-even production, the OTIS MIS network has generated adequate revenue through its OTIS-line services. As soon as a customer places a demand, a pre-assigned team takes over, customizes the offer, and organizes the delivery. The OTIS-network allows supervising the production process on-line, assembling, testing, and installing the product at customer's site. Evidently, The OTIS-line service enables high availability, product monitoring, and prompt product maintenance and support. Highly responsive OTIS-line team capitalizes on the efficient *workflow* and the benefits of the information-centric, enterprise paradigm online.

Network Efficiency vs. Total Cost of Ownership[68]

Undoubtedly, the understanding of network efficiency represents an important issue that has to be viewed from the sustainable enterprise change perspective and the global integration trend. The *network efficiency* is usually defined as a measure in terms of the *data overhead* experienced or present during *data transmission* through the network. It is also proportional to the length of the *data message*. Due to the consistent trend of integration of services throughout the network and the convergence to global enterprise paradigms, it is evident that a single network type could not possibly provide a unique, efficient, network solution. The enterprises usually implement local networks based on *Ethernet* or *Token Ring* configurations. Both solutions are constantly driven by the business demand. Should they evolve and introduce complex and more sophisticated networking alternatives, such as *FDDI* support, *xDSL,* integrated *frame relays*, or *cell relays* ATM communication? These alternatives provide enterprises a wide networking support and allow them efficient integration of *Intranet* networking solutions, such as Novell *IntranetWare*, Microsoft *Outlook*, or IBM *Lotus Notes* . For more; see Case 5: Novell NetWare at Beveridge & Diamond.

---

[68] Gartner Group Report http://www.gartner.com/

As mentioned earlier in Persistent Transactions: Thin vs. Fat Systems and presented in *Case 10:* Insignia Solutions apply NTrigue with Citrix WinFrame the thin-client/server option may eventually reduce the *Total Costs of Ownership* (TCO). The reduced TCO may allow the deployment of many business-critical applications over heterogeneous environments without compromises such as loss of application performance, data security, or lack of administrative control.

The introduction of the latest IT not only changes the end-user practices, but eventually the network efficiencies change too; see *Table 7*. Obviously, replacing previously obsolete IT solutions with more up-to-date technology often requires substantial new financial investment, with even more challenging know-how. Since more advanced, this usually requires a subsequent technology change and change management assistance. This in turn drives into a spiral of new capital investments. Only few solutions offered nowadays claim to have overcome that vicious investment circle by providing minimal *total ownership costs*. In fact, it means turning the high capital investment-costs into controllable, but lower running service-costs. Eventually, a new solution arrives based on customisation and the *economies of scope* rather than the *economies of scale*. For more, please see the *Gartner Group Report*[68].

Table 7. Network Efficiency [69]

Enterprise network type	Bandwidth Mpbs	Efficiency (%) 300B message	Efficiency (%) 1200B message	Overhead & delay due to
Ethernet	10	57	84	Msg. Confirmation
Token Ring	4	84	95	Token propagation
TCP/IP	0.064	43	75	Acknowledgements
Frame Relay	2	53	82	Relay confirmation
Fast Ethernet	100	65	88	Msg. Confirmation
ATM relay	155	77	87	Cell propagation

Network Costs

As usual, the cost of enterprise networking technology may become prohibitive. In order to stay competitive, it is essential to control all the costs, which means containing enterprise-networking costs as well. Due to stable IT trends to date and the increase of cost/performance ration, the actual networking costs are going down every year with every new IT generation. However, the costs of services including the product turnover are constantly increasing. This is due to the increase in the user's pool size, expansion of the distribution channels, introduction of open standard system configuration, a widespread procurement of integrated applications, and the appropriate network management required for enterprise paradigm support. One way out is to seriously take care of the enterprise *life-cycle management.* Not only it reduces the costs, but also provides cheaper open standard IT technology. It also maintains a powerful and flexible environment to the enterprise users.

---

[69] Tanenbaum, 1989; Stallings, 1996; Renaud, 1996

Still, there are many roadblocks on the way, mainly inconsistencies due to the software-driven technology, loss of control by MIS managers, large non-quantifiable costs, etc. In order to ascertain the competitiveness of the enterprise paradigm shift, it is important to get insights in the *TOC* trend[70] presented in the following *Table 8.*

Table 8. Enterprise Trends [70]

Features/Year	1987	1995	1997	2002 (*estimated*)
Avg. desktop pool	600	2300	2600	6000
Apps/desktop	1 á 2	3 á 4	5 á 6	6 á 10
Type of users	Power user	Power user: 30% high touch user	Power user: 20% production user	Power user: 20% i-Net; developer
5 years costs/seat Client & C/S ($K)	16	Client: 44 C/S: 66	Client: 20 C/S: 35	Client: 10 C/S: 25
Complexity	Standalone	Networked	Integr../multimedia	Web/multimedia

Total Cost of Ownership (TCO)

Whenever used for cost containment the IT primarily focuses on proper resource allocation to its core business processes. It is feasible to maintain high service level and still achieve technology advantage by controlling its *Ownership Costs; see* Figure 22. There are two cost items. The *tangible costs* are clearly visible. A substantial part of the invisible, i.e. hidden costs is known as *the Iceberg Factor.*

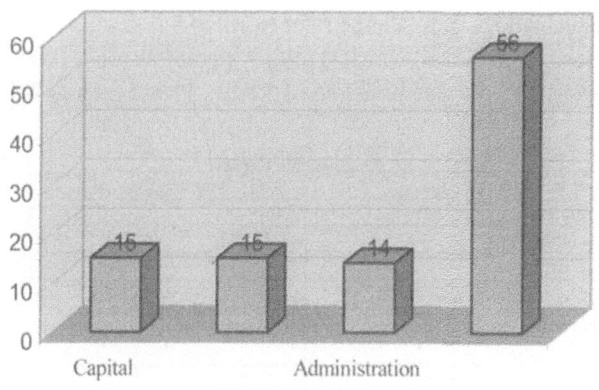

Figure 22. Desktop TCO Breakdown[70]

---

[70] Adapted from Gartner Group, 1995

Visible Costs

Much easier to identify are the *visible* costs. They usually entail:
—   Initial purchase price of the equipment, hardware and software included
—   Licensing and support contracts, but also including the staff training costs
—   Networking connectivity costs including fixed and dial-up connection fees

Table 9. Breakdown of TCO – Operations (56%) [70]

Itemisation	TCO - Operations (56%)
Peer Support	4
Supplies	7
Data Management	14
Application Development	15
Formal Learning	12
Casual Learning	18
"Futz" Factor	30

Invisible Costs

The invisible costs are more difficult to identify since being hidden within the costs of the operating environment; *see Table 9*. Due to changes in the user's culture when interacting with enterprise technology they need to adapt or change appropriately. These costs depend on:
—   Proper utilisation of infrastructure, software and hardware included
—   The appropriate support, or lack of it. Please refer to *Table 10*
—   Overcome the technology gap. Please refer to *Table 5*
—   Reducing the lost *mind-shares*, which is often reflected as user's downtime
—   Costly and boring enterprise administration burden. Please refer to *Table 11*.

Table 10. Breakdown of TCO - Support (15%) [70]

Itemisation/Percentage	TCO - Support (%)
Help Desk	20
Documentation	3
Newsletter	1
Configuration review	1
Data extraction	10
Vendor liaison	7
Standards development	6
Product introduction	6
Product review	1
Applications consulting	13
User group	1
Learning	3
Planning	2
Utilisation review	2
Service/PM	16

Maintain Information Technology

Maintaining the Information Technology during its lifecycle involves many tasks that may contribute to the TCO. Starting from planning an introduction of IT, through acquisition and installation, continuing the users' training, IT support and management, to finally disposing of the old IT, replacing and recycling any of the obsolete IT equipment, and components in accordance to the regulations.

Table 11. Breakdown of TCO - Administration (14%) [70]

Itemisation	TCO - Administration (%)
Asset management	3
Security	17
Legal	2
Purchasing	3
Formal audit	27
Internal audit	4
Policies & Procedures	31
Installation	5
Moves & changes	8

Network Change and Managing Complexity

As mentioned before, the IT cost containment enables us to focus on enterprise scarce resources and its core business processes. It is therefore of no surprise that the distribution of resources and the change of network architecture remain the key issues in any enterprise network management. Matching business processes to enterprise network solution is therefore an important decision in any enterprise design process. There are few common decision strategies that could help us decide. However, one should be careful and avoid the *silver bullet* decision trap, since there is an all but universal enterprise networking solution.

There are few networking alternatives based on the well-known *space-to-time tradeoffs* that have to be carefully examined. The enterprise architecture decision also comes as the solution that reduces the inherent *complexity* of the network and as usual it is constrained by the level of acceptable operational *risks*.

However, few important questions such as, the enterprise *availability, reliability, distribution,* and *scalability* remain uncompromising and are to be carefully examined. The availability and reliability issues are discussed in Enterprise Platforms. Due to inherent complexity, large enterprise networks in particular, are concerned with the *resource distributions* problems caused by the *scalability* of the enterprise and the *network growth.*

Network Growth

Nowadays, the IT providers offer ready-made solutions for the deployment of a small network, most often a single-site enterprise, supporting just few standard desktop applications. It rarely entails custom-made transaction-oriented database applications. Most cost-containment alternatives take the advantage of *industry-*

standard hardware and common end-user, Intranet, or office *software-packages*. For instance, *MS Windows 2000/NT/XP* desktop platform with *MS Office* and with/out Novell *IntranetWare* support might be a suitable solution for a small to medium size enterprises (SMSE). However, following a fixed enterprise growth pattern, immediately after a relatively smooth start, the enterprise eventually starts growing, expanding the established relationships throughout and spreading well beyond its established business community. For instance, it may be necessary to introduce few enterprise File & Print servers, a backup server, e-mail and messaging services support, or provide for higher throughput Internet services, etc. Usually, solving one problem often brings about another one, and a new challenge all over again. For example, the introduction of Fast Ethernet® or the ATM-based solution may abruptly change the normal evolutionary growth into a sudden and abrupt enterprise development that might be difficult to predict and support. Likewise, in pursuit of a global enterprise networking solution, the scaling up or the growth of the enterprise may challenge the enterprise *scalability* beyond the resolution point hence becoming a problem with several implications:

— Sustain the *network bandwidth* by providing servers to maintain the overall control over the network traffic, either by reducing the unnecessary traffic, or by applying call-back approach that enables *client-pulling* instead of *server-polling* networking

— Provide *sufficient resource capacities* by distributing the data processing over multiple, sometimes, redundant capacities. For instance, introducing specialised File & Print servers, applications servers, or transaction servers etc. may divert the processing demand off the main servers. Further load distribution may be achieved by partitioning, introducing network tiers, or satisfying the processing power demand by adding *Server Arrays*. This efficient server architecture is often coupled with SMP processor technology, either through a special MOM link, or by sharing a scaleable RAID storage memory. Gaining larger network bandwidth is also possible through *UTP* and *fibre optic cables,* which allow for very high communication capacities. This is especially true if matching with the *ISDN*, xDSL, *frame relay,* and ATM *cell-switching* technology is to be achieved.

— Manage the *enterprise complexity* growth. The enterprise complexity issue goes hand in hand with the network *reliability*. It is well known fact that the reliability of a complex system depends on how reliable is its weakest component. However, as pointed out in Enterprise Platforms, the availability of enterprise networks depends heavily on the decision approach applied in order to manage the increased system's complexity. Not only in networking, this is especially true for software systems. The *OO* approach may provide a solution that could be exploited at the system's hardware level and communications design. In fact, it is based on the *divide and conquer*, or system *decentralisation* approach. Once applied to software applications the object-oriented *encapsulation* follows the *keep-it-simple-stupid* (KISS) method in order to resolve and manage the software complexity. In fact, it simplifies the actual system down to its basic constituent parts. Then, the system is re-assembled using as few as possible standard building components, sharing them across the systems. The resulting system provides ample cost-performance benefits without compromising the system's security, reliability, or availability. For more, please *Case 20: Transition Associate and Lotus Notes at Foulks Lynch Virtual College.*

Resource Distribution

During our review of network architectures in Network Architecture and throughout the elaboration of the Enterprise Business Model we have mentioned the data distribution problem, i.e. *how to and where to allocate* data resources. The common rules of thumb suggest *following the business process distribution and reducing as much as possible the distributed data movement.* The solution eliminates any excess data transfers using existing *data caches.* Yet another approach uses *data on demand* as *byte-size.* In anticipation of user's responses, the Internet browsers apply for instance, the *look-ahead* approach. Still another efficient use of available channel capacity can be achieved by applying highly efficient data *compression* methods, e.g. lossless vs. lossy. It helps preserve the valuable network bandwidth. In fact, depending on the approach and intended *space vs. time* trade-off there are three available alternatives for data distribution:

-   *Replicated,* with multiple data copies reside on some enterprise servers that enables distribute the overhead of query processing among servers at the expense of less frequent, but efficient propagation of frequent data updates. Appropriate enterprise architecture helps the data updates apply correct data locking and synchronisation mechanisms. The three-tier architecture in *Figure 9* is often regarded as the most appropriate. In fact, the third-tier server layer is acting as a commit manager and is responsible for implementation of the *two-phase commit* (2PC) transaction protocol.
-   *Partitioned,* which maintains the data locally by providing distributed partitions throughout enterprise servers at the expense of some communication overhead and somewhat reduced bandwidth due to the remote data access and complex query processing. However, it allows exploiting the *time vs. space locality of data references* by implementing the efficient data caches at local servers. The three-tier architecture could help, but as in most cases, the third-tier server layer apparently performs the role of *information broker.* Actually, it provides and disseminates the *whereabouts* of data information instead of the actual data. In fact, applying the enterprise architecture beyond three tiers and creating multi-tiers helps managing the system's complexity. It allows the hierarchical data organisations to distribute various data levels of desired granularity among enterprise tiers. For instance, let a workgroup server for the Geographical Information Systems (GIS) maintain local municipal data. A site server may be responsible for the municipalities' databases, and a headquarter server can keep track of the overall view of the regional data and provides the GIS *meta-data support* (i.e. data layout, data descriptions, or type and data organisation).
-   *Federated* approach applies to cases where data distribution of enterprise servers may be restricted due to complex transactions. Often, it runs by more than a single application. Usual multi-client *data locking* schemes prevent the two-tier

servers to efficiently manage the data distributed through several database servers. In fact, the federated data application servers may often require the transaction manager support. Larger enterprises, running several applications simultaneously, have solved the problem by relying on three-tier network layout, i.e. allowing the application server to control the transaction logic via TPM or *Transaction Process Monitors*. BEA *Tuxedo*, IBM *CICS*, and IBM *Encina* offer this approach. For more, please refer to *Case 24:* CoreLAN - TP Services with BEA Tuxedo [TM]. In fact, the use of TPM simplifies the underlining application complexity type. It transforms the *many-to-many* enterprise relationship into a *many-to-one-to-many* by suitable introduction of a *transaction monitor* creating essentially, a new focal point in the enterprise architecture. Having a global focal point, one may argue that the *transaction manager* introduces a single point of failure, therefore reducing the reliability of the whole enterprise. Fortunately, this is not the case, since the transaction manager is designed to deliver a robust multi-server, multi-application transaction support. Thanks to the network management overall *performance*, global *transaction synchronisation*, *balancing the load* across the enterprise servers, and providing a secure system's *recovery,* the role of the TP Monitor becomes even more indispensable.

Bibliography

Enterprise management software helps Food Lion control far-flung IT empire; *Tony Seideman*; **Stores**, New York; Dec 2000; Vol. 82, Iss. 12; pg. 56

IT and business management should put their heads together; *Bruce Taylor*; **Computing Canada**, Willowdale; Jan 15, 1999; Vol. 25, Iss. 2; pg. 32, 1 pgs

Apps aid in e-business management; *George V Hulme*; **InformationWeek**, Manhasset; May 15, 2000, Iss. 786; pg. 101, 1 pgs

E-business relies on enterprise management; *John Soat*; **InformationWeek**, Manhasset; May 8, 2000, Iss. 785; pg. 128, 4 pgs

Computer Associates Looks To E-Business Management -- Company to focus on Jasmine ii at CA World user conference; *Rutrell Yasin*; **InternetWeek**, Manhasset; Apr 10, 2000; pg. PG.12

Small Business Management: An Overview; *Mohsen A Derregia*; **International Small Business Journal**, London; Apr-Jun 2000; Vol. 18, Iss. 3; pg. 97, 3 pgs

Enterprise management systems; *Anonymous*; **Manufacturing Systems**, Oak Brook; Sep 1999; Vol. 17, Iss. 9; pg. 64, 1 pgs

A New Dimension to enterprise management; *Monique Delage*; **Midrange Systems**, Spring House; May 10, 1999; Vol. 12, Iss. 7; pg. 8, 1 pgs

Compaq boosts Web-based enterprise management app; **Network World** *Robin Schreier Hohman*; Jul 6, 1998

Enterprise management: Selecting the right product; **Telecommunications** *Ryan P Kluft*; Jul 1998

Win 100: Business management; **Windows Magazine** *Joel Patz*; Summer 1998

Tivoli to stress enterprise management; **Computing Canada** *Andrew Brooks*; Jun 22, 1998

Integrated enterprise management: A look at the functions, the enterprise, and the environment--can you see the difference?; **Hospital Materiel Management Quarterly** *David M Lehmann*; May 1998

CHAPTER 8

ENTERPRISE DEVELOPMENT

Objects, CASE tools and Enterprise JavaBeans

Case 11: CA AllFusion Harvest Manager Tool with IBM's WebSphere Studio

CA TO INTEGRATE ALLFUSION HARVEST CHANGE MANAGER TOOL
WITH IBM'S WEBSPHERE STUDIO

(Copyright © 2002, AllFusion, Endeavor & Harvest product names used herein are trademarks of Computer Associates International, Inc. Used by permission herein.)
http://www3.ca.com/press/pressrelease.asp?id=1904

**CA Solution To Provide Change and Configuration Management for IBM
WebSphere Studio eBusiness Development Projects**

ISLANDIA, N.Y., February 14, 2002 – Computer Associates International, Inc. (CA) today announced that it will integrate AllFusion Harvest Change Manager with IBM's WebSphere Studio, enabling organizations to maintain the integrity and improve the quality of their eBusiness applications.

The integration will provide IBM WebSphere Studio developers with seamless access to the uniquely powerful software change and configuration management functionality of AllFusion Harvest Change Manager. Unlike other change management products, AllFusion Harvest Change Manager will enable IBM WebSphere Studio application developers and managers to establish customisable software development life cycles. These life cycles tie IT development to business processes and reduce the risk and time-to-market associated with developing and deploying new systems.

"AllFusion Harvest Change Manager is already a strategic component of our current development environment, ensuring that mission-critical systems are developed and maintained quickly and according to exact standards," said Mark Dyviniak, Director of Quality Assurance at Farmers Insurance Group, a leading U.S.

insurance provider. "We are excited about the prospect of applying these same capabilities to our upcoming implementation of IBM WebSphere Studio."

AllFusion Harvest Change Manager provides flexible, powerful process control to support and automate the full range of IT development tasks required by complex eBusiness projects. By strengthening control over all stages of software development activity, AllFusion Harvest Change Manager improves the reliability of traditional and web-based applications, while increasing developer productivity.

"As businesses push IT to quickly deliver competitive advantage, time-to-market is more critical than ever," said Clive Burrows, principal analyst at Ovum. "In the face of such accelerated development cycles, the integration of a robust change management solution like AllFusion Harvest Change Manager into eBusiness development processes is essential to ensure optimal organizational efficiency and application quality."

AllFusion Harvest Change Manager features a user-friendly web interface and comprehensive, integrated change management functionality, providing scalability and security across the enterprise. Designed for distributed and heterogeneous environments, AllFusion Harvest Change Manager provides broad support for many leading development environments in addition to IBM WebSphere Studio to simplify integration of the change management discipline into the developer's environment.

"For customers to get maximum business value from their change management tools, they need those tools to support all of their strategic development environments," said Ricardo Antuna, vice president marketing, data management and application development solutions, CA. "By integrating AllFusion Harvest Change Manager into IBM WebSphere Studio, CA is demonstrating its commitment to delivering this wide-ranging support."

Integration between AllFusion Harvest Change Manager 5.1 and IBM WebSphere Studio will be available for beta testing next month.

About Computer Associates

Computer Associates International, Inc. (NYSE: <u>CA</u>) delivers The Software That Manages eBusiness. CA's world-class solutions address all aspects of eBusiness management through industry-leading brands: Unicenter for infrastructure management, BrightStor for storage management, *e*Trust for security management, CleverPath for portal and business intelligence, AllFusion for application life cycle management, Advantage for data management and application development, and Jasmine for object-oriented database technology. Founded in 1976, CA serves organizations in more than 100 countries, including 99 percent of the Fortune 500 companies. For more information, visit http://ca.com.

Throughout the presentation of enterprise paradigms, the prevalent application processing has established a specific relationship between the *clients,* the *servers,* and the *communication network* as constitutive part of enterprise network that has been reviewed in number of cases. Introduced historically by the traditional mainframe paradigm, the enterprise centralised its legacy applications and integrated its processing activity at the *server side,* i.e. the mainframe.

Subsequently, most of the applications processing in the contemporary enterprise network of SMSE shifted gradually to the *client side* i.e. the desktop and the PC. The integration of application processing achieved through the interoperation software and hardware devices or *middleware* has enabled users easy access to data distributed all over enterprise servers. Moreover, due to the proliferation of enterprise paradigms worldwide, there was and still, it is necessary that the networking technology supports the integration and migration of different vendor specific networking platforms. It mainly relates to Microsoft *Object Linking and Embedding* (OLE), *Dynamical Data Exchange* (DDE), *Distributed Computing Environment (*DCE), the OMG *Common Object Request Broker Architecture* (CORBA), and the suite of Sun Java 2 Enterprise Edition (J2EE) standards.

Apparently, most of the enterprise paradigms are variations on two basic types, *client-based,* and *server-based* computing. The application integration at the client side uses the application calls approach for distributed applications spread across the enterprise. Having taken care of the applications, it brings about an important question: *How do we integrate the data that reside at the server side?*

The enterprise database servers naturally integrate common data, often used by several applications. Are there any rules that can help distribute data to servers throughout the enterprise network? The question becomes even more general. How do we allocate distributed enterprise resources and maintain the integrity of the operations and information throughout the enterprise? It might be worthwhile mentioning some *rules of thumb* though:

1. Whenever possible run compute-intensive processes at the client side.
2. Let servers take care of shared resources such as common or static data.
3. Whenever possible try to maintain locally owned dynamic data.
4. Let servers manage large data transfers rather than clients poll the server.
5. If feasible trade time to memory to preserve critical network bandwidth.
6. Bear in mind that a throughput chain is as fast as its slowest component.
7. Abolish bottlenecks by distributing the load across bounds: *space and time.*
8. Reduce performance bottlenecks by avoiding unnecessary resource locking.
9. Maintain remote network administration via distributed services or agents.
10. Share security services whenever necessary to reduce the operational costs.

We also know that whenever the complexity of enterprise is contested, the straightforward solution is to follow the *enterprise business processes'* flows. Actual implementation of suitable enterprise architecture however, may involve several development strategies. At our disposal is an advanced IT as the enabling technology: *business process reengineering*, platform *downsizing*, *outsourcing*, cut-off of production applications and *streamlining*, and *distributing* some business processes and administration burden across the enterprise.

In order to maintain the information leverage by integrating and streamlining diverse business processes it may require a new way of enterprise organisation. Usually, it is referred to as *business process re-engineering* (BPR). However, there exists a clear distinction between *software re-engineering,* and *business process re-engineering.* The former is used mainly to enhance the availability of existing applications, which might be difficult to maintain. Thus, valuable legacy databases and associated applications often ought to be modified according to the ever-changing needs of the evolving business processes. Some software re-engineering methods commonly used to achieve this goal are the *Reverse engineering* and *Forward CASE engineering.* Applying reverse engineering produces a specification data for application development used by CASE tools to generate a new application code. Forward engineering however, makes use of the existing application layout, various data flow charts, data structures, entity-relationship diagrams, and functional decomposition diagrams in order to convert the application into new source-code application. Most often it caused by the migration to a different DBMS, a new OS, new hardware platform, or some other specific considerations, security issues for instance.

Business Process Re-Engineering

Business Process Re-engineering (BPR) *represents* a process of transformation, change that is used to redesign, rethink conventional enterprise processes, inventing, or introducing a new way the business processes are to be carried out. The forefathers of BPR, Michael Hammer and James Champy[71] have set forth the following seven rules.

1. Organise around processes and outcomes, not tasks and departments.
2. Have the output end-users perform the process.
3. Have those who produce the information process it.
4. Centralise processing and disperse the data across the enterprise.
5. Integrate parallel activities whenever possible.
6. Empower workers and use the built-in controls.
7. Capture data once, at its source.

Essentially, the BPR applies the information-engineering principles to enterprise networks. The conventional *data - function* separation and legacy relationships are redesigned into new, contemporary data-driven, a *change-process* induced paradigm. First introduced in 1970s by James Martin and Clive Finkelstein, the change-process approach has received substantial attention. Alongside, the BPR has re-gained its popularity within the industry[72]. Presently, there are two main developments in the BPR implementation. An alternative is the *evolutionary, incremental change,* which relies on the continuous improvement approach.

There is also the *revolutionary change approach,* a radical re-engineering advocating *'erecting a phoenix from the aches of the old enterprise'.* Instead of evolutionary, continuous changes, it rather maintains the revolutionary changes following a fresh clean-up stage, i.e. the *'green field approach'.* In fact, it completely abolishes the old system's behaviour introducing sudden changes,

---

[71] Michael Hammer, James Champy, 1993, *"Re-engineering of Corporation"*

[72] IMD International, 1995 Report, *Heineken Netherlands, BV (B): Transforming IS/IT to Support Supply Chain Management.*

creating a business environment with improvements resulting mainly from the revolutionary radical changes. For more please check the MIT90's Framework [73]. In order to sustain the IT changes at the highly competitive market, the BPR has gained support from the quest for *ISO 9000 certification.* For BPR deployment, the developers may rely on a suite of efficient development tools. For instance, SAP R/3, the market leader in *Enterprise Resource Planning* (ERP), followed by Oracle, Baan[74], PeopleSoft, and JD Edwards are providing efficient BPR support. There is also a suite for *Component Based Development* (CBD) supported by UML-based CASE tools, Objectory, Select®, or Dynasty®. A system modelling and simulation tool for decision support like Ithink®, or Cortex-Pro® an *Artificial Neural Network* (ANN) tool, assisted by a SPSS® statistical package might be instrumental too. For more, *see* Application Development Environment.

The BPR involves not only the redesign of the entire enterprise, its business processes, management systems, and enterprise structures, but individual tasks, values, and common beliefs too. Most importantly, it introduces a new *cultural change* within the enterprise fabric. This also means that changes are introduced to the existing, old applications in order to facilitate the deployment of the new technology. In the process of enterprise re-design, more than ever, it is important that the management maintains its strategic focus, helping the enterprise meet the new visions and accomplish the goals[75]. For more see *Case 17:* Tarantella Web-Enabling Software.

The practice shows however, that the real changes do not sustain unless there is a full commitment and support by the top and senior management. Some familiar examples of re-engineering business processes are the deployment of *Electronic Data Interchange* (EDI) alternative, a paperless document imaging and archiving system by *XEROX*, the electronic banking by eCash[76], or the Web-based trade e-payment system using *SmartCards[77]; see Case 18:* What is Enterprise Networks?

Function-Data Separation and Data-Driven Processes

For long time, the traditional system engineering has relied on function-data separation in the enterprise application design. In brief, the system designer identifies the core system functions by conducting an application workflow analysis. Then follows the systems mapping by associating the relevant data to its functions. Well-known methods for this type of software engineering are SADT [Ross, 1985], RDD [Alford, 1985], or SA/SD [Yourdon, 1989]. The main engineering idea can be traced back to the *Von Neumann* computer architecture that has data separated from data-driven computing processes. A data-driven system executes computations in order manner following the data dependencies.

[73] Scott Morton, M. S. (ed.). *The Corporation of the 1990*s, Oxford University Press, Oxford, UK, 1991

[74] Invensys plc, UK, acquired Baan due to its financial fiasco, http://www.baan.com/cgi-bin/bvisapi.dll

[75] Top 5 Critical Success Factors for Organisations Starting 3-Tier Development, Cayenne Software, http://www.cayennesoft.com/products/wpaper/top5.html

[76] eCash, formerly *DigiCash*, is market leader in P2P e-Banking, http://www.ecashtechnologies.com

[77] MasterCard®, SmartCards technology for e-Banking, http://www.mastercard.com/ourcards/smartcard

Two kinds of data-driven computation are the dataflow and the demand-driven approach. Accordingly, any system or enterprise business process for instance, performs certain functions using information as raw data that is either sent for processing, or has been exchanged among functional entities. There are few major problems related to this approach. First, the application maintenance is not simple. For, due to system's requirements the system functions are to maintain global knowledge of its data structure, respect the data-dependencies including the way data is actually stored or internally represented. Thus, any modification in data representation or its structure initiates a chain reaction and propagation of changes to all functions related to the data that results in rather unstable system. Moreover, the end- users usually do not think of processes in terms of *how,* but rather, *what* do they represent or perform. Furthermore, the need for timely response and frequent alterations of existing applications increases due to constant adaptations to changes in the business environment. E. Yourdon, the recognised authority in the application system development, has emphasised the importance of application change. The *probability of change* reported [Coda, Yourdon, 1991] is lowest for problem domain entities and its related structures; average for passive attributes and sequences of behaviour; and highest for system interfaces and added new functionality.

Consequently, the business process-aware paradigm considers data as integral part to the process behaviour and intrinsic system functionality. The prevailing system development methodology today introduces *objects* and *object-oriented paradigm* (OOP) in the application development arena. It assumes that business processes are easily identified and considerably well defined within a structured problem domain. Besides, the users are much better acquainted with business process descriptions and could easily formulate *what* certain processes are performing, usually using simple natural language descriptions, avoiding vague interpretations, and eventual misunderstanding. This distinctive feature of the contemporary application development tools is usually referred to as the reduced *semantical gap of* misconception. OO development approach produces rather stable model of enterprise business-processes. Accordingly, the interactions are defined globally using standard interfaces, allowing frequent and cumbersome changes to be performed locally without disturbing the rest of the system.

Vision for Enterprise Maturity

The enterprise requires sound vision and a lot of determination and commitment from the top and senior management in order to introduce a new development process. For, unless planned properly, the changes about to be introduced may bring in the ambiguity that leads to undesired uncertainties, fears, and tensions. Unless prepared and trained properly, the inexperienced user once faced with the introduction of new technology might be rather confused and prone to failures. It might also be interpreted as the existential threat that is closely related to the changes introduced by the enterprise environment. As a reaction to change and the opposition to what follows, the end-user's resistance is therefore inevitable.

An important step therefore, is to prevent the anticipated resistance to change and to technological innovations. The management should take proactive approach, introduce training, and take a lead in technology ownership to prevent any undesired reaction to change. This in turn encourages users to get actively involved in the process of change and provide full support to overcome problems associated with change. The *setting up users' mind* approach enables to adopt the shift and embrace the ownership of technological change. It also provides the opportunity to overcome a *mind change* and ensure successful *process of change*.

However, most important is to sustain the *cultural change*. Foremost, it ought to be backed up and fully supported by the firm commitments of the senior management. Ensuring a critical mass of supporters is yet another important step. This helps finding our own way out of the eventual resistance to change. Once the responsibilities are re-assigned and the individual tasks are re-organised, the enterprise could free up almost a full mind-share of fellow supporters. The new *mind-sets* can now foster the IT use for strategic advantage. Essentially, this in turn empowers the users, integrates applications, emphasises constant change of resource distribution, and increases the productivity. In fact, these changes and continuous improvement together with the procurement of current *standards* through the enterprise are required in order to maintain the lowest *TOC* of IT.

Therefore, an enterprise keen to develop successfully some business capabilities requires an outstanding maturity. The *Capability Maturity Model*[78] (CMM), brought about by the *Software Engineering Institute* (SEI) at Carnegie Mellon University, is the leading assessment methodology for enterprise maturity that mainly takes in consideration the assessment of software development processes. Accordingly, the CMM study [Hamphrey, 1989] acknowledges five levels of enterprise maturity:

1.   The *initial* or lowest level of maturity, at which an enterprise maintains no written description and performs risky, undocumented software development processes. It refers to enterprise management as 'heroes and champions' to make things happen.

2.   The *repeatable level* at which an organisation applies certain documented software development methods but lacks the project management control support. New software development methodology, usually introduced haphazardly, may easily turn the enterprise back to the initial maturity level. The enterprise management requires some experience and determination to repeat the success of any previous project.

3.   The *defined level,* at which commonly there exist elaborated documented software development processes. Several specific software process groups are engaged in, following the formalisation, development, and refinement. This level of maturity is usually considered as the necessary condition for introduction of new development methods, tools, or paradigms throughout the enterprise.

---

[78] http://www.sei.cmu.edu/cmm/cmm.html

4. The *managed level*, at which there exists a formal quality monitoring process based upon adopted certified software development metrics. The software development process is managed, supervised, measured, and able to control allocated enterprise resources. Consequently, the gain in enterprise productivity and efficiency comes along with the high quality of software development applications.
5. The *optimising level* or the highest maturity level, at which there exists a regular feedback control over the entire software development process. It makes use of the data acquired systematically from the monitoring process. It leverages on the results from the development process and enables the enterprise to efficiently respond both, to the *process change,* as well as to new developments in *technology change.*

According to CMM 1996 report, only few percent of software development enterprises in US have attained the maturity levels higher than level 3. The findings just prove our assumptions that a lot of effort, basic preparations, and follow-up in technological advances, have to be carried out prior to embarking on new enterprise developments. For more, please refer to the *SPICE project* [79].

IT Enabled Business Processes

The enterprises have accepted the IT enabling role and have reviewed the necessary steps that need to be taken in order to introduce changes to the network environment. However, there is no simple answer to the question: *How an enterprise could actually implement advanced IT for the benefit of the business?*

Despite budget constraints, internal maintenance problems, raising IT ownership costs, unawareness of business process changes, technology obsolescence, and permanent market changes, a strive for survival is what actually drives the enterprises to look for the advanced IT and gain the competitive advantage. In order to contain the raising of overall costs, many enterprises have opted for *outsourcing* of its IT operations, or have transformed them into smaller, usually self-sustained supporting units. There are many alternatives to outsourcing. All of them have one thing in common, a trade-off between the IT strategy focus and streamlining the core business processes by containing the costs of operations. Many enterprises with strategic IT systems are determined to keep the IT strategy in focus while still maintaining the cost-effective operations.

As emphasised earlier, the theme of the day is that the IT-enabled enterprise is to provide full client networking support with lowest *total costs of IT ownership.* This brings about the process of change and the way the enterprise responds to that change. However, we should keep in mind the importance of enterprise-wide *integration.* We should not forget that the *entire network* not only servers provide reliable *distributed* services throughout the enterprise. Last but not least, the *network management* should be able to run in decentralised mode allowing

---

[79] http://www.sqi.gu.edu.au/spice

efficient monitoring and complete administrative support from any enterprise network site hence, providing unconstrained *remote network control.*

Development Methodology

We are witnessing constant change of enterprise environment. Since applications are performing tasks the way users communicate or organise their work, their best practices are to be modified accordingly, in order to accommodate to ever changing requirements. To negotiate these modifications, system developers are trying to modify the existing systems, but more often, the new ones are developed instead. The importance of having an organised approach to the system development has been clearly emphasised in the previous SEI CMM review. To appreciate the difference that exists in the application development today, a short review of the *Object Oriented System Engineering* (OOSE) will be presented. Presently, the UML-based OOSE approach entails one of the leading tools in object oriented system development methodology.

The OOSE approach originates from the *OO programming*, *conceptual system modelling*, and *component* (or building block) design. Closely associated with OO programming, the conceptual modelling is related to information modelling. It is often used modelling technique for data modelling and database design too. The system component or building block design renders the required system functionality expressed through particular *method* invocations. Methods and data are *encapsulated* in building blocks components, and higher modular complexes. They communicate among each other via *messages* sent through well-defined standardised set of *system interfaces* [80].

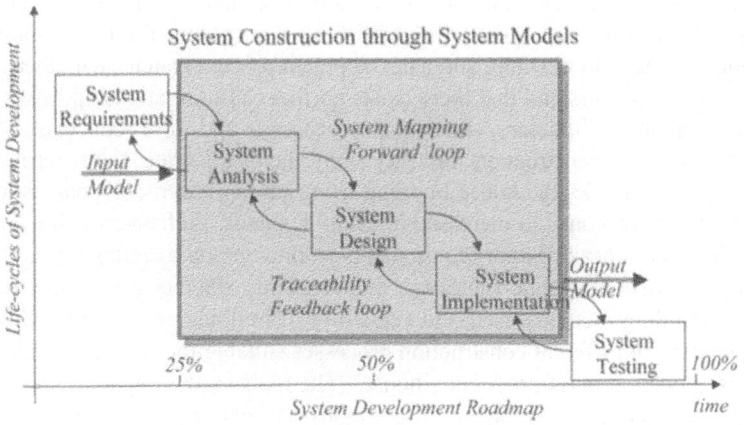

Figure 23. Development Processes and System Models

---

[80] The *Interaction State Diagrams* idea originates from *Ericson* AB. [Jacobson and all, 1995]. It was introduced in 1960s since when this approach has been in wide use not only by telecommunications but by software industry too.

Enterprise Process Identification: Modelling

In fact, the OOSE development approach represents a voyage through model building. The OOSE development methodology assumes incremental system changes and gradual system development through sets of refined models (see *Figure 23*). Each model manages a specific system *complexity* and reduces its *uncertainty* during the development process. This is achieved through evolution sequence of several development models:

1. The *requirement model* entails system's functional requirements.
2. The *analysis model* produces a simple but resilient view of the system.
3. The *design model* captures specific system features hence refining the previous *'what-is'* system model in order to meet the specific requirements of the implementation environment.
4. The *implementation model* aims at actual *'how-to'* system implementation.
5. The *test model* finally, verifies, and validates the system to be deployed against the specified development criteria.

Subsequent transitions between models can easily be followed using the *traceability* of distinct objects between development models. It is attributed to OOSE *seamlessness* property, i.e. the ability of the design process to easily adapt to changes, an important feature of contemporary applications development.

Usually system developers produce many alternative models of an application in order to arrive to the model that suits best the developing criteria and complies with the system requirements. The richness of modelling techniques used to produce all these models defines the *system architecture*. The *development process* therefore, represents a particular implementation of the development methodology that also requires specific development *tools.* By analogy, a PC desktop editor and a simple printer are sufficient for small-volume document printing. However, professional publishing software and an offset or even a printing plant is usually required for publishing newspapers for large-volume distribution. System architecture and a development process match each other.

It is important to understand that there exists normal causal relationship between the development architecture, methods, processes, and tool concepts. An example from the construction industry may help illustrate their intrinsic differences. Worldwide, the house building using prefabricated components has been appropriate response to increased housing demands. Prefabricated building may easily meet rather different requirements from common dwelling houses, to administrative offices, public buildings, or even large warehouses. Despite the variety of building methods used, the versatility of building architecture allows implementation of different construction processes suitable for either, individual, as well as, industrial mass-production houses. The tools used though, are specific depending whether an individual or an industrial construction applies. The choice of tools especially, makes significant differences when used for industrial, often a mass-scale production. Likewise, OOSE system development tools claim being well suited for industrial, mass-production of component-based systems.

Regarding the development costs from system version to version, the costs are expected to accumulate throughout the development cycle, as can be inspected from *Figure 24*. In order to help estimate system development costs we could apply the COCOMO approach developed at USC, California. The COCOMO (COnstructive COst MOdel)[81] is interactive software tool that assists in planning and schedule the estimation of software development projects. COCOMO helps develop a model of projects in order to identify potential problems in resources, personnel, budgets, and schedules both before and also during the phase when the potential software package has been developed.

Enterprise Design: Prototype vs. Rapid Development
To begin with, it is important to determine the right system requirements. Due to lack of knowledge, combined with high *complexity* of system development, dynamical and frequent changes in enterprise environment, even sophisticated CASE tools and sound CBD methodology can still introduce vague decisions, design *uncertainties,* hence raising the *development risk.* Depending on the level of uncertainty and the development risk, the developers may apply several approaches in order to reduce the uncertainty in system development. There are few system development alternatives:

– The *waterfall* system development is traditionally used if uncertainty in the system requirements is low. Usually, this is when the specified requirements are explicit from the outset. The system development process caries straightforward. Following clear requirements, the analysis process continues with construction and finally concludes by testing of the complete system. A subsequent system maintenance is often considered a normal phase in the system life cycle. In more complex cases, the development may iterate between the development stages in order to refine the system functionality. Sometimes, it may produce a staged output, usually due to time constraints, or induced responses to specific market demands (e.g. a demand for a fast response to negotiate market demand, or to maintain a long-lasting market presence). Essentially, it solves the software development *process control problem.*

– The software *packages* customised system development approach represents an alternative widely offered by professional system developers, ASP, and commercial software houses. Software packages are offered for specific application domains, supporting any HW/SW platform, wide scope of price - performance features, and entailing wide system functionality, e.g. SAP R/3. Usually, the packages are developed, supported, and maintained for the market, sometimes specific, but unknown customers. Due to the economies of scale and scope in the development process, most software packages have affordable price/performance for the functionality that is offered, but still require some specific end-user customisation. Today, ready-made software packages offered by ASP are easily downloadable via Internet, providing a remote version control and full Web-publishing support. This approach in contrast, solves the system in-house development *resource problem.* For more, please check Case *17:* Tarantella Web-Enabling Software.

---

[81] Dr. Barry Boehm, <u>Software Engineering Economics</u>, Prentice-Hall (1981), and Ada COCOMO (1989)

- The *incremental* development is a system development approach that is mostly used if system requirements are vague, not specifically clear, sometimes with missing clues, or often unknown system requirements. It allows building the system progressively, in *versions* of applications with increased complexity, reducing the uncertainty in stages, as the knowledge accumulates; *see Figure 24*. Moreover, the system brought about during the usual maintenance and system change is considered as a subsequent system version rather than a maintained system. It is frequently used approach in order to help solve system development *time-to-market problem*.

- The system *prototyping* is yet another important system development approach. It is used in combination with other system development alternatives in order to reduce the uncertainty in development, either by simulation, or rapid modelling of missing system functionality. It is regularly used to make customer's demands clearer, to simulate the required but often missing system parameters. The prototyping is to solve the understanding, knowledge lacking development or the *know-how problem*.

- *Rapid Application Development* (RAD) allows implementation of some specific development criteria. Supported by *interactive development tools,* it provides less robust analysis and allows basic functionality with acceptable system performance, which can result in rapid, easily modifiable system. Sometimes, it is combined with the system prototyping in order to develop missing project proposal features, or a feasibility study. In cases with anticipated end-user involvement both RAD and the interactive *end-user development* are used to solve the *time-resource problem*. For more, please check *Case 25:* Cognicase: Sold! Maximizer Enterprise for Notes Wins Bid for Management Solution.

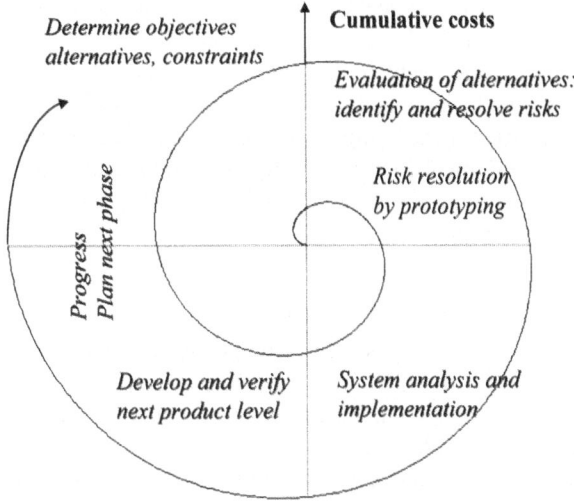

Figure 24. Boehm's Spiral Development Model [81]

Enterprise Network: Allocate Resources to Processes

An important decision in developing enterprise systems is to maintain focus on architectural, logical issues, before getting down to the implementation details. It is of utmost importance therefore, to first allocate functional requirements among clients and servers. Applying simple *rules of thumb* we could allocate clients to processes, eventually, distributing as much as possible processing to the client side. We may proceed with the identification of available enterprise devices and resources as shareable virtual network servers. The distribution of real resources to virtual servers develops naturally. For instance, following the previous analysis of business processes, data and applications are allocated to data and application servers. Thereafter, the network tiers are introduced. We should keep in mind that the goal is to reduce complexity, negotiate the network bandwidth, and balance evenly the eventual processing overload. Constantly checking on validated requirements, system availability, performance and reliability, safety, and security issues, the enterprise architecture emerges within several iterative trials. Having done so far, the resulting enterprise architecture and selected networking technology are put in place, verified, tested, and set ready. Then, the network is gradually loaded.

Enterprise Verification & Validation

Following the integration tests, interoperability, and performance benchmark tests, the proposed enterprise architecture is amply scrutinised, verifying the requirements and validating the decisions. It may take several iterations to arrive at adequate enterprise architecture. Whenever changes are to be introduced, applying a seamlessness design to system features about to be modified could help trace them back to the logical design. Having made the necessary changes we may return and repeat the development process.

The use of CASE development tools can help us guide through the iterative design process, especially in documenting, system's administration, maintaining the development process, hence, improving the overall design efficiency. In fact, any new system requirements, modifications, or maintenance changes are to be treated alike, consistently, improving the quality of new versions of the existing enterprise system; *see Figure 24*.

Application Development Environment

Essentially, there are two types of development demands. *Business* users primarily care for flexibility, GUI support, safety and security, or simplicity of accessing applications and data. However, *professional* developers look for advanced development tools that support complex development processes, particularly mission-critical applications. The latter often requires a GroupWare development support, a workbench of reusable code, and a CASE tool library associated with a repository of system building components.

Development Tools

Modern development tools can efficiently generate complete applications. Traditional applications were often based on 3GL, programming languages such as COBOL, C or database schema scripts, and common GUI program interfaces (menus, buttons, icons, dialog boxes, etc.) for *point-and-click* operations support. This kind of application development is dying out since it is time-consuming and often unreliable, as it is prone to errors. However, for a small, in-house project development, it is advised to use a standard query-and-report provided by many off-the-shelf database development tools. Among the products that support this type of application development is Microsoft's SQL Server, SyBase® EA Server[82], NetWare[83] v.5.1 by Novell, SQLBase from Centura[84] Team Developer (CTD), Web Developer, and Net.DB (formerly Gupta Corporation.), etc. They provide the plug-and-play support and widespread development expertise for MacOS, OS/2, Windows *2000/NT*, UNIX/Linux, or NetWare platforms. Competing alongside Oracle[85], the market leader in the traditional relational database applications, is also Informix[86] 4GL, now Ingress II[87], following the acquisition by CA along with the sophisticated object-relational Postgres[88] database. Today the PostgreSQL is the most advanced open-source database

---

[82] SyBase® EA Server http://www.sybase.com/products/applicationservers/easerver

[83] True Internet Technology by Novel NetWare 5.1 http://www.novell.com/products/netware

[84] Centura Software Corporation, formerly Gupta Corporation, http://www.centurasoft.com

[85] Oracle9i Database: The Next Generation http://www.oracle.com/ip/deploy/database

[86] Informix 4GL Product Family Overview http://www.informix.com/4gl

[87] CA Ingres II: The Platform for Integrated Enterprise Applications, http://www.ca.com/analyst/124

[88] PostgresSCL http://www.sai.msu.su:8000

server that is freely distributed with Linux distribution. For more please check it out at PostgreSQL.org [89] Web site.

Integrated data management software with front-end applications supported by the 4GL development tools that do not necessarily require a substantial programming language experience are common nowadays, e.g. *EASEL Workbench*[90] *from* Easel Corp., or the Centura Software's *SQLWindows* (formerly Gupta Corp.). Other tools, such as the CA COOL: Joe[91] tool (formerly the first UML compliant *ObjectTeam*[92] by Cayenne Software Inc.), acquired by Sterling and by Computer Associates in April 2000, is specialised in the collaborative OO application development. The COOL: Joe is a leading *Enterprise JavaBeans* (EJB) development environment with strong architectural design and component-based modelling capabilities. Sybase *PowerBuilder*[93] and *MS Visual Studio*[94] (VB, Visual Basic v.6 based) provide widely recognised development support for client/server enterprise applications, real-time embedded systems, and e-Business solutions in heterogeneous enterprise networking environments. The SyBase *PowerBuilder93* also claims market leadership in enterprise development offering significant productivity enhancements and broad support for Web-based component standards. It achieves tight integration with Sybase *EA Server*[82] both for development and for deployment of enterprise Web solutions.

CASE Tool Support

Computer Aided System Engineering (CASE) usually entails a development tool that provides end-users full professional support in developing complex applications. Most CASE tools support interactive development, 4GL, GUIs, component libraries, RAD support, and application generators either with optional or automatic code generation. Some, such as OOSE Objectory, Select®, Dynasty®, and similar followers of the world's leading visual modelling tool *Unified Modelling Language* (UML) by Rational Rose[95], introduced by Booch, Jacobson, and Rumbaugh [1996] have taken full advantage of the OO distributed paradigm, shared, and collaborative component-based, application-development environment.

The legacy applications are also supported by platform independent, graphic oriented, decomposition simple, Entity-Relationship, and data-flow diagram representations. Not only the tools have improved the quality of application development and raised the developer's productivity, but have also enabled the *Component Based Development* (CBD) through implementation based on

---

[89] PostgreSQl.ORG, http://postgresql.rmplc.co.uk/info.html

[90] Easel. Corp. http://www.rodley.com/articles/Easel/Easel.html

[91] CA, COOL:Joe Enterprise JavaBeans for eBusiness, http://www.cai.com/products/cool/cooljoe.htm

[92] UML compliant OMG CASE tool http://www8.techmall.com/techdocs/NP971208-5.html

[93] SyBase PowerBuilder tool, http://www.sybase.com/products/internetappdevttools/powerbuilder

[94] Microsoft Visual Studio Enterprise, http://www.microsoft.com/catalog/display.asp?subid=22&site=736

[95] Rational rose ...world's leading visual modelling tool, http://www.rational.com/products/rose/index.jsp

distributed components - *Java applets* and *ActiveX*. The CA COOL: Gen[96] has integrated *Information Engineering Facility* (IEF) by Sterling Software (formerly by Texas Instruments) and the *Application Development Workbench* (ADW) by Sterling Software (formerly KnowledgeWare) in a CASE tool that helps developers deliver Web-enabled applications, integrate legacy software with new systems, and design and construct software components. It is worth mentioning the CASE tool by DataDirect ®, a division of Merant[97], the market leader in Enterprise Application Development, formed by the integration of Micro Focus and Intersolv. (Just for the record, the *Excelerator II* CASE tool by Intersolv was the leading application specialised for OO development support in OS/2 LAN). Merant provides valuable suits of integrated application development CASE tools. The Merant Egility ™ products address a complete spectrum of software solutions needed to take business to the Internet. Merant E-Solutions® rather, applies Merant Egility ® products in order to assist implementing a sustainable Internet strategy. It is evident that the CASE tool market itself is subject to fast and dynamic integration changes along with the technology it is keen to support.

Distributed Transaction Environment

Managing a *distributed transaction processing* (DTP) environment is even more challenging, since eventually, it brings about some rather complex problems.
- Distributed database *synchronisation*.
- Distributed *locking* that may require *deadlock* detection and prevention.
- Managing *recovery* and backup operations.

As mentioned, earlier, *Transaction Processing Monitor* (TPM) is designed to provide reliable support for DTP environment. BEA *Tuxedo* is the industry-leading e-business transaction platform that enables rapid development and deployment of e-commerce systems. The BEA *Tuxedo*[98] product, (developed at AT&T Labs and later acquired from UNIX System Laboratories (USL), formerly Novell's subsidiary), requires an Application TPM Interface support in order to provide location transparency, load balancing, transparent data formatting, context-sensitive routing, and priority processing. BEA *Tuxedo* Enterprise TPM support comes from BEA *Jolt*, BEA *Manager* and BEA *Builder*. BEA *Jolt* is a Java-based interface that extends BEA *Tuxedo* capabilities to the Internet. BEA *Manager* enables developers to administer, integrate and manage e-commerce applications. BEA *Tuxedo* Builder enhances and extends the development tools, such as Visual Basic, SyBase PowerBuilder, MS Visual C++, and Rational Rose. It runs on Windows, MacOS, OS/2, UNIX/Linux, and many other proprietary mainframe platforms. More importantly, BEA *Tuxedo* assures that transactions maintain its ACID properties. The *Atomicity, Correctness, Isolation,* and *Durability* are important database features that create transaction identifiers,

---

[96] COOL:Gen High-Powered eBusiness Solutions, http://www.cai.com/products/cool/coolgen.htm

[97] Merant Solutions Overview, http://www.intersolv.com/solutions

[98] BEA Tuxedo, http://www.bea.com/products/tuxedo/index_tux.html

provide status tracking, resolve deadlocks, implement database persistency by *two-phase commit* (2PC), and co-ordinate the transaction recovery processes. For more, check *Case 24:* CoreLAN - TP Services with BEA Tuxedo ™.

IBM Transarc's *Encina*[99]®, (grew out of 'Camelot' research at MCU), is the world's leading TP Monitor for large-scale distributed computing. IBM *Encina*, acquired by IBM's fully owned subsidiary Transarc Corp., helps develop DCE and supports *Distributed File Systems* (DFS). The *Encina* DTP is based on OSF's X/Open Consortium DCE technology. According to the IBM Transarc, 'The *Distributed Computing Environment* (DCE) is a cross-platform, comprehensive, integrated set of services that supports the development, use and maintenance of distributed computing applications'. *Figure 25* similarly as *Figure 58* presents DCE architecture as a 'fully integrated, production-ready distributed computing environment'. The *Encina* ++ is the enhanced distributed object application development environment reducing the development costs and time to market. It uses DCE and reusable object components in order to provide resource-location transparency, multi-treaded environment with complex nested transactions, security, transparent communication, and management support. *Encina* together with other TP Monitors, including CICS on Open Systems platforms, provides enterprise-wide solutions on a range of platforms from PCs running Windows and MacOS to powerful mainframe UNIX-based systems.

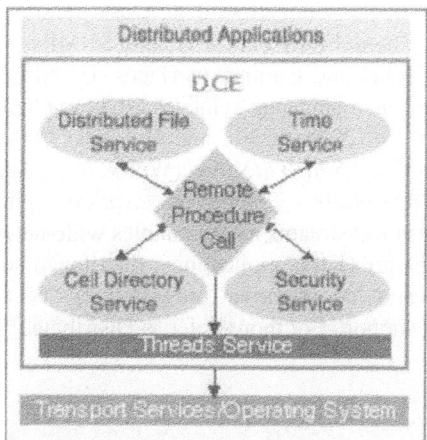

Figure 25. The DCE Architecture [100] at IBM Transarc's Encina

Java-based CBD and EJB-Distributed Applications
Recent data, IDC Report 2000[101]; *see Figure 26*, shows that the Java environment is extending over the Internet platforms. Win/Tel (MS Windows

---

[99] IBM Transarc. Encina Product Info., http://www.transarc.ibm.com/Product/Txseries/Encina/index.html
[100] DCE Product Overview, http://www.transarc.ibm.com/Product/DCE/DCEOverview/dceoverview.html
[101] IDC Report, 2000, http://www.linux-mag.com/2000-11/future_04.html

and Intel) is covering almost 89%, Macintosh Apple 5%, and Linux some 4% of the desktop market share. The situation in the server market is a bit different; see Figure 27. MS Widows is gaining almost 37%, followed by Linux 24%, NetWare 18%, and Unix almost 15%. Proprietary servers OS cover the rest of the market share.

Desktop Market Share

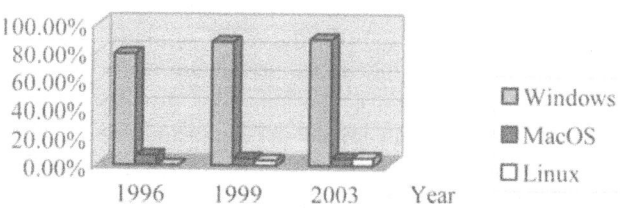

Figure 26. Desktop Market Share (IDC Report, 2000)

The related Internet applications need a support for variety of media types: text, images, video, or movie performing as in their own native environments. Java programming language overcomes most of these problems by encapsulating the necessary Internet protocols within few of its class libraries, hence enabling a unified implementation model for FTP, HTTP, and SNMP protocols, as well as a lower-level network socket and naming interfaces. Based on *Abstract Window Toolkit* (AWT) classes, Java language achieves GUIs implementation for Xerox PARC '90, Macintosh '84, X/Motif '88, and Windows 2000/NT environments too. Inherently tied to the *World Wide Web* (Web) *Java* language also provides interactive use of Java objects - *applets* or *JavaBeans* embedded in HTML applications. Its uniform I/O streams model enables wide-network distribution of new *Enterprise JavaBeans* (EJB) applications, distributed solutions, multi-user multi-treaded tasks, and co-operative programming hence, providing full distributed processing support. For more, refer to Distributed Application.

Server Market Share

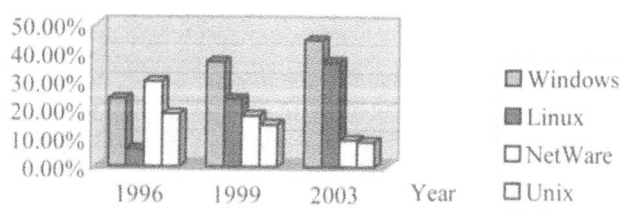

Figure 27. Server Market Share (IDC Report, 2000)

Program distribution, its version control, and application maintenance are just few problems of distributed legacy applications, which are practically solved using Java browsers and EJB component-based development environment. EJB brings about a component-based model that helps solve these problems. EJB's entity and session beans provide EJB development applications a control over the *entities*-database components and its *sessions* - typical transaction model components. In addition, an EJB-based application entails the following features:

– Transaction model support
– Database and file access persistence
– Concurrency control
– Client authentication and access control
– Resource management for threads, network, and database connections
– Bean life-cycle management for creating, finding, caching, and destroying beans
– External configuration of bean runtime properties
– Dynamic deployment of beans at the running server

To date, Java and EJB become a leading trend in distributed CBD enterprise application. As mentioned in earlier cases, many contemporary DCE applications claim Java support, such as CA COOL: Gen, BEA Tuxedo, IBM Transarc's Encina++, etc. See *Case 24:* CoreLAN - TP Services with BEA Tuxedo ™.

Case 12: Nortel Networks Solutions to Power Taiwan's new eASPNet

NORTEL NETWORKS SOLUTIONS TO POWER TAIWAN'S NEW EASPNET
Establishes First Mover Advantage in Asia ASP Market with Supply, Integration
August 31, 2000
http://www.nortelnetworks.com/corporate/news/newsreleases/2000c/08_31_000
0402_easpnet.html

TAIPEI, Taiwan - Nortel Networks* [NYSE/TSE: NT] laid claim to first-mover advantage in Asia's Application Service Provider (ASP) infrastructure market, announcing a US$26 million contract to be chief supplier and prime solutions integrator for eASPNet (www.easpnet.com), Taiwan's new ASP and Internet Data Centre (IDC).

Recently formed by a consortium of blue chip Taiwanese and Asian companies, eASPNet plans to offer enterprise customers - initially in Taiwan and eventually across Asia - a full range of eBusiness and ASP services. At approximately 105,000 square feet, eASPNet expects to be one of the largest carrier-grade IDCs in Asia.

Under the agreement, Nortel Networks will design and build for eASPNet a robust and highly reliable carrier-grade IDC environment to host the business-critical applications it intends to deliver to its customers.

"There is enormous enthusiasm for the Internet economy in Taiwan and China, and eASPNet's 'rent-an-application' model offers enterprise customers access to high-value eBusiness applications at significant cost savings, as well as the freedom to focus on core business issues," said Yu-Lon Chiao, chairman, eASPNet. "Nortel

Networks' traditional networking strengths and its global leadership in eBusiness and the Internet make it the ideal ally to implement Taiwan's largest IDC, and to function as an end-to-end solutions integrator for our business customers."

"We are working with eASPNet to bring the economic and competitive benefits of a world-class ASP solutions portfolio to Taiwan's small and medium-sized businesses, as well as to implement eASPNet's advanced IDC hosting and network infrastructure," said Robert Mao, president and chief executive officer, Nortel Networks China. "Both ASPs and IDCs play key roles in fuelling the Internet economy. This association with eASPNet is another significant step in strengthening our regional and global lead in building the high-performance Internet."

In association with several industry allies, Nortel Networks recently unveiled a Managed Application Services initiative, bringing together the elements ASPs require to enable a powerful and efficient strategy and solutions portfolio.

This initiative is intended to accelerate time-to-market and free resources for critical customer and market-related tasks; tune ASP networks for peak application performance, creating platforms for rapid rollout of new services and optimisation of the end-user experience; deliver top-level service management allowing ASPs to generate new revenue streams and offer differentiated services with guaranteed service levels; and provide single points of accountability.

The Nortel Networks end-to-end IDC solution consists of industry-leading network infrastructure and management software integrated with IT (information technology) infrastructure, storage and other components from Nortel Networks allies. Part of the IDC solution is the Nortel Networks Preside* Managed Application Services platform, enabling ASPs to cost-effectively offer a variety of hosted eBusiness applications to enterprises of all sizes, and to deliver end-to-end application management all the way to the desktop via a common platform.

eASPNet is a full e-Service Provider offering trusted end-to-end managed Internet Data Centre and Application Service Provider services in the Asia Pacific region. eASPNet is enabling innovative Internet hosting and application rental services to enterprises of all sizes with best in class technology partners and corporate alliances. eASPNet is formed by a group of global blue-chip corporations aiming to build a long-term sustainable and profitable business.

Nortel Networks is a global Internet and communications leader with capabilities spanning Optical, Wireless, Local Internet and eBusiness. The Company had 1999 U.S. GAAP revenues of US$21.3 billion and serves carrier, service provider and enterprise customers globally. Today, Nortel Networks is creating a high-performance Internet that is more reliable and faster than ever before. It is redefining the economics and quality of networking and the Internet, promising a new era of collaboration, communications and commerce.

Visit us at www.nortelnetworks.com.

*Nortel Networks, the Nortel Networks logo, the Globemark and Preside are trademarks of Nortel Networks

Bibliography

How Uncle Sam is involved in e-business development; *Daniel W Gottlieb*; **Purchasing**, Boston; Nov 2, 2000; Vol. 129, Iss. 8; pg. 42, 2 pgs

Tracking the e-business evolution; *Lisa C Rabon*; **Bobbin**, Columbia; Sep 2000; Vol. 42, Iss. 1; pg. 14, 3 pgs

Is Domino an e-business development environment?; *Mark Buchner*; **Midrange Systems**, Spring House; Jun 26, 2000; Vol. 13, Iss. 9; pg. 40, 1 pgs

Exec drives business development; *Laura Petrecca*; **Advertising Age**, Chicago; Feb 7, 2000; Vol. 71, Iss. 6; Midwest region edition; pg. S8, 1 pgs

E-business evolution; *Gregory Dalton*; **InformationWeek**, Manhasset; Jun 7, '99, Iss. 737; pg. 50, 7 pgs

Database 'toolbox' cuts enterprise development time; **Control Engineering** *Anonymous*; Aug 1998

PART III

ENTERPRISE NETWORKING

Case 13: Corvis All-Optical Network

CORVIS: WHAT IS THE ALL-OPTICAL NETWORK
http://www.corvis.com/
(Reprinted by permission of Corvis Corporation)

Corvis products give communication service providers the capability to build a single-layer, transparent all-optical network.

Over the past decade, the volume of data traffic transported across telecommunications networks has grown rapidly and now exceeds the volume of voice traffic. Data-intensive applications such as Internet access, e-mail, e-commerce, web-hosting, remote access and other data services have placed significant strains on the capacity of the existing network infrastructure. This increase in traffic volume is forcing both incumbent and emerging service providers to design, build and add capacity to their networks.

How it Works

All-optical networking is a revolutionary technology designed to fundamentally change the way data traffic is transmitted. Today, transmission equipment takes electrical signals generated from communication devices such as phones and computers and converts them to optical signals or light waves that are transmitted along a strand of fibre. As the light wave, or optical signal, travels over the fibre, it degrades. Once it does, equipment in the network must regenerate the light wave by converting it into an electrical signal and then back into a light wave before it can continue through the network.

Typically, this equipment, called regenerators, are placed every 300 to 600 kilometres (186 to 373 miles) along the network to strengthen the light waves—a costly process. In an all-optical network, light waves can travel ultra-long distances—up to 3,200 km or almost 2,000 miles without being regenerated.

The Corvis all-optical network solution offers three key elements that differentiate it from other optical solutions available in today's market:

Ultra-Long Optical Reach:
transport of optical   signals over ultra-long distances

Terabit Optical Switching:
true optical switching, eliminating all OEO conversions

Integrated Network Management:
a complete network management package that remotely controls and monitors all aspects of the network.

Solutions for the Internet Economy

All-optical networks are better equipped than traditional networks to handle the traffic demands that are anticipated from tomorrow's Internet driven economy. Because of their high efficiency and straightforward architecture, all-optical networks can carry very large amounts of data over ultra-long distances, at a dramatically reduced cost. This allows network operators to offer more value-added services, such as video conferencing, real-time video on demand and other high bandwidth applications—making it easier for the world to communicate at the speed of light.

There are some new developments at the communications front as it is presented in the opening *Case 13:* Corvis All-Optical Network. In fact, the technology substitution takes place along the new developments and the expected IT change. The traditional circuit switching technology, used by frame relays and ATM cell-relays slowly but certainly is replaced by digital packet routing communications hence, paving the way to the ubiquitous presence of mobile and wireless communications. Most of these advances in the communications technology have prompted enterprise users to pay greater attention to the introduction of new IT, adopting it fully into the common everyday use. It also requires prompt update of its best business practices. In many respects, the present process of IT-change represents an important technological trend known as the *convergence of technologies*, e.g. communications and computing, television and computing, etc. It closely relates the information processing and the computer technology to date. Still, it is even strongly associated than ever with communications, connecting people, messaging, and information exchange. The new enterprise paradigms are coming in along with it, blending the IT-change together and essentially, changing and shaping up the traditional enterprise-networking environment.

In this part, following closely the topics[102] from [Stallings & Slyke, 1996], we will review some of the communications technologies related to the IT developments. In fact, some fundamental communications issues inherent to the enterprise networking are going to change. Its importance rises beyond simple networking. Not only it is the enterprise environment changing, but the existing best practices change too, hence allowing enterprises greater freedom to communicate, operate effectively, and integrate its *virtual enterprise* activities, spanning them across space and time dimensions.

To begin with, the Chapter on Communications Networks we will review some basic networking and communications issues related to and allowing for global *connectivity*, i.e. starting with *HDLC, TCP/IP* networking protocol for instance, and the *ISDN* network architecture concept. The latter, represents an important set of integrated digital communications protocols, which has influenced several networking platforms. We follow with the review of most recent advances in higher bandwidth networking, such as, *frame,* and *cell* relays packet switching technology enabling high-speed communication throughout wide area networks.

Due to the importance of the Wide World Web, the Internet networking and the *wide area networks* in general, the Chapter on Wide Area Networks will elaborate on some of communications alternatives, such as, *packet* vs. *circuits* switching. It is an important IT trend that determines the prospects of enterprise-

---

[102] William Stallings, R. van Slyke , Business Data Communications, Prentice Hall, 1996.

wide networking. We are also aware that the digital technology is in process of convergence heading towards all-optical IP switching. It will allow bridging rather than managing the IT gap that exists between *conventional* enterprises confined to its local area networks and the new breed of *Web-based* enterprises.

The emergence of *virtual enterprises* spanning across local area network boundaries gives rise to the Intranets and wide area enterprise networks. Due to the importance of network implementation issues, we will elaborate on the *local area networks* concepts in Chapter on <u>Local Area Networks</u>. In particular, we will present the alternatives related to the networking topology, choices of media and cabling, and the differences between the two widely accepted *media access control* (MAC) protocols such as the *Ethernet* and the *Token ring* standards.

With the importance of distributed networking in mind, the subsequent Chapter on <u>Distributed Network Management</u> will elaborate on distributed network management issues, in particular, the modern system management alternatives, such as, manager of network managers and manager of managing agents. Special attention is paid to *CORBA* framework and *X/Open* management standards.

CHAPTER 9

COMMUNICATIONS NETWORKS

Open Systems

Case 14: CallWare's Callegra Advanced Messaging System

CALLEGRA™ UNIFIED MESSAGING

http://www.callware.com/unified.html

(Reprinted by permission of CallWare Technologies)

A software-based communications solution that resides natively on your company's network, Callegra instantly adds value to your existing messaging platforms and programs by integrating voice and fax messages to create a universal mailbox, accessible by phone or PC.

Callegra is a complete, software-based voice and fax messaging solution that makes communicating easy, saves money and increases productivity - all while leveraging existing equipment investments. A client/server-based application, Callegra unifies phone, fax, voicemail, and email into a single integrated application for unified messaging with Internet access. Callegra simplifies business communications by integrating with operating systems and applications people already own and are comfortable with: Windows 95/98/ME/XP, Windows *2000/NT* and leading email and groupware applications. Callegra combines the ease and familiarity of the telephone system with the power and flexibility of the computer network, to allow computer control of telephone and fax messaging functions.

Callegra's extensive voice messaging features may be all your company requires at the moment. However, Callegra can easily take you from an advanced voice messaging foundation to the productivity-enhancing benefits of unified messaging - and beyond. Simply add modules as needed to take advantage of a vast array of features that make communicating easy.

Callegra for Innovative Solutions Advanced Messaging

Callegra is a powerful voice messaging and automated attendant solution that easily expands to offer additional advantages such as integrated speech recognition, fax services, browser based voice and fax messaging and email integration. Its

145

proven telephone system integration combined with its rich feature set is designed to improve overall company communication, increase productivity and deliver next-generation telephone applications. Companies that deploy Callegra into their network infrastructure immediately create new business opportunities by protecting themselves from lost call possibilities, improving the flow of company information and increasing productivity. With Callegra any company is well positioned to accelerate toward the forefront of today's competitive arena. Callegra-enabled companies confidently look toward the future knowing they have invested in a communications platform that is continually updated with all the growth potential their company could ever need. The demands for efficient communication collaboration are now tougher than ever before. Callegra offers a growing list of unique capabilities that help deliver modern communication tools to the entire enterprise. After all, one major factor in determining the success of a business today is how well it communicates.

A Powerful Core: Callegra Engine

As a fifth generation voice processing engine, Callegra harnesses the strengths of the telephone system combined with the power of today's data networks to provide a robust voice messaging and automated attendant foundation. Its intuitive and familiar Windows 2000 interface makes administration straightforward and simple. The Callegra solution provides the ultimate in messaging performance and the strongest foundation for expanding into the advanced communication features of unified messaging.

- Microsoft Windows 2000 Support
- Dynamic GUI Icons
- Multi-Tenanting
- Extensive PBX Integration
- Multi-PBX Capability
- Multiple Caller Integration Methods
- Dialogic & Brooktrout Voice Boards Support
- AMIS Compliant
- Global Distribution Lists
- Direct To Voicemail Transfer
- Greeting & Passcode Lock
- Enhanced Tracing
- System Maintenance & Optimization
- MWI Controls
- Box Alias Table
- Dial String Translation
- System Utilities
- System Scalability
- Online Licensing & Upgrades
- Online Help & Documentation
- Fax Tone Auto-transfer

Intuitive graphical interfaces ensure fast and easy system set-up and administration.

Efficiency for Everyone: Mailbox Users

In today's dynamic marketplace, where being competitive means receiving instant information and delivering immediate responses, one thing remains constant–efficient communications is a hallmark of high profitability. Callegra provides the most contemporary mailbox tools to empower employees to manage their calls efficiently–despite diverse work hours, travel requirements and changing workloads throughout the organization.

- One Touch Record Service
- Call Screening
- Multiple Notifications for Voice and Fax Messages
- Email/SMS Notification
- Notification Control
- Alternate Busy/NA Extensions
- Extension Number Control
- Message Escalation
- Dial Sender (internal and external)
- Personal Distribution Lists
- Wake-Up Call
- Speed Dial
- Message Parameters & Controls
- Message Reply & Forward
- Message Delivery
- Remote Programmable Greetings
- New User Tutorial
- Deleted Message Recovery
- Multiple Address Messages
- Scheduled Personal Greetings
- Personal Caller Options
- Personal Box Operator

Communication Techniques

Signal Encoding

Essentially, there are two distinct ways of *transmission* of signals: *analogue and digital transmission,* i.e. continuous and discrete way of signal transmission, respectively. The two-by-two signal encoding matrix*; see Table 12,* shows all four possible ways of representation of information and signals during the transmission.

Table 12. Signal encoding

Signal/Transmission	Analogue	Digital
Analogue	Analogue	Analogue/Digital
Digital	Digital/Analogue	Digital

In the *analogue* case, the transmission maintains continuous values of signals over some interval of time; for instance, a continuous pattern of signal's intensity in voice, or in video communications. However, in the *digital* case, it takes discrete values at certain time instances, such as the case of representation of *binary data, text, digits, bitmaps,* etc. Similarly, an *analogue* signalling refers to continuously varying electromagnetic waves, in contrast to *digital* signalling that assumes sequence of pulses.

As usual, it is quite natural to talk about advantages or disadvantages of a particular communications technology. Digital technology in general is cheaper, more flexible, and much easier to maintain. Due to programmable features, it's less susceptible to noise interference, but suffers more signal attenuation than the analogue one. Unlike analogue amplifiers, the digital repeaters applied to extend signals over larger distances are not subject to cumulative noise effects. Due to readily applicable encryption techniques the digital technology also provides higher data integrity, security, and privacy. Standard modem data rate ranges in modules of 1.2 Kbps until 56 Kbps (1.2, 2.4, and 4.8, till 56 Kbps). Higher digital rates are based on 64 Kbps channel rate. The V.21 to V.34 denote modem standards recommended by the CCITT international body.

Signal Transmission

Regarding signal transmission, both analogue and digital information can be represented and propagated by either analogue or digital signals. Aside from other differences, most importantly, the analogue information occupies a limited signal bandwidth and can be represented directly by electromagnetic signal. A signal conversion device, known as *codec* (i.e. coder/decoder) is used to convert analogue into digital signals.

Digital information too can be represented by either analogue or digital signals.

Likewise, a *modem* (i.e. modulator/demodulator) is a device used to convert a series of binary information into corresponding analogue signals by modulating information onto some carrier signal. It is also possible to represent digital data directly using appropriate binary signals. In case of analogue encoding of digital information the modem that modulates a signal and the carrier signal may implement several modulation techniques with different transmission properties:

- *Amplitude-Shift Keying* (ASK) - uses two signal's amplitude levels, or a presence and absence of a signal. In general, it is susceptible to sudden gain changes due to environmental inference noise and is rather inefficient modulation techniques.

- *Frequency-Shift Keying* (FSK) - applies two different signal frequencies. It is less susceptible to environmental noise and employed for higher frequency range (4-30 MHz), often implemented in radio transmission, GPS, *wireless* LAN, etc.

– *Phase-Shift Keying* (PSK) - uses signal's phase shift or its inverse. It is highly noise-resistant and most efficient modulation technique to date, but for a price. Combined with either PSK or ASK it is used for higher data rates over voice-grade lines, known as *multilevel signalling.* To emphasize multi-bit per channel transfer rate it is measured in *Baud* instead of usual *bps - bits/second* data rate.

The conventional analogue encoding of analogue information occupies the same signal bandwidth. However, applying distinct modulated carriers, e.g. *amplitude, phase,* or *frequency,* produces new analogue signals shifted to different frequency bands and allowing more efficient transmission, thus permitting either *Frequency-Division Multiplexing,* or *Broad Band Multiplexing.*

The following *Figure 28* illustrates the digital encoding of analogue information in case of voice and TV signals. According to the *sampling rule* that preserves a *lossless transformation* of information, *the sampling rate should be at least twice the highest frequency in the analogue signal.* For example, applying twice data sampling rate to a 4 kHz *voice signal,* or similarly to a 4.8 MHz *TV signal* and implementing usual *Pulse Code Modulation* (PCM) with at least 8 bits/sample for voice and 10 bits/sample for video, results in digital signal of 64 Kbps and 96 Mbps, respectively.

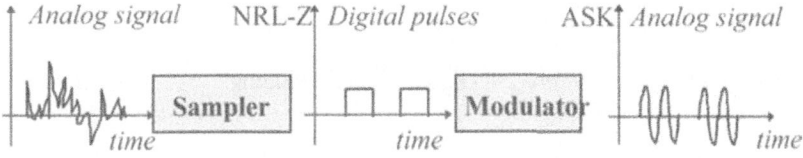

Figure 28. Digitising Analogue Signals

The most common and easiest scheme for *digital encoding* of *digital signals* is the *NonReturn-to-Zero-Level (NRZ-L);* see *Figure 28.* A positive pulse is used to represent a binary 0; similarly, a negative pulse represents binary 1. Common disadvantages of this scheme are difficulties associated with bit detection and synchronization problems. More efficient alternatives are *biphase-coding* schemes such as *Manchester* and *Differential Manchester; see Figure 29.* Using at least one transition per bit, twice the NRZ modulation rate, it is easier and more reliable in presence of noise or change of polarity. Moreover, it provides self-synchronization mechanism too. The Manchester encoding takes care of the detection of the order of incoming bits, i.e. its length and arrival. Differential Manchester resolves as well the synchronization problem of transmission. There are few ways of achieving the *synchronization* in transmission:

– *Asynchronous* – simple, a character at a time mechanism, with timing maintained within the characters. Having up to three detection-bits per character (0 for start and 11 for stop) makes it less efficient, generating more than 30% overhead.

- *Synchronous* - a separate mechanism that uses timing clocks within data signal or is often accomplished by the Manchester encoding. It is more efficient for sustained higher throughput resulting in less than 0.6% HDLC overhead.
- *Frames* - corresponds to a higher synchronisation level and entails beginning and ending data blocks. Usually, it is achieved using some specific *characters* or *bit patterns,* the so-called *pre/post-amble flag bits.*
  For instance, the overhead of one Mbytes-character message transmitted over 9.6 Kbps line using only two start/stop-bits per character results in 208s overhead. A synchronous transmission overhead is 5s for 48-bit flag per Kbytes-characters block-frame, making it the most widely used in network transmissions scheme.

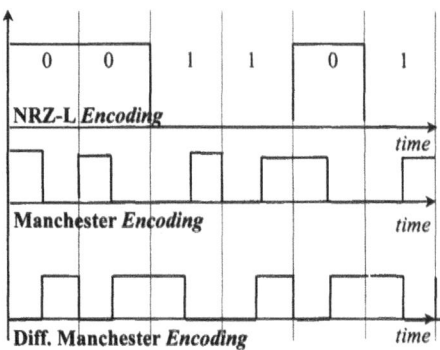

Figure 29. Digital Signal Encoding

Communication Interface

The Data Terminal Equipment to Data Communication Equipment or (DTE-DCE) *interface* that defines standard characteristics for network communications is shown in *Figure 31.* It specifies the *mechanical, physical* communications features (male/female plugs), or *electrical* features regarding timing, voltage levels, code/decode data rates. *Functional* features entail data, controls, or timing signals. Similarly, *procedural* attributes specify the sequence of events required for serial data transmission, etc. For instance, a *serial RS-232-C* connection is still used by variety of terminals and computer connections. *RS-232-C* can connect slow data-rate devices to a network through a modem and analogue communication line for data rates less then 20 Kbps and distance less then 15m. The coding associated with binary 1 or binary 0 may equal to -3V and +3V, respectively. Often, it is used for slow date-rate, dial-up connection, or private transmission line using asynchronous communication connecting two devices.

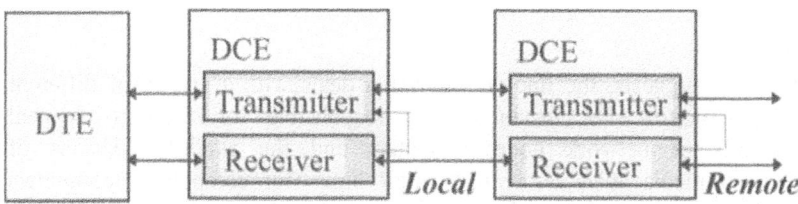

Figure 30. A Local/Remote Loop-Back with RS-449 [105]

The *RS-449/422/423* with 37-pin connector and *loop-back control; see Figure 30,* is yet another *serial* interface connecting terminals or computers modems to a network analogue line for greater data rates (0.1 -10 Mbps) and 1 km distance.

Figure 31. Communication Network [105]

Centronics is also a standard interface that connects block-data devices through parallel connections and synchronous transmission for disk drives, CD-ROM, tapes, etc. A new *Universal Serial Bus* (USB) standard has been introduced, connecting Mbps data-rate devices directly to the data bus. The USB is external peripheral interface standard allowing Mbps communication between a computer and external peripherals over inexpensive cable using biserial transmission. USB is going to replace the existing serial ports, parallel ports, keyboard, monitor connectors and possibly low-speed scanners, and removable hard drives
In a sequel, usually there is an ongoing discussion over the *paradox of standards.* It is their apparent tendency to freeze the current technology that soon makes it vulnerable of becoming obsolete. Often, standards prematurely follow eventual advances in technology. An interesting case is the current, rather efficient ISDN standard. Its full adoption is still questionable, lagging behind much older and inefficient RS-232 or X.21 serial interface standard that are still in common use.

HDLC Networking Protocol
In order to access computer networks it is necessary to resolve any network differences and complexities. Mainly, they exist due to fast changes in ICT, i.e. communications technology, and the evolving enterprise networks. The communication *data link* layers are replacing network interfaces in fact reaching beyond simpler transmission data-line interfaces. On the other hand, the network

communication *control* layer, referred to as *data link control protocol,* takes care of line configuration, flow control mechanism, error detection, and error control.

Line Configuration

As the name suggests, the line configuration deals with a variety of different network topologies. For instance, it is responsible for different physical arrangements of network node computers and the available options of transmission media such as, *point-to-point* links (for computer-to-computer) communication, *multipoint,* and *multidrop* links (used in traditional computer-terminal networks); *see Figure 32.* The data exchange supported is either *full-duplex* (simultaneous), or *half-duplex* (one direction at a time, or alternating communication transmission mode).

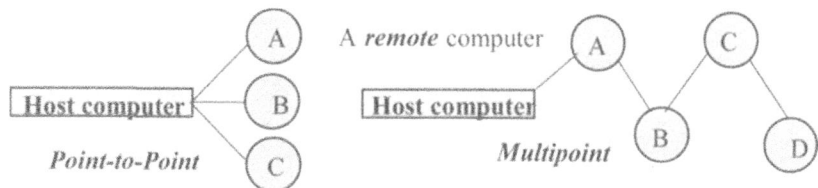

Figure 32. Computer/Terminal Line Configurations

Flow Control

Flow control is a technique used to assure correct data transmission. There are several methods of implementation:

— *Stop-and-wait,* is the simplest but often inadequate; used whenever there are a large numbers of smaller-size frames or messages.
— *Piggyback,* incorporates efficiently the *acknowledgement* frame onto the data frame sequences. It is used in a two-way data exchange (two communication windows at a time). In contrast, a *stop-and-wait* link with mere 0.1s to 0.3s transmission-to-delay ratio may achieve only 33% utilisation transmitting a 100-bit frames at Mbps data rate over 40 km line.
— *Sliding-window protocol* enables efficiently sending or receiving multiple-frame windows simultaneously by maintaining lists of sent and received frames rightly.

Error Detection

Error detection depends on the increased *redundancy* introduced into the data streams. Both receiver and transmitter cooperate during the exchange of error correction frames. There are few alternative schemes:

— *Parity-check* (either even or odd) is the simplest error-detection scheme.
— *Frame Check Sequence* (FCS) used in synchronous transmission is more efficient. Commonly, it applies a powerful overall check by adding a *Cyclic*

Redundancy Check (CRC) code to a frame, implemented as a 17-bit or 33-bit contingency prime (the control remainder is 16, or 32 bit long, respectively).

Error Control
Following the *error detection* the flow control uses *Automatic Repeat reQuest* (ARQ):
–   *Stop-and-wait ARQ* is usually for simple but rather inefficient communications.
–   *Go-back-N ARQ* is based on the efficient *sliding-window* flow-control protocol.

Link Control
The link control protocol provides both the data flow as well as the error control. The *data link control protocol* entails two modules used for synchronous, but rarely for asynchronous transmission:
–   Data link module - organises data into set of frames.
–   Control bits provide for reliable frame delivery.
For instance, the *High-level Data Link Control* (HDLC) is data link protocol used in most point-to-point and multi-point/drop lines, in full, or half-duplex operations, primarily for computer-to-computer (peer-to-peer and master/slave) connections.
There are several HDLC protocol types associated with different network node types (*primary, secondary, combined*), specific link configurations (*unbalanced, balanced*), and data transfer operation modes (*normal-response* NRM, *asynchronous-balanced* ABM, *asynchronous-response* ARM); *see Table 13*. Since HDLC represents a predefined *frame structure; see Figure 33*, it also provides some special fields for data control embedded into various types of *Information, Supervisory,* and *Unnumbered* frames. Consequently, there exist corresponding frames and control field formats. *Table 13* shows some commonly used protocols related to the HDLC protocol.

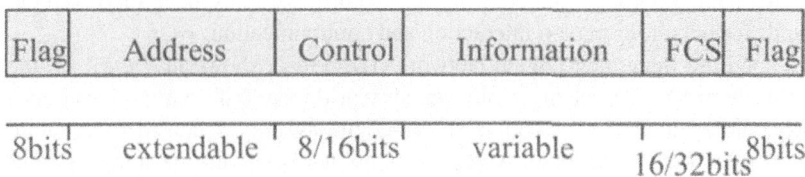

Figure 33. HDLC Frame Structure

Every communication that involves HDLC frames, such as the exchange of S, U, or I frames between two stations entails three phases:
–   *Initialisation* of the data link.
–   *Exchange* of user's data and control information under flow and error control.

— *Termination* of operation followed by disconnection of the communication link.

Table 13. HDLC Related Data Link Control Protocols

HDLC	Widely used by	Internationally ISO supported protocols
SDLC	SNA networks	IBM proprietary protocol akin to HDLC
BSC	IBM 3270	Binary Synchronous Communications
LAP-B	X.25 PSN	HDLC based Link Access Protocol
LAP-D	used in ISDN	LAP-B based D-channel Common Signalling
LLC	LAN addressing	HDLC based Logical Link Protocol

Integrated Digital Network Services -ISDN

Integrating the same digital technology for voice, data, images, and video makes the ISDN protocol a merger of two emerging technologies: *digital computing* and *packet switching communications*. There has been an increasing demand for efficient, timely collection, digital processing, and dissemination leading to the ISDN development of integrated systems for transmission and processing all types of data.

To contain the evolution and impact of ISDN, the international community led massive standardization effort for almost twenty years. ISDN were to be compatible with all kinds of communications equipment, telephones, computer terminals, PCs, attached to network anywhere and connected to the existing communications systems. The current trend is favourable. The increasing demands for computer connectivity followed by wireless and mobile communications led to ubiquitous mobile devices and portable computers. The impact of computer technology is evident everywhere. Data volume has increased dramatically due to the richness of multimedia types. *Natural Language Processing* (NLP) technology, voice and pattern recognition, and artificial intelligent systems penetrated irresistibly. Large enterprises followed by SMSE and entrepreneurial enterprises, all motivated by *paperless society* demanded more efficient computers. Global businesses and virtual offices promoted the so-called *smart buildings*. The smart office building integrating voice and data, environmental controls, and security systems, have increased the demands for person-to-person interaction and communication.

Based upon the Integrated Digital Network (IDN) idea, shown in *Figure 34*, the ISDN technology has been implemented worldwide with variable success. Clearly, the architecture of equivalent analogue system is considerably more complex than that of integrated system of digital networks. For instance, in order to allow general operation, *Space-Division Multiplexing* (SDM) input lines must connect to any output line, hence, both inputs and outputs must share the same frequency band. Thus, at any switching node the incoming *Frequency Division Multiplexing* (FDM) signal is to be de-multiplexed, transformed back to base-voice frequency, in order to allow any subsequent SDM switching to take place.

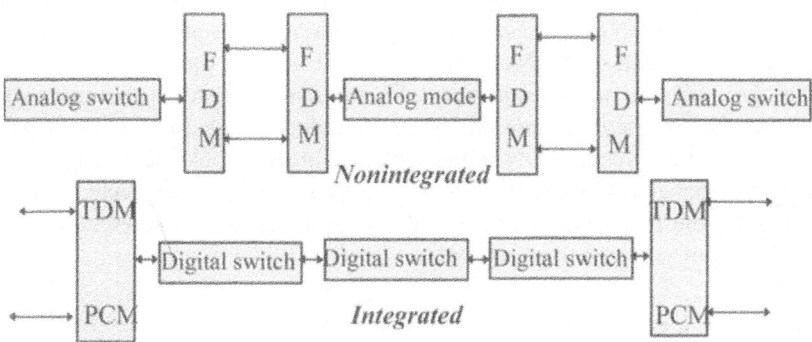

Figure 34. Integration of Transmission and Switching [105]

Thanks to the miniturialisation trend to date, both costs and physical size of the devices implemented in digital technology are falling continuously. The maintenance costs are all but fraction of those implemented in analogue circuitry. The use of digital repeaters also enables longer distances over lesser-quality line. The cumulativeless noise transmission provides higher data integrity. Due to the *economies of scale* achieved by integrating voice, data, images, and video signals together with the digital treatment has also rendered higher transmission security and privacy. Moreover, higher bandwidth Gbps transmission rates using satellite and fibre optic channel constantly demand more economical, and higher degree of multiplexing, which is readily provided by digital *Time Division Multiplexing* (TDM) rather than analogue FDM. The most recent advances in communications technology such as xDSL still give a chance to FDM and QAM communication to digital network local loop offering viable alternative solutions.

ISDN concept

The ISDN is conceived to provide support for voice and non-voice applications with a limited set of standardized facilities. Since planned for switched, as well as for non-switched applications, it is applicable for both CSN and PSN users. However, the initial reliance on 64 Kbps connections turned to be too restrictive for future ISDN development and actually led to the introduction of B-ISDN. Eventually, ISDN has introduced intelligence into network services beyond its initial call-setup phase. In fact, the ISDN follows the layered OSI protocol architecture and supports a variety of network configurations. Actually, it is able to run on more than one physical configuration. For instance, the user makes access to ISDN through the local interface or a *digital pipe* of some determined data rate. The user may at any time employ less than the maximum pipe capacity agreed. Accordingly, the fee charged is for the capacity used rather than by the connect time, as it used to be the case with other conventional communications channels. It also delegates the responsibility for full or optimal technology utilization to the service provider. The key objectives achieved are *standardization, service transparency, support* for leased, switched and multiplexed services (HDTV, PBX or LAN), *cost-related tariffs,* and its *smooth technology migration.* The principal benefits of ISDN are *integration of voice* and *variety of data-rates,* higher *efficiency* due to the economies of scale, *tailored services* that meet the users needs, *competitive advantages,* and reduced risk of *obsolescence.* Interestingly, the overall ISDN implementation process took the International Standard Organizations more than twenty years. Due to the unexpectedly long deployment, the ISDN presently came almost to the edge of obsolescence as a consequence of yet another *paradox of standards.*

ISDN Transmission Structure

The digital pipe between a provider's office and the ISDN subscriber carries a number of communications channels. The basic *B channel* of 64 Kbps is supported by a data *D channel* of 16 or 64 Kbps. A higher bandwidth *H channel* goes up to A1-level (2,044 Kbps in Europe and the rest of the world) or to T1-level (1,544 Kbps in the US). The channels form well-defined transmission structure offering *basic* and *primary* access packages to the end user:

- *B channel,* or a *basic* user's channel, provides digital data/voice or mixed low-rate traffic services designated to the same user's end-point. It also provides leased line equivalent connections to CSN, or PSN.
- *D channel,* known as common signalling channel, carries signalling information to control CSN over associated B channel for set-up calls over all B channels at customer's interface. In addition it may be used for low data rate PSN traffic, such as low-speed telemetry, or when no signalling information is required.
- *H channel* is intended for higher bit rates multiplexing a number of B channels together with a D channel (e.g. 31 B channels and a D channel makes an A1-level of 2.048 Kbps data-rate). It is used to provide high-speed trunk lines or subdivide accordingly the TDM schema for fast facsimile, video, high-speed data, high-fidelity audio, and multiplexed low-rate data.

Broadband ISDN

Following the introduction of ISDN, the efforts were directed toward the global network concepts incorporating LAN, PBXs, and broadcasting networks, a trend usually referred to as the *Broadband ISDN* (B-ISDN). The B-ISDN is in response to the increased user's demand for video services, higher data rates required for image and digital video, an order of magnitude beyond those delivered by usual ISDN. In order to meet the high-resolution digital video requirements, the B-ISDN has introduced an upper channel rate of 150 Mbps for simultaneous support for one or more interactive services (conversational, messaging, or retrieval), and broadcasting, distributive services up to a total of 600 Mbps subscriber-line data rate. To date, fibre optic remains the one and only appropriate transmission media technology for widespread support of B-ISDN.

Open System Interconnection - OSI

Following the review on networking protocols it is evident that some sort of application software module is required to support a computer communications. The *Open System Interconnection* (OSI) is an important international standard that provides that support. In general, a structured set of modules implementing more than two communications functions is often referred to as *communications architecture*. The HDLC protocol for instance relies on its modular structure of communications architecture. More complex networking used for instance in file transfer applications across networks may still require a different type of network architecture, please see *Figure 35*

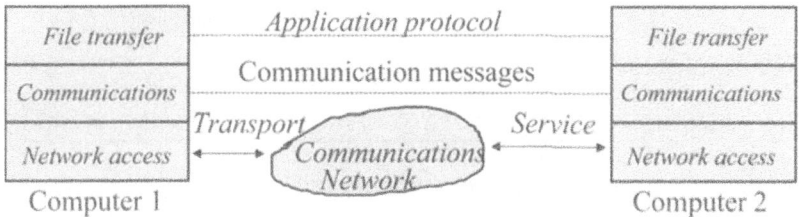

Figure 35. Network Communications Architecture [105]

The simple three-layer communications model presented in *Figure 35* entails three different agents: an *application, computers,* and a *network*. The *network access* is for instance, X.25 for PSN, or IEEE 802.3 for Ethernet LAN. The *transport layer* assures reliability, and application independence. The *application layer* enables higher logical application support, (e.g. email, file transfer, etc).

The modules at corresponding levels on different computers communicate to each other via protocols. A *protocol* represents just a set of rules or conventions governing the way the networked systems cooperate, for instance via HDLC, or X.25 protocol. The data from the next higher layer framed with the control information represents a *protocol data unit - PDU*, e.g. Transport PDU Network PDU; *see Figure 36.*

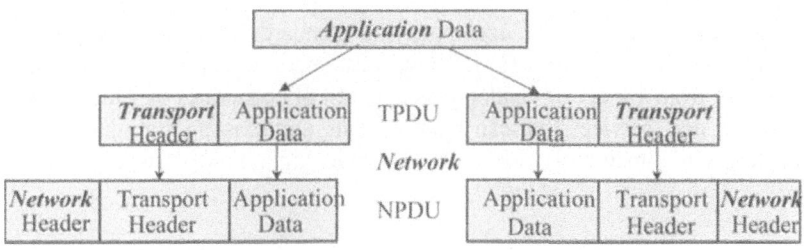

Figure 36. PDU - Protocol Data Unit [105]

The OSI Architecture

The computer vendors community has adopted the concept of *Open System architecture* and implemented a common set of conventions, which have enabled communications among computers from different vendors, different data formats, and data exchange protocols. Supported by *International Standards Organization* (ISO), this standard referred to as the *Open System Interconnect* (OSI) represents a *communications architecture* model for linking *heterogeneous* computer platforms across networks.

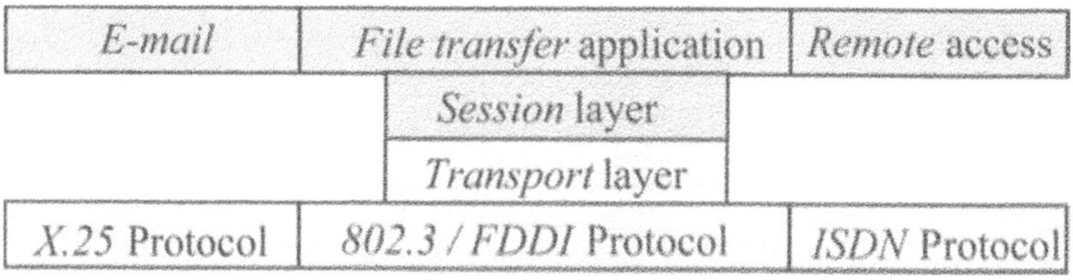

E-mail	File transfer application	Remote access
	Session layer	
	Transport layer	
X.25 Protocol	802.3 / FDDI Protocol	ISDN Protocol

Figure 37. OSI Model [105]

Few instances of *OSI model* are presented in *Figure 37*. The *system* represents a computer including the software, terminals, and any other peripheral devices. A *distributed application* is any activity that involves the exchange of information between the two *open systems*[103]. For instance, it can be remote login of a user on another computer, or sending an e-mail to another end-user, etc. Hence, the OSI model associates layers and services performed at each layer; see *Table 14*.

Table 14. OSI Network Architecture

Layer	Functions of Network Protocol Layers	Example
Physical	Unstructured bit stream transmissions	RS-232
Data link	Data transfer across physical link service	HDLC
Network	Upper layers are using it to connect systems	X.25
Transport	Transport data transfer, error/flow e.g. TCP/IP	TCP part
Session	Applications/Communications control structure	TLI
Presentation	Standardised application interface	GUI
Application	Provides services to users of OSI environment	e-Mail

The OSI architecture and the accompanying standards at each layer provide undeniable benefits to customers. It allows customers to acquire new hardware and software from variety of vendors, take benefit of economies of scale, market competition, new services that can readily fit in, and existing communications architecture, e.g. e-mail tools, document exchange, login, news casts, ect.

---

[103] What is Open System, http://www.sei.cmu.edu/opensystems/what.is.open.system.html

TCP/IP Architecture

Transmission Control Protocol/Internet Protocol (TCP/IP) is the two-layered networking architecture similar in many ways the OSI model; see *Figure 38*. TCP/IP was introduced as the networking standard of the ARPA (DoD) networks that later evolved into *Internet* and the *Web*. TCP/IP is by far the most widespread and popular networking technology in use by all network users today. Vendors offer networking benefits to customers providing TCP/IP networking standard support across networks and with proven track record of tens of years of reliable service. TCP handles data delivery and sequencing, error checking, and retransmission implemented as fast *connectionless datagram* communications. It enables connections to applications on other systems, most often OSI-based networking architectures. The IP handles the data delivery of packets, controls error detection, and error messaging. Even though TCP/IP is installed on far more networks today than OSI, it is *de facto* standard not a certified networking standard. Despite of its low efficiency when compared to other, either connectionless, or connection-based network protocols, for instance PSN X.25, FR, ATM, its popularity has been attributed to the low costs, widespread use, and reliability; see *Figure 38*. Due to its roots and links with UNIX kernel operating systems, TCP/IP is the natural networking protocol connecting UNIX-based system. MS *Windows 2000/NT* and recent versions of Novell *IntranetWare* provide full support to TCP/IP networking standard. For more on TCP/IP standard and addressing schemes please see Internet Hierarchy.

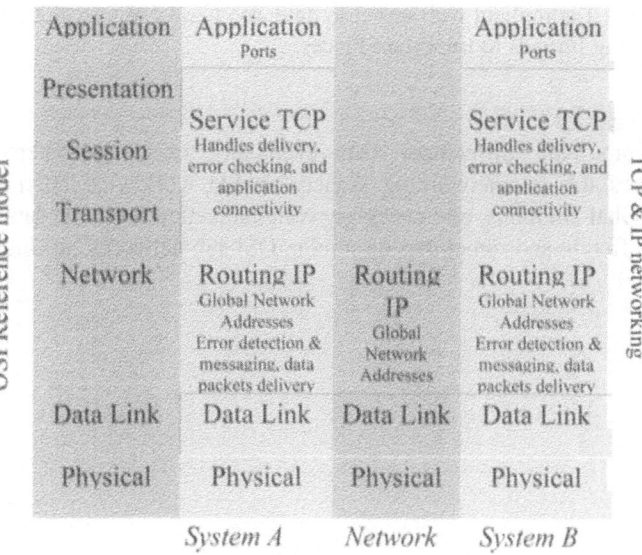

Figure 38. TCP/IP Architecture

The Web: HTTP & HTML

The World-Wide-Web, W3C, or the Web is a hypertext distributed global information retrieval system in public domain administrated by CERN [104], the High-Energy Physics laboratories in Geneva, Switzerland. A broader definition comes from Tim Berners-Lee, CERN, and the founder of W3C: *"The WWW is the universe of network-accessible information, an embodiment of human knowledge"*. The worldwide network of Internet servers makes use of specially formatted documents formatted and supported by *HyperText Markup Language* (HTML) protocol. In order to address documents anywhere in the Web, the HTML makes use of *Uniform Resource Location* (URL) links to other sub-documents, as well as graphics, audio, and video component files. The URL and IP addressing (see Internet Hierarchy) allows jumping from one document to another simply by clicking on the hot spots. Browsers like IIE, Netscape, and Mosaic are computer applications. Not all Internet servers are part of the World Wide Web. Alongside HTML, the underlying Web protocols are the *HyperText Transfer Protocol* (HTTP) and the *eXtentsible Markup Language* (XML) introduced most recently. It is important to note that the HTTP is a *stateless* protocol hence, responsible mainly for message formatting and its transmission via the Web, whereas the HTML is only responsible for Web page formats and presentation. To date, most Web browsers and servers support HTTP ver.1.1, which improved performance allows persistent connection for transmitting multiple files through the same connection path. Cookies, Java, EJB, ActiveX, and technologies alike are used to improve the HTTP shortcomings. The S-HTTP is an extension of the HTTP and is designed to deliver the Web messages securely. *Apache server* by Apache Group is powerful, flexible, and most widely used HTTP/1.1 compliant web server to date; see *Case 1:* Linux Success Stories: Linux Making Inroads in Important Places.

Internetworking

To overcome the differences that eventually exist in system network architectures the internetworking devices enable worldwide internetworking, provide global solutions, and necessary communication logic for data exchange between different and sometimes dissimilar, OSI sub-networks; see *Figure 39*.

---

[104] www.w3.org

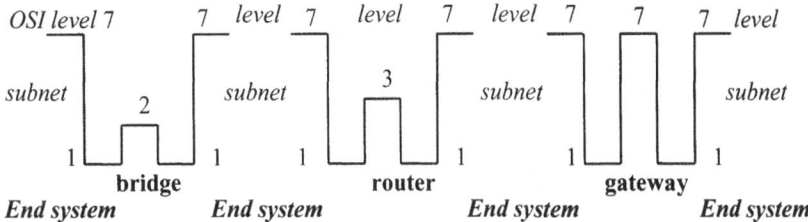

Figure 39. Internetworking Devices

The *bridge* is used to connect two *similar* networks that use *identical protocols*; it performs address filtering between the two LANs (up to OSI Layer 2). Among the benefits are increased reliability, security, performance, etc. The *router* however, enables to connect two *dissimilar* networks that use *different protocols*. Operating at OSI protocol Layer 3, it is transparent for different addressing schemes, packet sizes, or interface alterations. It also increases the flexibility and reliability across interconnected networks. The *gateway* allows for coexistence of OSI with dissimilar proprietary networks, SNA for instance.

Bibliography

New Offerings Aid Partner Relations -- PeopleSoft and Kovair release software to help businesses tackle strategic communications; *L. Scott Tillett*; **InternetWeek**, Manhasset; Jan 29, 2001; pg. PG.22

E-commerce: Small-business communications; *Anonymous*; **Fortune**, New York; Winter 2001; Vol. 142, Iss. 12; pg. 246, 1 pgs

Teligent delivers high bandwidth communications to businesses in Ohio; *Anonymous*; **America's Network**, Duluth; Sep 2000; pg. 32, 2 pgs

Small business: Communications; *Anonymous*; **Fortune**, New York; Winter 2000; pg. 182, 2 pgs

Portals Improve with Age -- Latest Software Tools Enhance Business Communications; *Peter Ruber*; **InternetWeek**, Manhasset; Dec 13, 1999; pg. PG.23

Betting the communications farm -- AMD to sell division, staking future on the tough MPU business; *Mark LaPedus*; **Electronic Buyers' News**, Manhasset; Oct 11, 1999; pg. PG.1

IBM offers e-business networking products; **AS/400 Systems Management** *Anonymous*; Jul 1998

There's no business like small business networking for Intel; **Computer Dealer News** *Shane Schick*; Feb 23, 1998

Newbridge Networks acquires UB Networks to strengthen enterprise networking market position; **Telecommunications** *Flanagan, Patrick*; Mar 1997

William Stallings, R. van Slyke , <u>Business Data Communications</u>, Prentice Hall,1996

CHAPTER 10

WIDE AREA NETWORKS

Last Mile Communications

Case 15: ACTnet Frame Relays Media Integration and Global Access

Bank's Network Cuts Millions from Phone Bills while Offering Global Access for Worldwide Sites

The Problem: Inadequate Communications Network for International Branches

When Banco do Brasil, the largest bank in Brazil with over 2500 branches, began expanding their international operations, they knew that process would most likely be an expensive, but necessary, investment to provide customers with the services they expect. What they didn't realize was that a technology on the horizon would soon provide a way for the Bank to meet all their data communication and network performance needs, while offering an opportunity to cut gargantuan telephone bills down to size.

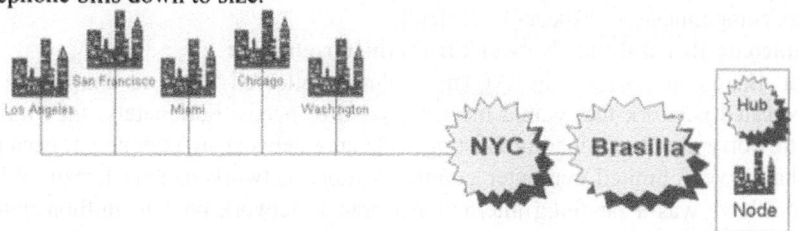

The Solution: An Integrated Networking System Called ACTnet

With 32 sites in 26 countries on four continents- and still growing- Banco do Brasil wanted a sophisticated network that also was cost-effective, easy to install and grow with minimal investment in equipment and staff. ACTnet met all those requirements and also provided a way to control rising telephone and facsimile costs, which had mounted to $4 million a quarter! By integrating telephone and fax calls among branches and between the branches and headquarters in Brasilia, Banco

163

do Brasil estimated they could cut 25-30% from their long distance telephone bills and realize a six-month payback on the cost of the wide area network.

Banco do Brasil - Completed Network

The Result: High-Performance Global Network Charts Future

The implementation of the ACTnet Network allows the Bank to control their communications except for exorbitantly-priced international mail service, there is now a high-throughput, low delay network.

ACTnet supports full LAN-to-WAN access and AS/400 data processing from every site, no matter how remote. Any-to-any telephone and fax connectivity means every person with access to a telephone or a fax machine at the Bank can communicate with any other employee over the network, eliminating all toll charges. Both these capabilities are critical to Banco do Brazil's future growth and success.

ACTnet Integrates Voice, Fax, Data and LAN Using Frame Relay

Combining advanced compression techniques with Frame Relay compliant technology, ACTnet supplied an innovative solution for the Bank. ACTnet comprises two Frame Relay switch models, the MS-1000 and MS-2000, and a Frame Relay network access multiplexer, the SDM-FP.

The MS-1000/2000 is a high-performance switch that provides up to 4 Mbps port data rate with greater than 20,000 packets per second throughput. Both switches are compliant with the full range of Frame Relay standards and offer distributed network intelligence, dynamic learning of network hub configurations and automatic rerouting in the event of trunk failures. The SDM-FP combines voice, fax, data and LAN input and compresses that information for cost efficient communications. The SDM-FP is a standards-compliant Frame Relay Access Device (FRAD), but unlike other FRADs, the SDM-FP translates telephone and facsimile calls as well as data into Frame Relay packets. Frame Relay not only provides a high throughput, low delay transport mode, it also allows for easy any-to-any network connectivity. Other vendors of integrated network solutions rely on point-to-point links, making voice and fax communications especially difficult.

Banco do Brasil Builds Network from the Ground Up

For Banco do Brasil, the ACTnet solution allowed them to implement a sophisticated network that would meet a myriad of needs. Fortunately, they didn't have to worry about eliminating existing wide area networking equipment, because they had a very limited computer communications network outside Brazil. What they did have was a far-flung international branch network on four million dollar monthly telephone and facsimile bills in the effort to communicate with and between the personnel at the remote sites and their customers. ACTnet targeted both problems.

Communication through networks has been a significant improvement enabling enterprises global access with two essential benefits:

– *Customisable* transmission media, affordable, shareable, *low operation costs*.
– *Full connectivity* of all networked devices and user's stations to a network node.

Historically, depending mainly on its scope of activity, there exist two specific types of communication networks, wide, and local area networks:

- Wide Area Networks (WAN) are covering larger areas than a building, such as metropolis, regions, or even covering areas all over the world, i.e. global WAN.
- Local Area Network (LAN) is usually confined to a smaller area, a building, or a cluster of buildings, such as university, medical, or a government campus site.

Global communications in WAN takes place through so-called, point-to-point networking device among parties, which are often remote, far apart. On the other hand, the link among mobile users is established through set of devices requiring either fixed or occasional communications links for a specific period of time.

Conversely, LAN communications has mainly been implemented using C/S broadcasting communications technology. Still, there are some point-to-point alternatives such as *Peer-to-Peer* (P2P). In either case the primary concern is the transmission speed and bandwidth rather than the wide connectivity and security. Historically, the prevailing communications technology used in networks was quite different. The voice-based WAN developed on switched communications technology. Many communications types have evolved, mainly common circuit switching, proper as well as the virtual ones. Recently however, communications technology development naturally led to the convergence of these technologies. To date, there is a spectrum of diverse, very much mixed communications, using broadcasting as well as switched communications. The global connectivity, along with the widespread organisational enterprise integration bridging across boundaries may finally remove the differences between the two network types.

Moreover, the network ownership represents yet another interesting feature that distinguishes the two types of networks. Despite global nature and connectivity concerns, the WAN is rarely owned by a single enterprise. In contrast, a LAN is often private, relying on its own investment in the networking infrastructure. Though, it is possible that the networking infrastructure be partly or completely rented or provided by a third party. Many users usually share the networking infrastructure and services offered by *Network Service Providers* (NSP). An interesting legal event, a legislature change, has influenced the future trend of the global communications market. The 1996 US Government liberalization of the information market allows companies in telecommunications not only may they provide telecommunications services, but may also offer information-related networking services. It allows them to compete equally with network service providers, hopefully, for the benefit of all users seeking services at the global networking market.

Switched Wide Area Network Communications
WAN or switched Wide Area Network communications represents a manifold of interconnected collection of *nodes* - computer servers or routers, and number of *links* - a set of communications media connecting nodes by *transmission paths*; see *Figure 6*.

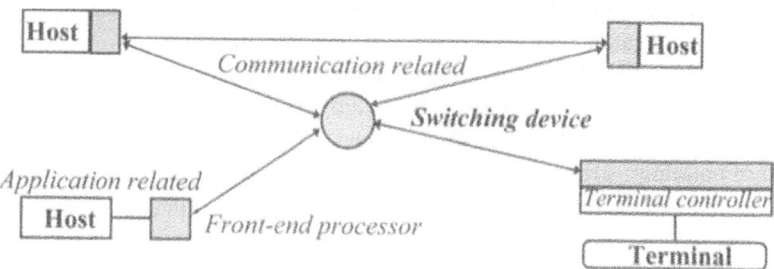

Figure 40. Generic Switching Node

Some WAN nodes perform internal information switching tasks, such as switching and routing, whereby, other nodes may perform some information specific tasks such as accessing, storing, processing, dissemination, or delivering of information. The node stations - *hosts* are generally linked by multipath *point-to-point* communications links. Although, reliable full network connectivity is highly desirable feature, fully connected networks are rarely found, mainly due to economical constraints. As mentioned earlier, *Circuit Switching* and *Packet Switching* are two distinct technologies used to implement network connectivity. With the growing importance of network communications and information technology in general, it is possible to specifically tailor public networks services to a particular, usually a private user, by means of specific communications software. Special networking services have been established that provide access to the so-called *Software Defined Networks*. Some examples represent EDI and the provision of advanced *800/900-dial and mobile telecommunications services* allowing customers various options to pre-planned communications services specific to tasks, time, location, network conditions, or to a particular situation-dependent response that the user would like to see applied to particular services.

Packet Switching Network

Packet Switched Network (PSN) is based on X.25, ISDN, Frame Relay, or cell-switched ATM protocols and represents the state-of-the-art in the wide-area broadcasting communications technology. Historically, PSN was the information technology planned for long-distance data communications. It concerns *message* broadcasting framed in packages, very much similar to an ordinary mail services, e.g. letter, parcels, etc. PSN sees the network as a distributed collection of PSN nodes. In fact, it is also assumes some inherent "*knowledge*" on their local status. This is important since it raises the question of awareness over the availability of a particular part of the network. Obviously, the node status information is difficult to maintain constantly, throughout the network, due to a variable time-delay between frequent, individual status changes. Consequently, a *PSN can never perform perfectly*. Thus, there is always a *delay* or a transmission *overhead* involved in its network operations. There are few WAN alternatives like public, *value-added*, and *private* PSN. The public PSN provides public data packet transmission services commonly used by large enterprises, government offices, and businesses in general. It provides a global *connectivity* to LANs too.

In PSN the data is transmitted in *short packets,* few Kbytes in length, depending on the case and according to the data frame standard applied, or HDLC; see *Figure 33.* Each packet contains a portion of user's payload data and some valuable data for control and routing information (e.g. error and flow control, etc.). Depending whether connectionless or connection approach has been implemented, there are two PSN communications:

- Datagrams
- Virtual Circuits

The network packet switching implemented by *datagrams* resembles an ordinary mail service for it requires no setup-time and transmits the packet independently. It is thereby a favourable communications type for short packets, often character-based computer-device messages. Since packets essentially follow separate paths they can easily survive and bypass node failures or network congestion points.

In contrast, the network packet switching implemented using virtual circuits resembles partly an ordinary phone call since it requires some setup-time so that all message-related packets could follow a pre-planned route. The actual routing is done once at the initiation, and then has been dynamically maintained by the network routing software. By setting up *logical* or *virtual* circuits has enabled implementation of more efficient packet sequencing and error control. The full network knowledge and timely propagation of individual network *node-status information* remains the prerequisite for a reliable WAN performance.

There are some advantages of PSN over switched communications; see *Table 15*:

- Ability to run *connectionless* transmission off-line without *data-rate conversion.*
- Achieve higher *efficiency* since resources are *dynamically allocated* or *shared.*
- *Heavy traffic packets* are apparently accepted without *blocking,* experiencing only some network slowdown due to actual time delivery.
- Overall *control over transmission* allows use of digital coding or priority scheme

The *CCITT X.25* protocol represents a PSN communication standard enabling transparent interfaces between attached devices and the network. It entails the first three *OSI* levels that allow for cooperation among communication network and end-user stations:

- At the *physical level,* for instance, it calls for X.21, or RS-232-C standard.
- At the *link level,* it may use the LAP-B frame sequencing as a subset of HDLC.
- At the *packet level,* it may actually provide *virtual circuit* services for packets.

Table 15. Advantages and Disadvantages of CSN vs. PSN

CSN	PSN
voice compatible	speed & rate conversion
common for voice and data	logical multiplexing
no training or protocols	complex routing/control
economy of scale for voice & data	efficient utilisation
subject to blocking & compatibility	appears non-blocking
set-up call delay	load dependent delay
not for short transactions	not for interactive/voice

Wide-Area Networks provide few alternatives for data communications. There is public PSN using X.25 interface, private PSN through leased lines, private leased lines either through dedicated or multiplexed lines, public CSN using modem dial-up lines for data communications, and private CSN via local PBX employing 56 Kbps analogue line or 64Kbps digital bundled as A1/T1 trunk lines. The cost/performance evaluation has to take into considerations both *data volume* (lengthy streams, fairly continuous, or continuous voice transmission) and *pattern* of data communication *traffic* (e.g. short bursts, sporadic, or occasional terminal-to-host transactions); see *Figure 41*. Other considerations may as well include *management decision features,* such as, network *strategic control, growth control, maintenance operations,* or *reliability* and *security issues.* Despite limited use of PSN for voice communications in the past due to existing variable data delay, there are alternative technologies such as *Frame Relays and* cell-relays ATM that have successfully overcome problems of WAN applications for commercial voice and data communications.

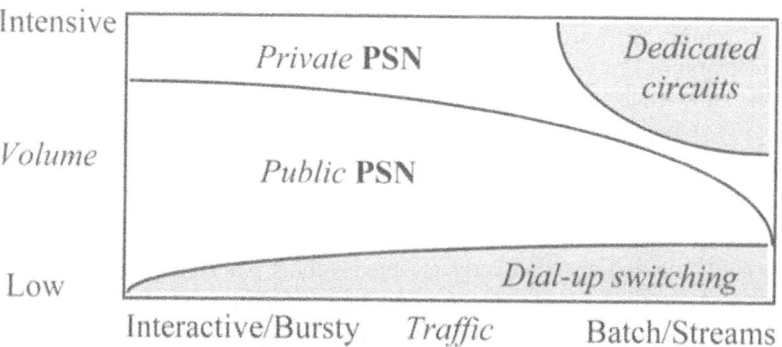

Figure 41. Data Communications Alternatives [105]

Circuit Switching Network
Circuit-Switching Networks (CSN) have been the dominant technology for *voice* and most recently for *data* communications. CSN use *dedicated* communications path between stations and dedicated channels over *physical links*. Same common examples include a telephone network, a PBX within an enterprise, private PBXs networks, etc. The analogue CSN is rather *inefficient* due to idle times, on-line access, and low data capacity. However, it provides unnoticeable *transmission delays* and *transparent* networks for the end-users. Developed for voice, it has been used for *data and voice traffic* and gradually has been converted to a *digital network;* see *Figure 40*. The basic circuit-switching operation takes three phases:
   1. *Circuit establishment*, set-up of channel capacity, or communications links.

---

[105] Adapted from William Stallings, R. van Slyke, <u>Business Data Communications</u>, Prentice Hall,1996

2. *Information transmission*, duplex, analogue or digital, for voice and data.

3. *Circuit disconnected* with automatic de-allocation of allocated resources.

Historically, *Space-Division Switching* (SDS) was used to set up and physically switch different signal paths. However, SDS showed undesirable blocking-feature due to physical constraints. It did not allow *any two devices share a switch simultaneously*. The solution was a *single-node network switch* using bus-based digital switch allowing virtual, transparent, full-duplex path between the users; see *Figure 42*.

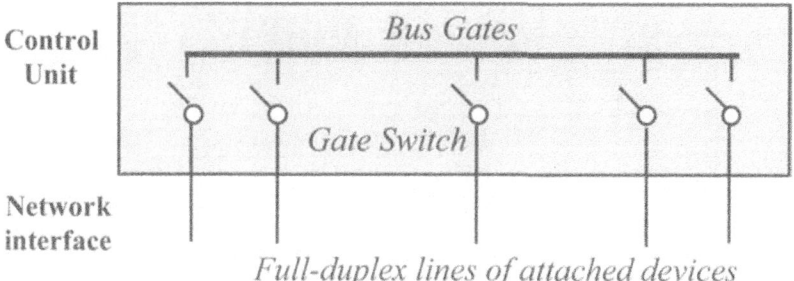

Figure 42. Bus-based Digital Switch [105]

A network interface and a switch control unit using *Time Division Multiplexing* (TDM) was necessary in order to connect devices to the network. An improved *multistage* network of switches allowed more complex control, overcoming the blocking or allowing *possibly blocking* feature. *Time-Division Switching* (TDS) and digital systems have replaced the space switching by applying time division instead. The TDM merges the lower-speed data into higher-speed bit-streams, comparable to streams created by digital images, audio, and video signals. Using pre-assigned *frames per time slots* it provides almost *non-blocking* feature. However, frame allocation on-demand introduces some blocking that needs to be negotiated; see *Figure 43*.

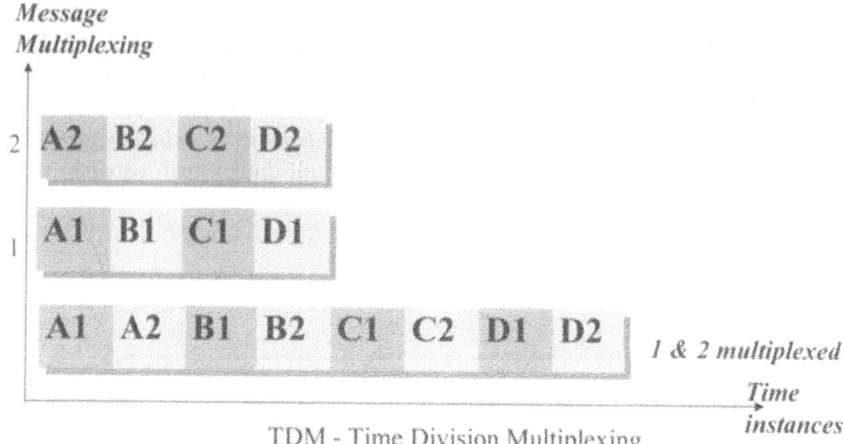

Figure 43. TDM Switching [105]

The circuit switching technology has its own disadvantages. Whether for voice or data calls, once the network resources are allocated to a particular *circuit* it displays few shortcomings:

— *Inefficiency* in case of *idle-line* situation (terminal-to-computer connection).
— Limited data transmission *capability* due to fixed incompatible data transmission features of communication devices. For instance, it only allows transmitting or receiving online at the same data rate using the same communications protocol.

WAN communications: PSN vs. CSN

In order to understand WAN communications it is interesting to compare both types of networks. *Table 16* features the advantages and disadvantages that result from the inherent differences in underlying communication processes of PSN networking types compared to CSN communications. The enterprise seeking global connectivity and moving the operations from conventional voice to *Intranet* or *Extranet* environments is to be aware of these features. The enterprise has to properly evaluate the advantages and disadvantages, and assess business perspectives, especially having in mind the consequences of convergence processes in information technology. The advantages of some alternatives of WAN communications will be discussed later in High Speed Networking: Frame vs. Cell Switching. Likewise, the following topics on Last Mile Alternatives: x*DSL, Wireless, Mobile, Bluetooth, FSO* and Optic-optic Network: Next Generation Internet (NGI) are already setting up and preparing the stage for future super networks.

Table 16. Comparison of WAN Communications Techniques [105]

CSN	Datagram PSN	Virtual-circuit PSN
dedicated path required	no dedicated path	no dedicated path
continuous transmission	packet transmission	packet transmission
interactive operations	interactive operations	interactive operations
no stored messages	packets stored	packets stored
pre-established path	established route	established route
set-up delay	packet delay	set-up & packet delay
no transmission delay	transmission delay	transmission delay
busy/blocking signal	not delivered note	connect denial note
overload blocking	delay due to overload	delay due to overload
scaleable node switches	router node switching	router switching nodes
full user responsibility	network responsibility	network responsibility
no speed/code conversion	speed/code conversion	speed/code conversion
fixed bandwidth	dynamic bandwidth	dynamic bandwidth
no overhead after set-up	packet overhead bits	packet overhead bits

Computer Telephony Integration

As mentioned, the nodes in non-hierarchical CSN architecture frequently apply *peer relationship*. Though flexible, more complex routing is needed in order to perform networking functions. Effective load sharing is also possible since enhanced switches could communicate the traffic status, hence allowing one or more network *management centres* to implement the *protocol,* the same control signalling techniques for its status exchange. As a result of implementation of CSN in enterprises, there is a widespread use of *private PBX network*. It entails subscribers, PBX sub-network, network trunks, and public communication links. Among many services it supports alternate routing, the end-user authorization, charge-back, voice mail messaging, exception reporting, etc. Most recently, the *Computer Telephone Integration* (CTI) represents a prevailing convergence trend of telephony, Extranet, databases, and computing technology. Some new interesting features are messaging, making and receiving calls using graphical GUI help, forwarding and conferencing; e-mail, call and data association, automatic logging for invoicing with call-back; speech synthesis with speech recognition, video-telephony integration, etc. It provides business efficiency and improved customer service, enhances personal and corporate productivity, introduces competitive differentiation via open communications and advanced networking services. Few examples include: *call centres* for customer support, *telebanking, telebusiness*, contact management, *helpdesk*, auto attendants, integrating the task *workflow* with *order-entry* processing, eCach/*SmartCards* transaction support, etc. see *Figure 44*. Among expected benefits certainly is increased productivity, reduced costs, enhanced workflow automation, protected investment in computer and telephony infrastructure, computerized telephony intelligence, improved customer service, etc. More on CTI; see Callegra case presented in Case 14: CallWare's CALLEGRA Advanced Messaging System .

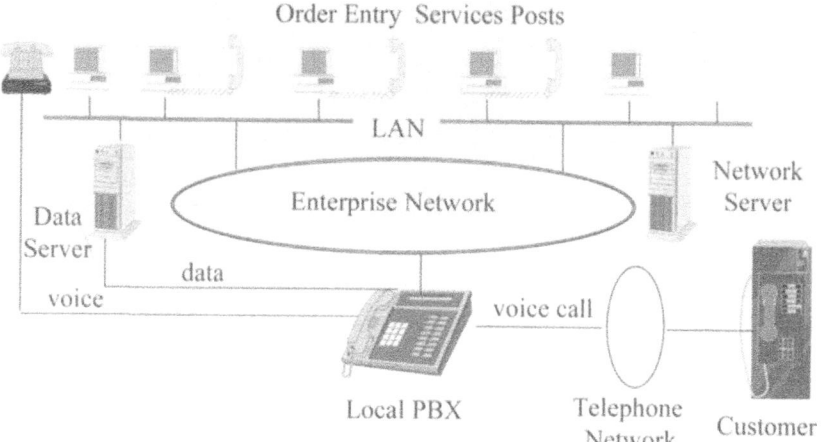

Figure 44. CTI for Order-entry Processing

High Speed Networking: Frame vs. Cell Switching

The ubiquitous wide area networking and advanced communications have changed traditional networking practices. For instance, PSN introduces digital communications at Gbps rates allowing integration of various information media types. New networking paradigms are evolving, providing Java applications on-demand and compelling prices are slashing *Internet Phone* (IP) services[106]. Also, integrated WAN information services allow low priced e-mail, exchange of fax and voice, voice-mail, or *video-on-demand* (VOD). The ISP, a new '*kids around the block'* phenomenon is mushrooming everywhere. However, the IP trend also raises the dilemma whether to separate the increased value added ISP services from bare networking services. Some consider the new challenging IP concept as a move toward pure IP switching by introducing extremely fast but "*stupid*" networks. In contrast, pursuing the sophisticated Intranet trend and similar "*intelligent*" networks[107] requires considerable investment in core network intelligence. In practice, most SMSE and other cautious end-users are suspicious of services that attempt to lock-in customers to large network carriers through so-called intelligent innovations. The communications tariffs and long distance carriers are also under constant pressure due to competitive and compelling flat-rate ISP services. The long distance carriers have recognised the strategic role of ISP by commissioning its services. This allows some ISP to even offer end-users free access to the Net[108]. Frame Relays or *frame switching* and ATM or *cell relays switching* are the two technical innovations enabling these changes. In

---

[106] "ISP evolution extends data service choice", CWI, October, 1998

[107] "Vendors face the transition to an IP world". CWI, October, 1998

[108] "Hybrid ISP scraps subs from business plan", CWI, July 20, 1998

fact, both came out of the ISDN standardization process, streamlining or adapting X.25 protocol for high-speed WAN packet switching.

Frame Relays

In response to high performance demands and in order to provide high-speed frame transmission in WAN packet switching networks, *Frame Relays* (FR) have introduced several small but significant modifications to the X.25 protocol. They have mainly affected the packet control signalling, by reducing the number of communications layers and simplifying the flow and error control. More reliable and higher quality of sophisticated digital technology has facilitated and enabled these changes. Streamlined HDLC frame data-link protocol for Frame Relays, as presented in *Figure 45*, makes FR several orders of magnitude faster and cheaper than the conventional X.25 protocol.

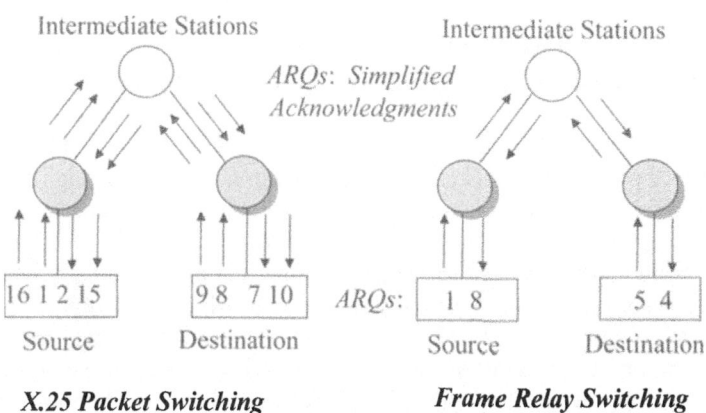

X.25 Packet Switching   *Frame Relay Switching*

Figure 45. Frame Relays vs. X.25 Packet Switching

Frame Relays protocol has considerably reduced the number of hops required for packet transmission, therefore requiring frame acknowledgments only by end-stations rather than from each and every intermediate station. It resulted in very efficient streamlining and simplification not only in the virtual circuit call management but also in the flow and error control of the X.25 protocol. It also enabled much higher PSN data transmission rate close to A1/T1 level. Due to the streamlining of the X.25 protocol by taking out its networking layer, has resulted in Frame Relays lacking the usual end-to-end flow and error control. However, it does not mean any serious disadvantage since, it has been already supported by upper OSI communications protocol levels, usually via particular application or networking service.

The advantage of Frame Relays over conventional X.25 packet switching is mainly in more efficient streamlined packet switching process and simplified overall functionality. This has resulted in reduced network interface time, lower delays, and enabled higher throughput. In fact, the results achieved are much higher WAN transmission rate and for the first time approaching that of LAN networks, please see *Table 17*. Among worldwide providers that support global, comprehensive, frame relay services with competitive pricing schemes of up to T1/A1 data rate are AT&T, BT, MCI, or ACT. For more, please refer to the Case *15:* ACTnet Frame Relays Media Integration and Global Access.

Table 17 Frame Relays vs. ATM

FR	ATM
mainly data also voice compatible	voice or data compatible
common with LAN data traffic	backbone LAN switches
missing error and flow control	simple routing/control
economy of scale for voice & data	virtual path multiplexing
subject to blocking & compatibility	appears non-blocking
call set-up delay	fibre optic preferably
not for short transactions	most efficient utilisation

Asynchronous Transfer Mode - ATM

The *Intranet* but especially the *Extranet* with widespread multimedia information services has placed enormous demand on wide area networks for higher networking throughput, *wider bandwidth,* and *higher data rates*. Following the convergence process of WAN toward LAN, and in fact achieving high data rates along with full symmetrical communications, the quest for Gbps-data-rate WAN is the driving force behind the promotion of the *Asynchronous Transfer Mode* (ATM) technology. We have seen that it is possible to substantially overcome X.25 overhead and promote Frame Relays beyond 2 Mbps networking access.

The ATM technology goes beyond it and well into Gbps-data-rate range. Similarly to previous enhancements for Frame Relays, the ATM has introduced even further improvements to the X.25 ISDN protocol. The ATM however, took slightly different approach. The ATM is implementing fast switching of information data flow with fixed length data packets over a set of logical/virtual connection circuits. The 53 Bytes long packet consists of 48 Bytes payload and 5 Bytes virtual switching address. The fixed-size packets, called *cells,* are found appropriate both for data and for digital multimedia traffic. It allows very fast cell *switching*, if fact, implementing Gbps data broadcasting through ATM virtual network channels; see *Figure 46.*

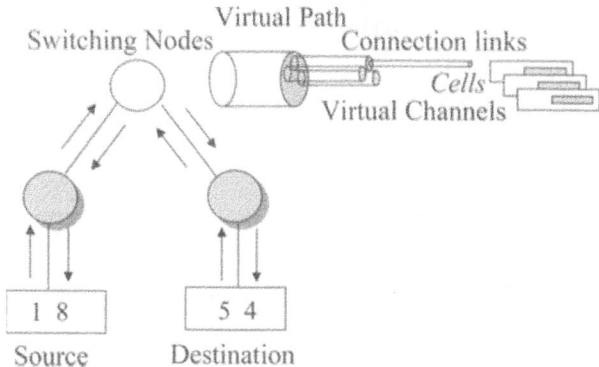

Figure 46. Frame Relays vs. ATM Cell Switching

Frame vs. ATM Cell Switching

ATM is packet-oriented communications that permits multiplexing, multiple, logical-connections over single physical interfaces. Similar to Frame Relays networking, the ATM error and flow control assumes to be provided by higher networking protocols; see *Figure 46*. Unlike Frame Relay, the rich ATM hierarchy is based on *virtual channel* and *virtual path* levels. The basic switching unit is logical connection known as the *virtual channel*. It is similar to X.25 virtual circuit or a logical connection in Frame Relays. The virtual path however, corresponds to a bundle of virtual channels having common source and destination points. In fact, separating *individual* logical connections (virtual channels) from a *group* of logical connections has resulted in simplified network architecture, enhancing network services, and significantly reducing the setup time for connection processing due to virtual paths; see *Figure 46*.

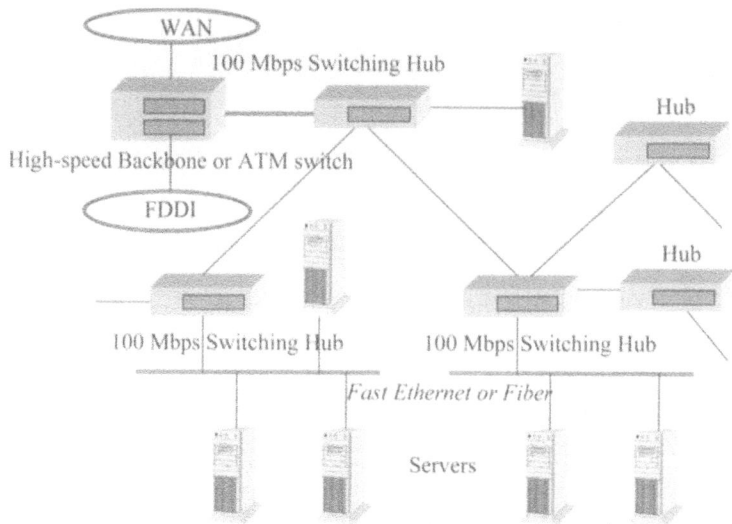

Figure 47. Networking Hierarchy

The ATM, or *cell-relays*, implements asynchronous transfer mode using fixed-size data cells. It also provides corporate customers more efficient short packet switching and option to set up either *Permanent* or *Switched Virtual Circuits* (SVC). Unlike PVC, SVC reduces queuing delays achieving flexible network platforms for mixed voice and data traffic, which can accommodate very high transmission rates and offer a dynamic bandwidth access[109]. The virtual path and virtual channel identifier may change during the transmission of the cells through the network; see *Figure 46.* Acting as routing data only, it is used locally by the network node routing. Usually, an 8-bit *Header Error Check* (HEC) control code is associated to any 32-bit header for single-bit error correction in the headers and double-bit header error detection. HEC error protection mechanism suits best in voice-based communications media considered to be prone to a combination of single-bit header errors and rare occurrence of large-bit burst errors.

Optic-optic Network: Next Generation Internet (NGI)

Most recently, the <u>NGI</u> trend is to integrate as much as possible communications traffic. All-fibre rings have been developed for voice traffic, which need not to connect every city to every other city. Signals travel around the ring until reaching the destination. By sending signals in other direction it makes possible for an alternative connection path and backup in case of disconnected loops. However, the drawbacks are that the ring has to have the same high bandwidth all around even though it may not be necessary for some slower rural networks. In order to reach the end-user switch the optic signal has to be converted into

---

[109] "Deutsche Telecom lunches flexible ATM service", CWI, November 2, 1998

electrical signal and back into light at every network node and/or ring junctures; see *Figure 48*.

The introduction of data traffic mainly through frame and cell relays has rendered the all-fibre rings obsolete as the networking core. A proposed solution is to introduce partial mesh. It makes only major connections necessary with multiple options so that the networking software can choose its own path by traversing the mesh and finding the alternative routes. Both market leaders Cisco and Nortel[110] have agreed on the fibre mesh technology providing a bit different solutions for implementation of its mesh structures.

Nortel is developing 1,000 x 1,000 *all-optical cross-connects* based on the Xros. Inc. micro-machine mirrors technology. Cisco on the other hand, relies on its *hybrid ring/mesh network* based on the wavelength router technology from Monterey Networks Inc. acquired recently. Both cross-connect and wavelength routers are expected to be used primarily in long-haul communications.

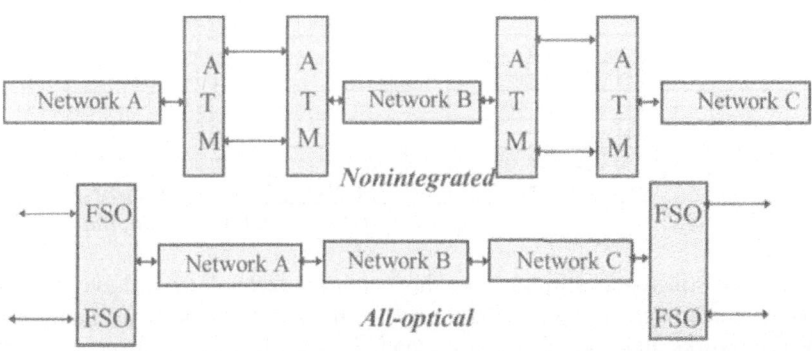

Figure 48. All optical integrated network routing

*Last Mile Alternatives: x*DSL, Wireless, Mobile, Bluetooth, FSO

Presently, there are few new high data-rate communications alternatives. Aside application field differences, all are based on the fundamental modulation techniques: *Quadrature Amplitude Modulation* (QAM), similar to *Carrierless Amplitude Phase* (CAM), and *Discrete MultiTone Modulation* (DMT). In CAM, the amplitude and phase changes are modulated onto a suppressed carrier signal (carries no information load). Less susceptible to noise or interference, DMT breaks down the information payload into 256 discrete frequency sub-channels based upon their ability to carry the specific signal transmission. Several emerging DSL schemes are competing with variable success as a WAN protocol of the best choice. The main differences are due to the trade-off between the signal speed and local loop distances. It also includes user *acceptability* (existing

---

[110] Cisco, Nortel Battle For Switching Core, Craig Matsumoto and Loring Wirbel, EE Times, Sep 1, 2000

standards), the best suited network *applications* e.g. HDTV - *High Definition TV,* the *performance* criteria, e.g. maximum rate, maximum distance over *Unshielded Twisted Pair* (UTP), and the availability of *symmetrical* (duplex) mode. The features of high-speed DSL protocol alternatives needed for local-loop support to ISDN/B-ISDN, FR, and ATM in global high-speed networking are presented in *Table 18.* For more; see Case 16: NetSpeed Copper-based High-speed WAN Link via ADSL . The following are the *last mile* technology alternatives [111]:

- High bit-rate Digital Subscriber Line (HDSL) is the most mature
- Asymmetric/Rate-Adaptive Digital Subscriber Line (R/ADSL) is operational
- Single-pair Digital Subscriber Line (SDSL) is suitable for video conferencing
- Very-high bit-rate Digital Subscriber Line (VDSL) delivers the fastest data rate
- ISDN-based DSL Web-access (IDSL) uses 144Kbps rather than 128Kbps
- Recent broadband choices include Bluetooth and Free Space Optics (FSO).

Table 18. Review of the '*Last Mile*' Communications [112]

xDSL Technology	Max Rate (Mbps) Download & upload		Max UTP Length (km)	Best for enterprise Applications
ADSL R-ADSL	1.5 - 8	.064 - 1.5	6 @ ≤2 Mbps 4 @ >2 Mbps	LAN, Intra/Internet, VoIP, VPN, VOD
VDSL	13 - 52	1.5 - 2.3	0.33 to 1.5	HDTV, Multimedia
HDSL	1.5T1 (2E1) duplex		4 to 5	LAN, PBX, F/Relay
SDSL	1.5T1 (2E1) duplex		3.33	LAN, PBX, F/Relay
IDSL	0.144 duplex		6	Internet access, VoIP
Bluetooth	1.0 to 10 duplex		0.05 to 0.3	Internet access, LAN
FSO	100 to 1250 duplex		10 to 25 (optic)	HDTV, WLAN, MAN

Adapted from DataComm International [112]

However, it still remains to see how this emerging technology will evolve and whether it can overcome present convergence problems, connectivity issues for global networks and become a viable standard that integrates high-speed WAN to LAN services.

To date, TeraBeam[113] and Conversant[114] offer highly competitive local-loop high speed alternatives using Free-Space Optic (FSO) *laser and fibre* technology[115]. The FSO provides an affordable Wireless LAN (WLAN) solution. FSO also enables simple LAN to WAN/MAN wireless connectivity commonly supporting data rates from 1.25 up to 160 Gbps using simple rooftop-mounted, line-of-sight laser transceivers. For more on TeraBeam Optical Wireless Networks (TOWN) technology please see Forbes' article[116] "Sleepless in Seattle".

---

[111] 3Com, March 1998, http://www.3com.com/technology/tech_net/white_papers/500624.html#Different

[112] DataComm International, 3/1997, p. 103

[113] http://www.terabeam.com/our/index.shtml

[114] http://www.conversant.com

[115] http://www.nwfusion.com/news/tech/2002/0722tech.html

[116] http://www.forbes.com/forbes/00/0501/6510148a.htm

On the mobile communications front there are significant changes too. Even though US has set the stage for the Internet, Europe and Asia are still leading the way in wireless and mobile domain. Due to their individual differences in mobile communications, whereby US uses primarily CDMA[117], while Europe and Asia use *Global System for Mobile* (GSM) Communications moving fast towards new 3G variants such as GPRS. It has enabled many *Short Message Service* (SMS), *Wide Area Protocol* (WAP) and Bluetooth[118] solutions to expand across the Web.

Bluetooth is a new technology standard for wide range of wireless devices to communicate with each other. The *Bluetooth Wireless Personal Area Network* (WPAN) falls under IEEE 802.15 allowing few Mbps communication bandwidth with minimal user involvement using short-range radio links. It is meant to replace cable connecting portables and fixed electronic devices. Its key features are robustness, low complexity, low power, and low cost. Bluetooth also offers wireless access to LAN, PSTN, mobile phone network, and Internet for a host of thin clients, home appliances, devices, and portable handheld interfaces.

Case 16: NetSpeed Copper-based High-speed WAN Link via ADSL

NETSPEED (AUSTIN, TEXAS) SPEEDRUNNER 100 ROUTER
http://www.netspeed.com/sr202.html
(Reprinted by permission of the Cisco Systems)
Netspeed's product, the *Speedrunner 100 router*, provides a corporate LAN link to the ADSL net via an Ethernet port and one RJ-11 ADSL jack that forwards downstream data at 2 Mbps for $1.295.

The *Speedrunner 300 inverse mux* has also an Ethernet or fast Ethernet port and three RJ-11 ADSL jacks providing adjustable transmission rate according to the length and quality of the phone line, for $8,995.

The *PCIrunner adapter cards* are slotted into remote PCs and come in both CAP or DMT versions together with drivers for Windows 95, Windows NT, and NetWare for $595 apiece. At $15 to $170 per month rent for a twisted-pair without voice channels running ADSL (up to 1 Mbps upstream and 8 Mbps downstream traffic) over copper lines is an alternative that provides much faster Internet connection and is much cheaper: compare $200-$400 per month for T1/A1 (1.544/2.044 Mbps) with at least $70-$150 per month for bare 0.128 Mbps ISDN BRI (Basic-Rate Interface).

Bibliography

Broadcom foresees mitosis of LAN/WAN business; *Bruce Gain*; **Electronic Buyers' News**, Manhasset; Dec 4, 2000; pg. PG.8

Services Hit The Accelerator -- Carriers prep IP, DSL services to speed enterprise access to the WAN; *Chuck Moozakis*; **InternetWeek**, Manhasset; Feb 1, 1999; pg. PG.6

Enterprise WAN equipment; *Andrew Cray*; **Data Communications**, New York; Jan 1999; Vol. 28, Iss. 1; pg. 54, 3 pgs

FMI Bolsters LAN/WAN Thrust With Key ASIC Design Win -- Develops Complex Chips For Foundry Networks; **EBN**, Manhasset; Jan 29, 2001; pg. PG.30

---

[117] Jennifer Gilbert – Crain Communications Inc., March 2000, http://www.adage.com

[118] http://www.intel.com/network/connectivity/products/wireless.htm

Network Infrastructure -- Cache And Carry -- Network Appliance's NetCache might be the best tool for improving end-user response time and decreasing WAN bandwidth; *Alan Zeichick*; **InternetWeek**, Manhasset; Oct 9, 2000; pg. PG.41

Network Infrastructure -- The Intelligent Edge -- QoSWorks 7000 allows IT managers to reallocate expensive WAN bandwidth; *Keith Schultz*; **InternetWeek**, Manhasset; Aug 14, 2000; pg. PG.49

Virtual private networks simplify communications; **Control Engineering** *Matt Bellm*; Apr 1998

WAN vendors collaborate to guarantee service; **InfoWorld** *Stephen Lawson*; Dec 21, 1998

Bottlenecks In LAN, WAN; **InternetWeek** *Salvatore Salamone*; Dec 21, 1998

Meet the invisible WAN; **Communications News** *John Mazzaferro*; Dec 1998

WAN vendors team to speed service advances; **Network World** *Jim Duffy*; Nov 30, 1998

Network too slow? Not all applications work well over a WAN; **InfoWorld** *Laura Wonnacott*; Nov 16, 1998

Choices multiply for converging ATM and IP in the WAN; **Business Communications Review** *David Passmore*; Nov 1998

Richter Systems builds own Internet-based WAN; **Network Computing** *Kelly Jackson Higgins*; Nov 1, 1998

LAN, WAN Views Merge In Network 'Swiss Army Knife'; **InternetWeek** *Tim Wilson*; Oct 26, 1998

NetReality WiseWan: WAN management meets WAN control; **Network Computing** *David Willis*; Oct 15, 1998

Fast Copper, Faster WAN Ports On Tap; **InternetWeek** *John Fontana*; Oct 12, 1998

Rules of the WAN; **Network World** *Gail R James*; Oct 12, 1998

Cisco Powers Into WAN; **InternetWeek** Oct 5, 1998

Cisco WAN switch blends data, voice and video; **Network World** *Jim Duffy*; Oct 5, 1998

Performance analysis of cell discarding techniques for best effort video communications over ATM networks; **Computer Networks and ISDN Systems** *Mehaoua, Ahmed*; Feb 1998

Communications networks in the U.S. and EU (European Union); **Managing Office Technology** *Anonymous*; Sep 1997

CHAPTER 11

LOCAL AREA NETWORKS

Convergence Issues

Case 17: Tarantella Web-Enabling Software

Tarantella is software that provides centralized deployment and management of server-based applications. It is designed for IT Professionals who need to provide users with instant access to applications and services. The standards-based Tarantella technology provides application access that can be custom-built to meet your needs.

Users can easily access their applications from Java™ technology enabled client devices, without the need for additional software to be installed on those devices. This approach drastically reduces the time to deliver applications, allows the applications to reach more users, increases manageability and moves the management of users and applications back to centrally located servers.

Tarantella uses an innovative, three-tier architecture that integrates diverse application servers and diverse types of client with little or no disruption to the existing environment. Applications continue to run on existing servers, and many existing clients, such as PCs, UNIX workstations, and Net work Computers, can all be used.

The Tarantella server acts a type of middleware storing information centrally about users and their associated applications. When a user connects to the Tarantella server, a WebTop (a dynamically created web page that is unique to each user) is delivered to the user. Users can access all the applications and data on the network through this WebTop with Tarantella managing all the connections, sessions and security.

Tarantella provides the option to use 'native' clients: software that does not require a Java Virtual Machine on the client, or a Java technology enabled browser. The Tarantella Native Client provides an application 'launchpad' interface that is consistent with the WebTop.

In contrast to public or sometimes mixed ownership WAN infrastructure, a *Local Area Network* (LAN) is usually owned by a single enterprise, the one that is actually using the network for its business purposes. Commonly, a LAN is designed to carryout much greater communications load and greater information bandwidth, often beyond 4-10 Mbps data rate (e.g. 10/100 Mbps is common Fast Ethernet data-rate.). In fact, it is to provide networking infrastructure for common data processing, data packet routing, and switching as in case of ATM switching hubs, digital data switching boards in CSN, and to support *plain old telephone* (POT) and digital voice communications used by the PBX. Naturally, LAN design is often influenced by rapid changes in IT and ubiquitous application of modern digital technology. As mentioned earlier in Computer Telephony Integration topics, the convergence trends of IT currently play important role in the choice of suitable enterprise LAN.

Prior to introduction of *Intranet* technology in enterprises, we should state few important differences between LAN and WAN:

- LAN has *smaller scope* since confined to a single building or a cluster of buildings in business, government, or university campus
- LAN is *owned by the same organisation* that makes use of it
- LAN *infrastructure* requires substantial *capital investment*, not only for equipment but also for upgrade, maintenance and support, and procurement of software
- LAN internal *transmission data rates* by default are much higher than in WAN. There are two distinct communications technology types applied in LAN
- *Circuit Switching* uses digital PBX mainly for voice but also for data switching.
- *Packet Switching* uses LAN broadcasting mainly for data frames but also for voice.

Historically, usual LAN transmission media were *multidrop or multiplexed lines.* Today, primarily shared *bus* or switched *peer-to-peer* lines are used for LAN communications.

The scope of LAN applications remains broad. Usually, LAN applications perform *data processing* (entry-order systems), *transaction processing* (point-of-sale, or database applications), *file and print services, remote batch processing, MIS, office automation services, CAD/CAM applications and CIM process control* in factory automation, *energy management services, multimedia and teleconferencing, electronic library and publishing services, back-plane server communications,* etc.

The ubiquitous penetration of LAN into enterprises and recently in individual homes is due to the appealing benefits of office automation, enterprise integration, and sharing of network ownership costs. The evolving technology along with constant and favourable price/performance trends in digital technology provide adequate support for common business needs. Moreover, the prevailing standardization of network interfaces provides additional flexibility, accessibility, safety, and network reliability.

However, even simple as it may look, LAN wiring is considered to be common cause of problems mainly due to missing or wrong implementation of existing standards, both hardware and software. *Thin-Ethernet* LAN is based on copper, *shielded* or *unshielded twisted pair* (UTP), 10/100 Base-T4, category #3-5 cable. It is the most common wiring solution that has replaced the traditional *multidrop terminal line*. Equally good in ordinary use is the *coaxial cable* 10 Base-TX. In most demanding multimedia cases, the *fibre optic* 100 Base-FX or higher proves to be indispensable.

Prior to the introduction of Internet technology in enterprise Intranets, LAN-based computer networking has been regarded as the only enterprise-networking alternative that provides flexible and cost/performance effective solution. The reason is that the LAN design relies just on few simple decisions:

− LAN network *topology* considers *bus* vs. *ring* solutions
− LAN communications *medium* options: twisted pair, coaxial, or fibre optic cable
− LAN network *layout* alternative is *linear* vs. *star* layout
− LAN *medium access control* option is CSMA/CD vs. *token-based* sensing.

LAN Topology: Bus vs. Ring

The ring network implements message broadcasting through close-loop device arrangements in a *ring*. High-speed communications ring represents a shareable sequential cable connection of either physical or logical neighbouring stations that allows exchange of payload data packets and a control data *token*. The user stations are connected to the ring through digital signal repeaters, which at any time could assume only one of the three states: *listen, transmit,* or *bypass* broadcast messages.

The *bus* and *tree* networks are implemented by *bus* segments as common, shareable, parallel communications media. In principle, a device attachment is irrespective of the physical or logical arrangement. However, depending on the functionality and/or performances of the attached devices, some preferential bus-access schemas are easily implemented and a specific priority established. The direct attachment to the bus/tree and *media access control* for data transmission is under the protocol control. The increased signal attenuation or segment communications misbalance may limit the network size.

LAN Media: Twisted Pair, Coax, Fibre

Besides wireless LAN, there are but few cabling alternatives for LAN implementation: *twisted pair* (shielded or unshielded), *coaxial* cable, and *optic fibre*. Copper media may apply either *baseband* signalling, i.e. occupying a single frequency band for digital pulses, or *broadband* signalling, i.e. sharing the available frequency spectrum among multiplexed analogue signals − communication *channels*.

Since the digital *baseband* signalling (e.g. differential Manchester) occupies the entire bandwidth in both bus directions, all but a *single repeater* is allowed for distances not greater than few kilometres. The cost/performance features are in favour of digital technology, not only because of lower initial investments, but also due to the lower maintenance and more mature knowledge infrastructure and support; see *Table 19*.

In contrast, the broadband analogue signalling provides multichannel bands with high bandwidth capability, due to well-developed frequency multiplexing technology. The unidirectional transmission allows both bus and tree topologies. It requires either dual cable or split frequency bus-terminators. If the main applications are in video or in audio domain, it is possible to apply ordinary signal amplification, therefore extending the bus or the tree network to greater distances of up to few tens kilometres. If necessary, it is possible to implement broadband signalling by complex tree topology applying two different approaches: *dual* cable, or *split* frequencies. A single cable split frequency configuration is cheaper, however the dual cable alternative has twice the capacity and does not require *frequency translation* at bus termination points.

Since, LAN performance is constantly maturing, not only the ring topology is improving (considered to be superior to a similar bus/tree topology), but also the bus-based LAN. Advanced *FastEthernet* networking technology, *EtherExpress* from Intel, provides high signal fidelity, lower distortions, full control over attenuation, thus extending the bandwidth from 10 to 100 Mbps using ordinary UTP cables. Despite its simplicity, 10 Mbps coaxial cables are lagging behind.

Table 19. LAN Topology vs. Transmission Media

Media/Topology Bandwidth (Mbps)	Ring	Star	Bus	Tree	Dual Bus
Twisted pair	4 - 16	4 -100	1 - 10		4 - 16
Baseband coax	16	70	50		
Broadband coax			1 - 10	1 - 10	45
Fibre optic	100	10 - 20	45		100

LAN Layout: Linear vs. Star

LAN layout design of local networks takes *linear paths* to form either a bus or a ring so that neighbouring stations are consecutively attached to a copper or an optic fibre cable through a local loop. Most recently, the IEEE 802.11 *wireless* LAN standard offers a flexible layout and some limited mobility; see WLAN Alliance. Alternatively, it is also possible that any station has its individual loop connected to a central switching hub. This arrangement makes a *star network* layout, which sometimes is considered as a point or a very short-length bus. Any optimisation of networking costs for a network design has to take into account minimal cabling costs, cable plant labour costs, flexibility for future upgrade, and maintenance costs. If cabling costs are of prime importance, the linear layout gives the most favourable solution since it provides minimal cabling length. Although twisted pair is cheaper than coaxial, and the coaxial cable (either thin or thick) is cheaper than the optic fibre cable still, not all solutions apply equally well or meet other LAN communications requirements. Sometimes, even smaller cabling costs could not compensate the uncertain and higher labour costs. Laying down the networking cable plant may often end up being more expensive than anticipated.

Moreover, in response to frequent relocation of stations and in anticipation of future growth changes, the cable plant still has to reach to every office in the building. Still, the cable plant maintenance, modification, and servicing will be facilitated provided the *star* layout is implemented at the expense of some larger cable length. It is very much similar to adding a conventional local loop for usual phone connections. Similarly, there are many issues that may go in favour of optic fibre cables such as: the highest bandwidth available, exceptional reliability, the highest security and almost impossible tapping due to non electric nature of signal transmission and lack of signal interference. Unlike traditional copper-based communications, the optic fibre is quite different. The advanced sophisticated fibre technology requires special equipment, often, different tools and practices, and unconventional know-how for everyday network operations.

Besides high cabling costs, eventual networking improvement has to take into account many other issues concerning network performance, expandability and future growth, system availability, flexibility to local environmental change, security, reliability, accessibility for servicing, maintenance and support knowledge, etc.

Medium Access Control: CSMA/CD vs. Token Sensing

Among common techniques that provide access to various communications media is the *Media Access Control* (MAC) allowing access to shared LAN media:

- CSMA/CD for bus and tree topologies (e.g. Ethernet, *FastEthernet*)
- Token bus and ring (e.g. bus or tree, and ring topologies in particular).

The usual implementation of LAN communications assumes that the common enterprise LAN environment is confined to an office building or cluster of buildings. However, LAN can also be used in a harsh factory environment connecting number of robot devices in an assembly plant. It is also possible to extend the LAN using gateways, bridges, routers, and switching devices such as ATM switches, and switching hubs. They represent the building blocks of enterprise networks, necessary to extend the LAN in high rise buildings, university campuses, government complexes, factories, warehouses, stations, ports, department stores, hospitals, metropolitan networks, etc.

CSMA/CD - *Carrier Sense Multiple Access with Collision Detection* protocol, or better known as the *Ethernet*, was jointly developed by Xerox, DEC and Intel. It constantly senses the carrier as the signal transmission is in progress. A similar road-traffic analogy may well be a *highway on-ramp* traffic protocol. The arriving cars are waiting to enter the highway at random. Constantly watching (*sensing*) the highway traffic conditions in order to prevent eventual collision, the cars enter the highway using the closest entry lane (*transmission*) provided the traffic is idle or the traffic conditions allow safe entry. Similarly, under heavy traffic conditions the network performance might suffer due to the random access behaviour and uncertain response times that is closely contingent on unpredictable and often stochastic network traffic density.

LAN *token bus* developed by IBM applies to bus or tree LAN stations organized into a *logical ring*. The analogy for LAN token bus MAC protocol resembles a *relay running race*. The runners form a circular ordering arrangement waiting for the *relay transfer* that allows them to start running at the first touch. A control item, a *token,* regulates individual access rights. Any runner (e.g. station) is allowed to run (e.g. to transmit, to respond to any polls, initialisation, maintenance, or recovery) provided it has got hold of the token. Due to circular arrangement (*logical* or *physical*), the token bus behaviour is fairly deterministic, quite different from the Ethernet behaviour. It takes at most a cycle to deliver a message and eventually release the token, therefore allowing other stations to seize control of the token bus and continue to communicate.

LAN *token ring* is simpler variation of the token bus. In fact, the end-user stations are organized into a circular *physical ring*. The analogy of its behaviour is very similar to a *luggage claim carousel* often seen at airports. It takes a cycle for the luggage claim ring to deliver any packet to any waiting passengers. Therefore, seizing the control packet – the *token,* enables any station to take control over the ring. According to the protocol, the station may change the token bits, replacing them with its own code when transmitting the message through the ring. Once the message packet has completed a round trip, the transmitting station purges it off the ring and restores back the token bits, essentially releasing the control over the ring. Once the token is back in the ring, it allows anyone else to carry on the communication. The average waiting time is less than half a cycle.

Fibre Distributed Data Interface: FDDI

Fast LAN networks allowing Gbps-bandwidth are often required for high-speed office, multimedia and video libraries, or graphic and publishing applications. Still, the main use of FDDI-based LAN remains the *extended* LAN. High-rise building enterprises rely on FDDI communications for implementation of *down links, back-panel* computer room necessary to connect *CPU clusters* in *NUMA* server architectures, or providing *main-to-main* computer bus links. Most of these *backbone* LAN solutions actually expand the LAN concept into the *extended LAN* confined to the local site and extending its high processing capabilities. In fact, using the optic fibre technology, or most recently the fixed wireless GSM, it is possible to extend LAN to distances beyond ten kilometres.

IEEE 802 Suit of LAN Standards

The IEEE 802 suit of LAN standards was developed jointly by the IEEE Committee and the ANSI and subsequently adopted as international standards by ISO; see *Table 20*. Responding to the growing user's interest in LAN, the IEEE 802 standard is gaining widespread and rapid acceptance by vendors. IEEE 802 standards are organized into a *three-layer protocol hierarchy*. First comes the

Logical Link Control (LLC) layer that is responsible for packet addressing and data link control. Then comes the *Media Access Control* (MAC) layer taking the responsibility for medium access. Finally, the *physical layer* is responsible for variety of physical interfaces.

Table 20. Review of LAN Standards

LLC layer	802.2: Acknowledged or unacknowledged connectionless, or connection mode				
IEEE	802.3	802.4	802.5	802.6	FDDI
MAC	CSMA/CD	Token bus	Token ring	Dual bus	Fibre
Mbps	10/100	10/20	4/16	45/100	100/200
Topology	Bus/star/tree	Bus/star/tree	Ring	Bus/tree	Ring

Private Branch Exchange (PBX) LAN Alternative

Parallel to the development of LAN technology for data processing was the evolution of digital PBX, mainly for voice that recently introduced some fax and data processing too. PBX LAN uses mainly digital switching and traditional telephone exchange systems.

Applying conventional a*nalogue* and more recently the contemporary *digital technology,* it seems to offer competitively almost similar communications services as LAN networks:

– *Analogue* PBX handles *voice directly* and makes use of *modems* for *data*
– *Digital* PBX handles *data directly* and uses *codecs* (coders/decoders) for *voice*.

The advanced digital PBX services are becoming predominantly *application oriented.* PBX is gaining attractiveness by common users and becomes strategically important for high-tech enterprises due to the convergence trends of computing and communications, for instance, offered through *Digital Subscriber Line* (xDSL). For more, please check Last Mile Alternatives: *xDSL, Wireless, Mobile, Bluetooth, FSO,* and CTI elaborated in Computer Telephony Integration.

Broadband Wireless

Moreover, the new *broadband wireless* communications has the potential to introduce significant widespread changes to communications industry and enterprise-wide users. It is especially true for users hooked in by VOD offers on the Internet entertainment market. The broadband wireless, in particular the *Multichannel Multipoint Distribution Systems* (MMDS), the *Local Multipoint Distribution Service* (LMDS), and the *Microwave Video Distribution System* (MVDS) provide cheaper networking access and are faster to implement. The MMDS operates at low microwave frequencies, at around 2.5 GHz, covering the range of some 40-50 km. The LMDS is operating at 28 GHz and provides asymmetric high capacity transmission of 1.5 Gbps downstream and up to 200 Mbps upstream traffic. The MVDS provides high capacity operating at 40 GHz, but with somewhat limited range of about 2 km.

The *mobile* telephony, *portable* computing, *wireless networking,* and *multimedia* contribute very much to the revival of digital PBX and its remote alternative,

Centrex PBX networks. Centrex networks offered by local telephone service providers provide all PBX services remotely. Centrex follows as a consequence of convergence of digital PBX and LAN technology. Essentially, LAN contribution is to provide much higher bandwidth and data-processing rate irrespective of the media types applied. However, PBX contribution comes as apparent leverage of *voice-related* applications, for instance *voice mail* and *teleconferencing*. It provides increased flexibility across applications, integration support, user-friendly access, and most importantly - the *customer satisfaction*.

Digital PBX vs. LAN: Convergence Issues

The following *Table 21* clearly shows what are the features of current convergence processes and relationship that exists between digital PBX and LAN technology in enterprises. The few features examined, like connectivity, availability, and reliability emphasize the differences that endure presently, or will eventually continue to influence the technological convergence processes. For instance, the growing number of customer call-centres and CRM helpdesks is evident success of CTI achieved through integration of media types, voice and data, text and e-mail, image and fax, and teleconferencing. Still, it is just the first step toward global convergence process and full acceptance.

The media-type issue still remains the predominant digital technology choice, addressing the richness of services that are available to users. We acknowledge that available data bandwidth represents significant communications constraint playing an important role in multimedia processing, voice on demand, and teleconferencing. Hence, the future of network growth depends upon the feasibility of future upgrade and our response to the demands for technology change. From users point of view, they look mainly on the reliability and availability of application that are most appropriate for the task.

However, it is the enterprise infrastructure investment that looks upon current spending as the necessary conditions in order to achieve basic connectivity and networking for core business processes. In fact, a reliable network depends very much on the installed infrastructure needed to provide high availability of services to the users.

Table 21. Digital PBX vs. LAN Convergence

Features/Networks	Digital PBX	LAN
Infrastructure TCO	Existing, upgrade related	Redundant, initially high
Reliability	High redundancy	Secure, highly redundant
Data types	Superior voice services	Superior data processing
Bandwidth	Mbps range	Gbps range
Future growth	Performance/cost effective	Optimal, global scope
Applications	Office, business oriented	Office, enterprise wide

Bibliography

FMI Bolsters LAN/WAN Thrust With Key ASIC Design Win -- Develops Complex Chips For Foundry Networks; **EBN**, Manhasset; Jan 29, 2001; pg. PG.30

Business: A LAN line; *Anonymous*; **The Economist**, London; Jan 13, 2001; Vol. 358, Iss. 8204; pg. 59, 2 pgs

Network Management Software -- Watch Your Web -- These four LAN applications monitor, measure Web servers; *Alan Zeichick*; **InternetWeek**, Manhasset; Dec 11, 2000; pg. PG.37

LAN switches gear up for Web explosion; *Morris Edwards*; **Communications News**, Nokomis; Dec 2000; Vol. 37, Iss. 12; pg. 90, 2 pgs

Wireless Lans -- Cut The Cord -- It's been a long time coming, but IT managers are finally ready for enterprise wireless networks; *Terry Sweeney*; **InternetWeek**, Manhasset; Nov 13, 2000; pg. PG.75

Wireless LANs work their magic; *Joel Conover*; **Network Computing**, Manhasset; Jul 10, 2000; Vol. 11, Iss. 13; pg. 69, 3 pgs

Remote Access -- Lan On The Cheap -- You can make the most of your LAN with cheap connection sharing, a firewall, and e-mail, Web and DHCP servers; *Rebecca Rohan*; **InternetWeek**, Manhasset; Apr 3, 2000; pg. PG.50

Taco Cabana's CIO chose to work LAN, WAN, not the land; *Alan Liddle*; **Nation's Restaurant News**, New York; Sep 20, 1999; Vol. 33, Iss. 38; pg. 50, 1 pgs

Small businesses: The big spenders on LAN hardware; *Warren S Hersch*; **Computer Reseller News**, Manhasset; Jul 12, 1999, Iss. 850; pg. 79, 1 pgs

LAN telephony matures, but benefits remain elusive; **Computerworld** *Bob Wallace*; Dec 14, 1998

Working the land--and the LAN; **InformationWeek** *Stuart J Johnston*; Dec 7, 1998

Wireless LAN: Emerging to maturing technology; **Health Management Technology** *Mary Carmen Cupito*; Dec 1998

A new look at LAN plumbing; **Telecommunications** *Terri L Dixon*; Dec 1998

Local Metropolitan Area Networks; **Telecommunications** *Doug Allen*; Dec 1998

Wi-LAN gets green light in U.K.; **Computer Dealer News** *Anonymous*; Nov 30, 1998

Baseband processor implements upcoming wireless LAN spec; **Electronic Engineering Times** *Anonymous*; Nov 30, 1998

Harris offers device for wireless LANs; **Electronic Buyers' News** *Darrell Dunn*; Nov 23, 1998

This LAN works on the slopes; **Computerworld** *Matt Hamblen*; Nov 16, 1998

Freeing the LAN from backup traffic; **Network World** *Robin Purohit*; Nov 16, 1998

WideBand--the multi-band LAN; **Computer Technology Review** *Roger E Billings*; Nov 1998

Broad wireless integration adds LAN, phone, tracking; **Security Distributing & Marketing** *Bill Zalud*; Nov 1998

Real flow control for LANs? Reducing the mismatch for ATM; **Telecommunications** *Jim Mollenauer*; Nov 1998

LSI Logic, eyeing LANs, fields Fibre Channel cores; **Electronic Engineering Times** *Craig Matsumoto*; Oct 26, 1998

Viva, LAN Vegas; **InformationWeek** *Clinton Wilder*; Oct 26, 1998

LAN, WAN Views Merge In Network 'Swiss Army Knife'; **InternetWeek** *Tim Wilson*; Oct 26, 1998

Former LAN OS developer shifts into CTI gear; **Computer Reseller News** *Margie Semilof*; Oct 19, 1998

Ethernet connects most LANs; **InformationWeek** *Anonymous*; Oct 19, 1998

Managing Mainframe And Lan Events; **InternetWeek** *Tim Wilson*; Oct 19, 1998

Wireless LANs find a home; **Wireless Review** *Ira Brodsky*; Oct 15, 1998

Elastic Networks stretches LAN protocol translator; **InfoWorld** *Laura Kujubu*; Oct 12, 1998

Lucent to boost wireless LAN reach; **InfoWorld** *Laura Kujubu*; Oct 12, 1998

Wireless LANs winning over users, vendors; **Computing Canada** *Steve Gold*; Oct 5, 1998

Standards boost wireless LANs; **Electronic Engineering Times** *Jim Zyren*; Oct 5, 1998

Compaq sweeps LAN servers; **Computer Reseller News** *Amber Howle*; Sep 21, 1998

Davicom offers new LAN card -- UMC spin-off is one of few to offer one-chip Fast Ethernet solution; **Electronic Buyers' News** *Mark LaPedus*; Sep 21, 1998

Local Metropolitan Area Networks; **Telecommunications** *Doug Allen*; Dec 1998

Building Local Area Networks with Novell's Netware, Versions 2.2 to 3.12, Third Edition; **Computer Retail Week** *Anonymous*; Sep 8, 1997

Local Area Networks Making the Right Choices; **Computer Retail Week** *Anonymous*; Sep 8,

Bibliography

CHAPTER 12

DISTRIBUTED NETWORK MANAGEMENT

Mangers of Managing Agents

Case 18: What is Enterprise Networks?

WHAT IS ENTERPRISE NETWORKS?

http://www.nortel.com/enterprise/whatis.html

Of all the network business groups in Northern Telecom (Nortel), Enterprise Networks has the broadest, most diverse product portfolio and customer base. Its mission is to deliver custom designed enterprise network solutions for businesses worldwide - from the smallest operation to major corporations.

Enterprise Networks serves its customers in two ways: by working directly with each business to create a private network solution with customer premises equipment and applications, and by developing network solutions for major carriers and service providers who offer communications capabilities to both business and residential customers.

To accomplish this goal, the group relies on an array of products that spans terminals, key systems, private branch exchanges (PBXs), and broadband multimedia switches based on the latest ATM (asynchronous transfer mode) technology. As a complement to its platform products, Enterprise Networks also provides a variety of strategic business applications that cover call centres, integrated messaging, mobility communications, Internet access, desktop multimedia, interactive voice response, telecommuting, and flexible voice recognition.

On a global scale, the quality and reliability of Enterprise Networks products have earned the group a market leadership position in several notable areas, including: data packet networks, PBXs, enterprise mobility, call centres, messaging, key systems, and public network-based virtual private networks for businesses.

Enterprise Network Solutions for Critical Business Needs

Enterprise networks represent an operational "lifeline" for businesses. The power of communications can be used to link and access partners, suppliers, customers, employee locations, markets, and resources on a global basis. New technology is helping, too, by transforming corporate networks from separate voice and data arrangements into consolidated networks that support sophisticated multimedia applications, high-speed data connections, integrated computer-telephony solutions, and wireless mobility for users "on the move."

As companies re-engineer themselves to stay competitive and prepare for the future, they are seeking comprehensive solutions that will improve efficiency, productivity, and revenue opportunities. Based on customer feedback, Enterprise Networks has focused its resources on several strategic application areas that are most beneficial in delivering tangible, financial returns to enterprises. This real-world business needs include:

- Network consolidation
- LAN internetworking
- Integrated messaging
- Call centres
- Telecommuting
- Distance learning/training
- Computer-telephony integration
- Remote/branch offices
- Multimedia conferencing
- Mobility
- Voice processing and speech recognition

To satisfy these critical requirements, Enterprise Networks integrates a mix of products, applications, and services to fit the diversity found in the business world. The result is solutions that support multiple industry market segments, functional departments within enterprise operations, and a variety of private and public LAN, WAN, and campus networking environments.

Multimedia Strength from the Network to the Desktop

Multimedia communications that combine voice, data, images, and video are becoming a necessity today. By combining these media in an integrated and interactive fashion, people can work, sell, learn, and exchange information more effectively. From this multimedia perspective, the scope of Enterprise Networks operations can be arranged into four business groupings.

Multimedia Networks - for enterprise and carrier customers that require high-performance ATM-based switching systems, frame relay services, and Internet access. In this segment, Enterprise Networks offers several product families to address customer needs:

- Magellan data and broadband multimedia switching systems, including: the Magellan Concorde and Vector ATM switches for carrier backbone network transport and network access respectively; the Magellan Passport enterprise network switch that handles ATM cells, frame relay services, LAN interconnections, and IBM SNA/APPN communications for carriers and business customers; the Magellan Access Switch offering multiple protocols for branch and remote office networking; and the Magellan DPN-100 frame switch:

- Rapport - a new product family that makes Internet dial-up access reliable and cost-effective for carriers and service providers, as well as their customers;

– Entrust - electronic signature and encryption software products to make secure network communications and electronic commerce a reality for businesses.

In our review of the basic enterprise paradigms, we have been certainly lured by the advantages offered by global networking. It promised the *efficiency* due to economies of scale and resource *sharing*, and ease of communications among end-users within the enterprise, just to name few features we have dreamed of. However, the moonlighting eventually stops there, since there exists the other, darker side of the moon, when it comes to integrating and managing enterprise networks. Even though thousands and thousands of enterprises struggle "out there", the enterprise networking is progressing at full speed ahead. However, getting enterprise networks work in an open multi-vendor environment the way we desire looks more like pioneering an unknown trail, than driving on an inter-city highway.

There are many reasons, often used as excuses, such as the novelty of the enterprise technology, or the difficulty of being globally connected and still feeling nutshell secure that has delayed the enterprise networks progress. A very simple reason usually cited at the end remains, the lack of unique *global open standards*. Consequently, it leads to the proliferation of the existing *de-facto* standards that serves a sole purpose only, that of, protecting the market share of IT suppliers and network system providers. This is even more emphasised in the field of enterprise network management, i.e. the *Distributed System Management* (DSM). It is important therefore that we briefly review some existing DSM standards that govern the enterprise networking in a *multi vendor* and *open platform* technology environment.

Manager of Managers vs. Manager of Managing Agents

As soon as the centralised paradigm of mainframe computers was about to be replaced by the enterprise-networking concept, the leading mainframe supplier IBM introduced the first standard in the domain of distributed system management - the *NetView*, as the *manager-of-managers* concept. This entailed an on-line hierarchical management system based on a centralised database that keeps track of the enterprise network resources information. DEC, AT&T, and others immediately followed suit introducing its own innovations in DSM, hence eventually started the proliferation of DSM networking standards. Yet another innovation came from the Novell's *NetWare*, Sun Microsystems, and Cabletron. Instead of complex hierarchical management model they introduced an original implementation of the *client/server (C/S) paradigm* in network management. The C/S relied on its ability to easily launch *program and proxy agents* throughout the network in a reflexive manner, i.e. from server to server. The *recursive* deployment of RPC or MOM agents has enabled network management to collect real-time information remotely, all over the network. It provided a flexible enterprise architecture integrating management functions that reside on multiple servers and maintaining back-end data either by peer-to-peer or manager-to-manager communications. The authoritative *Object Management Group* (OMG) backed by the *X/Open* consortium put forward the most recent step in the evolution of *DSM platform* to set up open *industry interface standards* for APIs.

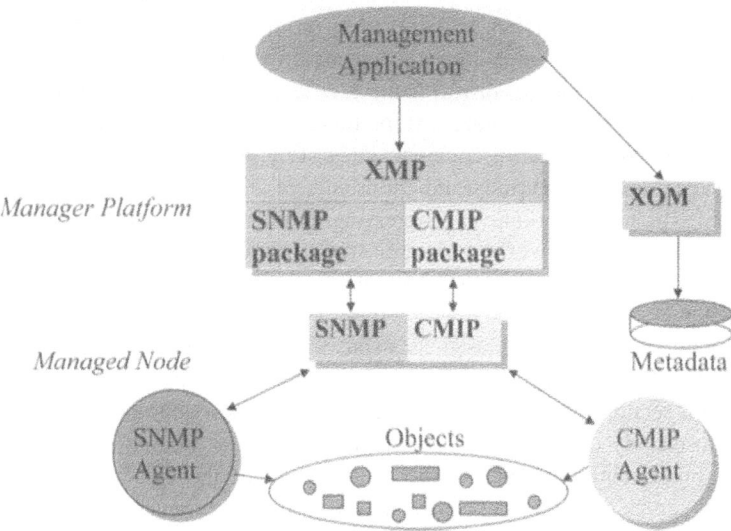

Figure 49. X/Open DSM Management Platform

X/OPEN Network Management Applications

The X/Open DSM platform; see *Figure 49*, entails several management components:

- *GUI & OOUI Interfaces* enable visual object presentation of managed resources
- *Management Applications* contain several domains that are usually provided by third parties: business management, problem management, change management, configuration management, operations management, and performance management. Several tools help manage the software, and collect massive data in real-time throughout the enterprise. For instance, the *performance-monitoring* tool gathers statistical data regarding resource utilisation; *inventory* management tool keeps track of enterprise assets (e.g. current status level of programs running on systems, servers, peripherals, routers, etc.); the *configuration* management tool assists in setting up some software parameters, or helps during complex systems fine-tuning sessions; the *security* tool monitors and manages the access to resources applying authentication and access protection mechanisms in normal operations usually by *firewall middleware*; the *fault* management tools identify fault conditions and launch corrective actions; *disaster* recovery tool provides a user interface for unattended scheduling of archiving and restoring actions, and assisting the disaster backup system. Finally, *software distribution and installation* together with *license management* tools enforce the procurement

of proper software standards and help download, publish, update, install, and de-install software and application packages throughout the enterprise network.

- *Basic Platform Services* enable applications to communicate with software agents, other applications, or event-driven services through open industry standard APIs.
- *Middleware Stacks* provide the communication infrastructure for software agents, applications, nodes, or operators (e.g. SNMP, CMIP, DCE, or CORBA standards).

Despite of its gradual acceptance, the aforementioned management applications have provided appealing features. Some DSM protocols such as, SNMP, CMIP, DMI, and CORBA have gained wider users' acceptance.

Internet Management Protocol - SNMP

Simple Networking Management Protocol (SNMP) represents the most widely implemented networking management protocol. On the Internet it gained support by the IETF. As its name suggests, the SNMP uses simple, unacknowledged, *connectionless* protocol (TCP/IP Datagram-based). Pooling the managing agents is implemented by *Terminate-Stay-Resident* (TSR), or by *Demon* background tasks. However, it is less reliable, unsecured, inefficient protocol, lacking some important network management features, such as, support for the *manager-to-manager* communications. Both SNMP and OSI's CMIP define resources as managed objects. A hierarchical (tree-based) *Management Information Base* (MIB) outlines the structure of managed objects. The MIB *schema* or the *Structure of Management Information* (SMI) defines the model and the naming conventions used. It also helps specifying managed objects for both, SNMP, and CMIP protocols.

In 1993, it was replaced by the improved SNMP2 standard that has been adopted as the new Internet protocol. Currently, a SNMP2 node can be both, *a managed,* as well as, *a managing* object. It allows implementation of new security features, *manager-to-manager* (M2M) communication, and the new M2M MIB in order to support the latest network topologies, bulk data transfers, etc.

OSI Network Management- CMIP

In order to provide a comprehensive solution to the network management in place of simple SNMP model, the OSI defines network-managed objects utilising the affirmed *object-oriented* framework. The *Complex Management Information Protocol* (CMIP) is a *connection*-oriented protocol running on top of a seven-layer OSI stack. It relies on both *manager-to-agent* and *manager-to-manager* communications. Instead of SNMP *datagram* communication, CMIP is session-based, more intelligent, and polls manager-to-agent event-driven interactions. CMIP is more secure and allows MIB use inheritance in defining managing objects. Despite small installed users' base, the CMIP remains better suited for the management of large, complex, multi-vendor enterprise networks.

Desktop Management Agents - DMI

Both SNMP2 and CMIP protocols demand rather large memory requirements, up to MByte of RAM, which has been somewhat restrictive for a growing number of desktop clients earlier. *Intel and Desktop Management Task Force* (DMTF) consortium responded by launching the *Desktop Management Interface (DMI)* protocol. It is its own *small software agent* designated to manage small desktop hardware, as well as, software components. DMI entails protocol-independent APIs based on multi-platform *Management Interface File* (MIF). The MIB is able to communicate with either SNMP2 or CMIP protocol. Using TSR in DOS or DLLs for Windows and OS/2, the DMI agents are able to load or unload the necessary components on demand in order to provide distributed management functionality consuming not more than few Kbytes of RAM. The low memory requirement has even allowed installation of proprietary agents on network adapter cards, for instance, the *3Com Ethernet desktop* card.

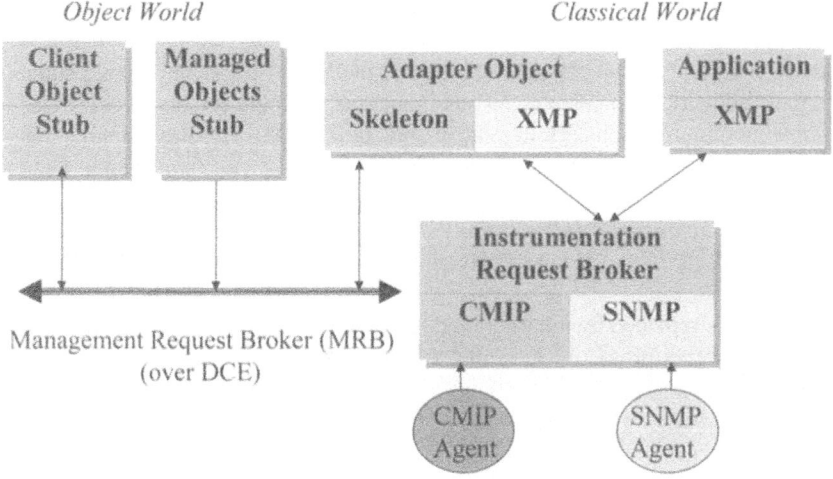

Figure 50. DME Object Management Framework

Network Object Management Framework

Recently, the DME *Object Management Framework* (OMF); see *Figure 50*, has provided complete advanced solution for network management in heterogeneous multi-vendor environment. The OMG *Common Object Request Broker Architecture* (CORBA) is a compliant framework that substitutes the traditional *manager-to-object* relationship with a *all-object* relationship. Thus, the CORBA object can take either of the two roles: *a client requesting a service, or a server providing services.* Based on the familiar DCE communication concepts among objects, it uses CORBA *Object Request Brokers* (ORB) to render exact services in distributed system management of asynchronous events; see *Figure 50*. The

CORBA standard is supported by the *Object Management Group* (OMG) and defines software boundaries that need to ensure the *interoperability* between independent distributed objects. The support comes from UNIX/Linux users too. The event-driven ORB static implementation is bound at compile time in the form of IDL precompiled *stub*. It is simpler, easier, faster, and more robust than other DSM. The dynamical method of ORB invocation however, manages objects at run-time resulting in more flexible environment. The traditional SNMP or CMIP are managed through special DME *Interface Definition Language* (IDL) *adapter object* encapsulations. Special IDL adapter objects are used to encapsulate the implementation of any management resource, for instance, defining a set of operations that emulate CMIP or SNMP calls. In order to avoid the proliferation of many special-purpose ORB object adapters, CORBA relies on the *Basic Object Adapters* (BOA) set for conventional ORB implementations. Despite its complexity, memory, and high processing power requirements, the DME OMF model represents highly sophisticated communication and interaction among self-managed objects, which may represent network resources, user interfaces, and managing applications. Moreover, due to continuing trends of inexpensive hardware, low-cost enterprise software ownership, and ever-growing demands for enterprise-wide networking, the overwhelming CORBA support is expected to bring about migration from simple SNMP and desktop-based DMI to sophisticated object-oriented ORB implementation. As mentioned in Java-based CBD and EJB-Distributed Applications, the EJB applications used to wrap legacy systems can run many clients: browsers, Java, ActiveX, CORBA.

Bibliography

VoiceXML for Web-based distributed conversational applications; *Bruce Lucas*; **Association for Computing Machinery. Communications of the ACM**, New York; Sep 2000; Vol. 43, Iss. 9; pg. 53, 5 pgs

Worst-case deadline failure probability in real-time applications distributed over controller area network; *N Navet*; **Journal of Systems Architecture**, Amsterdam; Apr 15, 2000; Vol. 46, Iss. 7; pg. 607

Designing a distributed database on a local area network: A methodology and decision support system; *H Lee*; **Information and Software Technology**, Amsterdam; Feb 25, 2000; Vol. 42, Iss. 3; pg. 171

Mass network flooding attacks (distributed denial of service - DDoS) surface in the wild; *Bill Hancock*; **Computers & Security**, Amsterdam; 2000; Vol. 19, Iss. 1; pg. 6

Communication patterns in distributed work groups: A network analysis; *France Belanger*; **IEEE Transactions on Professional Communication**, New York; Dec 1999; Vol. 42, Iss. 4; pg. 261

Distributed file systems for storage area networks; *Brad Kline*; **Computer Technology Review**, Los Angeles; Fourth Quarter 1999; pg. 34, 8 pgs

Distributed cooperative Web servers; *Baker, Scott M*; **Computer Networks**, Amsterdam; May 17, 1999; Vol. 31, Iss. 11-16; pg. 1215, 15 pgs

BinderBus seeks to spark distributed network revolution; *Anonymous*; **Control Engineering**, Barrington; May 1999; Vol. 46, Iss. 5; pg. 9, 1 pgs

WDAI: A simple World Wide Web distributed authorization infrastructure; *Kahan, Jose*; **Computer Networks**, Amsterdam; May 17, 1999; Vol. 31, Iss. 11-16; pg. 1599, 11 pgs

Gigahertz wireless LANs expand mobile-design palette; **Electronic Engineering Times** *Ann R Thryft*; Dec 21, 1998

SiGe fires up 5-GHz wireless LANs; **Electronic Engineering Times** *Modest Oprysko*; Dec 21, 1998

Bottlenecks In LAN, WAN; **InternetWeek** *Salvatore Salamone*; Dec 21, 1998

PART IV

ENTERPRISE COMPUTING

Case 19: Transition Associates wins Lotus Beacon Award at Hughes
Christensen

Knowledge management lets Hughes Christensen drive change in its market
sector with a new business model that achieves massive increased value for its
customers.

The challenge in brief:
Introduce a radical consultancy-led business model to a product oriented
company within the highly competitive oil drilling market.

Summary of the solution:
Use Lotus Domino knowledge management to drive the creation of a specialist
and highly skilled consulting team within a sales focused organisation.

Benefits for Hughes Christensen
- **Accurate consultancy every time.** Domino knowledge management tools help
global Hughes staff provide consistent consultancy world-wide; financial risk and
deployment costs for companies adopting specialised one-off systems are reduced.
- **Rivals outdistanced.** Hughes is the first company in its niche to provide full-
service consultancy - a key differentiator against rivals in a highly competitive
market
- **Streamlined knowledge infrastructure.** Domino provides an easily updated
system for sharing learning, customer feedback and best practices. Integrating their
knowledge management systems into a single infrastructure company-wide ensures
consistency of information and services.
- **Global distributed learning.** Use of Domino based learning tools ensures that
not only is new knowledge quickly propagated world-wide, but can be learned at
best pace for individual staff.

More about the challenge
A specialist oil- and gas-industry tool provider, Hughes Christensen was
interested in introducing a revolutionary approach to its market by shifting from a
product sales-led focus to a high-end consultancy operation. The company knew it
had a great deal of unique expertise to sell, but this was locked up in the heads of
key employees. Hughes wanted this expertise to be available to all staff, but was
puzzled about the best way to do this. Nigel Meany, director of engineering services,
explains: "We developed a number of knowledge sharing alternatives, including an
expert system, but we still weren't achieving the business transformation we were
looking for.

"Our problem came to a head," he continues, "when a customer asked us to create a reference system of best practices. The skills we learned during Hughes' expert systems project were useful for eliciting a lot of practical knowledge from our engineers, but we weren't satisfied with our delivery of this. We ended up with a manual the size of a telephone directory, which like all reference books was destined to sit on the shelf unused".

The solution

To find a better solution, Hughes Christensen turned to Transition Associates. Hughes posed to Transition an open-ended question: "How do we utilise our knowledge by some other means than as a reference book?"

Transition Associates proposed creating the "Drilling Performance Guidelines" using Lotus Domino software. Meany explains that Domino allows a much looser arrangement of knowledge than traditional expert systems. "It delivers decision support rather than a rule-based decision-making program, complementing the existing expert system. This makes it an attractive knowledge sharing tool for our in-house experts, who otherwise worry that sharing their knowledge makes it less valuable."

The Drilling Performance Guidelines system is flexible too, he says, with users actively encouraged to challenge the knowledge offered there. "The project team meets three times a year to discuss these challenges, and to update and refine the system as new knowledge comes to light. So we have a live, up-to-date document - not a static, quickly outdated and expensive to replace paper manual."

As service provision became more critical to Hughes' business, the company decided it needed to provide alternatives to in-house class training. "Bringing people to our Aberdeen headquarters for up to a month at a time is expensive," says Meany. "Transition helped us create a less costly way to spread learning - a distributed learning environment based on Lotus Domino. Now learning materials used on our courses remain available as valuable support materials for consultants across the globe."

This new development has been so successful that Hughes' parent company, Fortune 500 Corporation Baker Hughes, has now taken ownership of the learning system.

The results

Supported by the Drilling Performance Guidelines solution, Hughes Christensen's new OASIS consultancy service has been able to provide its customers with some highly impressive returns on investment. Oil-drilling specialist BP Norge realised an ROI on Hughes Christensen's engineering services of 600% by saving nearly seven million dollars on a drilling optimisation project in Norway. Another customer saved 75 days of work thanks to advice offered by a team that included Hughes Christensen Says Meany, "With drilling operations costing up to $350,000 a day, that's a huge saving in an industry that may deal in large numbers but is also desperately keen to be cost-effective.

According to Meany, the Drilling Performance Guidelines gives Hughes a unique business edge. "Our knowledge management system is a true market differentiator. It allows us to develop solutions for our customers much faster. And we can demonstrate the system to clients, which inspires confidence in them about our entire organisation. It also raises the levels of knowledge of all our staff, so that unlike other companies we do not have to hire and retain very expensive hot-shot individuals. Instead we have many quality individuals on board, who don't have to have had all experiences themselves".

So impressed are Hughes Christensen's customers with the Drilling Performance Guidelines system that many of them have asked for access to it, or even to license it themselves. Initial concerns about passing on knowledge to customers have been replaced by the realisation that this is an excellent opportunity to place Hughes' best practices within the oil industry as a de facto standard.

With its best practices being adopted by customer organisations, Hughes Christensen will be an obvious choice to help further develop the processes that give this knowledge its value. "Sharing our expertise with customers," says Meany, "gives Hughes Christensen an opening to sell further services and products into the user organisations."

Nigel Meany is adamant that "Hughes Christensen's OASIS service couldn't have grown as fast as it has without knowledge management, and could not maintain its leadership without being able to develop the systems further. We are very happy with them".

Award winning
Nigel Meany is full of praise for Transition Associates, who provided the vision and the creativity to design and deliver his company's solutions. A Lotus Premium Partner that specialises in Domino solutions for knowledge management and distributed learning, <u>**Transition Associates**</u> **won the coveted 1999 Greatest Business Impact - Lotus Beacon Award for its work with Hughes Christensen.**

Enterprise computing represents an important activity encountered in every segment of enterprise organization. The opening *Case 19:* Transition Associates wins Lotus Beacon Award at Hughes Christensen and the following *Case 20:* Transition Associate and Lotus Notes at Foulks Lynch Virtual College illustrate the complexity of computing massive data, processing information coming from within the enterprise Intranet, or through the external information channels that keeps users constantly aware of the environment. In our quest for knowledge, acquiring the necessary know-how from the Web and network resources often requires appropriate set-up of enterprise computing at any level of the enterprise.

Having in mind the importance of information system needed to support decision-making processes, and the executive and knowledge-based systems throughout the enterprise, it is imperative that we turn our attention to the fundamental building block of any information system, the *Database Management System* (DBMS).

Evolution of Database Systems

During the last twenty years, enterprise computing has experienced an overwhelming enthusiasm for all sorts of database systems. As it is pointed out in Chapter Working with Databases, the Databases have changed and evolved to meet the need of business applications. Considering the interest and key position of *relational databases* among users in general, there are two significant periods in the evolution of database systems:

- *Pre relational* are mainly based upon data organized as inverted files, hierarchic structures, and networked databases
- *Post relational* are related to semantic data paradigms, object-oriented, expert systems, extended, and many other types of particular interest to certain groups of users, applications, or databases in support of CASE tools, multimedia, desktop publishing, document archiving, help-desk applications, CTI, etc.

The following Chapter Database Functionality essentially provides a review of some basic features of relational database systems in order to facilitate our understanding of specific requirements put forward by the enterprise community, common office productivity tools, and database applications.

Respecting the present trend set by the Web, Intranets, and applications that rely on databases for the implementation of distributed enterprise computing across enterprise boundaries, in Chapter Distributed Application Interoperability we are elaborating on establishing the requirements for distributed computing. Our interest is also motivated by the efforts, and in many instances, the success achieved to overcome problems that are associated with integration and wrapping up of legacy applications, highly dependent on former, predominantly relational database concepts.

Finally, in Chapter Business Intelligence we are addressing some modern trend in the decision support. An intelligence issues based on the availability of right information and timely data at the right place, or should we say, the right and knowledgeable end-users. Hence, introducing Data Warehouses within the enterprise, and Business Intelligence through the Web, the databases technology has advanced past the critical development point enabling enterprises wide range of technologies for distributed computing support.

CHAPTER 13

WORKING WITH DATABASES

Conceptual Views on Data

The client
Foulks Lynch is internationally acknowledged as the leading name in professional accountancy publishing and home study courses. Foulks Lynch is part of the Nord Anglia Education Plc group, one of the world's leading education based businesses.

For over 100 years, the name Foulks Lynch has been associated with the highest quality of accountancy training material. A new chapter began in 1993 when study materials of an innovative design were introduced. These publications rapidly acquired an enviable reputation and in 1995 when ACCA (Association of Chartered Certified Accountants) decided to outsource the production of its publications, it was only natural that Foulks Lynch was chosen as the Official Publisher for ACCA.

Foulks Lynch publications include all the necessary study guides and revision aids for the following professional qualifications :
- ACCA (Association of Chartered Certified Accountants)
- CAT (Certified Accounting Technician
- CIMA (Chartered Institute of Management Accountants)
- AAT (Association of Accounting Technicians)

The business issues
Foulks Lynch was already providing students with top class distance learning, so that learning could be "anywhere, any time". But they wanted to make use of advances in web usage to develop interactive online courses which would supplement the hard copy study textbooks, to give students an enhanced learning experience.

They selected Transition Associates to assist them in their goal to develop course packages with an online tutor for each student, interactive online study and revision material, discussion rooms, bulletin boards and CD-ROM.

Foulks Lynch wanted to become self-sufficient in as many aspects of the project as possible, and so Transition Associates worked with them as mentors, developing best practice procedures that could be adopted by Foulks Lynch to progress the project efficiently and successfully

The solution

The courses are hosted on a Lotus Domino server running Lotus LearningSpace and are accessed across the Internet, using standard Web browsers. This provides a convenient way for students world-wide to access the e-learning environment and its resources. Lotus LearningSpace enables a feature-rich, secure, interactive learning system to be developed far more rapidly than with standard Web technology.

Transition Associates was appointed by Foulks Lynch during March 2000. Initially, work consisted of planning and installing the technical infrastructure (Lotus Domino and Lotus LearningSpace) and developing technical processes for creation of the online course content. Over time, Transition Associates undertook a series of mini-projects:-

- Due to the volume of content for 21 ACCA courses, MS Word templates were developed to ensure that content, which was to be written by textbook authors, would follow a consistent format that would allow easy loading into LearningSpace.
- A workflow process was developed and integrated with the CourseBuilder functionality that LearningSpace contains, to ensure control and management of the loading, editing and publishing process.
- A set of templates were tailored, using a Foulks Lynch branded look and feel, together with home page splash screens which lead students into the courses. From the home page, students can also access a bulletin board and their personal planner, developed by Transition Associates to enable planning of their study up to their exam.
- Each course is brought to life with a number of interactive Flash objects, developed by Transition Associates, and each course contains a re-usable self-assessment object which is fed with questions and answers from a text file. This allows each instance to offer a different set of questions and answers under the control of a non-technical Foulks Lynch administrator.
- A procedure was developed whereby each course can be quickly converted to run from CD-ROM, with the look and feel of the LearningSpace courses, so that distant students can work the non-interactive elements of the course without needing to be continually connected to the Internet.
- Foulks Lynch already had a web site with e-commerce, so Transition Associates developed integration software that enables courses purchased on the main Foulks Lynch web site to trigger an automatic registration process on the Lotus Domino server. This means that a student can receive an email containing login details within minutes of purchase, without any manual intervention - thus

removing the need for manual administration processes and ensuring 24*7 registration availability.

The Lotus Domino server is hosted by BT Ignite, to ensure reliable 24*7 access to a global user base. Transition Associates' partnership with BT Ignite smoothed the way for Foulks Lynch to select and engage with BT Ignite with confidence and minimum effort.

Throughout the project duration, which culminated in the last of the 21 ACCA papers going live in November 2001, Transition Associates provided proactive guidance and assistance as required, gradually leading Foulks Lynch into self-sufficiency in all repeatable tasks.

Solution highlights

- Enabled Foulks Lynch to enhance its level of service significantly, by providing online features such as access to tutors, to supplement the traditional distance learning methods.

- Transition Associates worked as partners with Foulks Lynch to ensure that Foulks Lynch costs were not increased by the large volumes of content required for 21 courses.

- Workflow processes enabled control and management of content loading, editing, and approval, through to published content.

- Reduced costs through BT Ignite hosting.

- Fully automated self-serve environment, requiring zero administration. Students are enrolled within minutes of purchase, any time, anywhere.

LOTUS DOMINO FAQ

http://www.notes.net/about.nsf/be90c830fcee2b5e85256405007e8937/004cb678c9b376be85256495006db5e8?

(Copyright © 2002, International Business Machines Corp. All rights reserved.)

Domino is about access to information, the reach of the Internet and content...with an attitude! Instead of the passive publishing of information, Domino actively manages the flow of information amongst the people in your organization. Domino applications reflect the collective personality of workgroups and the tasks that make them productive and it works the Web just like you do. It has development tools, a database, data access tools, security, messaging, workflow, agents, directory, standards, tools for offline use. But best of all Domino has attitude...your attitude. Because applications are not about what everyone else does, but what you do.

What is Domino?

Domino is new server technology which transforms Lotus Notes into a world-class Internet applications server, allowing any Web client to participate in Notes applications securely. Bridging the open networking environment of Internet standards and protocols with the powerful application development facilities of Notes, Domino provides businesses and organizations with the ability to rapidly develop a broad range of business applications for the Internet and Intranet.

What are the key features of Domino?

Domino makes it possible to use Notes' rich application development environment to develop, manage and host Web applications.

Domino provides interactive Web client access to dynamic data and applications on a Notes Server. This means that Web clients may:

– Securely access a Notes server
– Access dynamic data and application based on time, database queries and/or user identity
– Create, edit and delete documents in a Notes database
– Search a Notes database
– View content in a Notes database with powerful Notes navigational capabilities such as the ability to expand and collapse views
  Domino extends Notes Access Control to include Web clients:
– Updated template of Notes Name and Address Book form includes new encrypted field to provide a Web client password
– Web client authentication via Basic Web Authentication (name and password)
– Web user may be added to ACL lists, groups and rights and assigned a "role"
– Database to field-level access control for Web clients
– SSL support for server authentication and encryption of data in secured sessions
  Domino serves HTML files stored in the file system.
  Domino runs CGI scripts activated by Web clients.

What are the benefits of Domino?

Domino reduces the complexity of creating and maintaining a content-rich Web site.

– Streamlines and automates the creation of content from multiple contributors/departments
– Easy, graphical page management database reduces tedious links and creates a more navigable site
– Eliminates need to train content creators in HTML; anyone with word-processing capabilities can author Web site content
  Domino delivers Web application developers a reach environment for creating secure mission-critical interactive applications.
– Graphical forms designer
– Broad range of application development facilities to serve the power user to the power programmer
  Point and click creation of agents and formulas to advanced scripting capabilities
– Integration with RDBMS and MQSeries
– Integrated messaging system providing backend infrastructure for business process applications
– Workflow
– Directory services for managing Web clients access to data and applications

- Roles-based access control down to the field level

Domino provides all the facilities required to build a Web site.
- Page management database
- Full-text search engine with automatic indexing of content
- Threaded discussion template
- Rapid application development of forms-based applications
- Registration template and directory services for secure Web client access

Domino makes it possible to synchronously manage mirror sites and distributed Intranets.
- Secure and automated bi-directional synchronisation of servers (replication) makes it easy to create mirror sites, distributed Intranets, and update content and receive information from Web sites hosted by ISPs.

Database: A Conceptual View on Data

Briefly, a database represents a repository of organized data collections persistently stored, hence providing users data access, retrieval, data manipulation, and data update.

Whether computerized, manual, or otherwise implemented, the users maintain certain conceptual views over the database organization that enables them to efficiently manage and control the underlying database complexity. During database evolution quite some database concepts were introduced. Some were radically different, others were very much original, yet some to be reinvented again, this time as sophisticated computerized database systems. For instance, the former hierarchical database concept has evolved into rather sophisticated *Lotus Notes* document-based database system.

Inverted files, hierarchical, semantic, relational, functional, logical, and object oriented, just to mention some of the most familiar concepts have reigned our imagination and views over massive data complexes. Despite its trivial flat-table concept, the relational database remains the most complete due to the underlying relational algebra that provides simple but effective manipulation and operation over data complexes. The *relational database* concept has been unanimously considered as the most mature of all.

Relational Database Concept

The most significant concepts that distinguish relational databases from other database paradigm are the *entity* and the *relationship*. The latter expresses the way entities relate to each other, in terms of its functionally building larger complexes, models also known as database scenarios; see *Figure 51*.
- *Entity* - represents a concept, real or virtual, associated with data it uses to describe as a distinguishable object, or an event of a process for which we would like to keep a persistent record in the database. For instance, the basic entities in *Figure 51* are UNIVERSITY, DEPARTMENTS, RESEARCHERS, REFERENCES, PROJECTS, REPORTS, and LIBRARY.

- *Relationship* - represents valuable information that relates entities denoted by named links and connecting items. It is often associated with data used for decision support, functional, or operational behaviour of an enterprise. In our example, in *Figure 51*, the relationship information is coded as 1, 2, and 3. The code 1 stands for a *reflexive* type that represents a recursive data structure too. This refers to the entity REFERENCES having constituent REFERENCES, which in turn may have their own REFERENCES. The code 2 denotes an ordinary *binary* relationship involving two entities. For instance, a DEPARTMENT consists of RESEARCHERS. Lastly, code 3 shows a *ternary* relationship involving three entities simultaneously, for instance, in case of a triple relationship REFERENCE - PROJECT – REPORT. It also means that only all three entities together may define consistently a particular project report referring to particular references, etc. The *persistency* and *properties* are the two important features associated with the database concept, commonly attributed to as database constituent parts:
- *Persistency* means that the data recorded involving input data, transient, output, or operational data is to endure the actual data computing process, and data manipulation.
- *Properties* may be simple or complex structures, closely associated with data types and data structures of corresponding entities and its relationships. For instance, EMPLOYEES have names, DEPARTMENTS have addresses, PROJECTS have start-dates, and BOOKS have ISBN numbers to be associated with, etc.

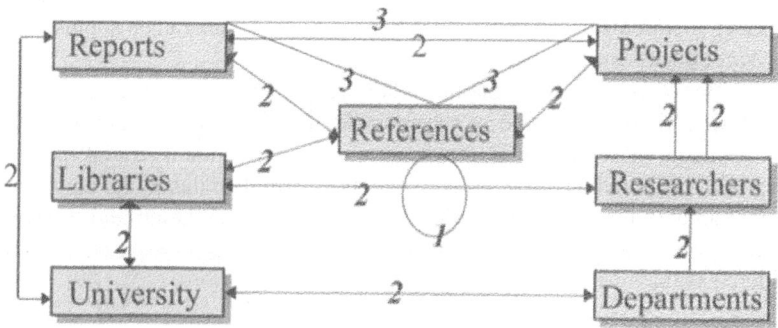

Figure 51. Relationship Types

Why Database?

It is a trivial question, but in a way it is a rewarding experience, arguing why do we need databases? Could we do without them? How complex are they really? Why are they so essential to business processes, individual decision-makers, or enterprises in general?

Considering databases as integral part of any enterprise computing, a building block of information systems we depend so much on, it is challenging to find innovative answers to these questions. For, there are many instances the databases are so good at that one could not do without. A database also underlines the way we humans perform certain activities, relying in many instances on our ability to make associations, in book keeping, information processing, or data archiving. In fact, it works well without databases provided there are small number of objects to remember, however, it is quite difficult and almost impossible when there are so many items, millions of them, very much alike, but nonetheless individually different. This is where databases are so good at: managing massive data complexity, keeping up with frequent changes, maintaining the links and administration records, responding to almost any trivial or complex query, being fast and reliable, and moreover, never complaining about anything.

However, there are few features we should be aware of when we discuss the advantages or disadvantages of dealing with databases:

- Whether distributed or not, they do provide an efficient *centralised control* over the enterprise information, establishing data procurement and the appropriate database administration. There are few advantages stemming from the centralised database control. The data *redundancy* can be controlled, reduced whenever possible, but also introduced in order to maintain the database responsiveness. By introducing appropriate *integrity* checks over the propagation of database updates most data *inconsistencies* can be avoided. Also, possible *conflicting* requirements can be balanced.

- *Procurement of standards* is yet another benefit of having centralised control over the databases. There are many applications based upon databases currently in use. Often different, sometimes even incompatible as they need constant updating and frequent maintenance. Enforcing standards in fact prevents the applications and databases from obsolesce.

- Allows *sharing* data between different applications, among sites, or many users.

- *Security* can be applied, especially for distributed databases, allowing restricted access to sensitive data, and controlling users access to the database.

- *Compactness* is introduced due to digital, electronic form, enabling enormous data volumes to be recorded, on a disk floppy, tape, disk, CD-ROM, smart-card ROM, or flash-memory for instance.

- The *drudgery* has been reduced than ever before. It is still possible to implement a database in a non-electronic form, a diary book, or paper cards for instance, with indexes, query holes etc. However, it only works provided there is small number of records and low data volume, often a size of modest telephone diary.

- *Fast retrieval* derives from database's digital implementation too. The data retrieval process is in fact based on matching operations over database complexes - tables, rather than individual item-searching and pair-wise comparisons, which is why data retrieval is extremely fast and relatively independent of the actual database size.

– Data *independence* provides databases with stability and reliability over eventual changes in software, hardware *platforms*, system *environment*, and *applications*.

Database Models

Database *models* are conceptual views on different data features. Models try to reduce data complexity by viewing data from different perspectives and allowing users different views. The database views can be set by many concurrent users in a number of different applications therefore, avoiding eventual conflicts and still maintaining *data consistence and independence*. The *conceptual* model of data establishes an abstract representation of data through the database irrespective of the way actual data is stored, linked, or otherwise accessed through data queries.

The *data mapping* provides a solution to the aforementioned problems. It maps data from one *domain* into another - the data *range*. The database concepts, or the way we perceive data and the way they relate, have to comply with certain requirements. They have to satisfy some constraints in order to achieve this kind of domain mapping and still provide respective database functionality and performance. The data mapping of a relational database is confined to a simple set (a manifold) representation. In fact, it is visualized as flat, table-like data structure. The relational database tolerates no hierarchies but simple, atomic, undivided data that allow no further subdivisions. In contrast, the object-oriented database constraints are influenced by encapsulation of data together with data processing. Consequently, the object data concept permits use of more elaborate hierarchical data structures. However, it allows objects to communicate only through well-defined interfaces for invocation of procedures and exchange of data, either through established inheritance, or through aggregation hierarchies.

The ANSI/SPARC database system architecture standard recognizes three data views. The *external* view is associated with individual users' views, for instance a product-in-stock database for mail-order transactions. The *conceptual* view however, deals with abstract data models and relationships, for instance, data records in a table. The *internal view* takes into consideration the way data has actually been stored internally, for instance, sequentially on a tape, or randomly on a disk, CD, flash-memory, etc.:

1. The *external* level is responsible for mapping individual user's views over data and its relations. It enables sharing a database system among users allowing them to maintain individual interactions. Usually, a data sub-language is responsible for mapping user's actions into appropriate database concepts. The data sub-language part that performs actions concerning data is known as *data definition language* (DDL). The other part of the language is responsible for actual *data manipulation,* (DML) for short. A particular language most frequently used either as standalone or embedded into a programming language is the *Structured Query Language* (SQL), sometimes implemented as the *Query-By-Example* (QBE) tool.

2. The *conceptual* level, as mentioned previously, provides data independent views over data structures. It applies abstract organisation types, irrespective of the way data is actually stored internally, sometimes also

constraining the real data in a way. The conceptual *schema* defines overall database conceptual views. For instance, we may look at the *Department* entity conceptually as a collection of records for number of departments (department occurrences). However, it may as well contain records of researchers (researcher occurrences) affiliated with each department.

3. The *internal* level is responsible for low-level representation of the entire database in terms of files, segments, even down to implementation of the actual data store onto memory pages, whether higher data structures such as hashing has been used, and many specific issues related to the physical database record. Often, the internal schema written in *data definition language* (DDL) also describes the internal view.

From the applications point of view, a *database* is usually considered as having a *back-end* and a *front-end*. The *back-end* is the part of the database usually hidden by the underlying platform, system, or the database environment. The *front-end* however, is responsible for the interactions with applications that directly or indirectly act with the data. User applications are usually built by conventional program languages such as VB, COBOL, or *Delphi*. In contrast to the traditional COBOL, a contemporary programming language like Delphi, or VB combines both visual and component-based design with optimising native-code compiler and scalable database access. More recently, databases are predominantly built using *fourth generation languages* (4GL), supported by *QBA programming* tools, smart queries-based spreadsheets, application and report generators, CASE tools, DBMS development packages such as *PowerBuilder,* etc.

Internal Level

We have mentioned that at the internal level a database management system is to resolve a very important issue concerning the actual data representation. This is all but an easy task, especially if we are to keep in mind the varieties and technological differences present in the implementation of various types of data stores, or the external memories with wide range of price/performance features. Still, it has to satisfy the data independence constraints due to endless changes of the environment and introduced by the underlying information technology.

Nevertheless, the *data representation* issue might be a bit out of our scope, it is important that the reader becomes familiar with the basic terms related to the data store for a persistent implementation of DBMS on usual external computer memories. Still, there are few issues closely related to the database organization. It is its functionality or behaviour that arises from usual database access whether by the file system, the operating system, or the disk manager for data clustering implemented on a particular data store. Basically, there are several ways to achieve data clustering on a physical data record:

- *Data page sets* as basic, but limited, physical addressable data units.
- *Data indexing*, as a solution to the minimal data relocation constraint.
- *B-trees,* implementing both fast query response and optimal data update.
- *Data heap* provides a quick response based upon B-trees and page sets.
- *Hashing* implements a fast response using random address-coding schemes.

- *Dynamic* data allocation is based on the dynamic address pointer chains.
- *Data compression* applies data compression (differential, hierarchic, or distributed Hoffman) techniques in response to minimal data store requirement. Sometimes, data clustering methods are combined together to provide better database response to user's requirements and meet different system constraints. For instance, the data heap structure implemented by data indexing and fast data access is quite common solution for neat addressable page-sets, minimal data relocation, fast query response and appropriate for frequent data updates. The trade-off for these database features comes as additional OS complexity or as a processing time overhead of a sophisticated OS file-system in order to provide a non-linear data organization support.

Conceptual Model: Relational Database Model

The Relational database concept has been conceived by E. F. Codd in 1970s [1970, 1972, 1974, 1979]. As a conceptual data model, the *relation* provides a two-dimensional view of a database, i.e. simple *table* consisting of columns and rows. For instance, the REFERENCE relation can be described meaningfully by several *instances* of its significant *attributes*. *Table 22* presents a relation REFERENCE (REF. #, TITLE, AUTHOR, PUBLISHER, ISSUED), as a table of 5 columns by 7 rows. In fact, there are 7 instances of a record of 5 attributes each. The REF. # is a unique number of a reference; TITLE - a title of a reference; AUTHOR - authors' names; PUBLISHER - publishers' names, and the date being ISSUED. The R (REFERENCE) is also called a relation of degree 5 with cardinality of 7.

It attains *no ordering* property. The attributes are restricted to *distinct* names, the values of which in general, are not unique and may come from overlapping *domains* of the relation. A particular KEY attribute of a relation represents any *non-redundant* subset of attributes (depicted underlined) that *uniquely* identifies any row in the relation (a table).

Closely aligned with and following the relational data representation by Codd is the *Extended Entity-Relation* (EE/R), a schema-based semantic database model by P. P. S. Chen [1976]. It received significant commercial interest especially in many CASE tools. During the last decade semantically enriched EE/R model by Chen has attracted considerable attention among wide user's community. Interestingly, the EE/R database design provides a *top-down* approach for entity mapping and transformation of its complex entity relations into basic relation schemes. For instance, every *entity* type is represented by a *relation* schema. An entity *attribute* becomes a simple, relation's atomic attribute. Accordingly, a *relationship* represents a named association of *entities*. The *functionality* of a relationship may be *one-to-one, one-to-many, or many-to-many*, usually denoted as (1:1), (1:n), or (n:m), respectively. Common relationships are presented in *Figure 51*. The *involuted* relationship – **1** involves a single entity, a part, or for instance, a marriage: one-to-one relationship between two instances of the same entity type - a person. The most common is the *binary* relationship – **2** involving two entities. *Triple* and *multiple* relationships - **3** similarly entail three or more entities. Complex relationships among two and more entities are subject to transformations that depend on the *functionality* of relationships and the *membership* classes (mandatory or obligatory) a particular entity is associated with. The model is implemented and used for computing, data transformation, and setting up the layout of an enterprise information system. Case 21: Dayton's Department Store Database shows the role and how important the EE/R database model design become today in solving numerous data processing problems.

Table 22. An Instance Table of the Relation REFERENCE

Ref. #	Title	Author	Publisher	Issued
cp01	The EE/R Model...	Chen, P. S.	ACM Trans.	1976
ce01	Relational Model of Data	Codd, E. F.	ACM Comms.	1970
ce02	Further Normalisation...	Codd, E. F.	Prentice Hall	1972
ce03	Recent Investigation ...	Codd, E. F.	Proc. IFIP	1974
ce04	Extending the Databases	Codd, E. F.	ACM Trans.	1979
dc01	Introduction to Databases	Date, C. J.	AWL	1990
dc02	Introduction to Databases	Date, C. J.	AWL	1995

Database Design: Top-Down Design vs. Bottom-Up Attribute Skeleton

Database development presented in *Case 21:* Dayton's Department Store Database illustrates the iterative database modelling process. In pursuit of a reliable interactive information system, the database designer tries to overcome the ambiguities or inconsistencies that are usually present in any database requirements. Once the model is validated, the testing and verification phases are the necessary stages that can indicate the presence or absence of inconsistencies in the implementation process. Therefore, a conventional lifecycle of the EE/R database development process usually is to include the following phases:

- Requirements analysis
- EE/R modelling (*entity, property, relationship, membership, subtype*)
- Entity classification (*entity, involuted, binary, ternary*)
- Relationships functionality (*one-to-one, one-to-many, many-to-many*)
- Transformation of EE/R model into a set of relational schemas
- Normalisation procedure (*Boyce-Codd Normal Form*)
- Building the skeleton of the EE/R model (*bottom-up attribute assignment*)
- Database implementation (*assembling components*)
- Testing (*verification and validation*)
- Maintenance and update.

Why Database Normalization?

There are many problems encountered during the database development that are either due to inconsistencies of the ideal, conceptual model, or the complexity and ambiguity present in the real case. A normalization procedure is therefore a necessary database refinement process. It applies the formalization of the relation modelling process that is constrained only by the lossless decomposition of entity information. The *normal forms* that are produced and the preservation of entity normalization achieved during this process are to sustain any subsequent lossless information transformation and allow for free, unrestricted database manipulation. Provided data retrieval performance is not seriously affected the normalization stays an efficient common procedure that refines the database development process, captures eventual ambiguities, inconsistencies, and uncertainties that may result from inaccurate application of an arbitrary entity relation model. It is important to recognize that the essential benefit of normalized database is the reduced data *redundancy* and the increased ability to perform database operations *without loss* of information. The normalization process involves several key elements:

– *Functional dependence* defines the existence of an association among attributes. For instance, attributes in R (REFERENCE) are fully related with values of REF. #

– The first, second, and third *normal forms* are commonly applied. They establish conditions and criteria for the removal of *complex*, *partial*, and *transitive* functional dependencies, respectively that may exist on the *prime* KEY attribute or relation in general. The normalisation performs exact non-loss decomposition of the original relation, thus increasing the number of normalised tables, usually less redundant relations.

– *Boyce - Codd Normal Form* (BCNF) establishes very simple and efficient non-loss decomposition criteria achieving more that all three normal forms together. It simply states that each *determinant* attribute, or group of attributes on which some other attributes of the relation are *fully* dependent, becomes a candidate *prime* KEY for newly reduced relation. However, due to database performance behaviour, it is up to the database designer to decide on the scale of actual non-loss information reduction. For instance, the relation BOOK (REF. #, AUTHOR, TITLE) due to the specific dependence of AUTHOR over TITLE of a book permits cases of books having the same titles, despite being written by different authors. A non-loss decomposition results in the two relations: TEXT (REF. #, TITLE), and WRITER (AUTHOR, TITLE). The attributes REF. #, and AUTHOR, thus represent the candidate prime KEYs for new third normal-form relations TEXT and WRITER, respectively. The fact that an author writes a specific title is stored only once in the database results in reduced redundancy. However, there are two, instead of single relation that may substantially influence actual data retrieval performance based on TITLE as a *foreign key* in implementing the query.

– There exist higher normal forms, such as, the *fourth* normal-form that removes eventual *multivalued* functional dependencies. Often, it is a result of ambiguities that have failed to be revealed at the *entity/relation* (E/R) modelling stage. Such is the case for instance, in the multivalued relation RESEARCH (PROJECT, REPORT, REFERENCE) presented in *Figure 51*.

There are however, some limitations in the implementation of database normalization process. The database refinement, reduced redundancy, or removal of functional dependencies and anomalies are all facilitating the database design process. Unless the *Database Integrity* is not compromised, normalization may not be always desirable and has to be sensibly controlled due to the adverse effect on the data retrieval performance.

Database Integrity

The database management system is responsible for monitoring, detecting violations during database manipulations, operations, transactions, and updating the database for the preservation of integrity of the database system. There are few integrity categories:

–   The *entity* integrity concern is maintaining a valid attribute domain mapping; it enforces the rule stating that there should always exist a non-empty domain for primary attributes, or in other words: *null prime attribute* values are not allowed.

–   The *relational* integrity maintains preservation of *key uniqueness*; it enforces the rule that no two instances of relation are equal, i.e. allow *no duplicate instances*.

–   The *referential* integrity maintains correctness and consistency of a relationship among relations. The rule allows neither *null primes* nor *null foreign-key* values.

Database Implementation

The following case shows Chen's EE/R design approach to database modelling.

Case 21: Dayton's Department Store Database

THE BRIDE WISH LIST

Dayton's Department Store has offered a computer-based *Bride Registry System* (BRS), which allows brides and grooms to generate a computer-stored list of the exact items they would like to be presented as gifts on their wedding. Once the list is stored in the computer database the gift-givers would be able to make use or the Dayton's BRS by simple keying-in the bride's name and thereby get access to the bridal "wish list". Once gifts are purchased, they are checked off the lists to avoid eventual duplicates.

A gift-giver has been identified by its gift-giver-#, and each list is identified by either bride-ID# or groom-ID#.

The Dayton's Department Store may keep more than one wish list, i.e. more than one bride or a groom may have their wish lists deposited at the Dayton's Department Store. The information required about a product code, the price, or manufacturer and stock status are constantly updated and maintained.

The Dayton's Store may also keep more than one item of any given product.

We begin with the requirements to design a database that can support the activities of the BRS by first creating appropriate data model. The data model closely follows the database design approach by Chen. It consists of an EE/R diagram design and a set of normalized tables. Please see *Figure 52*.

The BRS database is to support the following transactions: store the details of the gift-giver; store the details in a wish list; purchase a gift-item; record the purchase of a gift-item; delete a gift-giver; delete the purchase; select a gift-item; update the price; change the gift status; finally, find the gifts wished by a bride.

Following the requirements and the necessary transactions, the entity attributes to be included in the database design are as follows: gift-giver-ID#, bride-ID#, gift-giver-name, gift-item-name, bride-name, manufacturer-name, item-code, item-price, purchase-limit, purchase-date, gift-status, and selection-date. We should emphasis that the item-code is composite attribute consisting of product-code, manufacturer-code, item-code, and check digit.

After several iterative attempts to accommodate the constraints, transactions, and using all the available attributes, the EE/R diagram is completed and presented on *Figure 52*. It consists of five binary tables: *MANUFACTURER, PRODUCT, BRIDE, GIFT-GIVER,* and *GIFT-ITEM.* There are five relationships too. The *Manufactures* represents a many-to-one relationship between PRODUCT and MANUFACTURERS tables. The *Wished-by* is a many-to-one relationship between tables BRIDE and PRODUCT. The *Selection* represents a many-to-many relationship between tables PRODUCT and GIFT-GIVER. The *Purchase* is a many-to-one relationship between tables GIFT-GIVER and GIFT-ITEM and finally, the *Stock* represnts a many-to-one relationship between tables GIFT-ITEM and PRODUCT; see *Figure 52*.

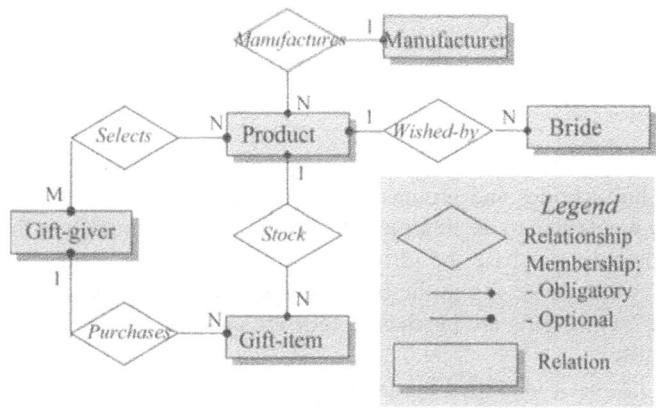

Figure 52. EE/R Diagram for the Bridal Case Database

The following headers make up a complete set of normalized relations including the prime-keys (<u>underlined</u>) and the corresponding attributes (within brackets).
GIFT-GIVER (<u>GIFT-GIVER-#</u>, GIFT-GIVER-NAME)
GIFT-ITEM (<u>BRIDE-#</u>, CODE, SELLING-PRICE)
PRODUCT (<u>CODE</u>, NAME, CURRENT-PRICE)
LIMIT (<u>GIFT-ITEM-STATUS</u>, PURCHASE-LIMIT)
WISH-LIST (<u>CODE, BRIDE-NAME</u>)
MANUFACTURER (<u>MANUFACTURER-CODE</u>, MANUFACTURER-NAME)
PURCHASE (<u>BRIDE-#</u>, GIFT-GIVER-#, PURCHASE-DATE)
SELECTION (<u>GIFT-GIVER-#, CODE</u>, SELECTION).
The database implementation starts with SQL *data definition* statements. The program coding for implementation of the database structure and required data

queries assumes that we are familiar with SQL *data manipulation* statements in some programming tool. *Oracle*, SyBase *EA Server*, DB2, CA *Ingress*, *FoxPro*, *Paradox*, *Access*, and SyBase *PowerBuilder* are few database development tools.

Database Manipulation - SQL

Database relations preserve some important properties under database transformations and database manipulation operations. As mentioned earlier, provided the *integrity* rules are in place, the *uniqueness* property of a database allows the records may easily change places and the attributes may swap its positions. In fact, it shows an interesting property that the database is lacking any notion of "*nextness*" in terms of its record order or their attributes' placements.

The implications are rather important with respect to database manipulation and general data processing. Unlike common individual data search procedures that usually apply to files, lists, or similar sequential files, performing a database query is implemented as simple logical operation over sets (manifolds) that entail database relations - tables and its related complexes (union, join, product, etc.).

The relational database manipulations are based on relational algebra operations. Basic relational operations on data sets include restriction, projection, product, union, intersect, difference, join, divide, a relational assignment operation, and a number of additional branch operators. The database processing therefore is much closer to *bit-pattern matching* process rather than individual compare-and-branch *item searching*. Therefore, it is of no surprise that database operations are rather efficient, fast, and almost independent of database size. However, it does depend on the implementation of virtual memory, the cache size, the external disk memory performance, the I/O channel bandwidth, or the size of allocated real memory. The database manipulation language usually referred to as SQL, or *Structural Query Language,* can either stand alone, or be embedded in usual programming languages. Some SQL implementations provide easier QBE, or *Query-By-Example*, i.e. database query programming using similar examples and likely scenarios.

Most common programming languages have included SQL to its database portfolio allowing embedded database access through native applications. Some database development tools also provide reporting facility, programming guide and support, also known as the *Fourth Generation Language* (4GL). The 4GL is a kind of higher scripting language supported by SQL pre-compiler that allows common users effortless creation and manipulation of complex databases, performing queries, and database processing. The XQL, a subset of the XML protocol, also makes use of the SQL database query functionality allowing fast data processing of dynamic Web based data.

In general, there are several distinguishable database types. The *base* tables and *views* are usually generated by individual applications providing end-users easy access to data. *Queries, temporary results*, and *intermediary* relations are also considered databases. *Snapshot* tables are important databases used not only by users but also by the DBMS in order to implement data warehouse functionality and some important database features. For instance, snapshots are instrumental during backup phases, fast database recovery, synchronization of transactions, creation of OLAP data warehouses, and data distribution via database replicas.

Alternative Database Models

There are several alternative database-modelling approaches that intend to solve the inherent data modelling problems either by extending it or entirely changing the relational data model. These new databases include *semantic modelling, knowledge base systems, nested relations, extendible systems*, and systems based on complex *database functional models*:

— *Semantic modelling* represents general modelling paradigm that incorporates the relational modelling. The idea is to try to identify a set of concepts that seem to be generically useful, that recur in some shape or form, and in a variety of applications. These concepts entail the notion of entity, primary keys, foreign keys, and domains at the basic level of relational model, and also kernels, characteristics, and associations of the RM/T database model defined by Codd.
— *Knowledge database system* is yet another modelling approach that refers to systems supporting "*objects*" in the OO sense. However, it usually implies implementation and database support containing logical rules of inference, also *well-formed formulae (wff)* instead of common data records. The knowledge is generated as a result of querying the whole database and exploring the inferences established among the logical rules. For instance, from the inference among the existing logical premises "*whales are mammals*" and "*mammals give birth to live offspring*" follows the knowledge "*whales give birth to live offspring*". Interestingly, in contrast to traditional databases that provide query for recorded data only, this fact appears even though it doesn't explicitly exist in the database.
— *Nested relations* are another way to increase the efficiency and functionality of the relational model. It is achieved by relaxing the normalisation requirement (i.e. First Normal Form is optional). In fact, the resulting complex records are recursive or nested relations. This objective is similar to the OO class concept.
— *Extended systems* provide the extendibility within the relational framework but paradoxically, sometimes disregarding the framework entirely. For instance, the extended OO database approach discards the relation concept entirely.
— *Functional models* represented by DAPLEX database are the original approach addressing the relational model by implementing one-to-one, one-to-many, and many-to-many mapping through functions. It uses typical mathematical notion and concept of a function and the domain mapping. The data integrity and the uniqueness properties are addressed by the system or at random by generating unique entity *identifiers*. This complex database model is mainly academic.

OO Databases

Most recently, the object-oriented technology represents just one of the many attempts to address the data-modelling problem. The *Object-Oriented* concepts are based on objects that *encapsulate,* both *data* and its processing – the object *behaviour. Objects* are unique replicated *instances* of a certain *class hierarchy.*

The data abstraction model of a class also includes object behaviour by specifying *operations* created either through *methods* that interact via public or private *interfaces* or *virtually* via protected interfaces through their inheritance channels. Effective data *integrity* and *consistency* checks may be enforced via incorporated procedures stored in their class definitions. A powerful OO *data abstraction, encapsulation, polymorphism* and strong *messaging* concepts apply best to CASE, multimedia, CAD/CAM, CAL, and similar AI applications. Most commercial relational DBMS claim extended support for object orientation. OO DBMS are still evolving under the research umbrella. *GemStone* and *Postgres* are the most prominent and the market leaders in the OO database domain. For more, please refer to the *Case 22:* GemStone OO dBase in CONDIS Project.

Bibliography

Database has big appeal to small business; *John Evan Frook*; **B to B**, Chicago; Jan 22, 2001; Vol. 86, Iss. 2; pg. 17, 1 pgs

Head-to-head comparison of 3 Web-based business database services; *Barbie E Keiser*; **EContent**, Wilton; Dec 2000; Vol. 23, Iss. 6; pg. 34, 6 pgs

Web database for e-business partners planned; *Ed Scannell*; **InfoWorld**, Framingham; Sep 4, 2000; Vol. 22, Iss. 36; pg. 5, 1 pgs

One 2 One to create business database; *Cordelia Brabbs*; **Marketing**, London; Jun 8, 2000; pg. 15, 1 pgs

New Web-based business service from Means Business taps concepts in books database; *Paula J Hane*; **Information Today**, Medford; Jan 2000; Vol. 17, Iss. 1; pg. 50, 1 pgs

Getting out of the HTML business: The database-driven Web site solution; *Kristin Antelman*; **Information Technology and Libraries**, Chicago; Dec 1999; Vol. 18, Iss. 4; pg. 176, 6 pgs

Jackson signs on at D'Arcy to grow database business; *Amanda Beeler*; **Advertising Age**, Chicago; Jul 10, 2000; Vol. 71, Iss. 29; Midwest region edition; pg. 34, 1 pgs

Distributed networks will eliminate vulnerable control centres; **Electrical World** August, 1998

The art of distributed network management; **Network Computing** *Dave Molta*; Sep 15, 1997

John G. Hughes, Object-Oriented Databases, Prentice Hall, 1991

CHAPTER 14

DATABASE FUNCTIONALITY

Concurrent Transactions

Case 22: GemStone OO dBase in CONDIS Project

CONDIS TESTPLAN
http://fbma.tuwien.ac.at/~e9027112/condis.html
(Reprinted by permission of the Author)

What is CONDIS?

CONDIS (Corporate Network Documentation and Information System) is based on object-oriented techniques. A first version was developed in a previous project under ESA (European Space Agency) contract. The main objective of the system is to provide network administration and planning tools for network administrators.

CONDIS is an object oriented software system with mouse driven graphical interface on SPARCstation or on MS Windows PC.

Network operator tasks are planning, configuration changes, inventory control and documentation. CONDIS is widely customisable, i.e. type of network elements can be configured and attributes can be changed and defined.

Network planning requires having an overview of the actual network configuration.

The planning task is supported by features such as:

– presenting the network configuration or parts of network graphically
– creating and deleting various network elects.
– manipulating properties of network elements like identification, administrative and operational state, type, transmission rate, etc.
– manipulating relationships between network elements such as connections, containment, element location (site, building, room), status, person, etc.

What are the Test steps?
1. Functionality Test
2. Performance Test
3. Timing test
4. Multiuser Test

The Test objects:

There are two configurations of CONDIS available:

1. PC-Client and Sun-Server
2. Sun-Client and Sun-Server
   The Test Environment.
   Installing and Configuring of the Test Environment: Gemstone (Server & Client) OO dBase

Server is Kyros (the old King of Persia) Technical data : WS: SPARCstation 20 Clock rate : 60 MHz CPU : sparc hostname : kyros hostid : 72728cbf Memory : 96 MB IP Address: 195.3.5.211 OS : Solaris 2.4	**Sun-Client machine is Darios** (another old King of Persia) Technical data : WS: SPARCstation 2 CPU: sparc hostname : darios hostid : 5540a62c Memory : 32 MB IP Address: 195.3.5.212 OS : Solaris 2.4	**PC-Client is hostname : PC5203** Memory : 16 MB IP Address:195.3.5.213 OS : WFW

WHY GEMSTONE?
http://fbma.tuwien.ac.at/~e9027112/gemstone.html

GemStone is a pure object database; it is not a compromise between the object model and the relational model. As such, it provides all the advantages of a complete ODBMS, plus the advantages of a mature commercial product:

As one of the first object databases, GemStone has a Well-developed set of predefined classes and methods.

GemStone uses a single, complete language for data definition, data manipulation, and query formulation, and it supports programming in other traditional and object-oriented languages.

GemStone supports multiple versions of schemas and data migration from one version to another, thus allowing concurrent revision and deployment an application in the same database.

GemStone is a production database system that supports large amounts of data and large numbers of concurrent users, and provides high-availability features such as on-line backup and easy recovery from system crashes and disk failure.

Gemstone Architecture for Condis-API

Production Database Systems

− *Scalability:* Gemstone can support hundreds of concurrent users and databases up to 10TBytes
− *High Availability*
− *On-line Backups*
− *Replicates*

Data replication in GemStone provides additional fault tolerance and provides for rapid recovery in case of disk failure:

− *Referential Integrity:* all database systems that use pointers and keys needs to address the issue of maintaining referential integrity.

> – *Multi-user Support*
> – *Security*
> – *Concurrency Control*

Concurrent Transactions Processing

Concurrent processing is an important feature in any database processing for it enables users simultaneous access, sharing data, and consistent updates of databases. A transaction represents a *logical unit of work*, atomic, but not necessarily single database operation and often requiring several database transformations. *Atomic* means that the changes are to be carried out complete, or not at all, from a *consistent state* of a database into subsequent consistent state. It is not necessary to preserve the database *consistency* at all intermediate instances. It should also ensure that the net effect of executing the transactions *concurrently* is not dependent on the order of execution. The *transaction* also represents a basic recovery unit used by the database *recovery* process.

The system that supports *transaction processing* is to provide a guarantee that whenever the transaction performs updates during system's failure (for whatever reason) *the updates are to be undone* before the transaction reaches its normal termination. The database system component that provides *atomic transaction* support is known as *Transaction Manager*. The *commit* and *rollback* actions are its essential operations. It makes use of a *recorded log* or *journal* of updates recorded on a persistent data store, tape, or hard disk taken *regularly* at the so-called *synchronization* points, or *randomly* during frequent update operations. Hence, performing *write-ahead log protocol* is an important DBMS routine. It establishes a *physical log* stored prior to any committed processing takes place thus allowing the subsequent restart to be able to recover from any incomplete transactions. It is important provision that protects databases from data loss.

Concurrency Control - Data Locking

Having executing *commit* or *rollback* operation the DBMS essentially establishes a specific synchronization point (*synch point*). In fact, it represents the *boundary* of *state of consistency* between two consecutive transactions. The d*ata locking* is common control mechanism that enables concurrent transaction processing. It locks the data that is about to be updated from reading or updating by any concurrent transaction. In a multiple-user environment lacking data locking feature tolerates concurrent transactions to interfere with each other's operation, hence creating concurrency problems such as *lost updates*, uncommitted *dependency*, or *inconsistent* data updates. The data locking mechanism prevents data loss and data inconsistencies by introducing data locks, eventually holding the concurrent transactions in a *wait state* until either the data lock is released, or subsequent *synch point* occurs. The transaction manager performs few actions:

– All updates made since the previous *synch point* are either committed or undone therefore eventually performing a *rollback* following the existing transaction log
– All previous data locks implemented for concurrency controls are released

– All open cursors are closed and current positioning in most applications is lost.
It is important to recognize the need to differentiate locks for concurrent access for data stores during record reading or updating. The compatibility matrix of correct reading and writing data locks is presented in *Table 23*. It applies simple *shared* and *exclusive* lock approach.

Table 23. Compatibility Matrix for Data Locking

Concurrent access: A vs. B	Data reading by A	Data update by A
Data reading by B	Shared lock	Exclusive lock
Data update by B	Exclusive lock	Exclusive lock

There are few significant drawbacks as a result of the concurrency control using data locking that may significantly influence the performance of database processing. Most importantly, the data locking facilitates the conditions for a *deadlock* event to occur. The deadlock is a state when two or more resources or transactions are simultaneously waiting for each other to release its lock. Not only is it difficult to detect the deadlock, but even more difficult to prevent it. Yet another problem comes from some relaxed data-locking schemes that try to implement data locking over higher data complexes and volumes. Implementing locks on larger data granularity may reduce the time overhead required by synchronization procedures. It may also reduce the frequency of occurrence of large-scale data-locking events. This is especially the case in multimedia and object-oriented database applications where *long-lived* transactions may occur (e.g. large GIS bitmaps, long music blobs, or CAD/CAM bit-images) and *larger data-store* transactions are common (e.g. large object classes and generated hierarchical data complexes).

Alternative Concurrency Control: Shadow copies vs. Time-stamping
Concurrency control in OO DBMS is therefore significantly different than in common relational DBMS applications. Most appropriately for many OO DBMS is the *optimistic* concurrency control with *shadow* object versions using object *time stamping* instead of data locking schemes. For instance, *GemStone* provides an optimistic concurrency control through shadow object versions. Due to the trade-off to reduce the time overhead, the time-stamp approach for maintaining shadow copies may result in increase of number of time-stamps required for every object in the database.

Two-Phase Commit: The Wedding Analogy
Two-Phase Commit (2PC) represents a commit and a rollback approach that ensures ACID properties of transactions. It permits a *consistent* execution of *atomic* transaction in *concurrent* database environment. *Distributed Management Environment* (DME) standard by X/Open group discussed earlier defines system structure and APIs to be used by TP Monitors; see *Figure 18*. The ISO/TP (ISO 0026) standard defines conditions for transactions abide by ACID properties:
– *Atomic*, follows simple *success-failure model*: either all actions happen or none

- *Consistent*, the transaction as a whole remains a correct database transformation
- *Isolated*, each transaction runs as though there were no concurrent ones
- *Durable*, the effects of committed transactions survive all failures.

The *success - failure* model commonly uses the analogy of a ship or an airplane command post procedure. There is usually more than one concurrent resource-officer responsible for instance, for steering, driving equipment, power engine, or navigation equipment. Much simpler is the wedding analogy that requires both the bride and the groom to commit and acknowledge their consent prior to the moment of their marriage being actually acknowledged. The TP system component, so-called TP *Coordinator*, guarantees that all the *multiple Resource Managers*, either *commit*, or *rollback* the updates for which they are responsible for, *all at once* that is, *in unison*. The *log-based restart* ensures a successful decision support even if the system fails during the transaction process.

Database Recovery

The Murphy's law, the motto cited at the beginning of Network Connectivity, is most appropriate for database environments. The reason is that the DBMS is to provide instantaneous recovery support. This not only applies to purely local failures, such as system power failure, but also to any global network failures. The *local* failures can affect all but the current transaction, whereby global failures may affect several, quite likely all the transactions in progress. The database failures therefore fall into two broad categories.

- *Soft*, or *system* failures without physical damage to the database.
- *Hard*, or *media* crash failures with partial or complete physical database damage.

The *crucial point* regarding the *system* failure is the *persistence* of *vulnerability* that affects the database consistency due to data loss, in particular, database cache, and data buffers. Due to the *uncertain state* of transactions at the time of the failure, it often has to be *undone*, which means, it is *rolled back* to its former stable and consistent state. Following subsequent system restart, so-called *check-pointing* procedure initiates the database recovery manager to perform *redoing* transactions, provided the transaction is successfully logged and backed up at the last *synch point* just before the system crash (hopefully).

Database Synchronization – check-pointing

The system recovery manager automatically initiates the *checkpoint i.e.* yet another synchronization mechanism. It represents a snapshot of transactions taken at certain prescribed intervals, often triggered by some specified number of updates written to the log. This means physically storing the contents of database buffers back to a *persistent database* on the hard data store. It also physically stores the corresponding checkpoint record back to the *persistent log* on disk or permanent media (streamer tapes or RAID disks).

A *media* failure represents a failure due to disk/tape crash or disk/tape controller. It is hard failure since some portion of the database has been physically destroyed. Recovery from such failures involves restarting and *reloading* the database from the *backup* copy. Using the transaction log it is possible to *redo* all transaction completed since the last *backup* synchronization point. In fact, there is no need to actually *undo* the transactions in progress since they have been corrupted anyway. This also shows the importance and the need of *backup* utility essential to *dump/restore* and *unload/load* frequently the complete physical database to and from a persistent data store.

Database Protection

Database security and integrity are two separate issues that concern database protection mechanisms. *Security* refers to the protection of database against unauthorized access, disclosure, alteration, or destruction. It ensures that users perform actions they are only *allowed* to. *Integrity* however, means maintaining the accuracy and validity of data. It ensures that users perform actions *correctly*. In both cases, the database system needs to be aware of certain specified *constraints* that *users must not violate* at any instance. The DBMS performs this function properly provided the authorization constraints are saved in the *system catalogue* and users' access request rights are checked against these constraints. Common mechanisms used are *passwords* and users' *identification* features.

Security Considerations

Database *security* means protecting the database against *unauthorized* users. It is accomplished by controlling users' access rights through checking the passwords and users' authentication. Whenever appropriate, it may involve introducing physical locks and controls. Setting physical locks to all system's access points, guarded entry, or implementing restricted entry, provides sufficient database security provided any remote access is disabled and the database stands alone, off the network. However, in a distributed database environment this is not the case since neither database access control nor users' authentication is feasible. Other problems are related to the need for frequent password change and secure password distribution through the network. A highly recommended practice is to make use of the *Public Key Infrastructure* (PKI) data *encryption* for password distribution through *Secure Electronic Transaction* (SET) protocol.

Integrity Issues

Whereas *security* means protecting the database against unauthorized users, the database *integrity* means protecting it against the *authorized* ones. Database systems today are typically *weak on integrity* since data integrity, accuracy, and correctness checking are still done by user-written procedural code rather than by the system itself. Obviously, it is preferable that the DBMS provides integrity checking, for instance, EE/R DBMS automatically checks on entity, relational, or referential integrity rules. Therefore, *integrity* constraints check upon conditions required by all *correct states* of the database. Most commercial DBMS tools today claim advanced integrity and security support.

However, security concerns have been raised following the recent reports by PGP, a market leader in security tools. A natural question may be raised how aware are we of network security threats and what could we do about it. For more, please see *Case 23:* PGP Security Extends PGP Wireless Platform Support to Windows CE and *Case 26:* Privacy Guide: Steganography.

Case 23: PGP Security Extends PGP Wireless Platform Support to Windows CE

PGP SECURITY EXTENDS PGP WIRELESS PLATFORM SUPPORT TO INCLUDE MICROSOFT WINDOWS CE
http://pgp.com/naicommon/aboutnai/press/pr_template.asp?PR=/PressMedia/091 12001-B.asp&Sel=1063

The First Security Solution for This Platform to Secure Data on Vulnerable Handheld Devices
Handheld Data Storage and Synchronization Made Secure for the Fastest Growing Computing Platforms

ATLANTA, Sept. 11 /PRNewswire/ -- PGP Security, a division of Network Associates, Inc. (Nasdaq: NETA), today introduced PGPwireless for Microsoft Windows CE, the first and only security solution for this platform. Extending the existing PGPwireless product line that supports Palm/OS devices, PGP wireless is now available for Windows CE devices. Additionally, PGPwireless for the Palm/OS version 2.0 is now available. PGPwireless provides security for data in storage and during synchronization on one of the fastest growing computing platforms.

According to a recent article from the Gartner, Inc, "by 2007, more than 60 percent of the European Union and U.S. population aged 15 to 50 will carry or wear a wireless computing and communications device at least six hours a day."* With increasing use of handheld devices to perform daily business and personal tasks, it's critical to secure and protect the privacy for this platform.

PGPwireless provides an effective encryption-based solution to protect information stored on handheld devices even if the device is lost or stolen. With PGPwireless only the owner can access the data.

"PGPwireless enables users to conduct secure business right from their handheld device, wherever they are," said Jeff Jones, vice president of marketing at PGP Security. "Then, when users return to their offices, PGPwireless easily and securely synchronizes data to the laptop, desktop or server. PGP Security provides the only privacy solution to exchange data securely between the broadest range of devices from handhelds, to PCs, to the mainframe."

The use of PGP encryption protects the integrity of data at all points of access on the enterprise network: handheld, laptop, desktop, server and mainframe platforms. Handhelds are now commonplace in the work environment, but few companies include these devices in their security policy. Users frequently synchronize these devices with their desktops so corporate information is easily transported outside of the security perimeter.

Pricing and Availability

* PGPwireless is available for $52/each for a two-year subscription for Palm/OS and Windows CE.

About PGP Security

PGP Security, a division of Network Associates Inc., is a worldwide leader in products and services focusing on solving privacy and data confidentiality issues, and has a strong history of setting security industry standards. PGP Security's breadth of security products, including firewall, encryption, intrusion detection, risk assessment and VPN technologies, address the full range of security and privacy issues, anywhere information is transmitted or stored. PGP Security's products secure over seven million users and include several of the industry's well-known security brands, including Gauntlet Firewall/VPN, PGP Corporate Desktop Privacy Products, the E-Business Server family of products, CyberCop Scanner, and PGP e-appliances/VPN. PGP Security's COVERT research team identifies and works to resolve serious vulnerabilities before attackers are able to exploit them. The findings are incorporated into the product offerings, ensuring protection from the latest vulnerabilities. For more information and software evaluations, visit http://www.pgp.com

About Network Associates

With headquarters in Santa Clara, Calif., Network Associates, Inc. is a leading supplier of security and availability solutions for e-businesses. Network Associates is comprised of four business units: McAfee, delivering world class anti-virus products; PGP Security, providing firewall, intrusion detection and encryption products; Sniffer Technologies, a leader in network and application management; and Magic Solutions, providing web-based service desk solutions. For more information, Network Associates can be reached at 972-308-9960 or on the Internet at http://www.nai.com

*source : Gartner "Wearing IT Out: The Growth of the Wireless, Wearable World", A. Linden, J, Fenn, April 2001.

Bibliography
A multi-granularity locking-based concurrency control in object-oriented database systems; *Woochun Jun*; **The Journal of Systems and Software**, New York; Nov 1, 2000; Vol. 54, Iss. 3; pg. 201

Step-change in partnering and real-time database systems; *Wouter Rensink*; **Petroleum Economist**, London; Oct 2000; Vol. 67, Iss. 10; pg. 34, 2 pgs

Similarity retrieval based on group bounding and the angle sequence matching in shape database systems; *P W Huang*; **The Journal of Systems and Software**, New York; Sep 30, 2000; Vol. 54, Iss. 1; pg. 9

Tips for transitioning to a new database system; *Wayne W Carley*; **Association Management**, Washington; Aug 2000; Vol. 52, Iss. 8; pg. 155, 1 pgs

EDI controls design support system using relational database system; *Sangjae Lee*; **Decision Support Systems**, Amsterdam; Aug 2000; Vol. 29, Iss. 2; pg. 169

TBA converts to new database system; *Anonymous*; **Texas Banking**, Austin; Aug 2000; Vol. 89, Iss. 8; pg. 26, 1 pgs

An atomic commit protocol for gigabit-networked distributed database systems; *Yousef J Al-Houmaily*; **Journal of Systems Architecture**, Amsterdam; Jul 2000; Vol. 46, Iss. 9; pg. 809

Transaction multicasting scheme for resilient routing control in parallel cluster database systems; *Inhwan Jung*; **Journal of Systems Architecture**, Amsterdam; Jun 2000; Vol. 46, Iss. 8; pg. 699

Issues and approaches to supporting timeliness and security in real-time database systems; *S H Son*; **Journal of Systems Architecture**, Amsterdam; Feb 2000; Vol. 46, Iss. 4; pg. 397

Extending a deductive object-oriented database system with spatial data handling facilities; *Fernandes, Alvaro A A*; **Information and Software Technology**, Amsterdam; Jun 15, 1999; Vol. 41, Iss. 8; pg. 483, 15 pgs

Principles of Multimedia Database Systems; *Goodrum, Abby A*; **Journal of the American Society for Information Science**, New York; Apr 1, 1999; Vol. 50, Iss. 4; pg. 382, 2 pgs

Active database systems; *Norman W Paton*; **ACM Computing Surveys**, Baltimore; Mar 1999; Vol. 31, Iss. 1; pg. 63, 41 pgs

OBJECTIVE: A benchmark for object-oriented active database systems; *Cetintemel, Ugur*; **The Journal of Systems and Software**, New York; Feb 1999; Vol. 45, Iss. 1; pg. 31, 13 pgs

EUTSTIS: A comprehensive database system to support transportation studies in an MPO; *Yanbing He*; **Institute of Transportation Engineers. ITE Journal**, Washington; Mar 1999; Vol. 69, Iss. 3; pg. 14, 1 pgs

OMG overview: CORBA and the OMA in enterprise computing; **Association for Computing Machinery. Communications of the ACM** *Jon Siegel*; Oct 1998

Borland shifts focus to enterprise computing; **AS/400 Systems Management** *Mayu Mishina*; Jul 1998

How interest in ERP led to expansion of Enterprise Computing section; **InfoWorld** *Sandy Reed*; Jun 22, 1998

Clustering: The path to open enterprise computing; **MC Technology Marketing Intelligence** *Pauline Nist*; Jan 1998

CHAPTER 15

DISTRIBUTED APPLICATION INTEROPERABILITY

Java ComponentWare

CoreLAN Communications - Tuxedo Consulting
TP Services with Tuxedo™
http://www.corelan.com/tux.html
(Copyright © 2002 Symcor Inc. All rights reserved. Reprinted by permission)

"CoreLAN specializes in the design, construction and implementation of high performance OLTP systems."

Transaction Processing Services

Tuxedo is one of the leading high performance transaction processing (TP) systems. Tuxedo™ is a shrink-wrapped solution offering guaranteed messaging, delivery and queuing of transactions.

CoreLAN specializes in the design, construction and implementation of high performance, high-volume on-line transaction processing (OLTP) and strategic decision support (DSS) architectures using open network, parallel DMBS object and three-tier middleware technologies. The company's experience places us at the forefront of delivering comprehensive TP systems based upon Tuxedo [TM].

CoreLAN is one of the only developers in Canada certified by EnterSoft, and BEA Associates on developing applications in Tuxedo [TM].

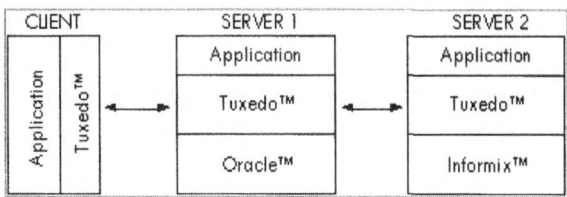

Figure 53. BEA Tuxedo

Tuxedo's "named services" allows an application to be layered and compartmentalised, thereby enhancing overall system performance and resilience. It

233

supports the concepts of a clustered application across multiple nodes, allowing for scalability and fault resilience.

If you wish to learn more about Tuxedo, check out <u>BEA's</u> web site. All contents Copyright © 1994, CoreLAN Communications, Inc. BEA Tuxedo is a registered trademark of BEA Systems. All Rights Reserved.

BEA Tuxedo - Introduction
http://www.bea.com/products/tuxedo/index.shtml
(Copyright © 2002 BEA Systems Inc. All rights reserved.)

BEA Tuxedo is a proven platform for building rock-solid, easy-to-manage enterprise systems that enable businesses to rapidly launch new products and services to maintain their competitive advantage.

Overview
Today's business environment demands Web and enterprise applications that will accelerate your entry into new markets, help you reach and retain customers, and enable you to introduce new products and services quickly. You need a proven, reliable, and scalable application infrastructure platform-one that can connect and empower all types of users, while integrating all of your corporate data and applications in a powerful, flexible end-to-end e-commerce solution. BEA Tuxedo takes the time, complexity, and risk out of developing and deploying this solution. BEA Tuxedo is an integral and proven component of the BEA WebLogic Enterprise Platform™ that businesses rely on to support their distributed, mission-critical applications.

Benefits
- Business-critical reliability. BEA Tuxedo has been tested and proven in thousands of the most demanding mission-critical applications.
- Virtually unlimited scalability. As demands increase, additional servers can be added on the fly without disrupting ongoing operations.
- Simplified development. You can focus on enterprise applications while BEA Tuxedo handles the underlying complexity of distributed applications.
- Unparalleled high-performance. BEA Tuxedo is designed for large-scale, Web-to-mainframe enterprise solutions.

Resources
- For customer success stories, see the <u>BEA Customers Web page</u>.
- For information about BEA e-business solution partners, see the <u>BEA Partners Web page</u>.

Distributed application computing nowadays encompasses a collection of sub-networks, connected together through some kind of wide area network communications in which each network site represents an enterprise Intranet site itself. Naturally, the sites have mutually agreed to cooperate together so that any user can access data and/or code from anywhere in the network, as if it were stored at the user's own site. It actually introduces the *concept* of a *virtual database* whose components are physically placed in a number of distinct real databases spread across a number of distinct network nodes.

Why is the distributed database concept desirable?
Since real enterprises are already segmented, at least operationally, into sub-networks, divisions, departments, projects, etc., very much likely their databases are physically distributed as well. In fact, eventual data distribution usually follows the ongoing enterprise business process reorganization. It maintains data at most suitable nodes closer to the enterprise business process that has created them or/and uses them.
The distributed database computing allows database structure to mirror the enterprise structure: *local data locally, remote data accessed when necessary.* Another fundamental principle of the distributed computing environment is that it is to be transparent and *look to the users exactly like a non-distributed system.*
The advantages are obvious. A combination of processing *efficiency* with closely stored data where it is most frequently used, and increased data *accessibility* throughout the enterprise network. Among the disadvantages, it is the increased system *complexity*, vulnerable system *security*, contingent *reliability*, negotiable centralized *control*, and the increased ownership *costs*. Not surprisingly, it is often advised to avoid distributed application computing whenever possible, and if still tempted to compromise over these issues make sure to secure the data that may jeopardize the entire business process.

Distributed Application Paradigm Shift
Distributed application computing is a phenomenon that closely follows the rapid development of enterprise-wide networks, the introduction of global networks, and the rapid growth of the Web. Undeniably, it has created great challenges that the business community could hardly resist. Challenges to provide global access to all end-users and make applications more suitable and responsive to changing business environment conditions. It enables all kinds of *"virtual"* concepts, from virtual databases to virtual enterprises, leveraging on existing resources and investments in IT.
The response to market challenges and user-driven IT demands has created a symbiosis among IT market leaders, vendors, IT professionals, and business process specialists to provide more adaptable, highly flexible, and functional distributed applications.
The result is the introduction of distributed application computing across enterprise networks. The re-engineering and developing new mission-critical applications also provides new solutions running PC and NC clients, sharing available resources across servers and mainframes alike. Its goal is simply to achieve flexible computing environment that can respond better and faster to current business needs leveraging on the IT investments.
The distributed computing environment constitutes of enterprise networks, supported by distributed computing middleware, and distributed applications.

The applications provide the necessary logic for the implementation of business processes allowing applications' code and data to move closer to users and processes that generate them.

The distributed application computing to date, represents a paradigm shift since it integrates advanced IT, distributed networks, high bandwidth communications, object-orientation development, and Java-aware distributed applications development tools. OMG *X/Open* together with *CORBA*, OSF *CMIP*, *DMI*, and *VE NIIIP* are just few important enabling standards for distributed application computing providing the necessary support by influential community groups.

Why Distributed Computing?

Undoubtedly, the distributed application computing leaves no choice when considering and deploying enterprise-wide applications. Clearly, the benefits include easier use of applications, reduced application development time and time-to-market, and increases enterprise opportunities. It also provides greater flexibility, requires less training, legacy applications integration, cost-effective learning curve, and higher end-user efficiency.

Evolution of Distributed Application Computing

It took enterprise community many years to accept the distributed computing applications as a viable enterprise-wide computing phenomenon. The evolution of distributed computing recognizes three important generations: *host-based*, *desktop-based*, and current *client/server* platform. Eventually, the *peer-to-peer* enterprise computing becomes its forth generation. *Table 24* presents a short overview of distributed computing evolution along with the representatives of TP Monitors that relate best to the distributed transaction model. For more, please refer to Case *24:* CoreLAN - TP Services with BEA Tuxedo ™.

Table 24. Distributed Computing Systems

Platform/Year	Networking	Computing	TP Monitor model/Apps
Host-based late 1970s	Shared Mainframe and Dumb ASCII terminals	Host - Mainframe Application processing	Two-ball: IBM's CICS; Novell's NetWare
Desktop-based mid 1980s	Shared Workstations & PC & ICA terminals	Desktop/Workstation application processing	TP multithreaded OS: Sybase EA Server
Client/Server early 1990s	Multiple Servers and PC Clients	Common Client/Server application processing	Three-ball router: IBM's IMS; Transarc's Encina
Peer-to-Peer late 1990s	Multi-tier Network and all type of Clients	Enterprise Network application processing	Three-ball SMP/cluster: BEA's Tuxedo

Host-Based

The host-based or mainframe distributed computing corresponds to former centralized mainframe system connecting a pool of dumb or character-based terminals. The end-users were operationally assigned to individual groups or departments, usually sharing data, files, and other resources (e.g. CPU time, main memory, communications devices, printers, databases and applications); see *Figure 54*. Nevertheless, the application processing was all but distributed. Applications were running on the mainframe under the control of the OS. Many host-based, mission-critical applications were deployed during these years, largely contributing to enterprise dependency on so-called, *legacy* applications. The term *legacy* applies mainly to the application development paradigms, programming languages, and development tools used to develop a variety of distributed applications. It involves inefficient many-to-many data processing.

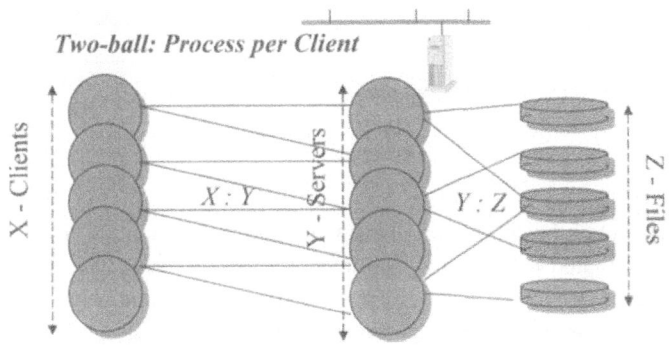

Figure 54. Host-based Distributed Computing [121]

Desktop-Based

During mid 1980s, is the emergence of individual end-users, stand-alone processing, and fairly powerful PC platforms evolved the distributed computing into another generation of *desktop-based* computing. The mainframe and mini-computer based two-tier networks provided the necessary networking and proprietary-connectivity to all enterprise users behind PCs and within individual departments. Applications were primarily running on individual workstations, sharing as before, all networking resources; see *Figure 55*. However, some smaller applications not restricted by CPU performance or memory footprint could run on a desktop thus paving the way for upcoming desktop processing. The increased network connectivity introduced sharing applications like *e-mail*, electronic *news, bulletin* boards, etc. Data s*ecurity* was not of any major concern.

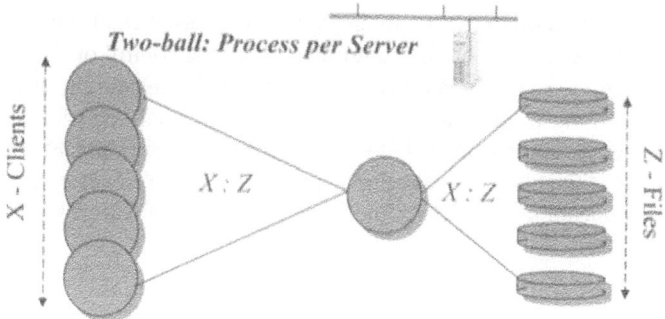

Figure 55. Desktop-based Distributed Computing [121]

Client/Server-Based

Thus far, so much has been said about Client/Server computing. It came on the wave of distributed computing phenomenon, hence freeing the end-users and allowing them an individual access to corporate decision support data and knowledge databases. It facilitated the entry of C/S technology through *remote* and *cooperative* processing. Servers run most of the applications, data processing, managing databases, providing networking, and sharing resources to individual clients' requests; see *Figure 56*. WAN and LAN played important role in establishing interconnection to Client/Server networks.

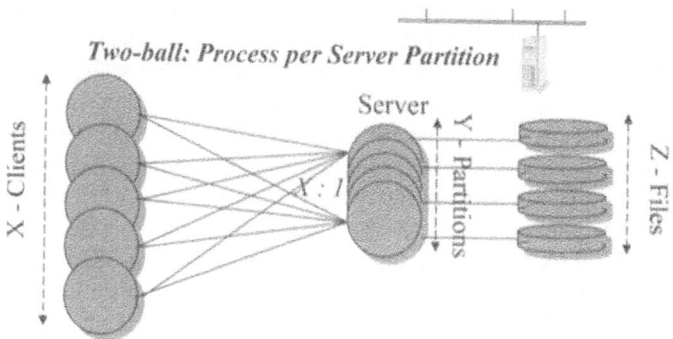

Figure 56. Traditional Client/Server Distributed Computing [121]

Peer-to-Peer Enterprise Networks

The new wave of enterprise distributed computing has just begun. We are witnessing the introduction of multi-tier network architectures, predominately based on peer-to-peer internetworking concepts. Suddenly, the network connectivity, middleware, and integration of applications across networks becomes of strategic importance. The distributed applications development, deployment, and maintenance are free of platforms, vendors, network and enterprise boundaries, proprietary restrictions, and building blocks choices. The application-to-application distributed computing to date is predominantly object-oriented. Based on DCE; see *Figure 57,* and CORBA compliant platforms, Java aware browsers, allow distributed processing and distributed development; see *Figure 58.* The enterprise-wide deployment integrates together the Web and corporate networks, enterprise-wide Intranet and Extranet, presumably on future thin-client devices and NC platforms.

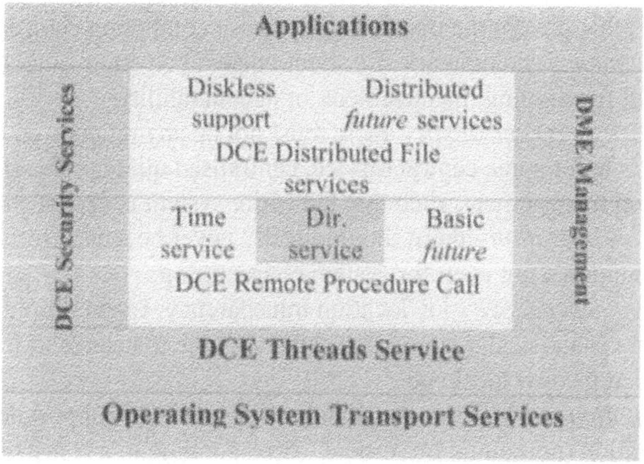

Figure 57. Distributed Computing Environment Services

Following the idea mentioned earlier, *the network* literally becomes a *virtual computer.* For more on networked PC please refer to the *Case 3:* Networked Computing with Beowulf Iridis Cluster. Any user can access distributed computing applications and data from anywhere as soon as being connected to the network. It provides unprecedented increase in number, data volume, and diversity of applications. The latter ranges from personal banking, e-commerce, and e-business. The Web also brings in remote home networking, virtual offices, teleconferencing, multimedia, integration of multiple applications, CTI-like convergence, technology conversion such as GSM using WAP, or SMS-based mobile e-mail, portable voice-activated computing, and much more. It turns out that the saying *'the sky is the limit'* is most appropriate description of the current developments in distributed-application computing world to date.

Distributed Database Computing
Distributed application computing has brought the power of computing to all platforms. However, the distributed databases represent its ultimate achievement. The users still need to access data on a local server in order to complete a task or

database application. In a distributed application environment however, both data and application code may reside on remote servers, sharing the computing load as well as the persistent data stores. The distributed application makes a request through its clients by initialising a chained process through multiple tiers of servers (e.g. MOM, RPC, or APPC-based). The result is that the data is sent through the network to the application as requested. The distributed transaction processing running across different database boundaries need special attention. This is due to the requirements for preservation of the **ACID** properties of transactional data. OMG *X/Open*, OSF *CORBA,* and other DCE standards are instrumental providing the necessary support to distributed database applications. In line with the challenges that are encountered in maintaining the distributed application computing environment, it is worth citing the *twelve rules* brought in by Date [1995] that govern the distributed database computing environment:

1. *Local autonomy* - no network site should depend on some other site for its successful functioning, management, or accountability.
2. *No reliance on a central site* - there must not be any reliance on a central *"master"* site for some central service, centralised query processing, or transaction management, such that the entire system is dependent on it.
3. *Continuous operation* - there should ideally never be a need for a planned system shutdown not even for system restructuring.
4. *Location independence* - i.e. location transparency. Users should not know where data is physically stored, but rather be able to behave as if data were all stored at its own local site.
5. *Fragmentation independence* - a database system is to support data fragmentation (horizontal or vertical, corresponding to a restriction or a projection database operation) provided a given relation can be divided up unto pieces or fragments for physical storage and reconstructed via suitable union or join database operation.
6. Replication independence - a system supports data transparent replication of a given fragment of a relation at a physical level by many distinct stored copies - replicas, at many distinct sites, allowing dynamic creation and removal.
7. Distributed query processing - outperforming the operations in non-relational database systems and introducing optimisation on data move.
8. Distributed transaction management - executing a single transaction on multiple sites through multiple processes - agents and preventing them against possible deadlocks, in case they are part of the same transaction, or imposing two-phase commit protocol for data recovery.
9. *Hardware independence* – desirable to run the same DBMS on different hardware platforms, and furthermore, to have them as equal partners.
10. Operating system independence - possible to run not only on different DBMS but different operating systems as well as on the same hardware.
11. *Network independence* - to be able to support multiple disparate sites, different hardware, or operating system platforms, on a variety of communication networks.

12. *DBMS independence* - all that is really needed, is to support the same interface on different sites, to be heterogeneous to some degree.

An overriding objective in distributed database systems is to *minimize the number and volume of messages*. It subsequently gives rise to several challenges:

1. *Database query processing*, implies that the query optimisation process itself needs to be distributed, just as well as its query execution process.
2. *Database catalogue management* - includes not only the usual catalogue data regarding relations, indexes, users, but also all the necessary control information to enable the system to provide the desired location, fragmentation, and replication independence (e.g. centralised, fully partitioned, partitioned, or any combination of all three).
3. *Update propagation* - introduces a common scheme of distribution, the so-called *primary copy* to all sites.
4. *Recovery* - based on the *two-phase commit* protocol (or some variant) optimises on number of messages.
5. *Concurrency* – is based on database locking and test, set and release lock messages, and primary copy strategy. However, it may lead to yet another problem – a *global deadlock* detection that may incur further network communications overhead.

ComponentWare - Java Applets

Most recent developments in the distributed networking technology are certainly related to new *componentware* application-development trends. Componentware represents a building-block approach in OO component-based development of distributed network applications. In particular, Sun *Java*, EJB, MS *ActiveX,* and the new brands of scripting languages such as *Visual Basic (VB), Perl* and alike, are instrumental in its promotion.

Typical business distributed applications most often run through multi-tier networks. Usually, client applications make requests to process data held in corporate databases. The use of Java-based applications in EJB environments clearly makes sense due to the widespread Web access and rather relaxed requirements for installation of applications. There are few advantages in this approach. Basically, the applications may easily be published and accessed through its *Uniform Resource Locator* (URL) Internet address. It provides full GUI client support and automatic EJB and Java applets version control.

The communications alternatives implemented among applet-clients and the application servers are HTTP, IP Sockets, *Remote Method Invocation* (RMI), COM and CORBA[119]. The HTTP based *Common Gateway Interface* (CGI), and IP Sockets are inferior to the RMI-based RPC and powerful MS DOC and UNIX CORBA platform; see *Figure 58*.

---

[119] For more, on the advantages and disadvantages, refer to A. Vogel, *"Building Distributed System in Java"*, Byte [Sept-Oct. 1995].

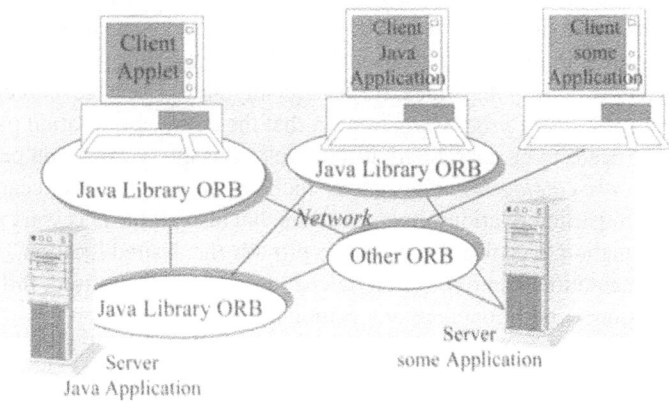

Figure 58. Distributed Java Applets using CORBA [120]

Distributed Transaction Processing

Since first CICS application on IBM mainframes, the distributed computing technology had a remarkable development, both in volume and in scale. In order to satisfy and to accommodate hundreds, yet tens of thousands of clients in huge volume of transactions per minute, it certainly makes a significant difference.

Simple distributed computing used on mainframes and old Client/Server systems apply very simple *one server-process per client* model. However, the two scalability problems emerged as main drawbacks. Firstly, it is the so-called *percentage problem*, when server itself becomes a precious resource. Secondly, it is the *polynomial explosion problem*, when a number of file connections literally overflow the server. As expected, as a response to the TP challenge the vendor's community resulted in proliferation of few basic distributed-transaction processing-models. The IBM CICS offered, so-called *"two-ball"* solutions, hence reducing the load by implementing only *one server-process per server* approach. In the *two-ball* TP model a client is expected to find and route the requests to the appropriate servers. Accordingly, TP OS implemented a private treaded library and built a private file system within the host OS. Other vendors like Novell's NetWare and SyBase followed suite. Please see *Figure 55.*

The newly introduced *multithreaded-TP* migrated on UNIX. It had the advantage of three times more efficient TP services and possible ten-fold increase in number of clients. However, the drawbacks of *the process-per-server* approach were its inability to scale up to the shared-memory SMP and cluster-CPU server systems, since only a single process was allocated to run the OS. It was also difficult to manage a single address process-space allocated to all joined applications. All but a single application failure could have crashed the server

---

[120] A. Vogel, Byte [1995]

system. In order to overcome the inherent scale-up problem, a *process-per-application-server partition* was introduced that allowed adding up servers for each and every new application. It is the most widely used approach to date that allows transaction scalability, such as CICS, NetWare, SyBase, and Oracle *TP Monitor*. Please see *Figure 56*.

Still, a more advanced approach, the *three-ball* TP model has introduced yet another layer, a process *router* that creates and manages the pool of application-server processes and brokers clients requests to servers; see *Figure 59*. This TP model multiplexes and runs several clients down to few standard server processes. The applications and routers can also benefit from SMP and cluster server architectures. It scales up by simply adding more routers. It also provides efficient load-balancing and transparent fail-over for clients. The first *three-ball* system was IBM IMS introduced back in 1970. IBM Transarc's *Encina*, Digital's *ACMS*, and BEA's *Tuxedo* have added many advanced features to this successful approach. For more; see *Case 24:* CoreLAN - TP Services with BEA Tuxedo ™.

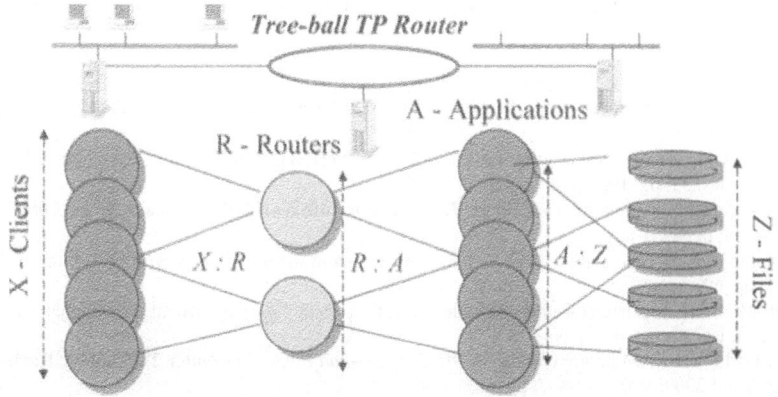

Figure 59. Peer-to-Peer Transaction Processing [121]

A client in the three-ball TP model usually performs data capture, local data processing and makes requests to a router. The router brokers the requests from a pool of clients to one or more servers. The appropriate servers execute these requests and respond. This concept has evolved into three generic applications: queued, conversational, and workflow TP server. The *queued* TP specializes in messaging applications such as e-mail, EDI, print spooling etc. On the other hand, the *conversational* TP based on multi-message exchange between a client and a server runs simple **ACID** transactions such as menu and forms-processing applications. Finally, the *workflow* TP server acts as a natural combination of both, the conversational and the queued transactional application server.

---

[121] Gray, Byte [April, 95]

Transaction application processing involving thousands of clients relies heavily on TP monitor's support. TP monitor manager considers databases, transaction queues, applications, communications, and servers as its available resources; see *Figure 18*. A TP monitor renders its servers' programs suitable packages (short-running of high-priority, and batch runs of low-priority) in response to collection of services generated by client applications. It also assigns the security attributes, defines users and roles, authenticates clients, and checks their authority on each request, rejecting those that violate the acknowledged security policy.

Bibliography

A framework and test-suite for assessing approaches to resolving heterogeneity in distributed databases; *H T El-Khatib*; **Information and Software Technology**, Amsterdam; May 1, 2000; Vol. 42, Iss. 7; pg. 505

An atomic commit protocol for gigabit-networked distributed database systems; *Yousef J Al-Houmaily*; **Journal of Systems Architecture**, Amsterdam; Jul 2000; Vol. 46, Iss. 9; pg. 809

Designing a distributed database on a local area network: A methodology and decision support system; *H Lee*; **Information and Software Technology**, Amsterdam; Feb 25, 2000; Vol. 42, Iss. 3; pg. 171

RosettaNet group to use XML for commerce interoperability; *Stannie Holt*; **InfoWorld**, Framingham; Jun 14, 1999; Vol. 21, Iss. 24; pg. 8, 1 pgs

Ishoni inks three DSL-interoperability deals; *Darrell Dunn*; **Electronic Buyers' News**, Manhasset; Sep 4, 2000; pg. PG.44

Lack of proven switch interoperability huts aggressors; *Kevin Tolly*; **Network World**, Framingham; Sep 18, 2000; Vol. 17, Iss. 38; pg. 32, 1 pgs

PKI Vendors Push For Interoperability; *RUTRELL YASIN*; **InternetWeek**, Manhasset; Aug 28, 2000; pg. PG.12

Vendors form DSL interoperability group; *Michael Martin*; **Network World**, Framingham; Aug 14, 2000; Vol. 17, Iss. 33; pg. 10, 2 pgs

BizTalk's interoperability coming from others; *Tom Sullivan*; **InfoWorld**, Framingham; Jul 24, 2000; Vol. 22, Iss. 30; pg. 32, 1 pgs

PKI: Struggling for interoperability; *Mike Fratto*; **Network Computing**, Manhasset; Aug 7, 2000; Vol. 11, Iss. 15; pg. 69, 4 pgs

IBM exec: Microsoft sees need for interoperability; *Lee Copeland*; **Computerworld**, Framingham; Jul 3, 2000; Vol. 34, Iss. 27; pg. 48, 1 pgs

A drive toward DVD-RAM interoperability at PC Expo; *Joshua Piven*; **Computer Technology Review**, Los Angeles; Jul 2000; Vol. 20, Iss. 7; pg. 58, 1 pgs

Fibre Channel switch interoperability; *Mark Ferelli*; **Computer Technology Review**, Los Angeles; Third Quarter 2000; pg. 40, 2 pgs

Switch interoperability brings fibre channel forward; *Mark Ferelli*; **Computer Technology Review**, Los Angeles; Jul 2000; Vol. 20, Iss. 7; pg. 54, 1 pgs

Conflict free transaction scheduling using serialization graph for real-time databases; *Victor C S Lee*; **The Journal of Systems and Software**, New York; Dec 1, 2000; Vol. 55, Iss. 1; pg. 57

Transaction management in databases supporting Web-based negotiations; *Waldemar Wieczerzycki*; **INFOR**, Ottawa; Aug 2000; Vol. 38, Iss. 3; pg. 245, 27 pgs

Distributed similarity search algorithm in distributed heterogeneous multimedia databases; *Ju-Hong Lee*; **Information Processing Letters**, Amsterdam; Jul 31, 2000; Vol. 75, Iss. 1,2; pg. 35

Transaction multicasting scheme for resilient routing control in parallel cluster database systems; *Inhwan Jung*; **Journal of Systems Architecture**, Amsterdam; Jun 2000; Vol. 46, Iss. 8; pg. 699

Electronic trading database counters costs, errors of paper-based transactions; *Michael Hartnett*; **Stores**, New York; Jun 2000; Vol. 82, Iss. 6; pg. 96

Priority and deadline assignment to triggered transactions in distributed real-time active databases; *Kam-Yiu Lam*; **The Journal of Systems and Software**, New York; Apr 1, 2000; Vol. 51, Iss. 1; pg. 49

SIRS Mandarin premieres new interface and databases, receives automation contract; *Anonymous*; **Information Today**, Medford; Feb 2000; Vol. 17, Iss. 2; pg. 37, 2 pgs

The Online Manual: A Practical Guide to Business Databases, 6th edition; **Database** *Deborah Lynne Wiley*; Aug/Sep 1998

Enterprise Databases BATTLE ON PART I; **Byte** *Karen Watterson*; Jun 1998

The use of patent databases by European small and medium-sized enterprises; **Technology Analysis & Strategic Management** *A Arundel*; Jun 1998

Database development methodology and organization; **Information Systems Management** *Purba, Sanjiv*; Winter 1999

The dissemination of good practices in database development work; **Journal of Database Management** *Becker, Shirley*; Summer 1998

Database development and working with a programmer; **Library Software Review** *Thomas L Kilpatrick*; Mar 1998

CHAPTER 16

BUSINESS INTELLIGENCE

Data Drilling, Mining and Slicing

Case 25: Cognicase: Sold! Maximizer Enterprise for Notes Wins Bid for Management Solution

SOLD! MAXIMIZER ENTERPRISE FOR NOTES WINS BID FOR MANAGEMENT SOLUTION

http://www.me4n.com/client/United/ME4N_UW_V500_MainEngine.nsf/0C7ADD3 472DBBAAC852565F90075D9CE/EA7B1E7DF8817EED85256AC0005350D6?OpenD ocument

In the words of Manheim Auctions CIO, Richard Deckard: "Our president wanted to have a detailed picture of the company each morning, almost at the touch of a button. With Maximizer Enterprise for Notes we can funnel all the latest information into a data warehouse ready for him each morning. He can see every aspect of the company."

The Challenge

Manheim Auctions is a leading auction house with an unusual speciality: wholesaling automobiles. Customers interact with Manheims four companies for sales, customer service and financing. The challenge was to find a system that would integrate the information of Manheim's four separate companies into one dynamic Customer Relationship Management solution.

Crescendo managing principal, Wayne Fleming recommended Maximizer Enterprise for Notes. Out of the box, Maximizer Enterprise for Notes addressed most of Manheim's needs.

The Solution

Richard Deckard, Manheims Auction's CIO, envisioned a system that would bring together the four individual companies.

The idea was to use the same customer master file to share information about customer service for marketing purposes, help desk issues, and for the sales force.

The idea was to use the same customer master file to share information about customer service for marketing purposes, help desk issues and for the sales force.

"I felt that the product had a significant portion of what Richard was looking for. One of the strong points was that it was open source code and customisable to any environment," explains Wayne Fleming. "We took a demo to Richard and he liked what we showed him.

The solution is a portal based system that integrates Maximizer Enterprise for Notes with an AS/400 back-end system and custom application development for collections, order entry, credit card processing and prospecting. These technologies combined provide a total Customer Relationship Management system, allowing four of Manheim Auction's businesses to manage and share information about its customers (car dealers), and facilitate workflow.

"The range of tools within the environment gives us endless ides of where we are going to go with this new capability," --- Richard Deckard, CIO Manheim Auctions.

The Result

The greatest benefit that has been realized from this solution is the ability for all users, from across all four businesses, to access and report on the same customer information. This has resulted in:

· Superior customer service through a unified help desk
· Enabling business units to leverage other business units' relationships with existing customers
·Effective performance measurement
· Call center now handles as many calls in one week, as they used to handle in one month – averaging 1,000 calls per week

"The solution delivered was the solution proposed. We got exactly what we asked for – on time and on budget," explains Deckard. It's no exaggeration to say this was the smoothest project I have ever worked on. The talent was right, the product was right, and the budget was right. It's as good as it gets."

The corporate data is strategically important to modern enterprises. Business people are literally drawn in data. Still, more than ever, a timely and accurately data access to corporate data resources is required in order to make correct and precise decisions. Among the IT achievements that have enabled these decision processes are certainly enterprise-wide networks, the client/server paradigm, global Web access, GroupWare technologies, and enterprise-wide databases. They have allowed managers promote imaginative decision-making approaches and introduce sophisticated business process re-engineering methods that helped refine the enterprise-wide business processes.

The enterprises are facing tougher competition due to the saturated market and the global reach trend enabled by the advances in Information Technology. The increasing customisation trends based on standardised of-the shelf products and services, together with the information revolution have revised the market driving forces. The common market feature to date is that *buyers are pulling rather than sellers pushing the market*. Moreover, the dynamic political changes and growing environmental consciousness are making the market picture even more obscured.

In order to do business successfully in such market conditions essentially, new marketing approaches are needed. Now, the emphasis is on quality of products and services, low costs and lean production, better response to customer's demands, closer relationship to customers and developing partner's alliances.

Inevitably, a new enterprise culture needs to be developed. The renewal of core business values and structure, along with re-engineering business processes, reduced enterprise complexity is required in order to stay competitive. In fact, it is the *information-driven* decision process that drives these changes. The information is on the desktop, the portable, at the palmtop, mobile phone, wherever we go. Not just any information, but *the one* actually needed. The one that makes the *difference,* sets our mind, right now and whenever we mean business. For some, *data warehouse* is the right answer to it "*helps turn data into a competitive tool*", advocates Computer World, [April 1995].

There is remarkable development in data warehouse technology mainly support of Web-based e-Commerce business applications and the need to generate customers' profiles, known as *Business Intelligence* (BI) trend. BI applications are in response to remain competitive by acquiring and preserving any valuable information about the market, its own decision processes, as well as the business processes of our competitors.

Data Warehouse Technology

So far, we have reviewed many of the current technologies that drive the IT change to date. In particular we have elaborated on the enterprise-wide connectivity, the LAN and WAN inter-networking, client/server paradigms, distributed databases, GroupWare etc. Data warehouses are logical step forward. It leverages on some unique database achievements, and the *ad hoc data access* of integrated *decision-support* tools.

The data warehouse looks a promising database technology providing increased accessibility of information to decision-makers. It helps directly manage business processes. In order to stay globally competitive, concerned business community responded immediately with appreciation, completely embracing the data warehouse technology. So, what is actually the *data warehousing*?

Data Warehouse (DW) is a data store that supports the business decision-making and ad-hoc data-retrieval process. It is closely related to database technology but it uses innovative decision making tools to analyse, distribute, and monitor customer-related information from a business decision-support point of view. For instance, it may provide answers to ordinary questions. *Who are the 20% highly profitable customers*? *How to serve them best*? But also to find intriguing answers to more sophisticated questions, sometimes even questionable, evoked from dubious legal, or ambiguous ethical reasons.

The data warehouses applications may include database-driven marketing, customer information systems with OLAP, risk management, customer monitoring and control, enterprise control etc. The industries directly influenced by data warehouse technology are financial and insurance services, manufacturing, distribution and transport, retail, public sector, procurement, communications, etc.

The data warehouse makes decision-relevant information easily accessible to decision-makers. It is often used as a collection of detail-data derived from operational business activities. In fact, it represents a snapshot of an on-line corporate database that is used to support the production, point-of-sale, or entry-order system, or a particular business decision-making process. Normally, the productive and operational business systems are constantly engaged in on-line transactions and should not be interrupted all of a sudden. However, operational database systems allow some necessary batch processing, mainly during the night, such as database backup, replication, and maintenance processing alike. It is then, the necessary snapshots used by the data warehouses are actually created. There are also significant differences in data manipulation types between operational and warehouse databases. The *operational* database allows almost any type of data manipulations, starting from installation, update, data retrieval, replace, to copying and replication. The transactions may require a structured access, sometimes a time consuming access detailed down to the record level, allowing consistent data updates and in-place DBMS that manage the database complexity. However the data *warehouse* mainly performs individual or ad-hoc access to data. There is no need of data updates or any complex database operations. Built-in database indexes are used to facilitate data retrieval process. Often, it may include larger data or greater time scope, depending on the actual decision scope and requested time frame.

The data warehouse is primarily used for *analysis-driven* decision support and ad-hoc data access, over large data scope, reloading data whenever extending the scope. Very simple database management is sufficient and often there is no need for complex operational DBMS support. Having operational database support is albeit beneficial.

The data warehouse entails large data stores (repository), often external data, data statistics reports and surveys, transformation of data structures according to the *meta-data* model, and usual relational DBMS providing relevant operational data. The meta-data model helps elicit the data since data derives from various sources and forms and there is a need for data description, data structuring, in general data modelling. Most often, the data warehouse performs interactive database processing, or *data mining* supported by decision-making system, tailored to the actual business process; see *Figure 60*. A market leader in warehouse database tools and the 1995 Byte award winner was *Impromptu and PowerPlay by* Cognos[122]. To date, due to proliferation, almost all database

---

[122] Cognos PowerPlay is the World's #1 Business Performance Measurement (BPM) analysis and reporting solution for OLAP data., http://www.cognos.com/products/powerplay/index.html

vendors support a sort of data-warehouse business solution. Note that it is called solution rather than software application since it is designed to solve problems.

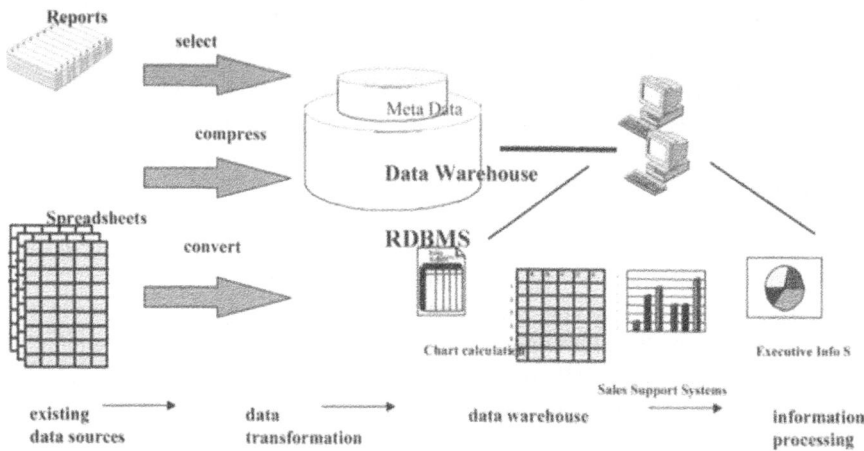

Figure 60. Data Warehouse [123]

The database model used in data warehouses is tailored according to the individual user's requirements for analysis and decision support. It includes a separate database replica storing permanent data for data warehouse purposes that does not interfere with the operational databases. This preserves the integrity and structure of operational databases, consistency and reproducibility of actual data. The actual query process is based on *meta-data* descriptions of operational data integrated into its permanent information base. A suite of statistical data models helps provide high data compression and multi-variant representation in support of information processing. In many instances the up-to-date data process may include time dimension, allowing for data filtering, time-series estimation, correlation, or prediction analysis:

There are several benefits of implementing data warehouses in enterprises.
- Enables business restructuring and supports business process re-engineering.
- Provides better product and customer services.
- Enables better insights in customer relationships.
- Remains a valuable tool for analysing market trends and helps align correctly new corporate strategies.
- Generates highly relevant information in support of decision-making from various data sources, information repositories and corporate operational databases.

---

[123] Siemens - Nixdorf, [1996]

– Helps control the enterprise information throughput, such as control of marketing and sales figures, reviews, public relations reports and press communication, etc.

Multimedia Technology

Data warehouse technology depends highly on the development of database technology. The benefit comes from advances in relational DBMS, such as faster parallel processing, parallel database loading and indexing, support of very large databases, multimedia database support, database partitioning, and scaleable Open System103. It is also closely related to high-performance connectivity technology. In our review, we will focus our attention on various document standards used in multimedia databases, meta-data, XML virtual catalogues, MMX enhanced multimedia processing, and spatial databases.

Document Standards: SGML, HTML, VRML, XML

Enterprises have established the Web presence and widespread Internet access. It brings about new dimensions in information presentation, the unlimited use of multimedia information, and the proliferation of multimedia databases. The unprecedented growth in multimedia information led the development of multimedia applications, multimedia production, packaging and management, including multimedia databases. While the use of multimedia content in business applications is skyrocketing, the growth is still taken up by low-cost, simple-to-use multimedia presentation tools.

The multimedia with real-time compressed video decoding and encoding, MPEG video with Dolby audio technology, digital video-disk (DVD) and 3D VR are just few new developments emphasising the true use of multimedia. Recently, several standards have been introduced based on *Standard Generalised Markup Language* (SGML). The well-known *HyperText Markup Language* (HTML) standard is just a subset of the SGML. The *Virtual Reality Modelling Language* (VRML) supports 3D presentations is widely used in graphical, publishing, design, and multimedia applications. The XML or *eXtended Markup Language* is the most recent extension to the suite of SGML standards.

Enhanced Multimedia Processing - MMX

To date, all major processor architectures claim support for faster processing and multimedia interaction extensions. Multimedia processing acceleration makes 2D, 3D graphics and video, audio, voice processing, and data communications several times faster. *Matrix Math Extensions* (MMX) and *Mips Digital Media Extension* (MDMX) contribute best to multimedia processing technology.

In fact, MMX processing adheres to the extension of *Single Instruction per Multiple Data* (SIMD) processing principle that allows processors to compute multiple sets of small operands and produce multiple results within single instructions. The ultimate goal is the integration of real-time processing of audio, video, 2D, and 3D data streams. Future developments are expected to follow the path of MDMX already implemented in high-performance graphic workstations by *Silicon Graphics*.

Labelling Data - XML

A significant difference between data warehouse and ordinary database results from the underlining data structure. The relational database model retains simple set structure that resembles flat, two-dimensional tables. As mentioned in previous discussions over Database Integrity, in order to support the data model it is important that the database preserves the integrity rules. The data integrity in warehouse databases is emphasised even more, due to possible differences in data formats that may exist in *data stores* or repositories. There are ways to overcome these differences and comply with common established standards, integrity rules, and formats. These set of rules, constraints, descriptions, and standards are also known as *meta-data,* since it represents *description data about the data.* Yet another problem is to capture the data provided through various standard document forms. Except SGML, all other document standards are rather unstructured and do not provide common way of data capture. For instance, an e-Commerce Web application that provides database access through interactive Web database may encounter major problems when using raw data from the HTML page that could only be resolved by a human intervention. Thus, price, product quantity, or delivery data have to be appropriately labelled in order to allow e-Commerce application make efficient use of relational databases tools. The XML document standard actually provides data labelling necessary for structured data formats required by databases. Moreover, XML enables the use of relational database tools including XQL, or the XML-based SQL. The XML enabled Web browsers, such as IEv5, are instrumental in e-Commerce support.

Spatially Enabled Database - GIS

An important asset of every enterprise is its data inventory, entailing customers' business data, operations surveys, sales figures, supplier's cross product data, etc. It is of vital interest in running the business. Technology to date, allows many alternative ways of data storing, but also provides ways for enterprise-wide data-access, data processing, data dissemination, and providing informative services.

An interesting alternative in data presentation is to visualise not only generic spatial data such as maps, two-dimensional figures and shapes, geographic objects, but also pure numeric data converted into two or multi-dimensional form for easier visualisation and analysis. It is the human eye that makes this difference. For, there is much evidence that the pattern matching for features or shape recognition in humans are superior due to the brain computing process in visual mode. This is due to parallel processing of our visual-retinal system, rather than our mind-based algebraic numeric processing capabilities. In fact, the parallel processing eventually takes place both in the visual-retinal system as well as in our neuronal signal transmission.

Many software vendors, database products, and data warehouse tools are providing very much similar visualisation of generic spatial data that are tailored for numeric data too. *MapInfo* and *ArcInfo* are among leading *Geographical Information Systems* (GIS) and spatial database providers. They allow users to store, access, and manage point-data on any database system that supports point-data features. This functionality is provided for spatial data and attributes residing on spatial servers across the network. It is also worth mentioning the *Unisys* spatial technology product *SpatialWare* that enables *MapInfo* to access spatial data stored on Oracle spatial database store and performs data mining and data analyses. The integration of these technologies provides unique, completely integrated relational database environment for business applications that are essentially based on spatial data representation features.

It also provides a robust implementation of spatial data, SQL data retrieval using *Open Database Connectivity* (ODBC) standards. It ensures to follow our current investment and instant business response, leveraging on technology change. In fact, having performed advanced spatial query pre-processing on spatial data, we may optimise the network data processing. Moreover, the on-line transactional environment allows spatial data to be visualised and disseminated throughout the enterprise network.

Actually, *SpatialWare* products provide centralised *spatial data warehouse* or in part a *spatial data repository* for efficient querying and analysis of spatial data. It builds on simple data-*points* that represent people, customers, addresses, and inventory objects in a region. The *lines* representing streets, networks, links, may include complex *shapes* of domains of aggregated *planar* objects, *regions* etc; see *Figure 61*. Hence, the spatial data warehouse provides integration of these concepts with other data resources, data surveys, external data, statistical reports that could be effectively data mined, data drilled, or *sliced-and-diced*. In fact, it allows for efficient integration of spatial database features and common data warehouse processing applied in traditional relational database environment.

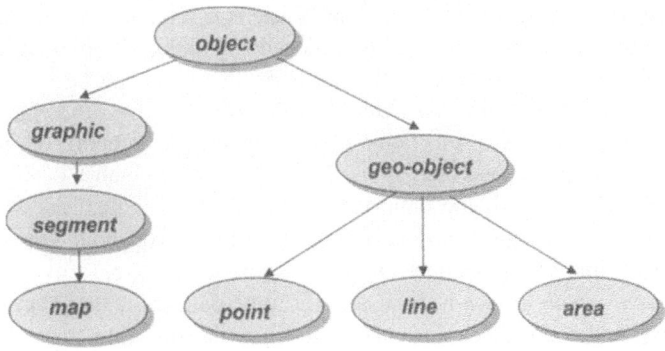

Figure 61. Spatial Data Hierarchy

OLAP: Data Drilling, Mining, and Slicing

We have seen so far that the relational database is primarily used to support business decision-making enterprise operations. Most business operations generate data in a regular manner, following timely scheduled processes. In order to monitor operational processes on-line without any loss of data, it is important that the data capture is as reliable and as secure as possible. Serious precautions should take place in order to perform regular data manipulation on operational database and prevent from eventual data corruption, data loss, or disable in any way the functionality of the database. Any exceptional data access, or ad-hoc data query is therefore discouraged. Instead, regular data retrieval is performed via standard and usually thoroughly tested SQL queries.

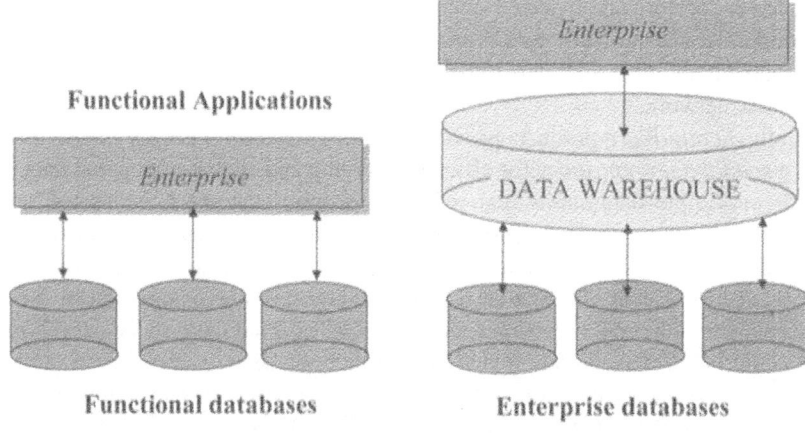

Functional Applications

DATA WAREHOUSE

Functional databases   Enterprise databases

Figure 62. Functional vs. Enterprise Database

In contrast, the data access to a data warehouse is essentially ad-hoc. Moreover, the ad-hoc optimised retrieval employs indexed and highly complex data queries. Usually, the data warehouse suits the needs of the whole enterprise, from front office operations up to the top management, providing *On-Line Analysis and data Processing* (OLAP) for random data queries in support of individual decision-making processes; see *Figure 62*. There exist a number of assorted but perplexing paths through the database generated by individual users. Most of them could at ease perform *data-mine* searches throughout the database, unlimited in time or data scope. Often the queries are after a tiny feature like *looking for a needle in a haystack*, specific time-patterns, data behaviour, data correlation, and complex dependencies hidden within the data store. Therefore, the introduction of *Artificial Neural Network* (ANN) applications represents a novel approach that allows implementation of advanced search methods, intelligent data drilling solutions, and helps performing arbitrary data retrieval or a specific pattern-recognition task.

The OLAP data queries that perform such database transformations, or data operations through multiple database levels in search of intelligent answers are often known as *data drilling* process. For instance, data drilling may start from a global worldwide sales data and perform search through sales by every country and any region looking for an individual data item. Likely, a *data mining* process may involve searching for data behaviour and data patterns throughout the multidimensional data space is known as *data slice and dice*. For instance, it helps finding best sales of a product in a store for a number of weeks.

Data Warehouse Development

The data warehouse is to satisfy and allow users to access information as transparently as possible in their quest for knowledge and in support of decision-making process. Since with wealth of information the capabilities increase, it is to provide scaleable open environment with robust query access and substantial intelligence to support both, guiding the user through data store and database management support. There are several steps we could follow in developing an efficient data warehouse.

− Identify the goals (global, individual, stakeholders, short or long term).
− Specify information and reporting needs.
− Determine the data store/repository structure and clarify its meta-data features.
− Specify database transformations and facilitate the use of data processing tools.
− Keep data volumes under control by reducing levels of summarisation as soon as timely data becomes obsolete or out of scope.

Data Warehouse Application Deployment

As any complex system the data warehouse involves many components, sophisticated and complex on its own. Therefore, the deployment of data warehouse should follow a rather systematic approach. Among important factors that may influence the deployment of *business-driven* data warehouses is the strategic vision, followed by tactical conception, a valuable data repository, and a rapid incremental implementation.

− *Strategic vision* for a data warehouse is expressed through set of business goals that the data warehouse can help achieve. The initiative starts with a vision and the expected business value of the warehouse approach, the identification of the target business processes, and the responses in anticipation of its impact
− *Tactical conception* represents a state of transition between the vision and the implementation, i.e. between *what* and *how to execute, perform*. It also develops a conceptual framework of tactics designed to meet specified business goals.
− *Data repository* and *meta-data* represent row data, database structure, and data description that help create the information environment we wish to explore
− *Incremental implementation* follows the Application Development Environment applied in *Figure 24*. In practice, this approach is most convenient for small enterprises, highly contained risk, low uncertainty, focused, and one familiar with rapid project development tools. It allows optimal project increments that provide identifiable business impact, based on manageable, fast deliverable units

Information and Intellectual Property Rights

The final notes are to address a very important intellectual property right issue in wide-enterprise networks. There are two opposing views: protectionist and information freedom. The traditional view maintains that the intellectual property is regarded as any other asset that needs to be protected at any costs. The important protection technology is to introduce new and improving standards to the existing information exchange MPEG suit such as MPEG3 to MPEG5. The solution argued is the case of Napster Web directory for music distribution; see *Case 7:* Peer-to-Peer Technology Exists Beyond Napster. The protectionists may also introduce some technical obstacles through various protectionist methods provided by Acrobat software as well as by *Pretty Good Privacy* (PGP) encryption software based on wide implementation of the RSA PKI encryption. Among such ideas is the *steganography* approach based on hidden encrypted copyright signatures within the binary-coded text, music score, video, or image. Similar protection mechanisms are already used in protecting the publishing of 'underground' hard sex comic books; see *Case 26:* Privacy Guide: Steganography

An interesting proposal[124] widely supported by the *dot.com* technology such as Superdistributed[125] is based on the idea put forward in the *Superdistribution; Objects as Property on the Electronic Frontier*[126] by Brad Coxis and earlier in the article Superdistribution: *The Concept and the Architecture*[127] by Ryoichi Mori. The idea *is to let information a freedom*. It asserts free exchange of information or any electronic form of intellectual property. It also makes use of the same information technology that has been used by pirates of intellectual property but this time for the benefit of authors of intellectual property. The appropriate electronic XrML labelling of information allows easy registering, tracing, and *disbursing* the usage of electronic replica of any intellectual property enabling it to be registered, monitored and managed, therefore accounted and traded rather than protected. '*Treat the ease of replication as an asset instead of a liability*', says Ryoichi Mori, JEIA head.

Case 26: Privacy Guide: Steganography

PRIVACY GUIDE: STEGANOGRAPHY
This Privacy Guide was originally written by Mr.Byte in 1997-1998
http://www.all-nettools.com/privacy/stegano.htm
*(Copyright © 1996-2000 TamoSoft, Inc. All rights reserved.
Reproduced by permission of TamoSoft, Inc.)*

When the Greek tyrant Histiaeus was held as a virtual prisoner of king Darius in Susa in the 5th century BCE, he had to send a secret message to his son-in-law Aristagoras to the Anatolian city of Miletus. Histiaeus shaved the head of a slave

---

[124] Mike Miron: '*The Internet is the world's biggest Xerox machine*', Xerox spin-off ContentGard CEO
[125] http://www.superdistributed.com/
[126] http://www.amazon.com/exec/obidos/ISBN=0201502089/virtualschoolA/
[127] http://virtualschool.edu/mon/ElectronicProperty/MoriSuperdist.html

and tattooed a message on his scalp. When the slave's hair had grown long enough he was dispatched to Miletus. That's how Herodotus describes one of the first cases of using steganography in the ancient world, the art of covered writing.

As the art developed it eventually became a science that has been helping people throughout the ages to disguise the very fact of information transmission. Ancient Romans used to write between lines using invisible ink based on various natural substances such as fruit juices, urine, and milk. Their experience was not forgotten: even nowadays children play spies and write secret messages that appear only when heated.

During the World War II the Germans developed the microdot. A secret message was photographically reduced to the size of a period, and affixed as the dot for the letter 'i' or other punctuation on a paper containing a written message. Microdots permitted the transmission of large amounts of printed data, including technical drawings, and the fact of the transmission was effectively hidden.

The wide usage of steganography during the war and the atmosphere of suspiciousness caused the institution of many restrictions that seem very funny today. In USA banned in advance were the international mailing of postal chess games, knitting instructions, newspaper clippings, children's drawings. It was also illegal to send cables ordering that specific types of flowers be delivered on a specific date, and eventually all international flower orders were banned by the US and British governments. In the USSR all international mailings were screened in attempt to detect any hostile activities.

The rapid progress of computer technology made all these restrictions obsolete. Nowadays everyone can make use of the advantages steganography can offer as a tool for hidden data transmission as well as for copyright protection. You can find more information on steganography on this site. Here we'll take a brief look at how steganography can help us protect our privacy.

Steganographic Software

Computer steganography is based on two principles. The first one is that the files that contain digitised images or sound can be altered to a certain extend without loosing their functionality unlike other types of data that have to be exact in order to function properly. The other principle deals with the human inability to distinguish minor changes in image colour or sound quality, which is especially easy to make use of in objects that contain redundant information, be it 16-bit sound, 8-bit or even better 24-bit image. Speaking of images, changing the value of the least significant bit of the pixel colour won't result in any perceivable change of that colour.

One of the best and most widely spread steganographic product for Windows95/98/NT is S-Tools (check this site for a huge list of steganograhic products and download links). This freeware program lets you hide files of any type in .gif and .bmp images as well as in .wav sounds. Moreover, S-Tools is actually a steganographic and cryptographic product in one, because the file to be hidden is encrypted using one of the symmetric key algorithms: DES (it's time has gone), Triple DES, and IDEA - the latter ones are very secure as of today. Working with the program is fun! You just drag the carrier file into the program window, then you drag the file you want to hide, choose an algorithm and a password, and here we go!

One can tell the difference between the clean and the loaded file only by comparing them, so if you look at the resulting file only, it looks totally innocent. For better security it is recommended that one uses images with many halftones and preferably unknown to the public because minor changes in them will not be noticed. Using Henri Matisse's *The Dance* is not a very good idea, because everyone (at least in our old good intellectual Europe) knows what it looks like, besides there are large spots of the same colour. Try using your dog's photo. Let's have a look at what we can do with this program:

http://www.all-nettools.com/files/sound1.wav .../sound2.wav

The left image in the first row (8.9K) contains no hidden data while the right one (11.2K) contains about 5K of password-protected text. In the second row the left sound file (4.6K) is also empty, while the right file contains 0.5K of text (the file size remained the same). Amazing, isn't it? Almost no distinctions. The ratio of the image file size and the text file size to be hidden depends on the image. Sometimes the maximum allowed text file size is even higher than the image size. Anyway, even if someone suspects that you are hiding something it's no help: without the password one cannot tell if an image has been processed by S-Tools.

Another good steganographic product is Steganos Security Suite (shareware). Unlike S-Tools it comprises a set of security tools including virtual encrypted drive, Internet Trace Destructor, clipboard encryption utility, shredder and several others. Steganos Security Suite employs AES and Blowfish encryption algorithms and is capable of hiding data in .bmp and .wav files after either finding them on your hard drive or creating them. As you surf the net your computer stores information about web sites that you visited, thus allowing other persons to trace your Internet activities. The Internet Trace Destructor included into Steganos Suite can erase traces of your Internet activities from your computer. Besides Steganos adds an option of sending files from your hard drive to the shredder which makes it impossible to recover them. Hey spies, get to the job!

A good file encryption utility with steganographic capabilities is Scramdisk. It is designed to create virtual encrypted drives and has an option to create a virtual drive out of .wav file and hide data inside it. The size of the encrypted partition varies between 25 and 50 percent of the original file size. The best thing about this program is that without knowing the pass-phrase it is not possible to prove that the file contains additional data.

Digital Watermarking

Speaking of commercial steganographic applications we should definitely mention digital watermarking which is a special technique of creating invisible digital marks in images and audio files that carry copyright information. These marks can be detected by special programs that can derive a lot of useful information from the watermark: when the file was created, who holds the copyright, how to contact the author etc. As you know tons of copyrighted material are reproduced, i.e. stolen on the Net every day so this technology might be useful if you are a designer.

There are many companies on the Net that sell watermarking products. One of the leaders is Digimarc that claims to have distributed over a million copies of its software. They offer a free download of PictureMarc which is a plug-in for Photoshop and CorelDraw, or stand-alone ReadMarc. Once you download and install it, you just open a file and read hidden watermarks embedded in it (if any). For those who want to go further Digimarc offers individual Creator ID (free for 1 year) that allows to embed watermarks in your own images before you put them on the Web. I believe many customers including designers, photographers and online galleries do it. Playboy magazine does it too. And then corporate users are offered to download MarcSpider that crawls the Web looking through all images and reports any unauthorized reproduction of them. Although in case of Playboy I can hardly believe anyone would put their photos on a site for commercial purposes because they can only attract schoolchildren...Anyway, it's up to them.

So it looks like the golden age of integrity is coming: authors no longer suffer from thefts, thieves take cameras, brushes, mice in their hands and start creating beautiful artworks themselves... but no! In spite of the manufacturers' claims watermarking didn't prove to be robust enough. Watermarks can survive a lot of things: brightness and contrast adjustments, applying special filters and even printing and scanning, but they cannot survive the manipulations of special programs such as StirMark and UnZign that appeared on the Net soon after the new technology was introduced. Apparently these tools are not targeted against any specific steganographic algorithm, they are rather benchmarks that help customers choose the most robust watermarking software. And the conclusion they lead us to is: as of today all watermarks can be destroyed without significant loss in picture quality.

"Well, now what?" the reader might ask. I don't know. Probably the algorithms will become more complicated or new image file formats will emerge. But any engineering entails reverse engineering, infinitely continuing the spiral of the technological progress. As it was written in my favourite book:
"What are your plans now?"
"My plans are whatever happens."

Bibliography

Shared Knowledge Builds Partnerships -- Managers use business intelligence tools to provide valuable data to suppliers and others; *John Webster*; **InternetWeek**, Manhasset; Oct 30, 2000; pg. PG.113

IBM tops in business intelligence, data warehousing; *Jim Martin*; **Midrange Systems**, Spring House; Sep 13, 1999; Vol. 12, Iss. 13; pg. 32, 1 pgs

Seeking business intelligence in a data warehouse; *Earl W Wilken*; **Graphic Arts Monthly**, Newton; Jul 1999; Vol. 71, Iss. 7; pg. 71, 1 pgs

Business intelligence: New gem in a data mine; *Earl W Wilken*; **Graphic Arts Monthly**, Newton; Mar 1999; Vol. 71, Iss. 3; pg. 93, 1 pgs

Business intelligence overview--data warehousing and a lot more; *Bernard Falkoff*; **Midrange Systems**, Spring House; Feb 9, 1999; Vol. 12, Iss. 2; pg. 27, 3 pgs

Mine your corporate data with business intelligence; *Samuel Greengard*; **Workforce**, Costa Mesa; Jan 1999; Vol. 78, Iss. 1; pg. 103, 2 pgs

Internet Business Intelligence: How to Build a Big Company System on a Small Company Budget; *Deborah Lynne Wiley*; **Online**, Wilton; Sep/Oct 2000; Vol. 24, Iss. 5; pg. 94, 2 pgs

It's 'think big, start small' with business intelligence systems; *Anonymous*; **Management Accounting**, London; Dec 1999; Vol. 77, Iss. 11; pg. 7, 1 pgs

System brings business intelligence to desktop; *Anonymous*; **American Bankers Association. ABA Banking Journal**, New York; Nov 1999; Vol. 91, Iss. 11; pg. 55, 1 pgs

Banks need data warehouses for customer management; **America's Community Banker** *Michelle Clayton*; Dec 1998

Data warehouses make ERP whole; **Computerworld** *Craig Stedman*; Nov 30, 1998

Hyperion simplifies data warehouses; **Computer Reseller News** *Shawn Willett*; Nov 16, 1998

Data warehouses can help operators uncover promotions that work; **Nation's Restaurant News** *Michael McCathren*; Nov 16, 1998

Data warehouses grow; **InformationWeek** *Beth Davis*; Nov 2, 1998

A framework for developing enterprise data warehouses; **Information Systems Management** *Murtaza, Ali H*; Fall 1998

Data warehouses win supporters; **Chain Store Age** *Jerri Lyn Jones*; Sep 1998

Data warehouses: Plan well, start small; **Computerworld** *Stewart Deck*; Aug 3, 1998

Data warehouses worth filling; **Network World** *Ellen Messmer*; Jul 20, 1998

Sybase ships integrated tools for data warehouses; **InformationWeek** *Rich Levin*; Jun 29, 1998

Data warehouses study helps dispel failure myth; **Computer Dealer News** *Anonymous*; Jun 1, 1998

Build partnerships first, then data warehouses; **Computer Dealer News** *Ron Cooper*; Apr 20, 1998

Realizing the strategic value of data warehouses; **Information Executive** *Barbara Gaskin*; Apr 1998

Data warehouses have need for clean data; **InfoWorld** *Paul Krill*; Mar 16, 1998

Data marts vs. data warehouses: Have your cake and eat it too; **Computer Technology Review** *John Zicker*; Feb 1998

Retailers cash in on data warehouses; **Software Magazine** *Deborah Radcliff*; Feb 1998

Data warehouses: Is bigger better?; **Insurance & Technology** *Tom Romeo*; Jan 1998

Data warehouses and data mining; **Internal Auditing** *Bodnar, George H*; Jan/Feb 1998

Data warehouses and marts; **Marketing Management** *Peter R Peacock*; Winter 1998

Office depot--developing a coherent data architecture; **Chain Store Age** *Anonymous*; Oct 1998

HP servers take aim at data warehousing, OLTP arenas; **Computer Reseller News** *Shawn Willett*; Dec 21-Dec 28, 1998

Data warehousing can give your customers a feeling of control; **Computing Canada** *Ed Karthaus*; Dec 7, 1998

Data warehousing and document management; **Document World** *Anonymous*; Dec 1998

Data warehousing market to grow by 30 per cent; **Computing Canada** *Kevin Restivo*; Nov 16, 1998

Paths to success in data warehousing; **Computerworld** *Fawn Fitter*; Nov 9, 1998

Data warehousing sales booming; **Computer Dealer News** *Kevin Restivo*; Nov 2, 1998

Users seek fix for data warehousing woe; **Computerworld** *Stewart Deck*; Nov 2, 1998

Oracle powering up XML, data warehousing; **InfoWorld** *Paul Krill*; Nov 2, 1998

Data warehousing; **Credit Union Magazine** *Patrick Totty*; Nov 1998

Data warehousing in the real world; **Credit Union Magazine** *Anonymous*; Nov 1998

Data warehousing: It's a zoo out there; **Computing Canada** *Anonymous*; Oct 26, 1998

Data warehousing demand puts premium on designers; **Computerworld** *Barb Cole-Gomolski*; Oct 12, 1998

Drug/convenience: Focus is on networks and data warehousing; **Chain Store Age** *Anonymous*; Oct 1998

Industrial-strength data warehousing; **Association for Computing Machinery. Communications of the ACM** *Arun Sen*; Sep 1998

Data warehousing hooks up with Internet; **AS/400 Systems Management** *Mayu Mishina*; Sep 1998

Data warehousing 101; **Chain Store Age** *Anonymous*; Sep 1998

Making sense of data warehousing; **Chain Store Age** *Anonymous*; Sep 1998

On-line retailers explore benefits of data warehousing; **Stores** *Ginger Koloszyc*; Sep 1998

Data warehousing; **Cornell Hotel and Restaurant Administration Quarterly** *Robert K Griffin*; Aug 1998

Building data repositories for business intelligence; **Software Magazine** *Peter Ruber*; Oct 1998

Seven steps to a meta-data repository; **Computerworld** *Shaku Atre*; Aug 24, 1998

CHIM clinical data repository survey uncovers expectations, inhibiting factors; **Health Management Technology** *Anonymous*; Jul 1998

HP revisits management data repository; **Network World** *Jim Duffy*; Nov 24, 1997

Implementing patient data repositories, a priority for health care professionals; **Health Management Technology** *Anonymous*; Sep 1997

BJC's $15 million Project Spectrum links four hospitals today, 4,000 remote physicians in the future, to central data repository; **Health Management Technology** *Anonymous*; Mar 1997

Appendix

Standards primarily set rules regarding what types of products are widely accepted in the networking environment. The two types of standards are *de facto* and *certified*:

De facto standards are products and results of widespread popularity among manufacturers, vendors, and users. These standards are often based on market share and market demand rather than certification exercised by well-known community groups or a recognised authority.

Certified standards on the other hand, are a result of a developer, a company or a vendor opening up a popular product to the wide user's community. Often, these standards are developed by formal professional groups, for instance IEEE in the *Ethernet* case, or OMG for X/*Open,* and OSF in the *CORBA* case.

Networking Standards Overview

OSI Model.

Open Systems Interconnection (OSI) entails several networking standards as common network architecture developed by the International Standards Organisation (ISO). However, due to pressures of powerful proprietary network vendors, the OSI has not been widely implemented, as the ISO anticipated. The OSI architecture is the standard seven-layer model for global networking. Each layer performs a function that adds to, or enhances a function of the layer below it. OSI covers all aspects of networking, from physical connections and wiring to applications support; see *Table 14.* Its major drawback is its inability to recognise the *Application Program Interface* (API). Since applications are often written for specific network protocols and specific platforms, often using specific APIs, OSI application layer protocol, clashes with other protocol APIs, causing protocol inconsistencies, which makes porting applications to OSI networks difficult, sometimes requires rewriting.

SNA vs. OSI

The Systems Network Architecture (SNA) is also a sever-layer networking architecture developed by IBM. Being a prime-networking model one might suspect that the OSI model was developed after the SNA. However, due to individual developments of both networking architectures there isn't a direct line up or correspondence between the SNA and OSI network layers. Despite both adhering to the 7-layer architecture there exists a substantial difference between the SNA and OSI. The SNA *layers simply do not line up with OSI layers therefore constitute a different protocol* that is to support IBM proprietary networking devices. These differences are so insurmountable that actually prevent simple SNA to OSI communications and therefore usually require multi-protocol gateways that emulate all the seven layers on both sides of the connection device.

IBM Proprietary System Network Architecture - SNA

SNA was introduced 1974 and represents a communications architecture designed by IBM to govern its proprietary *Systems Network Architecture* (SNA). The SNA was designed to provide networking facilities for IBM platforms only. It defines network elements or configurations possible within the SNA and underlined communications architecture of associated protocols supporting the SNA.

From user's view point network elements are terminals and applications. Host systems may contain communication logic or apply network *front-end* processors. In SNA hierarchy, *nodes* are hosts, terminals/controllers and communication processors may be interconnected by direct transmission lines or by networks - X.25 PSN. SNA provides a formal set of rules to manage communications implemented as a collection of software modules in various network nodes: *network addressable units* (*NAUs*), a logical network components providing communications and *system services control point* (SSCP), possible *Network Management, logical unit* (LU) and *end-user interface.* NAUs communicate with each other by means of *sessions* - a temporary liaison between NAUs for data exchange in controlled mode.

SNA Communication Architecture

SNA entails a set of seven layers performing communications functions see *Table 25*

Table 25 SNA System Network Architecture

SNA layers	Function
Physical control	physical node interface: serial/parallel
Data link control	manages data transmission single link
Path control	creates logical channel between NAUs
Transmission control	regulates session data flow
Data flow control	dialogue control: full/half duplex
Presentation services	provides data transform/format
Transaction services	provides distributed transaction processing

Novell IPX/SPX

SPX/IPX architecture is another proprietary network standard supported by Novell for Novell local area networks. Under pressure of Windows NT, OS/2 and other NOS most recent versions of Novell *IntranetWare* have endorsed TCP/IP in support parallel to its own IPX/SPX standard.

Novell *NetWare* and most recently, *IntranetWare* is a family of products designed to integrate LANs and WAN in an easily used network environment. Due to its share number of LANs, IPX/SPX represents *de facto* standard for LANs and Novell the market share leader for NOS. Novell refers to its NetWare as its networking architecture for providing a comprehensive platform for network computing.

Banyan VINES

Banyan *VIrtual NEtwork System (VINES) has* been developed to support medium size and large networks and network interconnections. A virtual network minimises the differences among clients, and servers. VINES can interconnect diverse network topologies through all types of communications media and provide complete support for OSI and TCP/IP network protocols.

DCE

Distributed Computing Environment (DCE) architecture represents the effort of *Open System Foundation* (OSF) task group to provide a common set of protocols which would provide user's community with wide variety of distributed functions across different platforms, irrespective of individual network protocols, or standards implemented. The *Figure 13* represents an overview of the most common network protocols used to implement distributed computing environment side by side with OSI network layers.

DME

Distributed Management Environment (DME) is a network management architecture that provides enterprises critical support for expansion of networks beyond local area networks and represents a valuable constituent part of a network comprehensive infrastructure management. SNMP and SNMP-2, together with DMI, CMIP and CORBA represent common network management standards used today.

Internet DME: *SNMP*

Simple Network Management Protocol (SNMP) and SNMP-2 as its most recent version are the two most common network management standards on *Internet* implementing the TCP/IP protocol for network management. Using SNMP a network administrator can address commands or inquiries to any SNMP computer or device on the network.

The *Simple Networking Management Protocol* (SNMP) is the most widely implemented networking management protocol. For the Internet it gained support by the IETF. As its name suggests, it represents simple, unacknowledged, *connectionless* protocol (TCP/IP Datagram based). Pooling managing agents is usually implemented by *Terminate-Stay-Resident* (TSR) or *Demon* background tasks. However, it is less reliable, unsecured, inefficient protocol lacking some important network management features such as support for *manager-to-manager* communications. Both SNMP and CMIP define resource as managed objects. A hierarchical (tree-based) *Management Information Base* (MIB) defines structures of managed objects. The MIB *schema* or *Structure of Management Information* (SMI) defines the model and naming conventions. It is used to specify managed objects for the SNMP and CMIP protocols.

In 1993 it was replaced by more improved SNMP 2 standard and adopted as the new Internet protocol. Now, a SNMP 2 node can be both, *a managed as well as managing object*. It allows new security features, communications *manager-to-manager* (M2M) and a new M2M MIB in order to support the new topology, bulk data transfers, etc.

OSI DME: *CMIP*

Common Management Information Protocol (CMIP) is more sophisticated object oriented network management used in OSI networks. It allows any device to report to the network manager if there is a problem. It is more advanced and with greater functionality then SNMP limited only to reporting network conditions.

In order to provide a comprehensive solution to network management, instead of simple SNMP model the OSI defines network-managed objects using a complex *object-oriented* framework. CMIP is *connection*-oriented protocol running on top of seven-layer OSI stack. It relies on both *manager-to-agent* and *manager-to-manager* communications. Instead of SNMP Datagram communications, CMIP is session-based, more intelligent using polling manager-to-agent event driven interactions. CMIP is much more secure with MIB allowing use of inheritance in defining managing objects. Dispite of its smaller installed base the CMIP is better suited for management of large, complex, multi-vendor enterprise networks.

OMG X/Open: *DMI API*

Both SNMP 2 and CMIP protocols have rather large memory requirements, up to a MB of RAM which has been somewhat restrictive for growing number of desktops clients. *Intel* together with the *Desktop Management Task Force* (DMTF) consortium responded with their own *small agent* designed to manage the desktop hardware as well as software components creating the *Desktop Management Interface* (DMI) protocol. DMI entails protocol-independent APIs based on multi-platform *Management Interface File* (MIF). The MIB is able to communicate with any of SNMP 2 or CMIP protocols. Using TSR for DOS or DLLs for Windows and OS/2 the DMI agents are able to load or unload the necessary components on demand in order to provide distributed management functionality consuming not more than few KB of RAM. The low memory requirement has enabled the proprietary agents to be installed on network adapter cards, for instance, the *3Com Ethernet* desktop card.

OSF DME: *CORBA*

The most recent DME *Object Management Framework* (OMF); see *Figure 50* provides a complete advanced solution for network management in heterogeneous multi-vendor environment. The OMG *Common Object Request Broker Architecture* (CORBA) compliant framework substitutes the traditional *manager-to-object* relationship with *all-object relationship*. A CORBA object can take either of the two roles: *a client requesting service or a server providing services*. Based on familiar DCE concepts for communications among objects it relies on CORBA *Object Request Brokers* (ORB) in providing precise services for distributed asynchronous system management events; see *Figure 49*. The CORBA standards supported by *Object Management Group* (OMG) has defined actual software boundaries needed to provide *interoperability* between independent distributed objects.

The event-driven ORB static implementations bound at compile time in form of IDL precompiled *stubs* are simpler, easier, faster, and more robust. The dynamical method ORB's invocations however, manage objects at run time hence provide more flexible environment. Traditional SNMP or CMIP are managed via special DME *Interface Definition Language* (IDL) *adapter object* encapsulations. The IDL adapter objects are used to encapsulate the implementation of any management resource, for instance, define a set of operations that emulate CMIP or SNMP calls. In order to avoid proliferation of many special-purpose ORB object adapters, CORBA relies on *Basic Object Adapters* (BOA) for conventional ORB implementations.

Despite its complexity, memory and high processing power requirements the DME OMF model represents highly sophisticated communications and interaction among self-managed objects used to represent network resources, user interfaces, or managing applications. Moreover, due to the continuing trends of cheaper hardware, more expensive enterprise software ownership, and ever growing demand of wide enterprise networking, the growing OMF CORBA support is expected to bring about migration from simple SNMP and desktop based DMI to sophisticated object-oriented ORB implementations.

Communications Protocols Review

The Telecommunications Act of 1996, http://www.ba.com/cgi-bin/AT-newsitesearch.cgi, (the "Act" or the "Telecommunications Act") has completely restructured the telecommunications industries.

IEEE 802 protocol suite
The IEEE 802 suit of LAN standards is developed jointly by the IEEE Committee and the ANSI and subsequently adopted as international standards by ISO. With the growing user's interest in LAN the IEEE 802 standards; see *Table 20*, have gained widespread and rapid acceptance by all vendors. The IEEE 802 standards are organized into three-layer protocol hierarchy. The Logical Link Control (LLC) level, is responsible for addressing and data link control. Media Access Control (MAC) is responsible for medium access, and Physical layer, responsible for physical interfaces.

ISDN/B-ISDN
The digital pipe between the central office and an ISDN subscriber is used to carry a number of communication channels. The B channel of 64 Kbps each is supported by D channel of 16 or 64 Kbps. Higher bandwidth H channel provide bandwidth of up to A1 (2,044 Kbps) or T1 (1,544 Kbps) in the US. Communication channels are grouped into transmission structure offering a *basic* or *primary* access package. Packages of higher multiples of B and D channels provide the user for higher bandwidth demand. Two B channels supported by a D channel known as a *basic* user channel provides the necessary bandwidth for digital data/voice or mixed low-rate traffic services which are designated to the same end point. It also provides leased line equivalent to the CSN or PSN connection services.

The D channel is known as common signalling channel. It carries the necessary signalling information required for the control of CSN over associated B channel and for set-up calls over all B channels at customer's interface. In addition it may be used for low data rate PSN traffic such as low-speed telemetry or when no signalling information is required. There are some interesting communication software solutions that cater on D channel bandwidth and make efficient use of it.

The H channel provides higher bit rates by multiplexing a number of B channels and a supporting D channel. For instance, 31 B channel plus a D channel add up to an A1 communication service with data rate of 2.048 Kbps in total. The later has been used to replace high-speed trunk lines or subdivide accordingly the TDM schema for fast facsimile, video, high-speed data, high-fidelity audio, or multiplexed low-rate data.

Broadband ISDN (B-ISDN)
The efforts directed toward the global network concept incorporating LAN, PBXs, and broadcasting networks are referred to as Broadband ISDN (B-ISDN). The B-ISDN represents a response of the standardisation community to the increased bandwidth demand required for video services, higher data rates for image and digital video, an order of magnitude beyond those delivered by the ordinary ISDN. Also, in order to meet the high-resolution digital video requirements the B-ISDN introduced an upper channel rate of 150 Mbps. Essentially, it can provide for a simultaneous support for one or more interactive conversational, messaging or retrieval services as well as broadcasting or distributive services up to 600 Mbps total subscriber line rate. From media point of view, fibre optic still remains the only appropriate technology for widespread support of B-ISDN.

CSN vs. PSN
For CSN vs. PSN please check *Table 15*

LAN vs. PBX
For LAN vs. PBX please check *Table 21*

FR vs. ATM
For FR vs. ATM please check *Table 17*

xDSL
For ADSL/RADSL, VDSL, HDSL, SDSL and IDSL please check *Table 18*

Mobile standards: *CDMA, TDMA, GSM vs. GPS, GPRS, WAP vs. SMS*
Code Division Multiple Access (**CDMA**) and *Time Division Multiple Access* (**TDMA**) are representatives of wireless technology protocols based on distribution of digitised signal samples across the entire bandwidth or time-slot channels respectively. It allows overlaying multiple calls over each other using unique sequence codes assigned to calls. CDMA is widely used in US.

Global System for Mobile **communications** (**GSM**) is a digital radio network for mobile telephony based on contemporary time/space-division technology protocols. The GSM communicates through a system of ground stations strategically located for best possible coverage. The cell-point's terminals send information through GSM base-stations to the cell-point server that calculates the position of the terminal and communicates the position back through the base-station to the end-user. Grace to the roaming agreements among network operators, service providers, the mobile users can freely move between countries. As of Oct. 1999, there are 369 GSM operators in more than 140 countries.

Global Positioning System (**GPS**) is a worldwide positioning system using a number of satellites orbiting around the globe. The accurate position of an object is obtained by triangulation using line of sight GHz. frequency signal from at least three satellites. GPS can not function indoors, whereas GSM not only operates indoors but can communicate its position as well.

The *third generation* (3G) or *Universal Mobile Telecommunications System* (**UTMS**) is a broad-bandwidth, IP-based packed-switching transmission of text, digitised voice, multimedia and video at data rates of up to and possibly higher than 2Mbps. It offers a consistent set of services to mobile computer and phone users irrespective of their global position. It is based on the GSM communications standard planned to get into operation in Asia and Europe by 2001. Until 3G is fully implemented users can use multi-mode devices that switch and benefit from currently available technology such as GSM 900 or 1800. Higher bandwidth of UTMS also promises richer video conferencing services and the realisation of long desired *Video Home Entertainment* (**VHE**) service.

General Packet Radio Service (**GPRS**) is a packet-based wireless communication mode already available that allows data rates from 56 up to 114 Kbps. It also provides a continuous connection to the Internet for mobile and computer users. Higher data rates will allow users to take part in multimedia and a bit reduced quality video conferencing. In addition to Internet the Protocol (IP), GPRS also supports X.25. It also complements the *Bluetooth* standard that replaces wired connection between devices with wireless radio connections. In a way, the GPRS represents an evolutionary step towards UMTS.

Wireless Application Protocol (**WAP**) is a protocol for the transmission of data over low bandwidth wireless networks. A technology that actually allows mobile users to access and browse the Web. It entails two essential components: WAP Gateway and a browser. The gateway allows connections of phones to the Internet, whereas the micro-browser uses the *eXtended Markup Language* (XML) document format together with *Wireless Markup Language* (WMP) to display pages irrespective of the user's screen limitations. The WAP getaway acts as a proxy interpreting requests from phone micro-browsers and retrieving content using standard XML to HTTP access. The WAP micro-browser is implemented in a mobile handset designed to handle WML code using the standard hand phone interface. Hence, the traditional Web applications that are going to provide WAP services need to translate their HTML and redesign the Web pages using WML.

Short Message Service (**SMS**) is GSM service that is very popular among mobile users throughout GSM markets in Asia and Europe. A single short message is not longer than 160 characters in length. It also supports non-text characters (binary format). The SMS is store and forward service, sent always via SMS centre. Unlike paging, it also features confirmation of message delivery. Since SMS is travelling across the data/signalling path rather than a dedicated channel, the SMS has no communications congestion problems. Another advantage of the SMS is that it can be sent and received simultaneously with the GSM voice, data and fax calls. SMS represents a rather efficient alternative to email. Unlike WAP, SMS is independent of hand-phones types or mobile network operators. SMS has been widely used and grows exponentially. Logica plc forecasts that the SMS will rise by 170%/year reaching in three years 100 billion SMS messages per month[128].

---

[128] *Logica* pls. Report June 2000, Consulting firm, London http://www.logica.com/news/press/pr704.html

Glossary

Application layer
The seventh of seven layers of the Open Systems Interconnection (OSI) model; it provides network access to users

Automatic flow control
The means of controlling the flow of data across a virtual circuit. This is done by setting the window size and the packet size. Automatic flow control can be negotiated in each direction on a per-call basis.

Backbone network
The primary connectivity mechanism of a hierarchical distributed system. It ensures that all systems that have connectivity to an intermediate system on the backbone have connectivity to one another.

Bandwidth
The carrying capacity of a circuit, usually measured in bits per second (bps) for digital circuits or in hertz (Hz) for analogue circuits.

Bridge
A device that connects two or more physical networks, forwarding frames between networks based on information in the data-link header. Because a bridge operates at the Data-Link layer, it is transparent to the Network-layer protocols.

Bus topology
The linear LAN used by Ethernet networks.

Circuit switching
A procedure for establishing a connection between two end devices. Once connected, it uses a non-sharable path through the network.

Client
A workstation or a user's computer in a network that relies on services provided by a server in order to perform or execute applications.

Client/server model
A configuration that uses distributed intelligence to treat both the server and the individual workstations as intelligent, programmable devices.

Control packet
A link-control or network-control packet for establishing encapsulation format options, size limits of packets, link set-up, peer authentication, or Network-layer protocol management.

Datagram
A packet of information and its associated delivery information, which is routed through a packet-switching, network.

Data-link layer
The second layer of the seven layers of Open Systems Interconnection (OSI) Reference Model. It is involved in both packaging and addressing information and controlling the flow of separate transmissions over communication lines.

Data Circuit Terminating Equipment (DCE)
Any one of the devices that is not a DTE, but is associated with a single network port. A DCE is responsible for establishing, maintaining, and terminating the connection with a DTE.

Data Terminal Equipment (DTE)
A generic term for any network-attached device at customer-premises or end user equipment operating in a packet mode.

Dial-up connection
A type of connection to a Public Data Network (PDN) used primarily by PC users to access data residing on remote hosts. The data transmission rate usually is slower than that of leased lines, and usually has an upper limit of 9600 bps.

End system
The computer of the Open Systems Interconnection (OSI) model containing application processes that can communicate through all seven layers of the OSI model. It's an equivalent to an end node.

Enterprise network
A computer network connecting the local and remote sites of an enterprise or corporation.

Ethernet
A system of high-performance coaxial cables widely used in the communications industry. Ethernet cables can be part of an AppleTalk network or a TCP/IP network, for example.

Fibre Distributed Data Interface (FDDI)
The ANSI standard for high-speed (100 Mbps) fibre-optic connections

Frame
(1) The data unit sent using a protocol, such as High-level Data Link Control (HDLC) or Link Access Procedure Balanced (LAPB), to provide Data Link-level communication between two nodes on a network. (2) A group of bits representing data from many channels, as in T1 communications. See also unnumbered frames.

Frame layer
An X.25 layer that transports data across the physical link, controls the interchange between the DTE and DCE, and corrects any link errors. Also called the Link layer.

Frame Relay network
A private line network that permanently allocates dedicated transmission resources between communication end points. A Frame Relay network uses statistical multiplexing, making transmission resources allocated only when active communications exist.

Frame switching/relaying technology
The process of quickly transporting HDLC (High-level Data Link Control) frames through a network.

Gateway
An internetworking device that operates from the network to application layers of the Open Systems Interconnection (OSI) model. Sometimes used as a synonym for router.

High-level Data Link Control (HDLC)
A bit-oriented, synchronous protocol that applies to the Data-Link layer of the Open Systems Interconnection (OSI) model

Header
The information at the beginning of a packet that defines control information, including addressing and control.

Integrated Services Digital Network (ISDN)
An evolving set of standards for a digital network that carries both voice and data communications.

Internet
The collection of networks and gateways that use the TCP/IP suite of protocols. Written in lowercase, it is an abbreviation for inter-network.

Internet Protocol (IP)
In the TCP/IP protocol suite, all packets are delivered by the IP datagram delivery service. Packet delivery is not guaranteed by this service. A packet can be misdirected, duplicated, or lost on the way to its destination. The service is connectionless because all packets are transmitted independently of any other packets. This is in contrast to a telephone network, for instance, where a circuit is established and maintained. TCP/IP applications using the IP datagram delivery service keep track of the delivery status by expecting to receive replies from the destination node, or by using one of the Transport-layer protocols within the TCP/IP suite.
IP defines the form that packets must take and the ways to handle packets when they are transmitted or received. The form the packet takes is called an I P datagram. An IP datagram is analogous to a physical frame transmitted on a network. A datagram has a header section containing the sender's and the receiver's IP address among other information, as well as a data section. Figure 2-3 shows the general form of an IP datagram. Each network type transmits IP packets in the data section of its physical frame.

Internet or IP address
A 32-bit address assigned to hosts using TCP/IP

Inter-network
Any interconnected group of networks, such as an interconnected group of TCP/IP networks. Network users in an inter-network can share information & network devices.

IP (Internet Protocol), IPv4 vs. IPv6
An Internet Protocol that provides TCP/IP datagram type delivery of messages. IPv4, the version of IP currently in use, designed in 1970, allowing 'only' for 4Billion network addresses isn't enough for today's demands. IPv6 promises significant benefits for users and allows greater flexibility for the introduction of new Internet services, e.g. mobile.
IPv6 uses 128bit address, vs. the 32bit-address range of IPv4, allowing for 2^{64}addresses. Microsoft made technical preview of IPv6 for Windows 2000. Nortel, Nokia, Ericsson, Cisco and other IP and Internet market leaders have already incorporated IPv6 into their forthcoming networking, mobile and wireless products to be delivered in 2000 and later.

Local Area Network (LAN)
A group of computers and other devices connected by a communications link that allows any device to interact with any other device on the network

LAN connectivity
The TCP/IP software provides connectivity for workstations and servers connected to LAN media such as Ethernet, FDDI, token ring, and ARCNET. An application for transferring files using TCP, for instance, performs the following operations to send the file contents:
The Application layer passes a stream of bytes to the Transport layer on the source computer.
The Transport layer divides the stream into TCP segments, adds a header with a sequence number for that segment, and passes the segment to the Internet (IP) layer. The checksum is computed.
The IP layer creates a packet with a data portion containing the TCP segment. The IP layer adds a packet header containing source and destination IP addresses. The IP layer also determines the physical address of the destination computer or intermediate computer on the way to the destination host. It passes the packet and the physical address to the Data-Link layer. The checksum is computed again.
The Data-Link layer transmits the IP packet in the data portion of a data-link frame to the destination computer. If the destination is an intermediate computer, then Step 3 happens again until the final destination is reached. At the destination computer, the Data-Link layer discards the data-link header and passes the IP packet to the IP layer.

The IP layer checks the IP packet header. If the checksum contained in the header does not match the checksum computed by the IP layer, it discards the packet. If the checksums match, the IP layer discards the IP packet header and passes the TCP segment to the TCP layer. The TCP layer checks the sequence number to determine whether the segment is the correct segment in the sequence.

The TCP layer computes a checksum for the TCP header and data. If the computed checksum does not match the checksum transmitted in the header, the TCP layer discards the segment. If the checksum is correct and the segment is in the correct sequence, the TCP layer sends an acknowledgement to the source computer. The TCP layer discards the TCP header and passes the bytes in the segment just received to the application. The application on the destination computer receives a stream of bytes, just as if it were directly connected to the application on the source computer.

Link Access Procedure-Balanced (LAPB) protocol
The Consultative Committee for International Telegraphy and Telephony (CCITT) bit-oriented protocol similar to the Synchronous Data-Link Control (SDLC) protocol.

Leased line
A dedicated communications line usually leased from a Public Data Network (PDN) vendor on a monthly basis. Current modem technology permits data transmission up to 19.2 Kbps on an analogue line. Direct digital service lines are available up to 64 Kbps.

Link layer
See Data-Link layer; Frame layer.

Modem
A device that performs modulation and demodulation, allowing data communications to occur in analogue form over telephone circuits.

Multiplexing
A method that allows a single communications circuit to take the place of several parallel ones; often used to allow remote terminals to communicate with front-end processor ports over a single circuit.

NetWare
A Novell network operating system that provides the ability to share services across dissimilar platforms. It uses the NetWare Core Protocol (NCP), Inter-network Packet Exchange (IPX), and Sequenced Packet Exchange (SPX) protocols transparently.

Network
A collection of interconnected, individually controlled computers, together with the hardware and software used to connect them.

Network architecture
A framework of principles to facilitate the operation, maintenance, and growth of a communications network by isolating the user and application programs from network details. Protocols and software are packaged together into a usable network architecture system that organises functions, data formats, and procedures.

Network layer
Third of seven layers of the Open Systems Interconnection (OSI) model; it ensures that information arrives at its intended destination and filters out the differences between network media so higher layers do not need to account for the distinctions.

Network topology
The arrangement of nodes in a network; usually following a star, ring, tree, or bus organisation.

Node
An addressable entity in a network. This term sometimes refers to a device itself. Some examples of nodes are Macintosh computers, printers, and file servers. The node acquires a unique 8-bit node number

dynamically when it connects to the network. It tries to use that address and node number again when it connects to the network the next time. If the node finds that its previous number is already in use, it tries again until it finds a unique node address.

Open Systems Interconnection (OSI) model
A seven-layer data communication model.

Packet
A group of bits transmitted as a unit of information on a network. These bits include data and control elements. The control elements include the addresses of the packet's source and destination and, in some cases, error-control information. In packet-switching networks, a transmission unit of a fixed maximum size that consists of binary digits that represents both data and a packet header.

Packet frame
A set of information added to a packet to ensure its proper transmission across the network. A frame consists of information in a format that is dependent on the physical medium on which the data travels.

Packet layer
An X.25 layer that controls call set-up and clearing, packet transfer, and network facility selection.

Packet-Switched Network (PSN)
A collection of interconnected, individually controlled computers that use packets to transmit information to each other. See packet switching.

Packet switching
A data communications process whereby messages are broken into finite-sized packets. The message packets are forwarded to the other party over different circuit paths. At the other end of the circuit, the packets are reassembled into the message, which is then passed on to the receiving terminal or device.

Physical layer
The first of seven layers of the Open Systems Interconnection (OSI) model; it details the protocols that govern transmission media and signals. In X.25, a layer of the interface that defines the physical interface between a DTE and DCE. It specifies the procedures used to establish, maintain, and release the physical connections or data circuits between network end points.

PPP (Point-to-Point Protocol)
An industry-standard protocol that enables point-to-point transmissions of routed data across transmission facilities between interconnected LANs using a synchronous or asynchronous serial interface.

Router
The software that connects multiple networks so that all the nodes on each network can access services and nodes on any other network. It operates at the Network layer (Layer 3) of the OSI model for forwarding decisions; for instance, an appleTalk router connects AppleTalk networks into an internetwork so that all the nodes on each network can access services and nodes on any other connected network. It receives and forwards AppleTalk packets on the networks to which it is directly connected.

Routing
The transmission of a datagram from one node to another on the same or a different network. It also refers to the paths that are chosen to transmit an IP datagram from its origin to its destination, based on the IP addresses contained in the datagram.

Segment
A LAN with no routers or bridges.

Server
A combination of controller software and mass-storage devices that allows computer users to share common files and applications on a network. A server on an AppleTalk network might be a Macintosh

computer running AppleShare software or an IBM PC (or a compatible computer) running the NetWare Communication Services Manager software.

Session layer
The fifth of seven layers of the Open Systems Interconnection (OSI) model; it allows dialog control between end systems.

Serial Line IP (SLIP)
An Internet protocol used to run IP over serial lines, such as telephone circuits or RS-232 cables, interconnecting two systems. SLIP is being replaced by the Point-to-Point Protocol (PPP).

Simple Network Management Protocol (SNMP)
The TCP/IP protocol that allows network management.

Statistical multiplexing
A method, usually through a time division multiplexer (TDM), that allocates line time dynamically to each of the various attached terminals, according to whether a terminal is active or inactive at a particular moment. Buffering and queuing functions are also included. It is also called a stat-mux.

Statistical Time-Division Multiplexing (STDM)
A method of data transmission that allows X.25 to maximise bandwidth use by dynamically allocating portions of the available bandwidth to active devices on demand. In contrast to time-division multiplexing (TDM), which dedicates a fixed bandwidth of the network medium to connected devices regardless of whether they are active, X.25 provides better throughput.

Sub-network
The portion of the backbone that is partitioned by repeaters, bridges, or routers.

Switched link
A service, such as switched 56 Kbps, providing for temporary file transfer or management. When the link is idle, the vendor uses the channel for other users. When your link becomes active, whatever 56-Kbps channel is available is switched to your link.

Switched Virtual Circuit (SVC)
A type of virtual circuit that is established dynamically using call set-up and call clearing procedures. A permanent SVC is left in a connected state until the user or application brings it down. An on-demand until more data is queued up for sending, at which point the connection is re-established.

Transmission Control Protocol (TCP)
One of the major transport protocols within the Internet suite of protocols, providing a reliable, connection-oriented, full-duplex streams; it uses IP for delivery.

Transmission Control Protocol/Internet Protocol (TCP/IP)
The protocol suite developed by the Advanced Research Projects Agency (ARPA). It includes TCP as the primary transport protocol and IP as the Network-layer protocol.

T1/E1
(T1) A high-speed leased line, transmitting at rates up to 1.544 Mbps (in United States).
(E1) A facility used to transport 30 voice channels at 64 Kbps of 2.048 Mbps (in Europe).

Telnet
A protocol in the TCP/IP suite that governs character-oriented terminal traffic.

Topology
The physical layer of network components (cables, stations, gateways, and hubs). Three basic interconnection topologies are star, ring, and bus networks.

Time-Division Multiplexing (TDM)
A type of data transmission that dedicates a fixed bandwidth of the network medium to connected devices, regardless of whether they are active. See also Statistical Time-Division Multiplexing (STDM).

Token-Talk
An AppleTalk network on a token ring.

Topology
The physical layer of network components (cables, stations, gateways, and hubs). Three basic interconnection topologies are star, ring, and bus networks.

Transaction
An indivisible unit of interaction in a DBMS or similar Client/Server based systems. It must be treated in a coherent and reliable way independent of other transactions.

Transport layer
The fourth of seven layers of the Open Systems Interconnection (OSI) model; it provides reliable, end-to-end delivery of data and detects transmission sequential errors.

TCP/IP Concepts
TCP/IP (Transmission Control Protocol/Internet Protocol) is a popular suite of standard networking protocols. These protocols are widely used, enabling dissimilar nodes in a heterogeneous environment to communicate with one another.

The general concept of connecting a network of dissimilar computers arose from research conducted by the Defence Advanced Research Projects Agency (DARPA). Within the framework of that research, DARPA developed the TCP/IP suite of protocols to communicate among networks and implemented an inter-network called the ARPA net, which later evolved into the Internet. The TCP/IP suite of protocols defines formats and rules for the transmission and receipt of information independent of any given network organisation or computer hardware. Although the protocols were developed for the Internet, TCP/IP is now the de facto standard as numerous private and public organisations use it for their networking.

The network, as conceived by DARPA and implemented with the TCP/IP suite of protocols, is a packet-switched network. A packet-switched network transmits information on the network in small segments, called packets. If one computer transmits a lengthy file to another computer, for example, the file is divided into many packets at the origin and then reassembled at the destination. The TCP/IP protocols define the format of these packets. This definition includes the origin of the packet, the destination of the packet, the length of the packet, and the types of packet, as well as the way computers on the networks are to receive and retransmit packets.

TCP/IP is a transport subsystem that brings TCP/IP connectivity to the NetWare operating system. This subsystem includes a collection of NLM files for NetWare designed to support applications requiring TCP/IP connectivity, such as the NetWare for NFS* (Network File System) product.

TCP/IP routing capabilities allow forwarding of IP traffic from one network to another. TCP/IP uses the Routing Information Protocol (RIP), Exterior Gateway Protocol (EGP), or Open Shortest Path First (OSPF) protocol to communicate with other routers. This allows all routers in the inter-network discover the inter-network configuration without human intervention.

In addition to routing services, TCP/IP provides transport interfaces for the use of higher-level network services. This interface is used by NFS and by third-party applications written for either the 4.3BSD* UNIX® socket interface or the STREAMSTM Transport Layer Interface (TLI).

TCP/IP supports Ethernet, token ring, FDDI, and ARCNET* networks through the Novell Open Data-Link Interface TM (ODITM) specification. Therefore, it works with any network adapters of these types supported by a NetWare LAN driver certified for version 3.12 or later.

Virtual circuit
A type of circuit that provides a connection-oriented service similar to that of circuit switching. In packet-switching networks, it is a circuit that appears to be a physical point-to-point circuit. It connects two end points, conveying sequenced data packets reliably; in fact, it shares the underlying links and relay systems with other users of the network.

Index

ACID iv, x, 16, 17, 19, 31, 43, 44, 45, 46, 50, 59, 62, 101, 137, 230, 245, 249, 286
Active Server Pages (ASP)............ 51
ADSL............... xi, 34, 180, 182, 272
ADSL/RADSL, VDSL, HDSL, SDSL 272
Advanced Program-to-Program Communication (APPC)............ 14
agents...13, 15, 39, 56, 62, 82, 88, 95, 99, 123, 146, 160, 197, 199, 200, 211, 212, 245, 269, 270
Amplitude-Shift Keying (ASK)... 150
Application Development. v, 59, 114, 125, 134, 136, 261, 286
Application Program Interface (API) 14
Application Service Providers (ASP) 26
Application Transaction Management 92
Artificial Neural Network (ANN) 260
Asymmetric/Rate-Adaptive Digital Subscribe Line (R/ADSL) 180
Asynchronous Transfer Mode (ATM) 176, 286
ATM .ix, x, 14, 36, 38, 112, 116, 117, 145, 162, 168, 170, 175, 176, 177, 178, 180, 183, 186, 189, 194, 195, 196, 272
Basic Object Adapters (BOA) 202, 271
Bluetooth Wireless Personal Area Network (WPAN)..................... 181
Boyce - Codd Normal Form (BCNF) 220
Broadband ISDN 159, 271
Business Intelligence (BI) 40, 106, 253
business paradigms........................... 2

Business Process Re-engineering (BPR) .... xvi, 68, 77, 93, 124
Capability Maturity Model (CMM) 287
Carrierless Amplitude Phase (CAM) 179
CGI 51, 96, 212
Circuit Switching Networks (CSN) 14
Client/Server iii, iv, ix, 13, 16, 19, 27, 43, 53, 93, 241, 243, 247, 280
Client/Server (C/S) 13
CMIP.... 199, 200, 201, 240, 269, 270
Commercial-Off-The-Shelf (COTS) 98
Common Gateway Interface (CGI) 51, 247
Common Object Request Broker Architecture (CORBA) 27, 123, 201, 270
Communications Service Provider (CSP)... 14
Complex Management Information Protocol (CMIP) 200
Component Based Development (CBD) 125, 136
Computer Aided System Engineering (CASE) 135, 287
Computer Telephone Integration (CTI) 173, 287
CORBA .viii, ix, 59, 96, 99, 100, 146, 199, 201, 202, 235, 240, 244, 245, 247, 268, 269, 270, 271
CTI... ix, 74, 173, 174, 191, 192, 194, 207, 244
Cyclic Redundancy Check (CRC) 155
Data Warehouse (DW)................. 253
Database Management System (DBMS) 207, 287
datagram 61, 162, 200, 276, 278

Desktop Management Task Force
   (DMTF) 200, 270, 287
Digital Subscriber Line (xDSL).. 191,
   287
Discrete MultiTone Modulation
   (DMT) 179
Distributed Management
   Environment 230, 269
Distributed System Management. 197
Distributed Transaction Processing
   .... vii, 60, 77, 91, 247, 287
DLL 59
DMI 199, 200, 202, 240, 269, 270,
   271
e-Business.... 1, v, viii, 26, 40, 62, 95,
   101, 103, 104, 105, 106, 107, 135
economy of scale ... 34, 111, 170, 176
economy of scope 111
Electronic Data Interchange . 62, 125,
   287
e-Market 106, 107
Enterprise Application Integration
   (EAI)....................................... 105
Enterprise Java Beans (EJB).......... 25
enterprise network xv, xvi, xviii, 2, 3,
   8, 13, 15, 16, 21, 25, 26, 31, 34,
   39, 46, 48, 57, 59, 61, 62, 67, 68,
   73, 74, 76, 77, 78, 79, 80, 81, 82,
   83, 86, 87, 90, 97, 98, 101, 103,
   104, 113, 116, 117, 123, 124, 129,
   135, 145, 146, 154, 164, 189, 195,
   196, 197, 199, 200, 234, 239, 240,
   258, 261, 270, 271
Enterprise Resource Planning (ERP)
   .... 105, 125
enterprise-wide network .... xv, xvi, 9,
   12, 32, 75, 88, 97, 146, 202, 239,
   252
Ethernet14, 21, 30, 32, 33, 35, 36, 38,
   47, 57, 111, 112, 116, 146, 160,
   182, 186, 187, 189, 190, 194, 200,
   268, 270, 274, 275, 276, 281, 286,
   287
expert systems 205, 207
Extended Entity-Relation (EE/R) 218

eXtentsible Markup Language
   (XML)....................................... 163
Extranet. 74, 75, 80, 86, 98, 100, 172,
   173, 176, 244, 287
File Allocation Table (FAT) 24
file servers............................. 26, 278
Frame Check Sequence (FCS) 155
Frame Relay .. ix, x, xi, 112, 165, 166,
   168, 170, 174, 175, 176, 177, 275,
   287
Frame Relays (FR) 175
Free Space Optics (FSO) 180
Frequency Division Multiplexing
   (FDM)...................................... 157
Frequency-Shift Keying (FSK).... 150
funnelling....................................... 59
Geographical Information Systems
   (GIS) 118, 258, 287
Global System for Mobile (GSM) 181
Graphical User Interfaces (GUI).... 17
GroupWare 48, 63, 68, 73, 75, 82, 87,
   88, 89, 100, 101, 103, 134, 252,
   253
GSM 38, 191, 244, 272, 273, 287
HDLC .. v, viii, x, 145, 152, 154, 155,
   156, 159, 160, 161, 169, 175, 275
Header Error Check (HEC).......... 178
High bit-rate Digital Subscribe Line
   (HDSL) 180
High-level Data Link Control
   (HDLC)............................ 155, 275
HTMLvii, 2, 3, 37, 51, 84, 85, 86, 96,
   101, 139, 163, 212, 225, 256, 257,
   273
HyperText Markup Language
   (HTML) 84, 163, 256, 287
HyperText Transfer Protocol (HTTP)
   163
Industrial Virtual Enterprises (IVE)
   99
Information Technology (IT)xv, 8, 12
Interface Definition Language (IDL)
   .... 201, 270
International Organization for
   Standardization (ISO) 160

Internet. iv, viii, xi, xiii, xvi, xviii, xx, 2, 3, 6, 13, 14, 15, 17, 24, 25, 26, 27, 30, 31, 32, 34, 35, 36, 37, 41, 42, 51, 55, 56, 61, 62, 69, 70, 71, 72, 74, 76, 80, 81, 84, 85, 86, 93, 95, 96, 116, 117, 132, 134, 136, 137, 138, 140, 141, 144, 145, 147, 162, 163, 174, 180, 181, 182, 183, 187, 192, 195, 196, 197, 199, 210, 211, 234, 246, 256, 262, 264, 266, 269, 270, 272, 273, 276, 279, 280

Internet Service Providers (ISP) ... 13, 25, 34

Intranet.12, 25, 26, 55, 56, 57, 62, 74, 75, 76, 80, 86, 97, 98, 100, 103, 112, 116, 172, 174, 176, 186, 206, 212, 238, 244, 288

IntranetWare 25, 39, 112, 116, 162, 269, 288

ISDN.v, xvi, 14, 34, 38, 57, 117, 145, 153, 156, 157, 158, 159, 168, 175, 176, 180, 182, 183, 271, 272, 275, 288

ISDN-based DSL Web-access (IDSL) 180

ISO 9000............................. 125, 288

J2EE .... viii, xx, 52, 123

Java Applets .... vii, ix, 246, 247

Java NC 48, 73, 82, 86, 288

Java RISC processors 86

Java Virtual Machine (JVM) .. 49, 70, 86

Kerberos 57, 288

Knowledge Management and Massaging (KM/M) 105

LAN......vi, x, 25, 36, 38, 39, 61, 136, 151, 156, 158, 159, 160, 166, 167, 176, 180, 181, 182, 183, 186, 187, 188, 189, 190, 191, 192, 193, 194, 196, 202, 243, 253, 271, 272, 274, 276, 278, 281, 290

LAN Server 39

Linux ....xi, 6, 7, 8, 13, 18, 22, 24, 27, 28, 29, 30, 32, 33, 47, 79, 81, 88, 90, 134, 137, 138, 163, 201, 288

Local Area Network (LAN) 167, 186, 276, 288

Local Multipoint Distribution Service (LMDS)................................... 192

Management Interface File (MIF) 200, 270

Massive Parallel Processing (MPP)90

Matrix Math eXtensions (MMX) 257, 288

Media Access Control (MAC) 189, 191, 271

Mergers & Acquisitions (M&A).. 110

meta-data..... 118, 254, 255, 256, 257, 261, 267

Microwave Video Distribution System (MVDS) 192

middleware 8, 15, 38, 46, 83, 99, 123, 185, 199, 237, 240, 244

Mips Digital Media Extension (MDMX)................................. 257

MMX 81, 85, 103, 256, 257

modems.......................... 18, 153, 191

Multichannel Multipoint Distribution Systems (MMDS) 192

Multilevel Organisation Memory (MOM)....................................... 20

Multiple-Instruction Multiple-Data (MIMD) 90

Natural Language Processing (NLP) 157

NetWarexi, xx, 11, 12, 13, 25, 39, 55, 56, 57, 61, 100, 102, 112, 134, 138, 182, 197, 240, 248, 269, 277, 279, 280, 281, 288

Network Computer 20, 32, 50, 82, 86, 288

Netware Directory System (NDS)103

Network Interface Card (NIC) . 20, 38

Network Service Providers (NSP) 80, 167, 288

Networking 1, iv, v, vi, vii, viii, ix, x, xiii, xv, xvi, 1, 2, 30, 34, 35, 37, 38, 39, 44, 48, 107, 114, 143, 154, 165, 172, 174, 178, 240, 268

Neugents 40

Next Generation Internet (NGI)..... vi, 172, 178, 288

Non Uniform Memory Access (NUMA).................................... 21

NonReturn-to-Zero-Level (NRZ-L) 151

NTFS 24

Object Linking & Embedding (OLE) 14, 121

Object Management Framework (OMF)............................ 201, 270

Object Management Group (OMG) 198, 201, 270, 288

Object Oriented System Engineering (OOSE)............................ 129, 288

Object Request Brokers (ORB).. 201, 270, 288

On-Line Analytical Processing (OLAP)...................................... 89

OOSE....................129, 130, 131, 135

Open Database Connectivity (ODBC) 258

Open System Interconnection (OSI) 159, 160, 288

Open Systems 98, 137, 147, 268, 274, 275, 277, 278, 279, 280

Packet Switching Network vi, 15, 33, 168

Packet Switched Network (PSN). 166

Peer-to-Peer (P2P)...................... 167

Peripheral Component Interconnect (PCI)... 18

Personal Digital Assistant 13, 67, 288

Phase-Shift Keying (PSK)........... 151

Pretty Good Privacy (PGP).......... 262

Private Branch Exchange (PBX) ... vi, 191

Protocol v, viii, 13, 34, 35, 37, 43, 52, 62, 98, 154, 156, 160, 161, 199, 269, 270, 272, 276, 277, 278, 279, 280, 289

Public Key Infrastructure (PKI)... 232

Publish-&-Subscribe...................... 59

Pulse Code Modulation (PCM) ... 151

Quadrature Amplitude Modulation (QAM).................................... 179

Query-By-Example (QBE) 217

Rapid Application Development (RAD) 132, 289

Reduced Instruction Set Computer (RISC)....................................... 20

Remote Method Invocation (RMI) 246

RSA............................. 57, 262, 289

Scaleable Coherent Interface (SCI) 21

SGML .... vii, 84, 85, 256, 257, 289

Short Message Service (SMS) 181, 273

Simple Networking Management Protocol (SNMP) 199, 269

Single Instruction per Multiple Data (SIMD).................................... 257

Single-pair Digital Subscribe Line (SDSL).................................... 180

SmartCards................... 125, 173, 289

Software Engineering Institute (SEI) 127

Space-Division Multiplexing (SDM) 157

SPICE project 128, 289

Standard 57, 60, 85, 150, 158, 256, 268, 288, 289

STandard for Exchange of Product data (STEP)............................... 98

Standard Generalised Markup Language (SGML)............. 85, 256

Steganography .... xi, 57, 233, 262

Structure of Management Information (SMI)............. 199, 270

Structured Query Language (SQL) 217

Switched Virtual Circuits (SVC) . 178

Systems Network Architecture (SNA)............................268, 289

TCP/IP ix, xvi, 14, 34, 35, 36, 37, 39, 57, 61, 99, 112, 145, 161, 162, 199, 269, 275, 276, 279, 280, 281

Teleconferencing .... v, 25, 97

Terminate-Stay-Resident (TSR) . 199, 270

Tier..........iv, viii, 45, 46, 47, 82, 125

Time Division Multiplexing (TDM)
.... 158, 171
Time-Division Switching 171
Time-Division Switching (TDS) . 171
Token Ring.............. 57, 60, 111, 112
Total Costs of Ownership (TCO) . 18, 112
TP Monitor 27, 44, 45, 58, 60, 62, 77, 82, 89, 91, 101, 119, 137, 230, 240, 248
Transaction viii, ix, 46, 48, 59, 77, 83, 92, 118, 136, 139, 229, 232, 235, 237, 248, 249, 250, 269, 280, 289
Transaction Processing Monitor
(TPM) 59, 136, 289
Transmission Control
Protocol/Internet Protocol
(TCP/IP) 161, 279, 289
Tuxedo.. ix, xi, xx, 27, 60, 62, 77, 92, 101, 118, 136, 139, 237, 238, 240, 241, 248, 289
Uniform Resource Location (URL)
.... 163
Universal Serial Bus (USB)......... 153
UNIX...xx, 13, 18, 23, 24, 25, 26, 27, 48, 61, 67, 76, 79, 81, 83, 85, 88, 109, 110, 134, 136, 137, 162, 185, 201, 247, 248, 280, 289
URL........................ 37, 51, 163, 246

VE NIIIP............ v, 98, 100, 240, 289
Very-high bit-rate Digital Subscribe
Line (VDSL)............................ 180
video-on-demand (VOD).............. 174
virtual offices 31, 80, 157, 244
Virtual Reality Modelling Language
(VRML) 85, 256, 289
W3C.................... 37, 86, 95, 163, 289
Wide Area Networks (WAN) 167
Wide Area Protocol (WAP)......... 181
Wireless Application Protocol
(WAP)............................... 17, 273
Wireless LAN (WLAN).............. 181
wireless networking 192
WLAN Alliance........................... 188
WorkFlow Management Coalition
(WFMC)..................... 98, 102, 290
World Wide Web (Web)............... 139
World Wide Web (WWW)............ 13
X.25 ... ix, 33, 36, 156, 160, 161, 162, 168, 169, 170, 175, 176, 177, 268, 272, 275, 278, 279
X/Open.... vi, viii, ix, xvii, 60, 61, 91, 92, 137, 146, 198, 230, 240, 245, 268, 270, 290
xDSL.... vi, 14, 26, 34, 112, 117, 158, 172, 179, 180, 191, 272
XML ... vii, 68, 84, 85, 101, 107, 224, 249, 256, 257, 266, 273

Website Bookmark

3Com Ethernet http://www.3com.com/solutions/ent_net/index.html 196

ACID http://cmsdoc.cern.ch/doc/swcr/docs/OODBMS
Acrobat viewer http://www.adobe.com/acrobat/readstep.html 2
Application Development Workbench (ADW) http://www.sterling.com/news/1996/19961104-add-a.html 131
ArcInfo http://www.realtime.net/virtual/esri.htm 253
Array Servers http://www.compaq.com/newsroom/
Asynchronous Transfer Mode (ATM) http://www.emap.co.uk/vc/ 173

BeBox http://www.metrowerks.com/press/be.shtml 18
BEA http://www.bea.com/products/tuxedo/index.shtml 234
Beowulf project http://cesdis.gsfc.nasa.gov/linux-web/beowulf/beowulf.html 30
BPR http://www-iwi.unisg.ch/iwi2/iswnet/index.html 76
Business process re-engineering (BPR)
http://www.datamation.com/PlugIn/issues/march1/03aev100.html 76

CA http://www3.ca.com/press/pressrelease.asp?id=1904 117
Callware http://www.callware.com/unified.html 141
Capability Maturity Model (CMM) http://ftp.centerline.com/technotes/technote/sei.frame.html#HDR4 97
CCITT http://incoma.com/cdrom/ccitt.html 144
Cisco http://www.kmj.com/cisco/cisco.html 37
Clarent Corp. http://www.acti.com/solutions/casestudies_bank.htm 161
Cognicase
http://www.me4n.com/client/United/ME4N_UW_V500_MainEngine.nsf/0C7ADD3472DBBAAC852565F
90075D9CE/EA7B1E7DF8817EED85256AC0005350D6?OpenDocument 247
Compaq ProLiant SMP http://www.compaq.com/newsroom/ 20
Component Pascal http://is.eunet.ch:80/customers/omi/ 99
Computer Telephone Integration (CTI) http://www.ie.utoronto.ca/EIL/eil.html 170
Computer Aided System Engineering (CASE) http://www.rai.com/soft_eng/indexes/case.html 130
Corvis Corp. http://www.corvis.com/ 138

DAPLEX http://www.cs.ncl.ac.uk/research/trs/abstracts/488.html 220
Database Management System (DBMS) http://ai.bpa.arizona.edu/papers/hicss27d/subsection3_5_1.html 202
DB2 http://www.darwintech.com/class/db2admin.html 218
Desktop Management Task Force (DMTF) http://www.dmtf.org/news/fact.html 195
Digital Subscriber Line (xDSL) http://www.probe.net/news/dsl.html 187
Distributed Transaction Processing (DTP) http://www.byte.com/art/9504/sec11/art3.htm 60

Electronic Data Interchange (EDI) http://ecworld.utexas.edu/ejou/edi/ 121
Ellipse http://www.cayennesoft.com/investors/reports/10k_896_02.html
Encina http://www.dstc.edu.au/events/TP/t3s1.html 115
Ethernet http://pullinaj1.newi.ac.uk/10quickref/ch4qr_1.html 14
Excelerator http://www.select-software.com/Products/_asp/Excelerator.asp 131
Extranet http://whatis.com/extranet.htm 72

Fast Ethernet http://www.intel.com/comm-net/sns/showcase/speed/hubs/whites/np0382.htm 20
Firewall http://www.gta.com/ 39
http://www.raptor.dk/whatsnew/lantimes/firetext.html 39
FoxPro http://www.microsoft.com/vfoxpro/ 80
Frame Relay http://www.construct.net/projects/pacbel/dedicated/transport/framerelay.html 56

Gartner Group http://www.gartner.com/ 70

GemStone http://fbma.tuwien.ac.at/~e9027112/gemstone.html 99
Geographical Information Systems (GIS) http://www.geo.ed.ac.uk/home/giswww.html 115
GroupWise http://www.gwmag.com/ 55
GSM http://www.issy.cnet.fr/a/cnet/domaction/clients/services/radio.html 178
Gupta Technologies http://www.netusa.com/pcsoft/library/p_178.htm 129

HyperText Markup Language (HTML) http://www.gcal.ac.uk/itsc/netinfo/htmldoc.htm 82

IBM http://www.csc.ibm.com/advisor/provensolutions/pcid/2622_362.html
IBM Lotus Notes
http://www.notes.net/about.nsf/be90c830fcee2b5e85256405007e8937/004cb678c9b376be85256495006d
b5e8? 207
IDG http://www.pcworld.com/news/article/0,aid,44670,00.asp 66
IEEE http://www.ieee.org/cur_soc_hps.html 1
IMS http://www.compapp.dcu.ie/databases/f175.html 236
Impromptu http://www.cognos.com/products/impromptu/index.html 150
Information Engineering Facility (IEF) http://www.ietf.cnri.reston.va.us/home.html 31
Informix http://www.informix.com/4gl 130
Ingress by CA http://www.ca.com/analyst/124 130
Intel http://www.intel.com/
Insignia http://www.insignia.com/products/ch.asp - compaq 69
Insignia http://www.insignia.com/NTRIGUE/users/96_11.html 107
International Standard Organisation (ISO) http://www.mcc.com/env/roadmap/roadmap.reg.html 60
Intranet http://www.cis.ohio-state.edu/hypertext/faq/usenet/client-server-faq/faq-doc-2.html 12
IntranetWare http://www.novell.com/text.html 25
ISDN http://www.datacraft.com.au/isdn/multi.html 14
ISO 9000 http://infomatique.iol.ie:8080/quality/publish/quality/ISO9002.HTM 120

Java http://java.sun.com/new.html
Java NC http://splash.javasoft.com/beans/ 47

Kerberos http://www.veritas.com/common/f/97042301.htm 57

Linux http://sunsite.unc.edu/linux-source/ 6
Local Area Network (LAN) http://www.tbi.net/~jhall/enetcfg.html 163
Lotus Notes http://www.csc.ibm.com/advisor/provensolutions/pcid/2622_362.html 99

MapInfo http://www.mapquest.com/ 253
Meta-data http://viu.eng.rpi.edu/ 115
Microsoft http://www.microsoft.com/
Microsoft Widows http://www.microsoft.com/Windows/embedded/ce/guide/casestudies/compaq.asp 72
Matrix Manipulation Extension (MMX) http://www-us-east.intel.com/procs/perf/spec95.htm 252
Motorola http://www.mot.com/ 11

National Industrial Information Infrastructure Protocols (NIIIP) http://www.rdrc.rpi.edu/virt-ent.html 93
Netspeed http://www.netspeed.com/products.html 19, 115
Netspeed Cisco http://www.netspeed.com/sr202.html 178
NetView http://www.networking.ibm.com/nva/nvaover.html 193
NetWare http://www.novell.com/products/ 11
Network Associates http://www.nai.com 230
Network Computer (NC) http://www.nc.ihost.com/ 19
Network Computer (NC) http://www.rutgers.edu/Accounting/anet/lists/ateach-l/0423.html 19
Network Service Providers (NSP) http://www.cerf.net/cerfnet//about/interconnect.html 79
Next Generation Internet (NGI) http://www.ntonc.org 169
Nortel http://www.nortel.com/enterprise/whatis.html 191
http://www.nortelnetworks.com/corporate/news/newsreleases/2000c/08_31_0000402_easpnet.html 134

NUMA http://playground.sun.com/pub/S3.mp/simple-coma/ 21

Object Management Group (OMG)
http://www.developer.ibm.com/library/aixpert/aug93/aixpert_aug93_OMG.html 193
Object Oriented System Engineering (OOSE) http://www.rational.com/ 124
Object Request Brokers (ORB) http://www.computerwire.com/bulletins/oo3636.htm 156
ObjectTeam http://www8.techmall.com/techdocs/NP971208-5.html 130
Oracle http://www.oracle.com/ 25
Open System Interconnection (OSI)
http://www-internal.amdahl.com/doc/products/oes/cb.uts/osifeat.html 154
OTIS Elevators http://www.elevator.com/pgpmod.htm 109

Paradox http://www.uic.edu/depts/adn/infwww/dinf0221.html 80
Personal Digital Assistant (PDA) http://www.aastore.com/aashopdirectory/gw/0cahwpo.htm 13
PGP http://www.pgp.com 230
Pool of servers http://cesdis.gsfc.nasa.gov/linux-web/beowulf/beowulf.html 88
PopC http://cesdis.gsfc.nasa.gov/linux-web/beowulf/beowulf.html 32
POSIX http://csrc.nist.gov/nistpubs/800-7/node8.html 24
Postgres http://www.sai.msu.su:8000 130
PowerBuilder http://www.powersoft.com/products/powerbuilder 130
PowerPlay http://www.cognos.com/products/powerplay/index.html 250

Rapid Application Development (RAD) http://www.adhere.on.ca/windsor/sdc009/sdc009.html 127
RSA http://www.racalitsec.com/prod-fr.htm 57

Southampton University Computing Services http://www.sucs.soton.ac.uk/research/iridis/ 29
Silicon Graphics http://www.sgi.com/ 252
Simple Network Management Protocol (SNMP) http://bit.csc.lsu.edu/~hendriks/snmp.html 263
SmartCards http://tavinstitute.guinet.com/index.htm 121
SpatialWare http://www.mapinfo.com/spatialware/spatial.html 253
SPICE project http://www.esi.es/Projects/SPICE.html 123
SQL Server http://www.sybase.com/Offerings/Servers/server.html 129
Standard for Exchange of Product data (STEP) http://www.eccnet.com/step/ 96
Standard Generalized Markup Language (SGML) http://www.sgmlopen.org/ 84
steganography http://www.sevenlocks.com/TOCSteganography.htm 257
Sun http://sunsite.unc.edu/ 7
Sun Microsystems Java workstations http://java.sun.com/faq2.html 7
Sun Microsystems http://www.sun.com/ 7
Sun Microsystems NC http://www.sun.com/servers/news/launch/ 7
SyBase e-Portal® http://www.sybase.com/products/ep/ep/ 129
SyBase EA Server http://www.sybase.com/products/applicationservers/easerver 129
SyBase PowerBuilder® http://www.sybase.com/products/internetappdevttools/powerbuilder 130
Symcor http://www.corelan.com/tux.html 233
Systems Network Architecture (SNA) http://www.csc.ibm.com/csoscs.htm 262

Tamosoft http://www.all-nettools.com/privacy/stegano.htm 157
Telecommunications Act http://www.ee.umanitoba.ca/~blight/telecom.html 265
Transition Associate http://www.transition.co.uk/tawebv2.nsf/lookup5/Hughes+Christensen 201
Transition Associate http://www.transition.co.uk/tawebv2.nsf/lookup5/FoulksLynch 205
Transaction Processing Monitor (TPM)
http://www.software.ibm.com/is/sw-servers/transaction/eaglwhtx.htm 59
Transaction Processing Monitor
http://www.software.ibm.com/is/sw-servers/transaction/eaglwhtx.htm 59
Transmission Control Protocol/Internet Protocol (TCP/IP)
http://learning.lib.vt.edu/wintcpip/trumpwsk.html 158
Tuxedo http://www.corelan.com/tux.html 60
Tuxedo http://www.beasys.fr/societe/historique.htm 115

Unified Modelling Language (UML) http://www.rational.com/uml/hot/ 130
Unisys http://www.unisys.com/ 11
UNIX System Laboratories (USL) http://www.vision.sco.com/brochure/supervision.html 131
UNIX SCO http://www.vision.sco.com/brochure/supervision.html 25

VE NIIIP http://www.rdrc.rpi.edu/virt-ent.html 95
Video On Demand (VOD) http://www.magic.ca/infohighway/vod.html 171
Vines http://www.banyan.com/david/txtweb.html 13
Virtual enterprise http://www.compchannel.com/e-cat/csbasics.htm 93
Virtual offices http://www.nortel.com/enterprise/whatis.html 31
Virtual Reality Modelling Language (VRML)
http://www.sdsc.edu/SDSC/Partners/vrml/software/browsers.html 83

W3C SGML http://18.23.0.23/pub/WWW/MarkUp/SGML/Activity 49
W3C OMG http://www.w3.org/OOP/9606_Workshop/submissions/38-W3COMG.htm 93
Webster Dictionary http://www.notredame.ac.jp/cgi-bin/wn.cgi 1
Windows 2000/NT http://www.csusm.edu/winworld/winworld.html
WinFrame http://www.citrix.com/sun.htm 17
Wireless LAN http://www.wlana.com/intro/wirels.html 144
Wireless http://www.telxon.com/defaultwire.htm 229
WorkFlow Management Coalition (WFMC) http://www.aiai.ed.ac.uk/project/wfmc/overview.html 96
WorldNet 1.5 Vocabulary Helper http://www.notredame.ac.jp/cgi-bin/wn.cgi 1

Xdrive Technologies, Inc. http://www.xdrive.com/ 41
X/Open http://xoweb.xopen.org/public/reqts/openb08s.htm 60

About the Author

Dragan Nikolik, Ph.D.
Maastricht School of Management, Maastricht, The Netherlands

Dr. Nikolik has joined the Maastricht School of Management (MSM) in 1993. He is Head of the IT/IS Professional Cell at MSM from 1999. Holds M.S. in Control Systems from the University of Southern California (USA), and Ph.D. in Biocybernetics and Electrical Engineering from the University of Ljubljana (Slovenia). As a Fulbright PhD Scholar at USC in Artificial Intelligence and Biocybernetics Dr. Nikolik took part in PhD research projects in AI system's modelling and implementation of computerized hearing aid implants at Children's Hospital, Los Angeles, and House Ear Institute, Los Angeles.

Presently, he is engaged in applied Artificial Neural Networks (ANN) to the BMI and Genetics research project at the University of Maastricht, the Netherlands. Dr. Nikolik has more than 20 years of academic experience both at MSM as well as Professor of Computer Science and Head of Computer Science Department at the University of Skopje (Macedonia). His main interests are in AI, ANN, Applied Information Technology, Computer Networks, and development of Databases and Information Systems.

The manufacturer's authorised representative in the EU is Springer
Nature Customer Service Centre GmbH, Europaplatz 3, 69115 Heidelberg,
Germany. If you have any concerns regarding our products, please
contact ProductSafety@springernature.com

Printed and bound by CPI Group (UK) Ltd, Croydon, CR0 4YY
23/04/2026
02095628-0002